SECOND EDITION

ADJUSTMENT, BEHAVIOR, AND PERSONALITY

LEONARD D. GOODSTEIN
RICHARD I. LANYON
Arizona State University

SECOND EDITION

ADJUSTMENT, BEHAVIOR, AND PERSONALITY

CARTOONS BY DAVID A. HILLS, Wake Forest University

**ADDISON-WESLEY
PUBLISHING COMPANY**

Reading, Massachusetts
Menlo Park, California
London
Amsterdam
Don Mills, Ontario
Sydney

Sponsoring Editor: Stuart W. Johnson

Production Editor: Barbara Pendergast

Designer: Judith Fletcher

Illustrator: ANCO/Boston and Joshua Clark

Cover Design: Richard Hannus

Cover Photograph: Marshall Henrichs

ISBN 0-201-02455-1
CDEFGHIJKL-DO-89876543210

*To
Jeanette
and
Barbara*

Preface
to the Second
Edition

In the four years that have transpired since the writing of the first edition, much has happened in the field of psychology, but much has remained the same. Our goal in this edition is the same as for the first edition—to provide a coherent and systematic approach to understanding human adjustment, using a social-learning theory orientation. We believe that social-learning theory is consistent with both the theoretical and the research traditions of American psychology. We further believe that of the major theoretical positions, social-learning theory provides the broadest and least confining point of view, based on the simple assumption that most human behavior is learned and that the understanding of the process of learning is a necessary foundation for understanding human adjustment.

Although social-learning theory serves as the basis of our analysis, we have tried to avoid being either narrow or doctrinaire. Thus, we have also identified other approaches to the study of human adjustment, and where appropriate we have tried to suggest how these alternative views might be understood or reconceptualized within a social-learning framework. We do not intend to convey the impression that the social-learning approach is without flaws; however, we do believe that it provides a unifed and integrated way of looking at the phenomena of human adjustment, leading to a clear understanding of a wide range of topics and processes.

The second edition contains a number of changes that reflect the changing nature of our field. In particular, Chapter 9 on adult adjustment reviews some of the very recent research on adult development, and Chapter 10 on assessment includes an overview of attribution theory as one way of understanding the processes by which we attempt to understand each other. A large variety of more minor changes throughout the text serve to update the research conclusions on many of the topics.

A number of colleagues have read the first edition of this text and provided detailed criticism, including Elizabeth Altmaier of the University of Florida, Gary Caldwell of John A. Logan College, Alan Glaros of Wayne State University, Henry Wellman of the University of Michigan, and Jeanne L'Okon of Tallahassee Community College. While we did not always follow their advice and suggestions, their work is sincerely appreciated.

We gratefully acknowledge the continued support of our publisher, Stuart Johnson, and Karen Guardino, his associate, in the development of this revision. LaVaun Habegger, Mary Redondo, and Helen Rubio, our secretaries at Arizona State University, have been continuously helpful in this project. Our wives, Jeanette Treat Good-stein and Barbara P. Lanyon, have continued to be uniquely helpful to us, in this project and in all our professional work.

Tempe, Arizona   *L. D. G.*
November 1978   *R. I. L.*

Preface to the First Edition

Psychology has become one of the most popular subjects on the college campus. Perhaps we should not be surprised that humans are fascinated by their own behavior. But many students are very disappointed by their first encounter with psychology. Rather than learning about human behavior, they find that psychology is the study of sensory processes, animal learning, statistics, and physiology. These topics are certainly important in any comprehensive view of human behavior; however, they omit the essentially human aspects that *are* psychology to the average person.

We have set out to write a text that takes the scientific principles derived from basic research and applies them systematically for the purpose of understanding everyday human behavior. It is our belief that a broadly behavioral view, one that is based upon the methods and insights of social-learning theory, can provide students with a relevant and useful understanding of their own behavior and that of others. We have attempted to follow the advice of George A. Miller, in his 1969 Presidential Address to the American Psychological Association, when he urged psychologists to "give psychology away to the people." In Professor Miller's view, there are a vast number of psychological facts and principles that, if generally understood and applied, would greatly benefit humanity. We have tried to heed this suggestion.

Our goal has been to present a coherent and systematic approach to the study of human adjustment, without being narrow and doctrinaire, on the one hand, or producing an encyclopedia-type reference book on the other. Although we are primarily committed to a social-learning orientation, we have included references to, and at times extensive presentations of, other approaches to the study of human adjustment, and we have tried to do so without distorting them.

A self-contained workbook is also available. The workbook contains the following for each chapter of the text:

- an essay (written from the student's point of view) that gives a commentary on the chapter;
- a series of review questions;
- a series of application questions;
- a "do-it-yourself" project that permits the students to apply the principles outlined in that chapter to their own lives.

The writing of this volume was made possible by a sabbatical leave granted the senior author by the University of Cincinnati, where he was a member of the faculty at that time. We gratefully acknowledge the strong support of Roger Drumm, our publisher, at all stages of this project. Ms. Olive Beard, the senior author's secretary at the University of Cincinnati, was more than devoted in her efforts to produce usable copy. Our wives, Jeanette Treat Goodstein and Barbara P. Lanyon, were supports, goads, editors, and reviewers in uniquely helpful ways. Our gratitude to them cannot be adequately communicated here.

January 1975   *L. D. G.*
                                                                                    R. I. L.

Contents

PART THREE

PROBLEMS OF ADJUSTMENT

PART ONE

FOUNDATIONS OF ADJUSTMENT

ONE

Introduction

The psychology of adjustment is the aspect of the science of human behavior that attempts to explain how people cope with the demands and problems of everyday life.

There are three major views of psychological adjustment.

- The moral view uses moral absolutes as guidelines.

- The humanistic view holds that each person is to be understood only as a unique individual with special worth.

- The social-learning view studies people's problem-solving behavior as they learn to master challenges to their well-being.

Adjustment is influenced by a variety of biological factors.

- Evolution has given human beings certain adaptive advantages.

- Important biological similarities and differences are the product of individual genetic inheritance.

- Heredity also influences interpersonal characteristics in indirect ways.

- Heredity is thought to play a significant role in the development of certain forms of mental illness.

- A person's future psychological adjustment can be affected by certain factors present at the time of birth.

PSYCHOLOGY IS OFTEN DEFINED AS THE SCIENCE OF HUMAN BEHAVIOR. THE **psychology of adjustment** is the particular part of the science that attempts to understand and explain the complex interpersonal behavior that people exhibit in their daily lives. Thus, psychologists who are interested in the process of adjustment attempt to use their knowledge of general psychological principles to improve our understanding of the different ways in which people attempt to cope with the demands of ordinary living. The psychology of adjustment, then, is the application of the principles of psychology to the problems of everyday life. The psychology of adjustment encompasses an enormous range of behavior, a range that would be extended even further if we were to include times and cultures other than our own. Let us examine six lives that illustrate this diversity and indicate some of the complexities involved in developing an adequate understanding of the processes of psychological adjustment.

Adele is a sixteen-year-old girl living in the ghetto of a large city. A high school dropout who is barely literate, she has never been gainfully employed. Adele is now pregnant for the second time, and she is seeking assistance from a public health agency because her mother refuses to take care of her any longer.

Bart is a twenty-year-old college junior majoring in political science. He is active in a variety of student activities and is now president of his fraternity. Bart has always been a good student without much effort and is planning a career in law. He has been engaged to be married since high school, and he and his fiancee have consulted a minister for premarital counseling.

Carl is a twenty-six-year-old man with a tenth-grade education. He is now hospitalized, for the fourth time in the past ten years, in the locked ward of the nearby state hospital for the mentally ill. Withdrawn and apathetic, Carl is unsure of where he is, and tends to be confused about the details of his life.

Donna is a nine-year-old girl who was referred to a developmental clinic for psychological and medical evaluation. Attractive and well groomed, she sits staring vacantly into space. Her parents have been unsuccessful in their efforts to have her fit into the normal classroom, and they explain that she had been rather ordinary in her development until the age of six, when she had a very high fever of undetermined origin accompanied by convulsions.

Ed is a twenty-three-year-old college graduate now living on a loosely organized rural commune. Ed has rejected traditional definitions of work and achievement, and he is seeking psychological counseling in a free clinic to help "get my head together." *He is alienated from his family because they neither understand nor approve of his new life style,* and he is both pleased by his freedom and lonely because he lacks any close interpersonal ties.

Frances is a forty-four-year-old housewife who seems to be stable and well adjusted except for an intense fear of thunderstorms. Because of this phobia, she listens to several weather forecasts each morning and inspects the sky almost continuously throughout the day. If there is the slightest possibility of rain, she cannot go out of the house. Rainclouds send her to the basement, shivering with fear, until her family assures her that all possibility of rain has passed. She has been doing this for twenty-five years.

These six case segments are a limited sampling of the enormous range of human behaviors and conditions which psychologists who study adjustment must attempt to explain. Most readers will be able to broaden this sample considerably with examples from their own experience. The central question with which we are concerned in this book is how we can understand human behavior. What are the primary factors that determine how people react to each other and to their environment? Why are some people better able than others to cope with life? How should we go about the extremely difficult task of making sense out of what people do?

We invite the reader to take up the challenge of this task with us, as we attempt to develop a framework that is both comprehensive and consistent for understanding human beings and human behavior. We will not succeed in achieving the degree of integration and consistency that we would ideally like, however, because the scientific data that will be our building blocks are incomplete and at times contradictory. Also, it is extremely difficult to step back and view people and their behavior in an objective manner, as we, both writers and readers, must admit to as many subjective biases as anybody else.

Clearly, the writers are committed to a psychological view of human behavior. But there are other approaches to the study of human experience, each equally valid in its own context. We are referring to such disciplines as literature, philosophy, religion, history, and mythology, each of which deals with the examination of human nature from a particular point of view. We believe that the psychological view is the one most likely to lead to the kind of understanding that enables us to cope with everyday problems and challenges to our well-being.

In most contemporary views of adjustment it is usual to stress either biological factors or psychological factors as the basic determinants of human behavior, separately or in some combination. Thus, the reasons an individual behaves in a particular fashion are usually given in terms of innate (biologically determined) factors, or experiential (psychologically determined) factors, or some combination of them. To refer to the brief case examples given above, it would probably be concluded that Donna's learning difficulties were a function of physiological changes following her illness. On the other hand, it is not likely to be suggested that Bart's behavior as a successful student and campus leader was determined primarily by biological factors. Instead, most persons would view Bart's actions more as a function of psychological factors, such as his early childhood experiences and his family background. Yet a reading of the latter part of this chapter will show that the role of hereditary factors in making Bart what he is cannot be ignored. The plight of Adele also appears to be a direct result of her socially deprived environment, although a closer examination would also be necessary to evaluate this interpretation.

The limits of available scientific knowledge often make it difficult to separate the determinants of a person's behavior. Carl, for example, is probably suffering from *schizophrenia*, and it is still unclear to what extent the origins of this complex and baffling disorder are biological and to what extent environmental. A number of experts regard schizophrenia as a hereditary disease, determined solely or primarily by genetics, while others believe it to be determined by psychological factors, such as early and severe parental rejection. Many psychologists, including the authors, take a middle-of-the-road position, viewing schizophrenia as involving a biologically determined predisposition which requires a particular set of experiences in order to develop into an actual schizophrenic disorder.

The highly specific phobia experienced by Frances is another kind of disorder that behavioral scientists do not fully understand, although it seems probable that the most important factors are specific events in the environment and the way in which the person reacts to them. The development of phobias is discussed more fully in Chapters 6 and 7, and in Chapter 11 we describe the way in which Frances was successfully treated for her difficulty.

The case of Ed presents yet another problem. Twenty years ago, most of us would have considered him seriously maladjusted because of his failure to conform with traditional American values. More recently, society's values have changed to the point where many people could comfortably view Ed's behavior as essentially normal. Thus, he would be seen as a person who is actively questioning traditional American values and trying to develop a role in life with which he can be comfortable.

Regardless of the particular view that one holds concerning human behavior, the basic importance of biological factors should be clearly underscored. We humans are first biological creatures, and our biological endowment as a species exerts a critical influence upon our behavior. For instance, as a function of being human, we are extremely helpless and dependent organisms when newborn, and must be fed, protected, and otherwise nurtured if we are to grow to full maturity. This dependency is characteristic of all humans and is a direct function of our biological endowment. This early dependency sets limits upon what can be accomplished by the human organism, and similar restrictions are imposed by the constant need for food, water, oxygen, warmth, and protection against disease and harm. What any person can become behaviorally is limited by the nature of the biological endowment of the species. There are individual and group variations in biological endowment, but there are definite limits that are characteristic of humans as a species. It should also be recognized, of course, that many of the human adaptive advantages over other animals are a product of our unique biological characteristics. Perhaps the most important advantage is the unique human capacity for thought, language, and speech.

We have taken the viewpoint that humans are best regarded as being on a continuum of complexity along with the other animals. Many people, however, believe that human behavior is not simply an elaboration of biological patterns present in other species, but is totally different. In this view, our uniquely human capacities for religious experience, philosophical speculation, and the control of our own destiny are seen as placing us distinctly apart from all other organisms. Readers should make their own decisions concerning the degree to which humans should be regarded as unique, and while the authors themselves emphasize the "continuum" viewpoint, it is not necessary for the reader to share this attitude in order to understand and appreciate the book.

THREE VIEWS OF ADJUSTMENT

Whenever assessment of the quality of human behavior is proposed, an immediate and basic question arises. On what basis is the judgment to be made? Who shall decide upon, and what guidelines shall be employed to evaluate, the adjustment value of a particular behavior? A clear example of these problems can be seen in regard to sexual behavior. Human sexual nature is one aspect of biological endowment, and sexual needs are biologically based. How should one behave in response to these biologically based impulses? Should they be denied or deliberately inhibited? Should they be responded to directly? Is masturbation an adequate coping response? Is homosexuality adjustive? The number of possible questions is endless.

To develop an adequate understanding of psychological adjustment, it is necessary to adopt some more or less consistent viewpoint concerning "basic human nature." Speculation about human nature could take us far afield into religion, philosophy, and other areas of thought and study which preceded the development of psychology, a relatively recent topic of study. Let us group these speculations under three headings and survey them briefly: the *moral* view, the *humanistic* view, and the *social-learning* view. It is the third view, the *social-learning* approach, that is favored by the authors and utilized as the primary focus throughout this book.

The Moral View of Adjustment

The answers to questions such as those posed above concerning sexual behavior were at one time quite simple. There were *moral absolutes* that provided the guidelines for

human behavior and thus for evaluating the quality of one's adjustment. These prescriptions for behavior have often been present as an integral part of formal religious doctrines, and some of them have influenced contemporary psychological thought.

The traditional Christian church probably holds the most influential conservative moral viewpoint in Western society. Whatever the nuances of the leading theologians have been, traditional conservative Christian thought has regarded humanity as basically evil, and has defined the goal of human life to be the return to the state of grace from which we originally fell. This is to be done by following a prescribed set of rules which comprehensively cover all behaviors and even thoughts and feelings. Transgressions are reported either to God directly or to his representative, and settling up is accomplished through a renewed commitment to obey the rules. Since human nature is, in this view, intrinsically evil, people are continually fighting a losing battle with their real or sinful selves. It is worth pointing out, however, that Protestant theologians have emphasized the human capacity for change (or self-redemption), implying that the ability to adapt to the demands of life is, to a large degree, within our own control. More contemporary liberal Christian theology tends to emphasize the acceptance of God's grace and the development of one's positive qualities in a constructive manner. This position is consistent with the humanistic view of adjustment, which we will consider below.

Freud and psychoanalysis. The moral view has permeated Western society for centuries, and it affects all of us to a greater or lesser degree. Sigmund Freud, the most influential pioneer in the study of human adjustment, was among the first to question the adequacy of the moral perspective as a basis for a complete understanding of human nature. Freud took the view that people are governed by instinctive, or biologically based, forces that lead to negative consequences. From his work with emotionally disturbed individuals, Freud developed his psychoanalytic theory, in which the basic "driving forces" are biologically based, undifferentiated sexual and aggressive energies or drives. These drives, and the ways in which the individual satisfies them, form the core of traditional psychoanalytic theory. In the process of psychosexual development, one learns socially acceptable ways to discharge these biological energies. In addition, Freud's theory holds that a portion of the energy comes to be controlled by the ego, that aspect of the personality which is conceptualized as being responsible for one's rational and mature development.

Freud's view of human adjustment reveals the legacy of other scholarly work from earlier days, particularly Newtonian physics. For example, the aggressive, or pleasure-destroying drive (or instinct) was set off against the pleasure-seeking drive, much in the manner of Newton's law of equal and opposite reactions. Freud also tried for some time to develop the notion of a life drive (Eros) with an opposing death drive (Thanatos), although these concepts did not play an important role in his theory of adjustive behavior.

Freud, like all scholars, was in many ways limited by the practical influences of the world around him. Had he found ready support and acceptance for his views, he might have been able to move even further toward the developments in modern psychology that have taken place since his death in 1939. As it was, his colleagues regarded him as something of a heretic, and he was ostracized from scientific and professional circles for much of his life.

In more recent years, most of Freud's theories have gained wide acceptance. Some of his views have been modified and extended; for example, several attempts have been made to restate his basic formulation in a manner that presents human motives in a more favorable light. One group of psychoanalysts, referred to as the neo-Freudians (Alfred Adler, Erich Fromm, Karen Horney, and Harry Stack Sullivan), placed much less emphasis on the biological or innate components of basic human needs, and concerned themselves more with needs produced by the demands of the interpersonal and social environment. Another group of psychoanalysts, usually referred to as the "ego psychologists" (Robert Lowenstein, Ernst Kris, Hans Hartmann, and Robert White), have moved away from Freud's focus on the biological primacy of human nature and have emphasized instead the adaptive and rational components, or the ego aspects of personality.

The Humanistic View of Adjustment

The *humanistic* psychologists offer a rather different view of human adjustment. In this view, with its strong roots in philosophy, literature, and contemporary liberal theology, people are seen as innately good, having special worth and being each uniquely different. Carl Rogers and Abraham Maslow are two major proponents of this position. It is particularly interesting that Maslow's view, like Freud's, places strong emphasis on the biological determinants of human nature, but then comes to the opposite conclusion about its basic direction. Maslow believed that all people possessed the potential for positive growth and, given a favorable environment, were capable of ultimately reaching the state of self-actualization, or fulfillment of their innate potentials. A rough analogy might be drawn between Maslow's view of the growth and development of personality and the growth and development of a seed into a plant and finally, given favorable conditions, into the flowers whose basic nature was originally contained in the seed. The "best" or most well-adjusted people are those who have developed successfully through their formative stages and have reached the highest stage, self-actualization, in which their basic potentials are expressed most fully and completely.

This humanistic view bears a considerable resemblance to the concept of physical maturation. Maturation refers to the development of a behavior as a function of the chronological maturity of the organism, without reference to practice or training. The swimming of tadpoles, the flying of birds, and the walking of children are all examples of maturation. Harmful circumstances—for example, the lack of adequate nutrition— can interfere with maturation, but otherwise the development of maturation-based behavior is a part of the inevitable development of the organism. In a similar way, the humanistic view of adjustment regards a person's failure to achieve self-actualization as the consequence of the interference of harmful or noxious psychological environments. Such aversive conditions include the lack of basic physical security, lack of emotional security and love, and lack of opportunity for the development of self-esteem.

Phenomenology. The humanistic view also tends to avoid the use of external frames of references to evaluate the quality of human behavior. This position is fundamental to one particular group of humanistic psychologists, the *phenomenologists,* who believe that a person's actions can be understood only through the internal frame of reference of that particular person.

Phenomenologists believe that it is not possible to decide for another person which behaviors are adjustive and which are not. Only behaving individuals can evaluate the adequacy of their behavior, using their own unique frame of reference. Just as cultural anthropologists have shown that moral absolutes differ from culture to culture, the phenomenologists believe that there is a similar limitation in the degree to which the same moral absolutes can be generalized from individual to individual. According to this view, individuals see the world through the selective filter of their own unique viewpoints, their own phenomenal fields. In order to predict an individual's behavior, it is thus necessary to have a knowledge of that person's phenomenal field. Each person's phenomenal field is constantly being restructured according to changing needs; parts of it, however, include relatively stable self-perceptions which form the self-concept. Thus, if someone knows that my self-concept includes viewing myself as helpful to others, that person will know that I can probably be persuaded to help somebody in need by appealing to that aspect of my self-concept.

In this view, the fundamental force motivating all behavior is the need to preserve and enhance the *phenomenal self.* In other words, behavior is adaptive if it meets the needs of the individual as perceived by the individual. Thus, if I am hungry and I eat, this is clearly adaptive from my point of view; if I am bored, then turning on my television or stereo may solve my problem.

However, the perspective of the behaving individual is frequently limited, particularly with regard to the long-term consequences of the behavior. It would not be adaptive, in the long run, if my playing the television or stereo disturbed you so much that you might later retaliate; or if I ate food which belonged to someone else. In other words, one problem with the strict phenomenological position is that the behaver is often unaware of the consequences of the behavior, and it is these consequences that are often critical in determining what most psychologists would regard as the adjustive quality of the response.

The phenomenological point of view raises a number of other questions for persons committed to an objective view of human behavior. How can an external observer

ever adequately understand the internal frame of reference of another person? How is it possible to enter the internal view of the behaver? How is it possible to see the world through the eyes of another person? Although the phenomenologists suggest that listening with empathy to the other person provides an answer to these questions, the necessary listening skills are difficult to develop. Also, the data gathered in this manner are not always as reliable as many psychologists would wish; that is, two different listeners often arrive at different conclusions after listening to the same material. In spite of the difficulties, however, some psychologists remain committed to this point of view.

Existentialism. Another specific humanistic position regarding adjustment is offered by existential psychology. Existentialists argue that we are each individually and uniquely responsible for our own destiny. Each person, thus, actively decides, or is continually deciding, upon a particular path of action. For the existentialists, life is a constant series of decisions, some of which may appear trivial or inconsequential. It is the pattern of these decisions, and their consequences, that really determines the quality of the individual's adjustment. In making these decisions, the individual's "free will" is emphasized above environmental influence, past experience, or internal psychological or biological states. Thus, each person is seen as actively deciding his or her own fate and as therefore responsible for the consequences of the decisions that are made. Much more is involved in the existential approach, which offers an extremely rich and complex view of the nature of the human experience.

Most objectively oriented psychologists have difficulty translating existentialism into a practical psychology for understanding everyday behavior. If behavior is a consequence of a free decision-making process, and if an analysis of behavior need not concentrate on prior experience or stable personality characteristics, then human behavior is beyond our understanding in traditional scientific terms. The interested reader will find more complete and sympathetic accounts in the works of Bugental (1978) and May, Angel, and Ellenberger (1958).

The Social-Learning View of Adjustment

The debate about human nature can go on endlessly. Most contemporary psychologists have preferred to organize their views around more specific questions of fact. As one such position, the social-learning view approaches the study of human psychological adjustment as the study of problem-solving, or *coping,* behavior. By coping we mean the degree to which individuals are able to meet and master at least three kinds of challenges to their existence: (1) direct challenges from the physical environment; (2) challenges stemming from their physical limitations; and (3) interpersonal challenges. The first of these, direct challenges from the environment, would include the adequacy or skill with which the individual copes with physical realities, such as extremes of temperature and climate, undersupplies of food or water, and animal or human predators. These challenges are defined by our biological nature: humans can withstand only a rather narrow range of temperatures, are prone to illness and disease, need food and water for survival, and can serve as food for other animals.

The second challenge to human existence involves people's responses to their own physical and intellectual limitations, such as physical weakness, defective vision or hearing, chronic illness, and other physical disorders, as well as a limited capacity for problem solving. These characteristics can be understood in large measure as individual differences in biological endowment from one person to another. Obviously, the adequacy with which individuals cope with such personal limitations is critical in determining the adequacy with which they cope with direct challenges from the environment, especially in primitive societies.

The third group of challenges includes those posed by the interpersonal environment: how successfully people cope with others in their environment, how adequately they interact with others to satisfy their personal needs, and how they cope with psy-

IT'S A "COPE OR BE COPED" WORLD!

Stevie Wonder, blind rock composer and
performer, is an outstanding example of how
individuals can successfully cope with their
personal limitations.

chological demands made by others. Although it has not always been the case, the
changing nature of our society has tended to emphasize interpersonal factors as most
important in the adjustment process. In each of the six case segments reported at the
beginning of the chapter, issues of coping with the interpersonal environment led the
person into an encounter with a mental health professional worker.

In sum, the social-learning view of adjustment regards an individual's adjustive
capacity as the ability to meet and cope with stresses and problems with a minimum of
disruption to the ongoing process of life, considering both the immediate and longer
term consequences of the behavior. In particular, this view relies on principles of learning as the most basic explanatory concepts in accounting for the way people behave.
This approach to adjustment bears a strong similarity to that taken by the above-men-
tioned ego psychologists in their attempts to update Freud's original views. The term
ego psychology, in fact, refers to a basic emphasis on the ego or problem-solving
aspects of personality. And contemporary thought in ego psychology, as developed
by Robert White, has introduced the basic concept of striving for competence as a
fundamental characteristic of adjustive behavior.

The authors' reasons for preferring the social-learning view of psychological adjustment are several. Perhaps the most important is that this view focuses upon observable events, and attempts to account for behavior in terms of these events with as little reliance as possible on hypothetical concepts not anchored in some observable data. Thus, in behavioral terms, deprivation of food leads to increased activity, a topic to be discussed in Chapter 2. Our identification of this increase in activity as "drive instigated" is based on the observable events of deprivation and activity. This approach is in sharp contrast to mentalistic explanations which employ the concept of *mind,* for example, a concept not anchored in observable data.

The social-learning position does not deny the existence of the phenomena that are called "mind," but approaches them in a particular manner. It uses people's *verbal reports* of such events as thoughts, intentions, and self-concepts as the basic behaviors that must occupy a central position in the science of human behavior. Recent research in both cognitive and behavioral psychology has shown the necessity of including these nonobservable events in any study of the conduct of human affairs. Self-reports are at the present time our only means of obtaining information about thought processes, and whether or not more direct ways will ever be developed is a question that as yet belongs in the realm of science fiction.

The reader should distinguish this social-learning approach to the study of human behavior, which is a moderate behavioral view, from the more radical behaviorist position of some writers (such as B. F. Skinner) who believe, for example, that nonobservable events such as thoughts are very difficult to study scientifically and therefore cannot occupy a central role in the science of behavior. While Skinner's contributions to behavioral psychology have been major and far-reaching, we reject the extreme aspects of his views in favor of a more moderate behavioral position.

We might compare our attempts to understand human behavior with the attempts of the six blind men to describe an elephant. Each of them touched a different part of the elephant and, failing to recognize the full enormity of the animal, described it as though their one part represented the whole beast. We can avoid making the same mistake if we continually bear in mind that any particular approach to understanding human behavior cannot encompass all its aspects. While the authors believe that the social-learning approach is the most adequate of the frameworks that are currently available for this task, other approaches also make their own unique contributions. And the future will certainly bring new approaches that will improve upon our present ones.

THE BIOLOGICAL BASIS OF ADJUSTMENT

As we have stated, this book takes a social-learning approach to the study of psychological adjustment by examining the problems or challenges which arise in the course of human life and the various ways of coping with them. Because our biological characteristics are part of us in the most basic possible way, we begin our journey into the understanding of psychological adjustment with a careful examination of some of the ways in which our biological makeup can influence our adjustment.

Heredity and Evolution

Many human adjustive behaviors are very different from those of other animals. Further, the adjustive behavior of twentieth-century humans is very different from that of their prehistoric ancestors. Both of these differences are the consequence of *evolution:* the first, of biological evolution and the second, of cultural evolution, the gradual development of the skills that are required for coping in a society of ever-increasing technological complexities. Because we are concerned in this chapter with the genetic determinants of behavior, we pause briefly to consider the nature of biological evolution.

Biological evolution provides one basic foundation for explaining how humans differ from other animals in their innate or inherent capacity for adjustment. In considering humans as different from other animals only in an evolutionary sense, we tend to disagree with many people who hold traditional religious beliefs about human creation, and also with those who are offended by grouping humans with all other living creatures.

What explains human dominance over other species? It is possible to trace the probable evolutionary development of the essential differences between humans and other animals, or more accurately, to report informed opinion about the manner in

which this development probably occurred (e.g., Washburn, 1960). For example, the development of bipedal locomotion (upright stance) was related to freeing the hands for use in carrying tools and weapons, during a time period when shortages of food made it necessary to develop new methods of food procurement. Such an evolutionary change had adaptive or problem-solving consequences, and was crucial for survival.

This and similar adaptive activities were performed best by those individuals with the most highly developed brains; in fact, perhaps the most important biological factor of all in human evolution is the evolution of the brain, particularly the cerebral cortex. The early human or perhaps humanoid inhabitants of our planet banded together into social groups in order to survive, and those members with the most highly developed brains were able to devise the most successful ways of surviving the many primitive stresses and hardships. To put it another way, the increasing complexity of social living during the early eras of human development led to the evolution of the human brain in its present form; and conversely, complex human society is possible only for creatures with human capacity for thought.

It is interesting to note that other creatures have evolved certain biologically adaptive capacities that humans do not possess. For example, many creatures are equipped to run faster and for more sustained periods of time. Some can fly, others can breathe under water, and many have much more acute senses of hearing and smell. But it is clear that humans are, on balance, best suited biologically to cope successfully with the widest range of environmental demands. Their problem-solving capacity enables them to compensate for other biological limitations and to live in diverse environments. Thus, in the sense of evolutionary adaptation to a variety of natural living conditions, it can be said that humans have made the most successful adjustment.

The Mechanism of Heredity

In considering the nature of human behavior, it is obvious that humans beget humans, just as each other kind of living thing reproduces its own species. Human genetic endowment, transmitted from parents to offspring, is the most basic determinant of human potential for both growth and behavior. How is this genetic information transmitted? What are the mechanisms of human heredity? Modern genetics is a fascinating area of scientific study, but it is also extremely complicated, so we must content ourselves with a summary of some basics of that process.

The moment at which the sperm cell of the male fertilizes the egg cell of the female represents the beginning of human life. The new human organism, at the moment of conception, has a complete genetic blueprint or set of instructions which will make possible the development of certain structures and certain behaviors under particular kinds of environmental conditions. In other words, at the moment of conception, when there is still only a single cell involved, the genetic endowment of that individual is set, including the potential for physical development, much of the behavioral repertoire, and the overall pattern of development throughout a rather predictable life cycle. This is not meant to imply, of course, that complex behaviors are directly inherited. Rather, genetic characteristics influence complex behaviors according to the principles of behavior genetics, as described on pages 29-31.

After fertilization occurs, the complex pattern of growth begins. The single cell, or **zygote,** divides into two cells, which further divide into four cells, then eight, then sixteen, and so on, all according to the elaborate blueprint set at the moment of conception. By the fifth week the organism, known as the **embryo** from the first week through the end of the second month following conception, begins to develop a spinal cord and backbone. By the eighth week the facial features are beginning to be distinguishable. From the third month onward the developing organism is called a **fetus,** and the predetermined pattern of development continues. By week eighteen hair on the head first appears, and by week thirty almost all of the organic systems are completely developed. Birth. however, does not ordinarily occur before week thirty-six.

The genetic code which sets this enormously complex pattern of development is found in the **chromosomes,** the tiny rod-like structures present in each cell. Each human cell contains twenty-three pairs of chromosomes, or forty-six altogether, except for the egg and sperm cells, which contain only twenty-three chromosomes, or one-half of each pair found in other cells. The creation of these germ cells involves the process of *reduction division*, whereby each mature sperm or egg cell receives only one of each pair of chromosomes from the parent cell, thus allowing the zygote to have forty-six chromosomes or twenty-three pairs, one half from each parent. Which particular chromosome of the pair is carried by a specific germ cell apparently is a random process, and this randomness accounts for the variability in genetic endowment. Biologists estimate that there are over eight million possible combinations of chromosomes from the mating of a given human male and female.

Within the fairly recent past, a great deal has been learned about the specifics of genetic transmission. For instance, it is now known that each chromosome is made up of long molecules of *deoxyribonucleic acid* (usually abbreviated DNA), which occur in two interwoven strands forming a double helix. The specific details of the genetic code are stored in the DNA helix in an ordered series. Each specific instruction is contained in a gene or combination of genes, which are strung along the helix much like pearls on a necklace. These **genes,** which are the individual units for transmitting heredity, control such diverse human characteristics as eye color, body size, and blood type.

Another aspect of genetic endowment involves the dominant or recessive nature of the genes. After fertilization, the genes affecting the various traits line up in pairs. For example, the genes for determining eye color, one from each parent, line up in the zygote to determine the eye color of the individual. We know that certain genes are stronger, or dominant, over others which are weaker, or recessive. In our example, if one parent has given a blue-eyed gene and the other has given a brown-eyed gene, the individual will have brown eyes, because in the determination of eye color, brown is dominant over blue. It should be noted, however, that the offspring, although brown-eyed, would have a recessive blue-eyed gene. Through reduction division such an offspring will itself produce some germ cells that have only a blue-eyed gene. Thus two brown-eyed persons might produce a blue-eyed offspring, because they would both have had recessive blue-eyed genes and through random genetic combinations could have produced two blue-eyed genes in the germ cells involved in mating. The probability of outcome of various genetic combinations can be determined by means of the Mendelian laws, which are named after Gregor Mendel, the nineteenth-century Austrian monk who discovered the principles of modern genetics. Because of the operation of recessive genes, it is impossible for persons to predict the exact characteristics of their offspring.

Biological Differences

Let us now turn our attention to biological or genetic differences among individual people in their adjustive capacities. We consider the general question: To what extent are differences in our capacities for successful adjustment genetically determined? First, there are obvious differences in physical stature from adult to adult which are determined by heredity. The man who is seven feet tall will have certain opportunities for adjustive behaviors that are denied to the great majority of us—for example, he is far better equipped to excel at basketball. On the other hand, he is faced with the prospect of adjusting continually to problem situations that do not exist for his smaller friends—difficulties in buying clothes, fitting into automobiles, walking through doorways, and a host of others, including interpersonal relationships. Then there are the myriad possibilities for the development of complex psychological problems stemming from the fact of being unalterably different from most other people in an obvious physical sense. Certainly peer acceptance becomes an important issue for very tall people, especially if they lack physical agility and coordination.

Even more severe problems exist at the other end of the size dimension. The social difficulties faced by those individuals who are unfortunate enough to be classified as dwarfs and midgets are so great that they tend to associate primarily with each other rather than with people of normal size (Weinberg, 1968). With the enormous importance that is placed on physical adequacy in Western culture, the opportunities for a dwarf to win adequate peer approval among the rest of us are few indeed. In addition, the sheer physical problems posed by being extremely short are often much more severe than those of being extremely tall.

We have used physical height as an example of genetic endowment because height is a human characteristic which is known to have a relatively clear hereditary basis. Although it is now known that nutritional deficiencies can prevent persons from reaching the full height of their genetic potential (see the work of Jean Mayer), height is ordinarily regarded as genetically determined. Height and other genetically deter-

James and Eileen Hagen are dwarfs and
must continually cope with problems relating
to their height, such as using stools to wash
the dinner dishes. Their daughter, Jill, is
normal in size.

mined physical characteristics are very important in determining the reactions of other
people to us and, consequently, our level and type of adjustment.

What other human characteristics with importance for psychological adjustment are
inherited to some degree or other? First of all, let us ask what human characteristics of
any kind are known to have a significant hereditary component. Eye color, physical
shape and structure, hair color, and propensity to baldness in males are some which
come immediately to mind. It should be apparent that there is no simple relationship
between any of these and problems of adjustment. In general, in each human society

or subgroup, there are fairly clearcut notions of what constitutes physical attractiveness. Persons who meet these criteria will evoke a more positive response from others
and will be more highly valued. On the other hand, such "beautiful people" might
come to feel that too much is expected of them and that they cannot meet these
expectations. Or, the easy availability of social rewards might prevent them from
developing adequate skills for coping with personal misfortunes of one kind or
another. Thus, the relationship between attractiveness and adjustment is complex and
requires careful analysis. In Western middle class society, for instance, it is claimed
that blondes have more fun; paradoxically, the originators of this commercial message
are working to nullify its validity by offering to make all women into blondes!

Heredity and Intelligence

We have seen that there are quite a number of physical characteristics related to
adjustment capacity that have a hereditary component. In other words, adjustment
potential may be influenced by inherited physical characteristics, and in some cases
markedly so. We now consider *psychological* characteristics in which there is a
significant genetic component. While the following discussion emphasizes the genetic
contribution to, or component of, each characteristic, it should be borne in mind that
scientists have found it extremely difficult to determine the relative amount of genetic
influence upon a characteristic as compared to the influence of environmental factors.
First, we consider **intelligence,** variously defined as the capacity for conceptual
thinking, for judgment, and for anticipating the consequences of one's actions.

   To what extent is intelligence inherited, and how do we know this? These questions
have not yet been fully answered, and the partial answers now available reveal the
complexity of the problem and the incompleteness of our knowledge. Let us examine

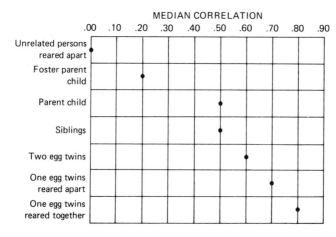

Figure 1-1. Correlation between the intelligence scores of people having different genetic relationships to each other. (From L. Erlenmeyer-Kimling and L. F. Jarvik, Genetics and intelligence. *Science,* December, 1963, **142,** 1477-1479. Copyright 1963 by the American Association for the Advancement of Science. Reproduced by permission.)

Figure 1-1, in which an attempt is made to summarize our knowledge in this area. This figure presents a number of **correlations,** or statistically derived numbers which indicate the degree of relationship between two sets of scores or other quantities. Let us take a moment to examine the concept of correlation. The correlation between degree of baldness and body weight, for example, is zero. That is to say, there is no relationship between these quantities. A perfect positive relationship—for example, the relationship between the size of people's left and right feet—would be depicted by a correlation coefficient of plus one. For an inverse relationship, the correlation coefficient would be negative, to a maximum of minus one.

Returning now to Figure 1-1, the point at the top left corner represents the correlation between the intelligence test scores of pairs of people who were selected at random. As expected, this correlation coefficient is zero. Now consider the point nearest the bottom right corner. This represents the correlation between the intelligence scores of identical twins who grew up in the same household. Since identical twins come from the same single fertilized egg, they share a common heredity. The inclusion of the qualification that they grew up together ensures that they were exposed to similar environmental influences. This correlation is high, indicating that identical twins are very similar in intelligence. The correlation for identical twins who were reared apart is also high but not as high as for identical twins reared together, indicating that the more similar their environmental influences, the more similar two people's IQ scores will be. Since identical twins are assumed to have the same heredity, it can confidently be said that the fairly high degree of relationship between the IQ scores of identical twins reared apart represents the influence of heredity on intelligence, while the still higher correlation for identical twins reared together represents the additional contribution of environment in determining IQ.

The point second nearest the top represents the correlation in IQ between foster parents and their children. Since there is no genetic similarity here, the existing small degree of positive relationship must be due to environmental factors, one of which is probably the fact that child placement agencies often attempt to place children with foster parents whose intellectual level is similar to that of the child's natural parents.

The remaining three points in the figure refer to pairs of people who have some genetic similarity to each other, but not complete similarity, as with identical twins. These relationships are moderately high, and the highest is for pairs of fraternal twins, whose genetic similarity to each other is no greater than for non-twin siblings. It can be appreciated, however, that twins, being exactly the same age, will experience more similarities in their environmental experiences than ordinary siblings. Thus, the difference between the correlations for fraternal twins and for ordinary siblings can be held to represent the differential effect of environment.

Environmental Factors in Intellectual Development

Our conclusion from a careful study of this figure is that within a stable population, heredity plays a major part in the development of intelligence. Environment also plays an important part, but in all probability a smaller one. One way to state the relationship is to consider that heredity sets the ceiling for the development of one's intellectual potential, a ceiling that can be approached if one's environment is favorable. Thus, an unfavorable environment might leave a person with a useful intellectual capacity far below the genetic potential. In other words, heredity sets the limit on a person's capacity for learning, while environmental influences determine what is learned, and to what extent one's capacity is utilized. A point to note, however, is that the range of environment involved in these studies has probably been limited. For example, it is unlikely that foster children were ever placed in extremely impoverished home environments. Scarr (1977), following a comprehensive review of the evidence on the genetics of human intelligence, has reaffirmed this conclusion, stating that "the relative standing of a person in his intellectual peer group depends more on genetic than on environmental differences, given rearing conditions in a humane range" (p. 1). Munsinger (1978) conducted an independent review and reached the same conclusion.

In very recent years it has been recognized that the degree of intellectual and other stimulation received by children in their earliest years is an important environmental determinant of functioning intellectual capacity in later life. Further, the amount and kind of intellectual stimulation available to any child is a function of a complex set of social factors. Included among these factors would be such things as the education of the parents, the family income, and the number of other children present in the home. It is clear, for instance, that magazines that are colorful and interesting to children are more likely to be present in the homes of better educated and more affluent parents than in the homes of poorly educated and less affluent parents. Also, the better educated parents will more systematically urge their children to interest themselves in these materials, and even more importantly, will reward them for this behavior.

One aspect of this problem that has received much attention is whether or not the lack of this kind of early intellectual stimulation can be remedied. The children's educational program *Sesame Street* and the various Head Start programs are deliberate attempts to provide children with the kind of stimulation which is conducive to intellectual development, and recent studies have demonstrated some success for them. It should be emphasized that psychologists have only recently begun to develop any kind of satisfactory understanding of how children learn and develop intellectually, so that the full range of possibilities for improving intelligence is as yet unknown. In fact, some psychologists have advanced the view that even intelligent people use only a small fraction of their intellectual potential, suggesting that it could be greatly increased with proper training. Let us hasten to indicate, however, that this is simply speculation, and that such methods are at present unknown, despite the many "improve your intelligence" magazine advertisements.

Hereditary factors in mental retardation. Just as there are a few people at the extremely high points of the intelligence scale continuum, who are considered to be intellectually gifted, so there are those few at the lower end, who are considered to be mentally retarded. Most of those at the lower end will be there because of the kind of hereditary and environmental factors discussed above. Also, mistakes are sometimes made in labeling a person as retarded because of inappropriate testing procedures. For most individuals who are severely defective in intelligence, it is now believed that there is some specific brain abnormality, although the exact causes can be discovered in only a minority of cases (O'Leary and Wilson, 1975, pp. 135-144). For a few of them, there is a known physical cause. For example, mongolism, now better known as Down's syndrome, accounts for about 10 percent of the institutionalized mentally retarded. Much more rare is Huntington's chorea, a hereditary illness which becomes apparent only in later life, and involves other problems such as difficulties in coordination.

We have dwelt on the subject of heredity and intelligence at some length because intelligence provides a good illustration of the manner in which evidence can be accumulated concerning the relative contributions of heredity and environment to a

Down's syndrome is a disorder caused by a chromosomal abnormality. Individuals with Down's syndrome seldom have an IQ over 50 and exhibit certain physical characteristics, such as a flat nose bridge, skin folds at the inner corner of the eye, and stubby hands.

human characteristic related to psychological adjustment, as well as evidence concerning their complex interaction. With this background, we can now examine some other factors in adjustment that may have some hereditary basis.

Heredity and Personal Characteristics

There can be no doubt that heredity does exert some influence, in one way or another, on personal characteristics and on individual modes of adjustment. One has only to note the fact that animal breeders have for many years worked at developing particular "temperaments" in various kinds of animals, particularly dogs. More specific evidence can be cited from recent studies of behavior genetics, which show that such characteristics as dominance and hoarding can be bred in mice. Although such studies could not be conducted with humans for obvious reasons, it is likely that the same principles apply there.

Although it is generally believed that the relationship between personal characteristics and heredity is complex and heavily influenced by environmental variables, several psychologists have chosen to defend the position that there is in fact a much simpler, direct relationship. Perhaps the best known of these is W. H. Sheldon (1942, 1954). In Sheldon's view, hereditary factors are of major importance in determining human behavior, and play a crucial role in each individual's development. Further, according to Sheldon, it is possible to classify individuals according to three dimensions or types of body build: _mesomorphy, endomorphy, and ectomorphy_, each with its associated interpersonal or behavioral characteristics. The pure mesomorph is mostly muscle and bone, with relatively little fat. The professional football guard or tackle would often be considered as close to the perfect mesomorph. Interpersonally, mesomorphs are characterized by a high degree of _somatotonia_, which is Sheldon's word for a high need for vigorous physical activity, love of adventure, and domination of others. Such people are also said to be somewhat callous and insensitive in their feelings toward others.

The second type of body build, endomorphy, refers to those individuals with a high proportion of fatty tissue and a soft, flabby build. The interpersonal characteristics of endomorphs are referred to as _viscerotonia_—love of comfort, sociability, food, and affection, and a relaxed, tolerant, even manner. The "jolly fat person" fits the stereotype of the endomorph. Ectomorphy is the third type of body build, and refers to individuals who are thin and small-boned with little fat or muscle. Ectomorphy is associated with _cerebrotonia_, Sheldon's word indicating a need for solitude and for avoiding attention, for overreactivity, and a general fear of people. One can think of the stooped, skinny, worried-looking, bespectacled bookworm as the typical ectomorph. It is uncommon to find pure examples of one or another of these three body build types; rather, an individual is assigned three numbers in the range of 1 through 7. Each number represents the amount of a type which is possessed by the person, and implies a similar proportion of the associated personality characteristics.

Sheldon's own work is open to the criticism that the evaluations of interpersonal characteristics and body build in his studies were both made by the same investigators at the same time and that, therefore, they found what they hoped to find. More recent research, however, has found some degree of support for a relationship between body build and certain personality characteristics (e.g., Cortes and Gatti, 1970). This work should not be taken as evidence for a cause-and-effect relationship between body build and personality. Rather, it is likely that body build affects behavior indirectly through differential learning experiences, as explained in the section below on behavior genetics.

In our society there is a certain amount of reluctance to accept explanations of behavior and personality that involve heredity. Explanations based on heredity run contrary to the Horatio Alger spirit: the notion that through hard work and determination one can accomplish practically anything. The resistance to theoretical views and to research findings that emphasize the importance of genetic determinants of any important human characteristic—intelligence, personality, and so on—must also be understood in this context.

Other psychological theorists are less extreme than Sheldon in their views of the relationship between heredity and personal characteristics. Raymond B. Cattell (1946, 1973), for example, believes that human behavior is best understood in terms of traits, or generalized response tendencies, which can be divided into overt, or **manifest traits,** and underlying, or **source traits.** Cattell notes that there are major consistencies in human behavior over time and across situations. For example, some people show conscientious behavior in a wide variety of situations, and such persons can be considered to possess the manifest or overt trait of conscientiousness. Underlying the manifest traits are the source traits, or mechanisms that are offered to explain the observed behavior. In Cattell's view, personality can best be understood as the underlying patterns of source traits possessed by the individual; that is, the underlying mechanisms determining his or her behavior. These underlying mechanisms are, of course, themselves formed by a variety of influences, and we are here concerned with those influences that are present at birth. Cattell, among others, argues that there are some very important source traits that are constitutional or hereditary. The major source traits which he regards as based on hereditary factors include gregariousness, fear, self-assertion, and self-indulgence. Cattell believes that the importance of heredity as a determinant of personality factors has been underestimated by American psychologists. Similarities can be seen between Cattell's view and other views that humans are motivated by biologically based drives. Freud, for example, took the view that sexual and aggressive drives were the basic sources of human motivation. What Cattell proposes in addition is that basic differences among individuals can be explained in terms of the different amounts of these biologically based drives, or traits, that different persons possess.

One of the important current debates in psychology involves the nature and importance of these so-called source traits. There are a number of psychologists (e.g.,

Mischel, 1968; Skinner, 1974) who have argued that source traits are principally environmental and that stability in human behavior is a result of the similarity of situations in which people find themselves. Psychologists of this persuasion insist that a better understanding of behavior will come from a more careful analysis of the situations or environments in which people behave, and how particular behaviors are learned in these situations.

The work of the British psychologist H. J. Eysenck (1947, 1970) should also be mentioned in this context. In Eysenck's view, our capacity for adjustment is determined by just two simple hereditary source traits or dimensions: autonomic reactivity (or emotionality), and conditionability. Autonomic reactivity refers to the degree of reactivity of one's autonomic nervous system, and is the source of the physiological basis of the personality dimension of *neuroticism*. Conditionability refers to the speed with which one's emotional reactions can be conditioned, and is the basis of the personality dimension of *extraversion—introversion*, a concept originally introduced to psychology by Freud's early colleague, Carl Jung. Eysenck believes that these two constitutional variables are adequate for a science of human behavior. There is little evidence as yet, however, in support of the hereditary aspects of Eysenck's framework, and the general usefulness of his theory is still to be demonstrated.

Buss and Plomin (1975) have recently proposed a new theory of personality based on temperament. To qualify as a temperament, first, a characteristic must be inherited; and second, it must show stability during childhood, be retained into adulthood, and be shown to have been present with adaptive value in our animal forebears. Buss and Plomin propose that four characteristics meet this definition of a temperament:

- *Level of activity,* or total energy output. Active people are typically busy and in a hurry.
- *Emotionality,* or intensity of reaction. Emotional people are easily aroused.
- *Sociability,* or affiliativeness. Sociable people have a strong desire to be with others.
- *Impulsivity*. Impulsive people tend to respond quickly rather than inhibiting the response.

As yet, there is little clear evidence to support the Buss-Plomin temperament approach to personality. However, it is an interesting and plausible idea, and should stimulate further research for some time to come.

Behavior genetics. We have already pointed out that one does not need a strictly hereditary viewpoint to support the belief that physical characteristics and personality are related. For example, Sheldon's mesomorphic children may be likely to develop into aggressive adults simply because, with their body builds, aggression is a behavior they perform well and for which they may be rewarded by others or by their own internal feelings of satisfaction. The complex relationship between heredity and behavior is the subject of a relatively new field of inquiry, **behavior genetics,** and much of the information in the present chapter would come under that heading.

There are two major principles that have emerged in behavior genetic research (see Wiggins *et al.*, 1971, Ch. 3), and the reader should bear them in mind throughout the first three chapters of this volume. The first principle, which might be termed **differential susceptibility to experience,** states that the same environmental treatment has different effects on people with different hereditary endowments. In the example given above, the mesomorphic boy may be little affected by a taunt from another child, because he knows he can silence the taunts if necessary. On the other hand, the weaker ectomorphic boy, with fewer physical resources at his disposal, might well be more adversely affected by exactly the same degree of teasing. The second principle, **selective exposure,** refers to the fact that one's hereditary endowment determines to some degree the environmental experiences to which one is exposed. Thus, "plain Jane" simply never receives the admiring glances that are freely bestowed upon her more attractive sisters, and so never learns how to react appropriately to them.

The principles of behavior genetics have been developed primarily through research with nonhuman creatures, such as mice and fruitflies, which can be bred selectively and exposed to specific environments. Behavior genetic research with humans cannot, of course, be conducted in this manner. Also, the most important genetic principles, the Mendelian laws, assume random mating and it is clear that human mating is not random. Humans are generally quite selective in their mating, and it cannot be determined how this selectivity modifies the application to humans of the genetic principles derived from species that randomly mate. Thus, without denying the importance of what is generally known about genetics, there is very little known about human behavior genetics that can be regarded as well substantiated.

Despite these problems, some relatively sophisticated research studies of pairs of individuals with differing degrees of genetic and environmental similarities have been reported. The research on intelligence presented in Figure 1-1 provides an excellent example of these methods. Characteristics such as intelligence are fairly straightforward to study, because everybody is a potential subject in one group or another. Imagine, however, the difficulty in studying the hereditary basis of schizophrenia when the frequency of this disorder in the population is less than 1 percent, and when such research involves the study of individuals who are both schizophrenic and twins—an extremely infrequent occurrence. And to locate a sample of such persons who were reared separately from their siblings is practically impossible. Yet, despite these great difficulties, such research has been reported (Heston, 1970).

Heredity and Deviant Behavior

Let us consider further the degree of relationship, if any, between hereditary factors and the various forms of serious psychological disturbance. A survey of the available evidence suggests that the degree of hereditary influence varies with the particular psychological disorder under consideration. The notion that there is a relationship between heredity and behavior pathology has been with us for centuries and is expressed in the view that insanity or other deviant behaviors run in families.

The most common serious psychological disturbance, schizophrenia, has been studied in considerable depth in this regard. To quote the writings of David Rosenthal (1971), an authority on the genetics of psychopathology, "the evidence . . . so strongly reinforces the probability of a genetic contribution to schizophrenia that such a view (that genetic factors are unimportant) no longer appears tenable" (p. 104). Rosenthal's summary of such studies shows, for example, that the likelihood of finding schizophrenia in a second twin if the first has schizophrenia is three to six times greater for identical twins than for fraternal twins. Perhaps the most common informed belief today is that many persons carry a genetic predisposition toward schizophrenia, but that certain unfavorable conditions in one's early childhood environment must also appear in order for the disorder to become manifest. It should be emphasized, however, that the picture is by no means clear.

There is also fairly strong evidence for a genetic contribution to another major psychological disturbance, **manic-depressive psychosis,** although studies of this disorder have not been as thorough as those of schizophrenia. (The reader should understand that this word does not refer to the depressive moods which are common to many people, but to mood swings so intense that the individual needs professional care, even hospitalization.) Once again, the exact nature of the disorder is not understood, and there is undoubtedly a large contribution from environmental factors.

A number of other disorders which are considered to be maladaptive ways of behaving, among them neurosis, alcoholism, and homosexuality, have also been studied from a genetic point of view. In general, it seems that there could be a genetic contribution in each of these types of disorders for at least some individuals, although the evidence is extremely sparse and inconclusive. The most common contemporary viewpoint on these disorders holds that there is no *direct* genetic contribution, and that any such influence would be part of a complex interaction with environmental factors.

Another area of psychological adjustment in which heredity has been traditionally considered to play a part is criminal behavior. Here, the popular notion of a hereditary influence is expressed in the idea of the "bad seed," or the "black sheep of the family." Criminal behavior is usually considered to be an outcome of an underlying disorder called **psychopathy,** although criminality is not the only possible consequence of psychopathy. Once again, no clear evidence of a genetic basis for psychopathy has been found; and conversely, it is well established that environmental factors are of considerable importance in determining criminal behavior. There are, however, four possible genetic influences that should not be overlooked (Rosenthal, 1971, pp. 136-137). The first three are indirect: (1) there is a higher incidence of brain abnormalities among criminals than in the general population, as indicated by studies of brain waves, more accurately called the electroencephalogram, or EEG; (2) criminals often tend to have lower IQ scores; and (3) their body builds are predominantly what Sheldon has termed mesomorphic—tough and muscular. All of these factors are known to have some hereditary basis, although abnormal EEG patterns are also often the result of disturbances to the brain occurring after birth, and intelligence may be adversely affected by early social and educational deprivation.

The fourth possible genetic influence on criminal behavior is both more direct and more controversial. It has been shown that there are some men who possess a genetic abnormality, which is referred to simply as the "XYY type." (Normal males are XY, normal females XX. The letters refer to sex chromosomes received from each parent.) These men tend to be taller, heavier, and stronger than average, and there is a higher proportion of them in prison populations than in the general population (Jarvik, Klodin, and Matsuyama, 1973). Scientists are currently studying this disorder to see whether there is in fact a meaningful relationship between this genetic anomaly and criminality. It should be emphasized, however, that the role of heredity in criminal behavior is generally agreed to be small, and that environmental factors are much more important. Thus, in contrast to the strong evidence of hereditary influence involved in schizophrenia, the evidence for such an influence on criminal behavior is unclear.

Limits to Our Present Knowledge

We have reviewed the scientific knowledge and opinion on the topic of the degree to which hereditary factors contribute to our capacities for psychological adjustment. We have seen that intelligence, which is traditionally defined as including memory, judgment, and ability for problem solving and learning, has a notable hereditary basis. There is a definite though smaller genetic contribution to one's predisposition to schizophrenia, and perhaps also to manic-depressive disorders. For other maladjustments, such as the neuroses, alcoholism, homosexuality, and criminal behavior, the direct contribution of heredity is currently regarded as minor. With regard to individual characteristics in the normal range, a variety of indirect connections can be developed, such as the relationship between aggressive behavior and physical size and strength, which has a hereditary component. The last decade has seen a resurgence of interest by researchers in behavior genetics, and it is hoped that a fuller understanding of the relationships of heredity and behavior will be forthcoming.

In spite of the fact that what is known about hereditary influences on one's capacity for psychological adjustment has been presented in a neat and systematic manner, the reader should not conclude that the process of gaining scientific knowledge proceeds as systematically. There are enormous difficulties in separating out the relative effects of heredity and environment on most human characteristics. This can be seen nowhere more clearly than in the current attempts to make an accurate determination of the extent to which negative environmental factors are responsible for the differences in intelligence-test performances between blacks and whites.

Most, if not all, of the formal measures of intelligence (or IQ tests) tend to reflect the individual's prior experience in problem solving. At the same time, both the problems to be solved and the solutions are rather different for middle class whites and ghetto blacks. Standard intelligence tests, constructed by middle class whites, tend to emphasize the problems and the problem solutions of white middle class culture. Such tests, with their marked cultural bias, often give an unfair appraisal of the problem-solving skills of blacks. Although there have been some recent attempts both to develop "culture-fair" and ghetto-based intelligence tests, most standard intelligence tests are biased. Indeed, one can argue that the entire concept of testing, with its emphasis on speed of performance, time limits, and comparisons among individuals, is culturally loaded. Scarr (1977), in her previously mentioned review of the evidence on the genetics of human intelligence, concluded that "black children are being reared in circumstances that give them only marginal acquaintance with the skills and the knowledge being sampled by the tests we administered. Some families in the black community encourage the development of these skills and knowledge, while others do not. In general, black children do not have the same access to these skills and knowledge as white children, which explains the lower performance of black children as a group" (pp. 40-41). For readers who want to know more about these problems, the writings of Jensen and his critics (Jensen et al., 1969), Herrnstein (1971), and Scarr (1977) offer thoughtful analyses.

Other Biological Problems in Adjustment

Heredity can be the basis for personal characteristics that offer both advantages and disadvantages for one's psychological adjustment. There is another group of personal characteristics which affect one's biological makeup from the time of birth, but which are the product of either the unborn child's environment or difficulties experienced at the time of birth. The reader is referred to Mussen, Conger, and Kagan (1974) for a more complete account of these factors.

First, it is known that deficiencies in the diet of an expectant mother can have negative effects on the fetus. Women suffering from malnutrition tend to have infants whose health is generally poorer than that of the children of adequately nourished mothers. Reported problems have included a higher incidence both of major illnesses, such as pneumonia and rickets, and also of such minor illnesses as colds during their first six months. There are also reports that stillbirths and deaths in early infancy occur more frequently when the mother has been undernourished. It is possible that severe malnutrition can also cause mental retardation in some instances, through its effects on aspects of brain development.

Better known dangers to an unborn child are those associated with the expectant mother's drug intake, certain diseases, or overexposure to radiation. Babies unfortunate enough to have been formed while their mothers were taking the drug thalidomide, before its disastrous effects were known, stood a high risk of being born with gross anatomical defects of the limbs. Babies whose mothers were given sedation during labor have been known to show signs themselves of sluggishness, and although

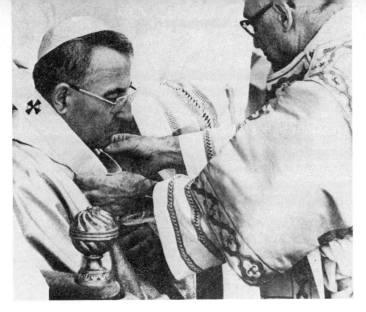

The late Pope John Paul I was born in the mountains of Italy and was the son of a bricklayer and a peasant woman. His humble origins did not hinder him from attaining the highest office of the Catholic church.

the effects have appeared to wear off rapidly, it is conceivable that permanent difficulties could occasionally result. It has also been reported that nicotine from an expectant mother's cigarettes can have an effect on the fetus such as lower birth weight, but researchers have as yet demonstrated no permanent effects.

Exposure to large amounts of X-ray radiation is known to greatly increase the risk of malformations in the newborn baby. Thus, expectant mothers who require X-ray treatment for a malignant growth produce children with a higher than average frequency of mental and physical abnormalities. And of course similar terrible effects on a larger scale followed the atomic bombing of Hiroshima in 1945, when many women who were close at hand and in the early stages of pregnancy gave birth to children with a variety of abnormalities.

Certain diseases in an expectant mother can affect the fetus. It is well known that mothers who contract German measles (rubella) early in pregnancy are more likely than average to give birth to children with a variety of problems including visual disorders, hearing disorders, and mental retardation. A pregnant woman suffering from syphilis may also give birth to a deformed or otherwise abnormal child, and pregnant women addicted to heroin give birth to children who are also addicted. Certain other diseases of the mother, such as diabetes, are also potentially harmful to the unborn child.

Perhaps the most fascinating and least understood effects are those associated with the pregnant woman's emotional states and psychological attitudes. It is known, for example, that prolonged emotional stress during pregnancy can have adverse consequences on the development of the fetus. Also, there is some evidence that women who are tense and anxious during pregnancy have babies who prove to be more difficult than average to care for, although this relationship is by no means a strong one.

We have seen how a variety of prenatal factors might serve to hamper the newborn child's ability to adjust well to the world. Certain factors during the process of birth occasionally also result in permanent physiological damage to the child. Perhaps the best known, though very infrequent, is *anoxia*, in which the brain of the newborn baby does not receive sufficient oxygen. This may result either from a failure to begin breathing, or bleeding caused by broken blood vessels in the brain. Anoxia in newborn babies is thought to be a cause of *cerebral palsy*, a name for partial paralysis and difficulties in movement associated with brain damage. Other causes of brain damage, accompanied at times by mental retardation, are certain illnesses such as meningitis, and, of course, direct injury to the head. The case of Donna, described at the beginning of this chapter, is a possible example of the effects of an illness resulting in brain damage. There is also a group of children who, though apparently normal in many aspects of intelligence, suffer from severe difficulties in certain aspects of school-work, such as reading. It is thought (e.g., Chalfant and Scheffelin, 1969) that the causes for the problems of many of these children are to be found in very mild degrees of brain damage, too mild to be identified by means of neurological or psychological tests, but very definite in their effects on the child's learning ability and general capacity for adjustment.

SUMMARY

1. The psychology of adjustment is the aspect of the science of human behavior that attempts to explain how people cope with the demands and problems of everyday life. To develop an adequate understanding of psychological adjustment, it is necessary to adopt a specific viewpoint regarding basic human nature. Three viewpoints have traditionally been held: the moral, the humanistic, and the social-learning. It is the social-learning view that forms the primary basis for this book.

2. In the *moral* view of psychological adjustment, moral absolutes provide the guidelines for evaluating the quality of one's adjustment. The traditional Christian church provided one such set of guidelines, in which the adjustment process was seen as a constant struggle against one's basically evil nature. Sigmund Freud, who was probably the most influential of all scholars in the field of psychological adjustment, also took a negative view of human nature, although later psychoanalytic scholars modified this view to increase the importance of social and cultural factors in the adjustment process.

3. The view that humans are innately good rather than evil has been put forward by *humanistic* psychologists, who consider that the highest level of adjustment is achieved when one has reached the stage of self-actualization, or fulfillment of one's innate potential. *Phenomenologists,* one group of humanistic psychologists, believe that it is possible to understand an individual only through his or her own subjective frame of reference. Thus, we must each ultimately judge for ourselves the adjustive quality of our actions. The *existential* view of the adjustment process emphasizes that we are all uniquely responsible for our own destiny, which is continually being shaped by the life decisions that we make.

4. The third view of adjustment, as a *social-learning* process, is the one taken in this book. We plan to study human problem-solving, or coping, behavior as people attempt to meet and master a variety of challenges to their existence, including (1) direct challenges from the physical environment; (2) challenges stemming from personal limitations; and (3) interpersonal challenges. The social-learning view of adjustment is similar in some respects to the contemporary view derived from Freudian theory known as ego psychology, which also emphasizes one's competence in coping with the environment.

5. The remainder of the chapter discusses those aspects of human biological makeup that influence adjustment in one way or another. First, we consider how the process of biological *evolution* has resulted in uniquely human adaptive advantages. Perhaps the most important difference in this regard is the superiority in the development of the human brain, and our resultant capacity for thought, language, and highly developed social interaction.

6. Next, we examine the mechanism of *heredity,* the manner in which characteristics are transmitted from one generation to the next. The genetic code, which determines the biological similarities and differences among individual members of a species, is found in the chromosomes, which are present in each living cell. Each offspring receives half of its chromosomes from each parent, giving it some of the genetic characteristics of each. The Mendelian laws enable some predictions to be made about inherited characteristics, but there are many complications in making such predictions.

7. An example of an inherited characteristic with many implications for one's adjustment is *height,* for it is obvious that persons who are extremely tall or extremely short encounter particular problems in coping with their environments. Another characteristic with a large hereditary component which has a vital influence on adjustment is *intelligence,* and there has been a considerable amount of research done in an effort to understand the exact nature of the contribution of heredity to this characteristic. Much of this research has involved an examination of the degree of relationship between the IQ scores of pairs of persons with varying degrees of genetic similarity to each other, such as identical twins and non-twin siblings. Very recently, attention has been given to understanding the effects of an intellectually deprived environment on limiting intellectual growth in young children.

8. Heredity also undoubtedly exerts an influence on *interpersonal characteristics*. Although views such as Sheldon's, which argue for a direct, causal relationship between body type and personality, are nowadays seldom entertained seriously, a variety of indirect relationships can be discovered. The two major principles which have emerged from research on the effects of genetic factors on behavior indicate that the same environmental situation has different effects on persons with different hereditary endowments, and that one's hereditary endowment is a factor in determining the environmental experiences to which one is exposed.

9. Heredity is known to play a significant role in the development of two major *psychological disturbances*, schizophrenia and manic-depressive psychosis. The possibility of some genetic contribution to other psychological and behavioral disorders has also been explored, but the effects, if any, are probably indirect and relatively slight. It is emphasized that enormous difficulties arise in any attempts to make a meaningful assessment of the influence of hereditary factors on behavior, and that scientific evidence in this area accumulates very slowly indeed.

10. There are a number of biological characteristics which, although not hereditary, are present at birth or in early childhood, and can have serious effects on an individual's capacity for psychological adjustment. One such group of factors are those which can adversely affect the unborn child, such as deficiencies in the expectant mother's diet, her use of drugs such as thalidomide, and exposure to X-ray irradiation. Emotional stress during pregnancy can also affect the fetus. Other problems can occur at the time of delivery, such as brain damage resulting from insufficient oxygen; and certain childhood illnesses can also lead to brain damage, with detrimental effects on adjustive capacity.

KEY TERMS

psychology	manifest traits
psychology of adjustment	source traits
zygote	behavior genetics
embryo	differential susceptibility to experience
fetus	
chromosomes	selective exposure
genes	manic-depressive psychosis
intelligence	psychopathy
correlations	

TWO

Learning and the Social Foundations of Adjustment

The foundations for learning to cope with the environment are set during the first years of life.

Learning is the process through which behavior is produced by special experience, stimulation, practice, and training.

- Learning can be both planned and unplanned; children learn both adaptive and unadaptive behaviors.
- Learning can take place by association, through classical conditioning.
- Learning can also take place by reinforcement, through operant conditioning.
- A third kind of learning process is modeling, or observational learning.

There are a number of basic concepts to master in understanding the learning process:

- drive, stimulus, response, and reinforcement
- generalization and discrimination
- response hierarchies and anticipatory responses
- extinction, spontaneous recovery, and punishment
- partial reinforcement

AN EXAMINATION OF THE BEHAVIOR OF THE NEWBORN HUMAN INFANT GIVES US some idea of its initial behavior repertoire, its unlearned reflexive equipment. These are the behaviors which have been produced by human genetic makeup, released by the genetic code discussed in Chapter 1, and they are further examples of the powerful influence of biology on human behavior.

Infantile dependency. Recent research studies of the newborn have shown that after only two hours the newborn will follow the movement of a light with its eyes, particularly if the movement is neither too fast nor too slow; will suckle on a nipple or finger placed in its mouth; will turn its head in the direction in which its mouth or cheek is touched; will lift its chin from its chest when it is stimulated; will cry, cough, blink, vomit, tense its body to loud noises, and change its position. The newborn infant can see, hear, taste, and smell, and is sensitive to pain, touch, and changes in position. In contrast to many other species, all these basic sensations are present in the human infant at birth. Puppies, on the other hand, are both blind and deaf at birth and their responsiveness to visual and auditory stimulation develops gradually. The normal human newborn is a relatively sensitive organism capable of a variety of responses.

Despite the newborn infant's sensitivity and behavior repertoire, its skills are not adequate to permit it to manage on its own. Compared with other species, maturation of the human infant proceeds at a slow pace. For a long period of time after birth the human infant can do little to care for itself. It must be fed, cleansed, and generally protected from the elements or else it will not survive. Other species produce offspring with sufficient unlearned behaviors to manage on their own or with a minimal period of nurturance. However, in humans, the unlearned behavior repertoire present at birth is not sufficient for survival, and without adequate parenting, human infants will die.

This infantile dependence is an important characteristic of humans and is a critical factor influencing the nature of human society. Adult humans must arrange their behaviors to care for their dependent offspring, otherwise the offspring would perish and the species would become extinct. The nuclear family, consisting of father, mother, and children, is the most common social arrangement for protecting and caring for the developing infant. Similar social groupings have been observed in primates (Mitchell, 1969; Van Lawick-Goodall, 1968), where there is a similar need for infantile protection. Animals whose mature behavior emerges earlier in the life cycle, such as cats and dogs, do not show such a social pattern.

Different human societies, both in the past and at present, show wide differences in the amount of time necessary for the maturing child to develop a set of behaviors that is adequate to cope with the environment. In all cases, however, maturity is not reached until many years after birth, and during this developmental period the child must be nurtured and protected. As societies become more technological and complex, the period of dependency is always lengthened. Thus the use of child labor, a commonly accepted practice in some other societies and in our own society at an earlier time, is now unacceptable to us.

Socialization. Although the behaviors that are regarded as indicating adulthood vary from society to society, the condition of the newborn infant and the pattern of its emerging behavior lead to certain universal problems of child handling. As Whiting and Child (1953) have noted, "In all societies the helpless infant, getting food by nursing at his mother's breast and having digested it, freely evacuating the waste products, exploring his genitals, biting and kicking at will, must be changed into a responsible adult obeying the rules of his society. . . . There is no clear evidence that any of these basic problems are in fact absent from the life of any people. Child training everywhere seems to be in considerable part concerned with problems which arise from universal characteristics of the human infant and from universal characteristics of adult culture which are incompatible with the continuation of infantile behavior" (pp. 63-64). Thus, in addition to the universal problems involved in producing control over these biologically based functions, there are the universal problems involved in changing the helpless, dependent child into the responsible, independent adult.

If we contrast the cases of Adele and Bart in Chapter 1, we can assume major differences in the patterns of socialization to which these two people have been exposed. Adele has not yet reached the status of a responsible independent adult, while Bart has done so. Ironically, Adele, who does not have the skills to manage herself, is about to have thrust upon her the responsibility for another human, a totally helpless one.

All societies make a clear distinction between behaviors that are appropriate for children and behaviors that are appropriate for adults. For example, no society expects very young children to control their eliminative processes but all societies do expect control from adults. There are wide differences in the toilet habits of different societies; for example, in Japan, Latin America, and certain other technologically sophisticated countries, it is common to see well-dressed men urinating against the side of buildings in major city streets. They would not, however, urinate in their clothing or in their living rooms. All societies have clear expectations about toilet habits and everybody is expected to follow them. The process by which the newborn infant is slowly and systematically trained in the expected behavioral traditions of its society is called **socialization.**

One way of looking at the phenomenon of socialization is to view it as the process by which the biologically determined, unlearned patterns of behavior are modified and changed into the learned patterns of behavior that are sanctioned or approved by the particular society. Socialization is the process by which the biological infant is transformed into the social person. Some psychologists have suggested that these universal biological needs account for most of the similarities among humans and the process of socialization accounts for the differences. This view, however, ignores the individual differences in behavior that are based on hereditary factors, already discussed in Chapter 1. In any event, it can be agreed that learning is the very basic process involved in the socialization of biologically based behaviors. It is the reliance on learning as a principal explanation that places this text within the social-learning approach to the study of human adjustment.

Understanding the process of socialization thus requires an understanding of the basic principles of learning, and we now direct our attention to an in-depth discussion of those principles, especially as they apply to socialization. In Chapter 3 we shall return to our discussion of the socialization process, paying particular attention to the various behavioral settings in which socialization occurs. First, however, it is necessary to understand the general process of learning.

THE PRINCIPLES OF LEARNING

We have already noted, both in Chapter 1 and earlier in this chapter, that certain behaviors emerge spontaneously as a function of the infant's biological makeup. The term *maturation* is used to describe these behaviors. Crawling, walking, and manipulation with the hands are examples of human maturational responses. These responses, the spontaneously occurring and unlearned behaviors of the organism, first appear in the unborn fetus and continue throughout the childhood years. It is important to remember that **maturational behaviors** do not require teaching or specific experiences in order to develop. The organism becomes capable of these responses as

Human infants are dependent for years
upon the care and protection of their parents. During this developmental period, they
are also socialized in the expected behavior
of their society.

a function of the growth of the central nervous system and other neural tissues as well as the growth of bones and muscles.

Attempts by adults to produce maturational responses in the infant prior to the time they spontaneously emerge have had little or no effect. Moreover, it is difficult to inhibit the emergence of these behaviors. For example, keeping infants in swaddling clothes or confined on cradle boards seems to have little effect on the emergence of walking. Dennis (1940) compared two groups of Hopi Indian children, one confined to cradle boards and the other allowed freedom of movement. For both groups the average age of walking was fifteen months, indicating that the cradling board did not have any retarding effect on walking.

Nevertheless, it is possible to interfere with the emergence of maturational responses, on either the physiological or the psychological level. As noted in Chapter 1, this can occur, on a physiological level, because of poor nutrition. On a psychological level, severe infantile deprivation—where the infant is never stimulated, rarely handled, and virtually ignored during the first year of life—can have a profoundly negative effect upon development. In a classical study, Spitz (1945) reported that such deprivation, occurring as a result of institutionalization, had widespread negative effects on the development of a group of children. Not only was there a marked deterioration in the intellectual and social development of these children as compared with children raised in more normal circumstances, as one might expect, but their motor development was also very much retarded. Under normal circumstances, however, maturational responses emerge without special stimulation or training.

What is learning? Learning is the process by which behavior is established through the influence of special experience or stimulation, as a result of practice or training. Learned behaviors do not occur without these influences. For example, human speech would never emerge spontaneously as a result of maturation, although there are maturational elements involved in learning to speak. The brain of the infant must mature and other physical development must occur before speech is possible, but these are not sufficient for the emergence of speech; adult stimulation and continued encouragement are also necessary.

It is important to recognize that learning is not always planned or deliberate. Although rearing children does involve a considerable amount of planned or intentional learning, such as teaching them to feed or dress themselves, much learning is accidental or incidental, as when a child learns to avoid the hot stove on which he or she has just been burned. While the parents may certainly wish that the child should learn to avoid painful objects, they rarely plan to arrange to have the child acquire this avoidance behavior directly.

Learning involves the arrangement of conditions, either intentionally or unintentionally, so that new or different responses are now made by the organism in place of some older responses or where no response at all was initially made. Learning is involved in a wide range of behaviors, from the simple process by which the child learns to avoid painful objects to the much more complex process of acquiring an understanding of arithmetic. Not only is normal behavior learned, but so too is much of what is considered abnormal behavior—fears, phobias, guilts, and the other signs that we regard as indicative of poor adjustment. It is because learning plays such a central role in the development of human behavior that we now direct our attention systematically to the details of this process.

The process of learning is extremely complex and is still not completely understood, even by those psychologists who have devoted their entire professional careers to its study. Also, there are several different theoretical approaches to the study of learning, and the differences in the theoretical assumptions, methods, and findings of these different approaches complicate our search for understanding still further. Any relatively brief explanation of the process of learning, such as this one, must be selective in its coverage and cannot delve into many of the theoretical issues that concern advanced workers in this field. The following presentation will focus on a few basic concepts of learning, those necessary for a basic knowledge of the ways in which human behavior is acquired, patterns of maladjustment are learned, and maladaptive or distressing behaviors can be changed.

One important theoretical issue concerns the number of different kinds of learning. Some psychologists argue that there is a single, general process of learning that accounts for the acquisition of all behavior, from the most simple to the most complex. While this is an extremely attractive position to adopt because it simplifies the problems of explanation, it appears to us that this viewpoint does not adequately account for some of the differences that are readily apparent among the phenomena of learning. It is quite possible that future research and theoretical work may point in another direction, but for our present purposes, we believe that it is most useful to talk about three kinds of learning: (1) **learning by association;** (2) **learning by reinforcement;** and (3) **learning by modeling or imitation.**

Learning by Association

One way of defining learning is in terms of the establishment of a "connective bond" or association between two events, an association that did not exist prior to learning. This learned response is not one which emerges as a function of maturation but is one which is created by special conditions. One of the special conditions for creating such a bond is to arrange a simple association between a **stimulus** and a **response.**

The original research into learning by association was done by the famous Russian physiologist and psychologist Ivan Pavlov. This process, which he first observed in the experimental laboratory is now known as **classical conditioning.** In Pavlov's experiments, a dog was taught to salivate to the sound of a buzzer, an "unnatural" response. Dogs do salivate naturally, however, to the sight and smell of meat. The response of salivation to food is innate and is part of the animal's unlearned, hereditary response system. This innate response of salivating is termed the **unconditioned response (UCR)** to the **unconditioned stimulus (UCS)** of the meat. Prior to conditioning,

the UCS always arouses the UCR. The bell, the **conditioned stimulus (CS),** is then presented a number of times immediately before the UCS. When the CS is finally presented alone, it then also elicits salivation, the **conditioned response (CR).**

The process of classical conditioning is probably the simplest kind of learning because it involves responses which are already part of the behavior repertoire of the organism. What happens in classical conditioning is that a new or arbitrary stimulus now evokes the response. Thus classical conditioning is sometimes described as **stimulus substitution.** The process of classical conditioning is presented in schematic form in Figure 2-1.

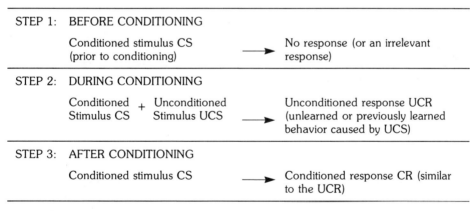

STEP 1:	BEFORE CONDITIONING	
	Conditioned stimulus CS (prior to conditioning) ⟶	No response (or an irrelevant response)
STEP 2:	DURING CONDITIONING	
	Conditioned Stimulus CS + Unconditioned Stimulus UCS ⟶	Unconditioned response UCR (unlearned or previously learned behavior caused by UCS)
STEP 3:	AFTER CONDITIONING	
	Conditioned stimulus CS ⟶	Conditioned response CR (similar to the UCR)

Figure 2-1. A three-step schematic representation of learning by association (classical conditioning). The association between the unconditioned stimulus (UCS) and the unconditioned response (UCR) exists prior to the conditioning process. This capacity of the UCS to elicit the UCR may be a function of some unlearned behavior pattern or may be the result of some prior learning. The association between the conditioned stimulus (CS) and the conditioned response (CR) is a learned one, arising from the pairing of the CS and UCS. As a result of continued pairing of the CS and UCS, the CS will come to elicit the CR which closely resembles the UCR, although they are not identical.

The reader may ask at this point about the relevance of classical conditioning for understanding human behavior. One important reason for studying classical conditioning is that this process is the basis for a good deal of human learning, especially the learning of anticipatory reactions such as fear. While the role of fear and anxiety in the adjustment process will be discussed in more detail in Chapter 4, it can be pointed out here that the learning of fear, which might be called a *conditioned emotional reaction,* tends to occur through classical conditioning.

An example of the learning of fear can be seen in a now famous experiment in which Watson and Rayner (1920) taught an infant boy, Albert, to fear a white rat. When Albert was initially shown the rat, he reached for it with no evidence of fear. While he was observing the rat, however, a loud noise (UCS) was deliberately set off behind him by the experimenters, causing an unconditioned fear response (UCR). When Albert was later shown the rat by itself he exhibited strong evidence of fear, a response which he had not shown before. The UCS of the noise had been paired with the neutral stimulus of the rat which thus became a CS for the arousal of the CR of fear. In the development of conditioned emotional reactions, stimuli that were originally neutral become CS's by being paired with UCS's that arouse innate emotional reactions. One important characteristic of conditioned emotional reactions worth noting is that these reactions, especially fear, can be learned through a simple association of the UCS and the CS. Many psychologists believe that most human fears, especially many of the so-called irrational fears, are acquired in this way. It is important to recognize that the CR is made not only to the original CS but to other stimuli that are similar, a process called *stimulus generalization.* Thus Albert became afraid not only of rats but also of other furry animals.

The acquisition of fear may also involve *higher-order conditioning.* In the case of Albert, he had learned to fear the rat by a process of simple conditioning. If the presentation of the rat was now simultaneously paired with the presentation of a flashing light, the flashing light would also become a CS for fear arousal, even though the light itself was never paired with the loud sound, the original UCS. This process of pairing stimuli without recourse to the original UCS is called **higher-order conditioning,** and is another important concept in explaining many complex human fears and other behaviors. The case of Frances in Chapter 1 gives a clear illustration of how intense circumscribed fears, or phobias, can develop and have important consequences for long periods in a person's adult life. We will return in Chapter 4 to a more detailed analysis of strong fear and the role of learning in explaining its persistence.

Learning by Reinforcement

Many psychologists have made a distinction between two kinds of behavior: *respondent* behavior and *operant* behavior. **Respondent behavior** includes responses that are commonly regarded as reflexes, such as salivation and simple knee jerks. Automatic, involuntary responses such as heartbeat and respiration that are under the control of the autonomic nervous system are also classified as respondent behaviors. All these behaviors may be influenced by classical conditioning, which is sometimes also called respondent conditioning. **Operant behavior,** on the other hand, is behavior which appears to be under the voluntary control of the organism. Included in the concept of operant behavior are all those responses which are under the conscious control of the individual, such as talking, walking, eating, and making love. These voluntary responses are mediated by the central nervous system and are developed and shaped through *reinforcement* learning. (A new field of study, to be discussed further in Chapter 6, involves the effect of reinforcement learning on respondent behaviors.)

A **reinforcer** is any event whose occurrence, following a particular response, increases the probability that the response will be made in the future. The question of *how* reinforcement increases the probability of a response is one that has been a source of continuing debate and research, and it is still far from resolved. The most common answer to the question of why reinforcers increase responses is that reinforcers reduce some drive, that is, meet some need or motive of the organism. Many psychologists take the view that when an organism is in a state of deprivation or is suffering some pain or injury, there exists a simultaneous state of psychological tension known as **drive.** (Deprivation refers to a failure to meet physiological needs, such as food, or psychological needs, such as affection and approval.) Drives serve to energize the organism and impel it to action. Most animals, when all their physiological needs are met and they are therefore in a state of low drive, will rest or sleep. Hunger, thirst, and the other physiologically based need states, the so-called primary needs, lead to increased levels of activity when they are not satisfied; these heightened levels of activity are taken to indicate heightened drive. The restless activity, or increased drive, exhibited by organisms typically leads to some behavior which reduces the need, and this behavior is then said to have been reinforced. When the organism is next in a state of high drive, there is now an increased probability that it will perform the same behavior.

Much human activity seems to involve other than primary, physiological needs. Human behavior more typically involves complex patterns of needs, or motives, such as money, status, achievement, and power. These human needs, and the behaviors that serve to reduce these needs, are acquired in the process of socialization. The process by which these *acquired* or *secondary needs* are learned will be covered in some detail in Chapter 3. For the moment, it is sufficient to understand that secondary needs exist and require satisfaction in much the same manner as primary needs or drives. Indeed, it is these secondary needs and their reduction that are the most important in understanding human behavior. This is especially true in the case of modern humans, who live in a technological society where their primary needs are routinely satisfied. The failure to meet these secondary or acquired needs is the most important source of adjustment difficulties in middle class society.

It is clear that the need satisfaction, or *drive reduction* hypothesis, which explains the effect of reinforcement in terms of meeting needs, either primary or secondary, is an oversimplified one. For example, it is difficult to explain curiosity or exploratory behavior in terms of drive reduction, unless we assume that there is a specific need for novelty and variety that requires satisfaction. On the other hand, it is clear that drive reduction does explain at least some kinds of reinforcement. Psychologists once referred to the drive reduction notion as "the law of effect," and it bears a close resemblance to the psychoanalytic notion of the "pleasure principle." It is also similar in some ways to the philosophical concept of hedonism, according to which pleasurable activities will be sought out and repeated. In analyzing and explaining behavior, most psychologists tend to rely upon drive reduction explanations of reinforcement and to look for the needs and motives that are being satisfied. We will return later in this chapter to some of the theoretical issues involved in understanding reinforcement.

Applications of reinforcement learning. In the case of Bart in Chapter 1, it is obvious that Bart has had a history of being systematically reinforced for making careful advance plans whenever there is an important decision to be made in his life. Thus, he has laid a careful foundation for his vocational goal, and now he appears to be planning carefully in preparation for a successful marriage.

A more extensive example involves the development of speech or vocalization in young children. When we mentioned the acquisition of speech earlier in this chapter, we pointed out that adult stimulation and encouragement, or reinforcement, was necessary for speech to develop. Let us examine the learning of speech more carefully as an example of learning by reinforcement. Although speech learning certainly involves a number of factors other than reinforcement, such as modeling, and is more complex than our present discussion might imply, few psychologists believe that speech would develop without reinforcement. For example, the existence of language areas in the brain has suggested to some psychologists that language and speech might be "preprogrammed" responses that are specific to humans. In the following discussion, we will concentrate our attention on the development of speech, not on the development of language.

The infant initially babbles a good deal, and in all societies the mother generally responds to this babbling while caring for the infant. The mother's presence and her caring for the infant are both powerful reinforcers for infant vocalization. As we noted previously, psychologists have established the powerful negative effects of failure to provide stimulation and caring. Early in the process of child rearing, the presence of the mother begins to arouse a strong, positive conditioned emotional reaction in the infant, another example of the classical conditioning process which we discussed earlier in the chapter. A pleasurable reaction is aroused in the infant when it sees its mother who has fed, bathed, clothed, and cuddled it—that is, has met the infant's fundamental human needs. Her presence can calm and soothe the infant, just as a stimulus that has been paired with some negative event can arouse crying and distress. The sight of the mother and her holding of the infant can now serve as reinforcers of other infant behaviors.

In the course of babbling, the infant will accidentally make a sound, or series of sounds, that the mother (or the father or another adult) regards as approximating a word. These "words" tend to refer to the parents, and are easily produced by infants, such as "mama" and "dada" in our language. The parent reinforces these sounds by repeating them back to the child and indicating pleasure at having the child make them. Thus, the child may be picked up, hugged, and otherwise reinforced for having learned its first words. When other adults become available, as when the father returns home from work, this entire process is repeated, further reinforcing the response.

In an early analysis by Mowrer (1950), it was suggested that, even earlier in the course of random vocalization, the infant makes a sound that is recognizably like a sound made by the parent. The infant now continues to make this sound over and over again, while alone, because it has a comforting, consoling effect. Because the sound has been associated with the comfort provided by the mother, the child can now enjoy itself by making the sound when it is alone, producing a conditioned positive emotional reaction. Thus, these self-produced sounds have become reinforcers. The more closely the sound resembles the one made by the mother, the greater is the degree of satisfaction or the stronger the conditioned emotional reaction. Thus the child begins a course of independent self-stimulation and self-contained learning. McNeill (1970) and others have noted that the child's accuracy in producing adult sounds increases with age, and that there is no evidence that adults systematically work on this accuracy, certainly not in the manner that a foreign language teacher works on new sounds with an adult student. To repeat, it is the child's own reactions to the sounds that are important, and these reactions involve self-reinforcement. Thus, it is not necessary to assume that the increase in accuracy is a result of continual reinforcement by adults, although the process may involve reinforcement.

Implicit in the preceding discussion of speech learning is the notion of *shaping* of behavior. **Shaping** refers to the procedure of initially reinforcing responses that only crudely approximate or resemble the response finally desired. Over time the least accurate responses are no longer reinforced, and only those behaviors that more closely resemble the desired final product earn reinforcement. Eventually only the desired response itself gets reinforced. Gradual shaping of behavior in this manner is necessary in developing complex behavior such as speech, where the final response that is desired cannot initially be elicited in its completed form. Good teachers of reading, music, or other complex skills recognize that all improvements in performance require constant reinforcement, and that they should continually raise their criteria for administering a reinforcer. No children who are learning to play the piano can be expected to play a Beethoven sonata after just a few lessons, but their early fumbling attempts, their practice of the scales, their playing of simple tunes, and their gradual improvement over time all must be reinforced if they are ever to achieve this behavioral goal. Good teachers and successful parents develop an intuitive understanding of the use of reinforcement—how often it should be given in order to sustain a particular level of performance, and when to raise the level of performance required for reinforcement. It is interesting to note that children generally acquire the capacity to self-reinforce at a very early age, and this response plays an important part in the shaping of new behaviors. Thus, we hear small children saying "Uh-uh" or "Oops" when they drop something, and saying "Good" when they believe they have met a parental criterion.

The concept of reinforcement also helps to explain why organisms ever learn anything at all. If an organism's behavior repertoire is adequate for meeting all its needs, then no new responses are necessary and learning will not occur. The learning of new responses only occurs when the organism's responses are not adequate to meet a need or motive—that is, when the behavior is not drive-reducing. For example, the mother of a mute four-year-old boy consulted a clinical psychologist when no physical reasons could be found for the boy's failure to speak. When asked how the child received the cookies that he wanted, the mother explained that he would stand in front of the closet in which the cookies were stored, pointing and grunting until the cookies were provided. He was able to have all his needs recognized and met in a similar manner. Under these circumstances, he was never required to develop verbal language. The mother was counseled to stop reinforcing the child's nonverbal language and to begin to shape his verbal behavior. This program proved eminently successful, although the boy emitted some additional behaviors, such as crying and pouting, which were distressing to the mother. This behavior, dysfunctional in terms of the mother's ultimate goal of speech development, must be ignored if the shaping process is to succeed. All too often, however, parents find such additional responses so upsetting that they are dissuaded from continuing their shaping of the desired behavior, and they again begin to reinforce the original responses. Whenever a normal and expected response has not developed in the repertoire of an individual, one should ask whether there has been a clear requirement for this response and if its occurrence has been adequately reinforced.

Learning by Modeling

In addition to learning by association and learning by reinforcement, a third major way in which new behaviors can be acquired and existing behaviors changed involves *modeling,* or *observational learning.* Such learning is also sometimes termed "identification," "imitation," "copying," "cognitive learning," or "vicarious learning." We shall most frequently use the term *modeling* to refer to the process by which individuals acquire new and potential behaviors through observing the behavior of others and without performing any behavior of their own. Modeling may occur through the direct observation of the behavior of others and the consequences this behavior produces, or from attending to symbols such as words or pictures that describe these events. Books, movies, and television are important sources for modeling in our society.

Much human behavior is acquired by these observation processes. As a specific example of observational learning, children typically learn the different behaviors

Children may acquire specific attitudes
through modeling, or observing and imitat-
ing, the behavior of adults.

which are exhibited by males and females in society with little or no direct training or
reinforcement by adults for practicing those behaviors. In our own society, for
instance, such sex-typed behaviors are clearly demonstrated by television, the movies,
and other mass media to which children are exposed, as well as by what they see at
home and in the neighborhood. Although some reinforcement may occur when the
behavior under question is actually exhibited by the child, there is none of the

systematic shaping of responses that characterizes learning by reinforcement. It is also clear that observational learning is different from learning by association, in that modeling involves the acquisition of new responses rather than the arousal of already existing responses by new stimuli.

The reader should distinguish between modeling and *identification*. **Identification** is the more complex process by which the individual attempts to take on through modeling the characteristics of another person whom he or she admires. The developing child often identifies with the same-sexed parent, imitates his or her behavior, and engages in self-reinforcement when there is a good match.

In viewing the case of Carl, as described in Chapter 1, many psychologists would argue that his apathy and unresponsiveness are at least as much a result of modeling based on the behavior of other patients as they are the result of a particular problem that resides within Carl. In a traditional hospital, Carl's behavior would likely be reinforced by staff, who would regard him as a patient who was easy to manage. In Chapter 7 we describe how the traditional function of the mental hospital as a custodial institution has now given way to active, community-oriented programs in which more appropriate models are available.

Among the behaviors which psychologists have shown to be learned by modeling are physical aggression, helping others, reduction of phobic fears, and even language style (Bandura, 1977). In typical experiments conducted in this area, the subjects, who are most often children, are initially tested to see if a particular response is already present, and are then shown a film or a videotape of another child or model engaging in that behavior and being reinforced for it. The subjects are then retested to see whether their observation of the model has affected their behavior. In one such study, Bandura, Grusec, and Menlove (1967) showed that children who had observed a model approaching a dog would themselves approach the same dog, although they had earlier exhibited fear reactions to the dog.

The development of the concept of modeling as a form of learning is rather recent, and the important, innovative work by Bandura (1971, 1977) and his colleagues has been largely responsible for shedding light on this process and exciting the interest of other psychologists. His research, and that of many other psychologists, indicates that it is not necessary to explain the development of all behavior in terms of specific reinforcements for individual responses and the laborious shaping of each new behavioral pattern. On the contrary, it is now clear that children may easily learn long and complex sequences of behavior through modeling. Indeed, there is considerable evidence that even lower animals can acquire new behaviors through observational learning without making any overt responses during the process. The later reinforcement for behaviors initially acquired by modeling is usually very important in establishing them as a permanent part of the individual's response system.

Some recent field studies have confirmed the importance of laboratory research on modeling. Lefkowitz, Eron, Walder, and Huesmann (1977), for instance, have reported that the more violent the television programs preferred by boys in the third grade, the more aggressive is their behavior, both at that time and ten years later. This relationship between early television watching of aggression and later aggressive behavior was found for both self-rating and peer ratings of aggressiveness. Early television watching seemed more influential than current television watching in this regard, since a preference for television violence in the thirteenth grade was not at all related to ratings of aggression at that time, nor were the early televison-watching preferences related to the later ones. These findings, obtained in a middle class American community, offer strong support for the importance of modeling as a factor in the development of human behavior.

Modeling appears to have three fairly different effects, each determined by different aspects of the process. First, modeling may lead to the acquisition of new behaviors which were not previously in the observer's response repertoire. For instance, a schoolboy basketball player might learn a hookshot by observing the performance of a professional basketball player. Second, modeling may have either an inhibiting or a facilitating effect. Observing a model's behavior and the resulting consequences may increase or decrease the frequency of responses that are already in the observer's repertoire. Thus, a child may refrain from crying while receiving an injection if she has seen an older sibling accept an injection without making a fuss; or she may make a fuss if the older sibling makes a fuss and is not punished for it. Third, modeling may serve an eliciting function, in which the observation of a model's behavior serves to elicit similar but previously learned responses from the observer. Contributing money while others are doing so or eating nonpreferred foods that others are eating are commonplace examples of the eliciting effects of modeling.

The process of modeling is not easy to understand, but psychologists are continually discovering more about it through research. At the present time, at least two general conclusions can be drawn from these research findings. First, the characteristics of the model are an important factor in determining the degree of behavior change. Models who are seen as having high status, prestige, and competence are more readily imitated than models who lack these characteristics. Models who behave warmly and supportively are also more likely to be copied, as are those who have some real-life power over the observer, such as parents and teachers. Similarity between observer and model in age, sex, and other obvious characteristics also tends to enhance imitation. Second, the observed consequences of the model's behavior are important in determining whether the responses are imitated. If the model's behavior leads to positive consequences, then more imitation will occur than if the model's behavior leads to punishment or negative consequences. Bandura (1977) has recently extended the concept of modeling to explain a number of important aspects of psychological development that are important for adjustment: language development, moral judgment, and the development of thinking skills. A considerable amount of further research will be needed before we understand just how much power the concept of modeling has relative to direct learning in explaining the acquisition of behavior.

It should be apparent that association, reinforcement, and modeling are not mutually exclusive learning processes. A behavior initially learned by modeling will almost certainly be directly reinforced at some time or another, a conditioned emotional reaction acquired by classical conditioning may serve an important role in reinforcing some new response, and so on. Also, it can be noted that psychologists might not agree as to which of these three kinds of learning was involved in the acquisition of a particular response. Nevertheless, the distinction is helpful in developing an adequate understanding of human behavior.

SOME DETAILS OF THE LEARNING PROCESS

We have sketched the characteristics of the learning process in broad outline. Before we begin an account of the way in which learning is the basis of the socialization process, the topic of Chapter 3, we need to examine some aspects of the learning process in greater detail. Because it is generally believed that the most important type of learning involved in socialization is reinforcement learning, we will emphasize that process in the following discussion, and refer to association learning (classical conditioning) and modeling when appropriate. Four important concepts to be examined are *drive, stimulus, response,* and *reinforcement.*

Drive

Earlier in this chapter we defined a drive as the state of psychological tension that exists when an organism is in a state of deprivation because one or more of its physiological needs is not met, or when the organism is suffering some pain or injury. This tension state ordinarily leads to increased activity, so that organisms that are highly active are assumed to be in a state of high drive. The tension is typically experienced as discomfort or emotional arousal. The theoretical notion of drive has been derived mainly from research on lower animals, in which very little attention has been paid to the role of psychological needs such as love, affiliation, and status. There is every reason to suppose, however, that the deprivation of these needs, which appear to be acquired in the socialization process, includes similar tension states or drives. Thus, drives can be considered as the tension states that result from the deprivation of either physiological or psychological needs.

Another way of considering drive is as a strong stimulus. The stronger a stimulus, the more drive properties it has. A slight awareness of hunger produces a modest level of drive, and an intense appetite produces a much higher level of drive. A low level noise has little or no drive properties in that it does not arouse much psychological tension, but a loud, persistent noise has strong drive properties.

While any stimulus may have drive properties, certain stimuli are more likely than others to arouse drive. These are the stimuli that are associated with the primary or in-

nate drives which stem from the biological nature of the organism, stimuli which are commonly referred to as "hunger," "thirst," and so on. As we have noted, in the case of humans, these are the physiological need states created by deprivation and by noxious stimuli which create pain. Ordinarily, the level of a primary drive is related to the amount of deprivation, so that the longer one is deprived of food or water, the higher the drive level. Obviously, however, a point is reached where the organism is weakened by prolonged deprivation, and is not able to respond to its physiological state with increased activity. Also, some physiological need states are not drive producing. For example, anoxia, or oxygen deprivation, does not lead to increased drive but rather to a state of mild euphoria and sleepiness.

Ordinarily, however, the longer the time of deprivation or the stronger the noxious stimulus, the stronger the drive. Drives ordinarily serve to arouse behavior and to energize the organism, and it is assumed that no reinforcement-based learning occurs without the presence of an adequate level of drive. With no drive or with a very low level of drive operating, the organism will not be impelled to action, and action is necessary in order for a response to be acquired through reinforcement learning. The role of drive seems to be less important in learning through modeling.

Stimulus

A stimulus is best thought of as any identifiable event, either internal or external, that has relevance for later behavior. While a drive, or more accurately, the drive-arousing properties of a stimulus, energizes the organism, there are other properties of the stimulus that determine the particular response that will be made. While hunger and thirst both arouse drive, their generalized energizing characteristic, they also have distinct properties which lead to different responses in each case. Given the opportunity, hungry animals will eat and thirsty animals will drink. Why not then simply use the notion of separate drives—that is, a hunger drive and a thirst drive? An examination of the organism's behavior when food or drink are not available provides a partial answer to this question. Whenever the need cannot be readily reduced, organisms that are hungry or thirsty both show the same restless, seemingly random behavior which is characteristic of a heightened drive. Under these circumstances, it would not be possible to determine which need is involved, but only that some need exists. Also, the effects of different need states are to some extent cumulative. Hungry and thirsty organisms will show a greater amount of restless activity than organisms which have been deprived only of food or of water for the same period of time. Thus it is useful to differentiate between the drive-arousing properties of a stimulus and the distinctive elements to which responses can be made, their discriminative or *cue properties* (Dollard and Miller, 1950).

When drive is aroused, it will always occur in a larger context, the environment in which the organism finds itself. For example, hunger pangs will raise the organism's drive level, and will lead to some response. The time of day, the availability of food, the presence or absence of other people, and their behavior—these are all part of the total stimulus complex at the time the drive level is raised and will determine what response will be made. All of us are undoubtedly aware of times when we recognized that we were quite hungry, but did not respond to this need because eating was not an appropriate response. Thus it is not only the drive level that determines the response, but also the distinctive elements of the stimuli to which responses have been learned, their acquired **cue value.**

To summarize, stimuli have two functions: drive and cue. The intensity of a stimulus determines its drive properties while its distinctive characteristics determine its cue value. For example, while both hunger and thirst are complex internal stimuli that energize the organism in the same fashion, they each have different, distinctive characteristics or cue properties, which lead to rather different behaviors: We may go to the cupboard to search for food when we are hungry and to the refrigerator for a cold drink when we are thirsty.

The unique language capacity that humans enjoy enables them to label these need states differentially, both to themselves and others, saying either "I am hungry" or "I am thirsty." This learned labeling of internal need states, which is only possible because of their differential cue value, facilitates the making of differential responses and also enables individuals to explain their behavior to others. One of the requirements of adequate socialization is to teach labeling of internal need states. This requirement is not always met in our society, however, particularly in the case of sex and aggression. It should also be emphasized that internal stimuli are not ordinarily discernible to the external observer, but are internal physiological states that are known only to the organism. Thus the individual's ability to label these states is very important in explaining one's behavior both to oneself and others. If a need state is not adequately lableled, the resultant behavior will often be seen as nonfunctional and pointless to both the responding individuals and the observer. An example can be found in the case of the university lecturer who often flies off the handle when asked even a polite question. This behavior seems pointless until we understand that he has very angry feelings about many important matters in his life, feelings which he cannot label because of his own desire to appear friendly and interesting to his students.

Generalization. It should be clear that the cue value of a stimulus refers to its distinctiveness, that cues may be internal or external, and that the distinctiveness of a cue may be verbally labeled. We may further note that stimuli may be similar to each other in their cue value or they may be quite dissimilar. The greater the similarity of cue value between two stimuli, the greater the probability that the same response will be made to the two stimuli. This phenomenon is known as **generalization.** Without generalization, no functional learning would ever occur, since the acquired responses could only be elicited by exactly the same stimuli involved in the learning process, rather than by a class or group of stimuli. We would have to learn how to tie each new pair of shoes, how to read each book and how to make change in each new store. The phenomenon of generalization is sometimes called *transfer of training*, to indicate that the effects of learning transfer from one situation to another.

Generalization permits us to make the same response to stimuli which are similar but not identical, and this has an obvious economic effect in the management of our affairs. Generalization also has its negative aspects. In our earlier example, Albert learned not only to be afraid of the single white rat, but his fear generalized to all furry objects. Since generalized responses can be nonfunctional, as in the case of Albert, or functional, as in the acquisition of skills, generalization should not be regarded as necessarily good or bad. It is best understood as a neutral characteristic of the learning process.

The process of generalization can be strengthened by reinforcing generalized responses. For example, we are reinforced with success when we discover that a particular response "works" in some new situation, as when we recognize that we can indeed correctly solve the problems at the end of the chapter in our mathematics text. Also, generalization can be enhanced by language, by applying the same label to different stimuli in order to evoke similar responses. Thus we can train children to exercise caution in the different stimulus conditions of approaching a hot stove and crossing the street by labeling them both as "dangerous." The use of labeling to enhance generalization is called *mediated generalization*. The verbal label serves as a cue for the desired behavior; in this case, caution.

Discrimination. Occasionally a generalized response is made when it is not desired, as when a very young child calls another man "Daddy." In this case **discrimination,** responding to a more limited set of cues, is desired. The child must learn that the response "Daddy" is appropriate to one male stimulus object, her father, but not to males in general. Differential responding depends upon the recognition that the two stimuli have different cue values, and this also may be enhanced by language. Mother

may point out that the other male is not Daddy by providing a different label, "Uncle Bob." Similarly, we may point out to a child how she may differentiate between dogs that are vicious and should be avoided and those that are friendly and playful, by identifying and labeling the cue differences between these two classes. Humans have an extraordinary capacity to respond to intricate and subtle patterns of cues, and this capacity to differentiate among cues is a critical factor in the socialization process.

The discriminations that a society teaches will vary greatly, depending upon the critical issues in that society. Since labeling enhances discrimination, a society's language should provide a clear indication of the important discriminations in that society. It thus should come as no surprise that Eskimos have almost two dozen words for discriminations among different kinds of snow, and that in the Cook Islands in Polynesia there are a dozen words for discriminating among coconuts. As a further example, in our own culture we use the same word, "uncle," for both our father's and our mother's brother. In those cultures in which the discrimination between maternal and paternal blood relationships is more important than our own, there are different words to identify these relationships.

Throughout our discussion of cues we have attempted to avoid the notion that behavioral psychologists describe the learning process in terms of simple reponses being made to simple stimuli. Human responses are complex, and responses are ordinarily made to patterns of stimuli and not to simple stimuli. Also, stimuli may be either internal or external, or some combination of them.

Response

We have noted that drive elicits activity and that cues determine the nature of this activity. To each situation the organism brings a variety of potential responses or behaviors. These responses are likely to occur in a particular order of probability, that is, in a **response hierarchy.** The nature of the response hierarchy is probably established initially by the organism's innate response patterns, but it may be markedly changed by experience.

The first responses made in a situation will be those which have been made previously to the cues present in that situation. If these responses do not lead to drive reduction, then the next lower response in the hierarchy will be made, and so on. In our earlier example of the nonspeaking boy, his original nonverbal responses led to satisfaction of his needs. When his mother now refused him a cookie in response to pointing and grunting, he made the next most probable responses from his hierarchy—crying and pouting. When these responses also did not lead to need satisfaction or drive reduction, still other responses were made, those yet lower in the response hierarchy. Ultimately, verbal responses or approximations of verbal responses were made. One of the problems frequently encountered in child rearing is the difficulty of evoking the desired response because it is low in the hierarchy, either because of slow maturation or because the parents are attempting to develop a response too early in the process of maturation. We will return to this issue in the next chapter.

As another example of response hierarchies, an English-speaking person who knows no Spanish, but who does know some German, might find himself thinking of German words when traveling in a Spanish-speaking country. English, the highest-order language response, is obviously inappropriate and is inhibited, and so the next highest response in the language hierarchy occurs automatically, even though it is not appropriate either.

When a number of responses are made from the response hierarchy, they can appear random and nonordered. This appearance of randomness occurs because the organism does not systematically move from response to response down the hierarchy, but rather will continue to try responses that are higher in the hierarchy. Also, the organism will attend to different aspects of the stimulus complex, producing different response hierarchies as it responds to different cues. The organism's behavior, as it moves through the response hierarchy in an effort to produce the appropriate or "correct" response, can be called *trial and error* behavior. The label trial and error behavior suggests that the responses are made in some random fashion; this, as we can see, is not the case.

The nature of the existing response hierarchy has important implications for the shaping of behavior which, as previously noted, involves changes in the standards for administering reinforcement. In shaping, the initial response to be reinforced must already be present in the organism's response repertoire, and must somehow be elicited so that it can be reinforced and then shaped over time. Sophisticated teachers and experienced animal trainers are both shrewd observers of the behavior of their students, and are usually able to develop techniques for producing the desired response. Thus, in teaching a dog to roll over, the initial response which must be elicited and reinforced is rolling over when the dog is already in a lying position.

In classical conditioning, the response of interest is always the initial response in the hierarchy. It is the initial response, the salivation in the case of Pavlov's dog, or the fear produced by the loud sound in the case of Albert, which now comes to be elicited by the new stimulus. The fact that no new response is elicited in classical conditioning causes some to regard learning by association as the simplest form of learning.

In learning by modeling, the nature of the response involved is not as clear as in learning by association or learning by reinforcement. Certainly, in order for any learning by observation to occur, the organism must make the response of observing the model behave in the first place. Some psychologists believe that organisms which learn through modeling have developed a response of compliance or have developed a kind of generalized copying response. However, the evidence that modeling depends upon the characteristics of the model appears to weaken that argument. Others have suggested that the major role of modeling is to reduce the response hierarchy of the observer, and eliminate some, if not all, of the trial and error behavior.

Anticipatory responses. A careful study of responses leads to the observation that behavior occurs in closely linked sequences. It is difficult to talk about a single response; rather, one should talk about a pattern or series of responses in a given situation. Further, it can be observed that certain responses are made shortly before the reinforcement is presented; these are called **anticipatory responses.** These anticipatory responses are quite important in the behavior sequence. On the positive side, they enable the sequence to be shortened; on the negative side, they produce anticipatory errors. The child who reaches out to touch a hot stove on which she has been previously burned, but withdraws her hand before she actually touches it again is an example of the shortening of a behavior sequence with functional consequences. On the other hand, a football quarterback who moves his feet in a certain fashion before throwing a pass, thus giving away his strategy to the opposing team, an anticipatory error, is not behaving functionally, nor are people who learn to close their eyes before pulling the trigger in order to avoid the gun flash.

For humans, an important set of anticipatory responses are language responses that are made nonvocally. These covert responses, the "things people say to themselves" (Farber, 1963, Meichenbaum 1977), are what we ordinarily mean by thinking. Thinking responses play an important role in human motivation and in reasoning and planning, two characteristics that are almost uniquely human. An individual might shorten and correct his or her behavior sequence by thinking, "No, turning left at this corner is wrong. The last time I turned left I ended up on the wrong street. I think that I should turn right." We shall refer to language and thinking responses at other points throughout this book, particularly in Chapter 6 when we discuss *repression.*

Reinforcement

The last aspect of learning to be discussed is reinforcement, which we have previously defined as any event whose occurrence following a particular response increases the probability that the response will be made in the future. On the basis of our discussion of learning so far, it is evident that prompt reduction in the strength of a strong drive acts as a reinforcement. It should be pointed out that the promptness of drive reduction is an important consideration; delayed reinforcements are less effective than immediate ones. Thus, the single piece of candy offered to children immediately after they do what the teacher wants is more effective than several pieces of candy given to them at the end of the day.

Extinction and spontaneous recovery. The fact that a response has been learned by reinforcement does not mean that it will always remain in the organism's repertoire, to be made whenever the drive and cue conditions for its elicitation are met. Reinforcement is necessary, at least on an intermittent basis, for the maintenance of the responses. When a response learned by reinforcement is repeated, but no further reinforcement is obtained, the strength of that response tendency will undergo a progressive decline until it no longer occurs. The decrease in the tendency to make a

Bingo relies on the principles of partial reinforcement to keep the participants playing even though the odds are against them.

response when it is no longer reinforced is termed **extinction,** and will eventually result in the elimination of the response. Just as people show individual differences in their rate of learning, so there are also individual differences in the rate of extinction.

The effects of extinction sometimes disappear over time. A dog that has stopped begging for table scraps because the behavior was no longer reinforced will occasionally demonstrate the behavior again. The tendency for an extinguished response to reappear after a period of time during which no reinforcements were obtained is called **spontaneous recovery.** Research on the learning process clearly indicates that spontaneous recovery is a regular, typical characteristic of behavior. This observation has led most psychologists to believe that any given response is elicited by a whole variety of cues, and that extinction only inhibits responding to some of these cues at any one time. Thus, responses that are apparently extinguished reappear from time to time, elicited by as yet unextinguished cues.

Spontaneous recovery is important in the socialization process, but it is not well understood by most parents. When a response which was thought to have been eliminated reappears, probably because of spontaneous recovery, the parents do not understand that such events are natural, but instead feel that their training has failed. Or they may become angry and pay a good deal of attention to the response rather than simply ignoring it and thus extending the extinction process to the current cues.

Punishment. In our discussion of reinforcement we have concentrated on positive rewards, or the satisfying of deprivations. What about **punishment,** the coupling of some noxious stimulus, such as pain, with a response? At first glance, it might seem obvious that noxious stimulation should inhibit the undesired response still further, and should thus facilitate extinction. While most psychologists would agree that punishment can interfere with responses, they are also quick to point out that punishment offers little in the way of cues about the nature of the correct or desired response. As we pointed out in our discussion of response hierarchies, responses will occur in a particular order unless there is some special cue to indicate a desired response, and no such indication is given by punishment. Indeed, the first several responses made by the organism may all lead to punishment, in which case a strong tendency to leave the situation will develop.

Punishment can lead to a variety of undesired and unplanned consequences. Thus, the father who routinely punishes a child in the evening for all of the child's misdeeds during the day may arouse a conditioned negative emotional reaction in the child. Thus the child will simply learn to avoid the father rather than learn the new behavior which the father would like. A child who is consistently punished in a situation because the desired response is fairly low in his or her response hierarchy may learn simply to avoid the situation, rather than attempt to produce a difficult response. Generally, psychologists tend to believe that the consequences of rewards are much more predictable than are those of punishment, and positive reinforcement is thus to be preferred. Whenever a punishment procedure is being considered for use in decreasing a

HER FINGERWAVING IS
BECOMING AN ANNOYING
NEGATIVE SECONDARY
REINFORCER FOR ME

particular response, it is highly desirable to first ensure that the individual has learned that there is an alternative response that will be rewarded.

Partial reinforcement. The frequency and regularity with which responses are reinforced, the *schedule of reinforcement,* is another important aspect of the learning process. If a response is not reinforced every time it is made but only some proportion of the time, **partial reinforcement** is said to be operating. Most responses that occur in nature are acquired under conditions of partial reinforcement. It is rare that real-life circumstances permit each and every response to be reinforced. We do not sink a basket every time we shoot, each date does not turn out to be successful, and each exam does not yield the grade we might like. Reinforcement in real life is sporadic, occurring after only some of our responses.

Psychological research has established an important fact about partial reinforcement: responses learned and maintained under conditions of partial reinforcement are very difficult to extinguish. One of the clearest examples of this phenomenon is the behavior of people playing the slot machines. This behavior may continue perpetually, in spite of inadequate payoffs, because of the intermittent and aperiodic schedules of reinforcement.

What is the reason for this unusual effect? One explanation might be that the person comes to view the reinforcement as following a series of responses rather than just a single response. Another, perhaps more likely, explanation is that because it is never clear exactly when the reinforcement is going to come, the person does not realize when reinforcement has ceased altogether and continues to believe that it will recur sooner or later, just as it has in the past. The mechanism controlling the payoff, or schedule of reinforcement delivered by the slot machines, takes account of this psychological principle. Thus partial reinforcement can be used to account for the occurrence of behavior that does not appear to be actively reinforced at that time, such as gambling while in a long losing streak. The best way to develop a strong and persistent response is to reinforce it only some of the time that it occurs, that is, to utilize the principle of partial reinforcement.

SUMMARY

1. The newborn infant possesses a set of unlearned or reflexive behaviors and is able to respond to a variety of sensations. This behavior repertoire, however, is not adequate to sustain life, so that the infant is dependent on other persons for an extended period of time. During these first years of life, the foundations are set for learning the behavior that will enable the child to cope with his or her environment, and in complex societies the *socialization* process continues for many years. Different cultures differ in the kinds of behaviors included in socialization, but there are certain training areas in child rearing that are more or less universal: feeding, elimination of body wastes, sexual behavior, and the handling of aggression.

2. The term *maturation* is used to describe behaviors such as crawling and walking, which emerge spontaneously in the developing infant and appear to be independent of its experience. The term *learning* refers to the process by which behavior is produced by special experience or stimulation as a result of practice or training. Learning is the foundation of the socialization process, and must be understood before socialization can be explained. Although much childhood learning is planned by parents and society, much is accidental or incidental; also, both adaptive and nonadaptive behaviors can be learned. Learning is a complex topic, and there are controversies about the best way to approach it. In this book, we talk about three kinds of learning processes: association, reinforcement, and modeling.

3. Learning by *association,* or classical conditioning, involves an unlearned connection between a stimulus (UCS) and a response (UCR). An arbitrary stimulus (CS) paired with the UCS eventually evokes a conditioned response (CR) that is similar to the UCR. The learning of fear in response to originally neutral stimuli occurs in this manner.

4. *Reinforcement* governs the learning of behavior that is under the voluntary control of the organism. Reinforcement can be defined as any event that increases the probability of the response that it follows. It is generally believed that reinforcement operates by reducing some drive, or psychological tension state, that accompanies physiological or other deprivation. Much human behavior seems to be motivated by the need to satisfy secondary or acquired drives such as those for money and achieve-

ment. An example of reinforcement learning can be seen in the acquisition of language. Certain sounds that occur in the infant's babbling are selectively reinforced by its parents, such as "mama" and "dada." It is also possible that the child repeats certain sounds because of their reinforcing value through being associated with the parents. Also important is the process of shaping, in which any approximation to the desired behavior is initially reinforced, and the standards are raised and narrowed as closer approximations become more frequent.

5. In learning by *modeling*, the individual acquires new and potential behaviors through observing the behavior of others. Children typically learn sex-typed behaviors in this manner, and some recent studies have indicated that children's observation of violent television programs can serve as models for later aggressive behavior. Modeling may lead to the acquisition of entirely new behaviors, it may alter the frequency of existing responses, and it may elicit previously learned behavior. Important in the modeling process are the characteristics of the model and the observed consequences of the model's behavior.

6. Four concepts of importance in learning, particularly reinforcement learning, are *drive, stimulus, response,* and *reinforcement.* Drives, which are strong stimuli, usually lead to increased activity on the part of the organism, that is, they serve to energize. The cue properties of a stimulus determine what response the energized organism will make. Thus, stimuli have two properties, drive and cue. The use of language to label the different cue properties of stimuli enables individuals to explain their behavior to themselves and others. *Generalization* refers to the phenomenon in which the same response may be made to two similar but not identical stimuli. This may be either functional, as in the transfer of skills to new situations, or dysfunctional, as in the generalization of fear. *Discrimination* refers to the ability to make different responses to similar stimuli. Both generalization and discrimination are enhanced by the use of verbal labels.

7. The response made first by individuals to a particular cue is the one that is highest in their *response hierarchy* to that cue. If this response fails to satisfy the need, a variety of less probable responses will be made, giving the appearance at times of trial and error activity. *Anticipatory responses* may serve a positive function by enabling a behavior sequence to be shortened or a negative function by interfering with the desired response. In humans, thoughts often function as anticipatory responses.

8. Reinforcement, to be most effective, should follow the response immediately. Responses that are not reinforced undergo *extinction,* although the *spontaneous recovery* of these responses suggests that they are merely inhibited and not eliminated altogether from the response hierarchy. Under some circumstances *punishment* facilitates extinction, but the effects of punishment are much less predictable than those of positive reinforcement, which is therefore to be preferred whenever possible. Under *partial reinforcement,* reward is given for only some of the correct responses. Behavior learned under a partial reinforcement schedule is very resistant to extinction, as in the example of compulsive gambling.

KEY TERMS

socialization

maturational behaviors

learning

learning by association

learning by reinforcement

learning by modeling

stimulus

response

classical conditioning

unconditioned response (UCR)

unconditioned stimulus (UCS)

conditioned stimulus (CS)

conditioned response (CR)

stimulus substitution

higher-order conditioning

respondent behavior

operant behavior

reinforcer

drive

shaping

identification

cue value

generalization

discrimination

response hierarchy

anticipatory responses

extinction

spontaneous recovery

punishment

partial reinforcement

THREE

Socialization and Personality Development

The process by which the infant is continuously trained in the expected behaviors of its society is called socialization.

The learning of socially relevant behaviors is motivated by acquired or secondary drives.

- Psychologists differ in their views about secondary drives.
- Self-reinforcement and conditioned reinforcement are important in practical human learning.
- Some organisms acquire certain behaviors through attachment.

Socialization takes place in at least six important areas.

- The feeding situation is the child's first major experience with its environment.
- All cultures have procedures for toilet training.
- Sex training is also universal, and is often associated with anxiety.
- All cultures train their children to control aggressive behavior.
- Children are gradually trained to be independent of their parents.
- Children develop prosocial or moral behavior.

The culture defines specific roles for each person through sex typing, age grading, and other processes.

Children are known to differ biologically in temperament.

SOCIALIZATION IS THE PROCESS BY WHICH THE INFANT IS SLOWLY BUT continuously trained in the expected behavioral traditions of its society. All societies have clear expectations as to how their members should behave, and although these expectations differ from society to society, the process by which they are communicated and monitored is always basically the same. No two persons have identical socialization experiences. Differences in socialization experiences contribute heavily to producing differences among people's enduring interpersonal characteristics, or personalities. The process of socialization and personality development, regardless of the particular behavior being socialized, involves the application of the principles of learning outlined in Chapter 2.

As an example, let us look at courtship behavior. Despite their obvious differences, we can explain each of the following forms of courtship behavior within the framework of socialization.

1. Informal Western. Male late adolescent meets female late adolescent. Strong psychological and physical attraction develops. Male asks female to marry. Couple cooperate in arranging for necessary legal steps and are married by legal authority (justice of the peace, for example).

2. Formal Western. Male late adolescent meets female late adolescent. Strong psychological and physical attraction develops. Male asks female to marry. Female tentatively accepts. Male formally requests permission of female's father who grants it. Formal period of betrothal ensues. Female's parents arrange for church ceremony with minister officiating followed by elaborate reception, with both families and many friends participating.

3. Formal Oriental. Father of infant son decides that a particular infant girl will be appropriate mate for his son. He arranges a go-between for marriage contract with father of girl. Contract emphasizes dowry for girl and financial resources of male's family. When appropriate time for actual marriage is reached at maturity of both partners, they meet at the formal wedding which has been arranged by the parents.

4. Certain primitive societies. Young man meets young woman. Strong psychological and physical attraction develops. They build hut and live together for a period of time. After she bears a healthy child, wedding arrangements are made by the elder relatives of the couple.

5. Australian Bushmen. Male meets female. Strong psychological and physical attraction develops. Relationship must be kept secret from all others, as adult members of the tribe would pronounce a death sentence on the couple if love interest was known. At a specified time, the couple elope in haste, pursued by the adults of the tribe. Amnesty is granted by tribe when couple reaches specified place before pursuers.

These particular examples indicate the diversity of behavior that is produced through the process of socialization and, incidentally, they also suggest the impor-

THINK OF IT AS AN AGENCY OF SOCIALIZATION

tance that is placed upon the control of sexual behavior, one of the several basic areas in which socialization universally occurs. In this chapter we systematically explore the major areas of socialization, and demonstrate the way in which the principles of learning explain the socialization process. The stable patterns of behavior which are produced by this process are what are typically called personality characteristics.

Beginning with the initial contacts between mother and child in infancy, virtually all of a child's interactions involve relations with significant **agents of socialization.** All of these people, intentionally or otherwise, transmit the culture to which they belong. These socialization agents have different degrees of importance at different times in the individual's development; parents, for example, are much more influential earlier in life, while influences outside the home grow in importance over time. As we explore the major areas in which socialization occurs, we shall also study socialization agents and the influences they exert on the developing individual. Agents differ in their influence depending upon the area of socialization. Parents, for example, are central in the development of the individual's attitudes toward the home and family, while peers play the more important role in developing the individual's sense of interpersonal competence and social skills.

In addition to these individual agents of socialization, there are other nonindividual agencies, both formal and informal, that play major roles in socialization: schools, churches, civic and public organizations, and (in our technological society) the mass communications media. All of these agencies transmit to the developing individual the rules, values, prohibitions, and sanctions of the society, together with its accumulated knowledge. The developing child observes the world around it, and takes for granted that the culture of which it is a part is the "natural" order of things. Consider the relative frequency with which children in our society observe a "nuclear" family consisting of a mother, father, and several children, in their direct experience at home and in the homes of their friends, as well as through television and movies. Clearly, the culture teaches that the nuclear family is the natural order of things. At the same time, the changing nature of the nuclear family in American society, with more married women working outside the home, is bringing about some interesting changes in the nature of the nuclear family. One obvious consequence of these changes will be the greater importance of nonfamily members—child-care workers, nursery school teachers, and the like—in the socialization process.

In all societies, correct or appropriate behavior is carefully defined, and deviations are usually taken seriously, with strong negative reactions following even minor transgressions. The ten-year-old son of an American professor teaching in the Netherlands was sharply criticized before his Dutch classmates when he picked

Many behavior patterns in our society which we take for granted would be unacceptable in other cultures. Communal bathing is common in Japan but would be considered scandalous by many in the United States.

up his luncheon sandwich with his fingers. "All nice boys know that you eat a sandwich with a knife and fork!" exclaimed the teacher. When the matter was brought to the attention of the boy's parents, who wanted to chastise the teacher, the boy asked them not to do it. "It's their country and they can decide how people ought to act," he pointed out. The point of this example is that socializaton is not a casual process, and each society regards deviation from their expected pattern as a serious matter. In fact, deviations are frequently seen in moral terms, and the persons who deviate are regarded as "bad," or "evil," or having "fallen from grace."

We are not suggesting that societies do not permit deviations. The parents of the boy described above could certainly have arranged to have their son eat his sandwich with his fingers. Once the reasons for the request were understood, it undoubtedly would have been seen as a minor and acceptable deviation, something those funny Americans do. But all societies consider certain behaviors completely unacceptable, since they challenge important basic values. If, for example, the boy had brought human flesh or feces to eat, this would have been totally unacceptable regardless of the explanations offered. Such deviations are sometimes called heresies, particularly if moral values are involved.

The Process of Socialization and Personality Development

Although there are various ways to organize the content of socialization, most social scientists are in fairly close agreement on the goals of the socialization process. These goals include the following:

1. Learning to inhibit and control biological impulses. Whereas the infant needs to be fed, watered, cuddled, and cared for, demanding instant gratification, the adult is expected to inhibit and control these needs. Children are allowed to show their unhappiness through tears and their anger through aggression, but adults are not. Learning to postpone or inhibit need gratification, learning to substitute the **reality principle** for the **pleasure principle,** in psychoanalytic terms, is one of the major tasks of the socialization process and one that occurs in all societies.

2. Acquisition of the secondary drives that are the culturally approved values of the society. Learning to value and seek intangible rewards such as status, achievement, security, and dominance, and learning the reward value of such tangible reinforcements as money and property are high priority goals of socialization in Western society. Further, culturally undesirable values such as narcissism, dishonesty, and idleness must be suppressed.

3. Acquisition of the skills and competencies that permit participation in the world of adults; in Western society, for example, the skills of reading, arithmetic, and social interaction. Although there are definite differences among cultures in the skills that they require for membership in adult society, all cultures require the development of skills that are not present in childhood.

4. Learning what particular social behaviors are appropriate, and what behaviors are inappropriate, to one's position in society. These *role* behaviors are socially defined as a function of: (a) sex or age; (b) occupation; (c) prestige position (chief, slave); (d) family, clan, or household; and (e) membership in common interest groups such as fraternities, teams, and associations (Linton, 1945). Thus we are socialized into knowing what behaviors are "proper" and "improper" for persons of different age, sex, vocation, family, and other groupings. Who has not heard the shocked remark, "How could a _____ do that?" with the blank filled in with "a person that age," "a nice girl," "a psychologist," "a Theta," "a person in his position," or some other role label. Of course roles can change as a function of the situation. For example, the parental role may be modified to a significant degree when a parent and his or her children visit the child's grandparents. Since the child's parents are now themselves in the role of children in their own parent's homes, they are faced with conflicting role expectations, a dilemma that frequently causes problems of adjustment.

Psychoanalytic Views of Socialization

Socialization is the continuous process of producing the behaviors that will meet social expectations. The process has a clear beginning in early infancy, probably in the first day of life, but there is much less agreement about when, or even whether, socialization ends. Some psychologists prefer to regard socialization as a process of early childhood, or at the most, of childhood and adolescence. In this book we take the view that socialization is continuous throughout life.

The most influential theory of socialization has been that of Sigmund Freud. His theory focuses upon the changes in the way individuals gratify their biological needs as a result of both social consequences and biological maturation. In the orthodox psychoanalytic view, these biological needs are regarded as basically sexual (with the concept of sexuality employed in a very broad manner), and the term **libido** is used to refer to these needs. The psychoanalytic theory of socialization involves a series of levels, or **psychosexual stages,** in which different zones of the body provide the major source of libidinal gratification until adult sexuality is achieved. These stages are **oral,** where gratification is gained primarily with the lips and mouth through sucking and biting; **anal,** where expelling and withholding feces leads to gratification; **phallic,** in which manipulation of the external sex organs produces gratification; and finally, **genital,** where gratification is gained through normal adult sexual behavior. There are two additional important concepts: the **Oedipal** stage, occurring at the same time as the phallic stage, in which gratification from the parent of the opposite sex is desired; and the **latency** period, following the phallic stage, where libidinal gratification is suppressed in the interest of learning about the surrounding world.

It is important to note two points about the psychoanalytic theory of socialization. First, the theory deals with socialization of the early impulse life of the individual, and Freud was among the first to point out the importance of these socialization experiences for later behavior. We return later in this chapter to a more detailed analysis of the socialization of the individual's early impulses. Second, Freud's theory assumed that all important socialization occurred during the first few years of life, and this assumption has influenced many other psychologists to adopt the view that socialization is a childhood phenomenon only. In keeping with Freud's emphasis on the socialization of early impulses, the psychoanalytic approach treats all the other, later goals of socialization as though they stemmed from these experiences. Thus, the acquisition of competence and the learning of social roles are seen as the by-products of impulse control rather than as separate phenomena.

A later psychoanalyst, Erik Erikson (1963), has proposed a broader and longer-term view of socialization. His theory involves a progression of **psychosocial stages,** in which individuals face an ever wider range of human interactions as they develop throughout their life spans. The broad outlines of Erikson's theory are presented in Table 3-1.

Although there are clear similarities between Erikson's views and those of the Freudians, Erikson's eight psychosocial stages place a greater importance on social

Table 3-1
Stages of Psychosocial Development (Socialization)
Adapted from Erik Erikson (1963)

Stage (Approx. age)	Psychosocial problem	Interactions involved	Favorable outcome from resolving problems
Oral-sensory (1st year)	Trust vs. mistrust	Mother or maternal person	Basic trust and optimism
Muscular-anal (2nd year)	Autonomy vs. shame and doubt	Parents or parental persons	Self-control and control over environment
Locomotor-genital (3rd-5th years)	Initiative vs. guilt	Nuclear family	Goal-directedness and purposefulness
Latency (6th year-puberty)	Productivity vs. inferiority	Neighborhood and school	Competence and skill
Puberty-adolescence	Identity vs. identity diffusion	Peer- and out-groups; leadership models	Central purpose and direction; integration of past, present, and future goals
Early adulthood	Intimacy vs. isolation	Sexual partnerships; long-term friends	Love and affection; closeness and sharing
Middle adulthood	Generativity vs. self-absorption	Home and family; work and leisure	Productiveness; concern about the future
Mature adulthood	Integrity vs. despair	Mankind; "my kind"	Perspective, satisfaction, and wisdom

and cultural factors in socialization, and they clearly extend over the entire life span, giving an emphasis that is not found in traditional early psychoanalytic theory. At each of the eight stages there are specific psychosocial issues to be resolved, and one's success at each stage results in the development of the skills and competencies necessary to cope with new problems. For example, during adolescence, the primary task is one of developing a separate identity as an independent human being, and learning role-appropriate behaviors that are distinctly different from those of childhood. The adolescent must develop a "central perspective and direction" that bridges the social values learned in childhood with the hopes and expectations of approaching adulthood. The difficulties that accompany this process account for the "identity crisis" of adolescence, a term first introduced by Erikson. Erikson's views of human behavior and the developmental process have been quite influential in establishing a broader view of socialization, and in kindling a greater interest in the socialization issues involved in adolescence and adulthood. We shall return to an examination of development in adolescence and adulthood in Chapter 9 where we will again encounter Erikson's important influence on developmental research and theory in the post-childhood years.

Is Socialization Necessary?

What would people be like without the effects of socialization? In some sense this question is unanswerable, since the pressures of socialization are inescapable. Also, as we have previously noted, the long period of human infantile dependency leads to a requirement for continued human care that can be provided only within a context of socialization. This question, nevertheless, has long fascinated philosophers and psychologists.

The study of unsocialized humans, humans without the experience of other humans, would shed light on a philosophical problem of considerable interest: the problem of "human nature." The two extreme positions usually presented are of humans as noble savages and as ravening beasts. Those who argue the former view take the position that humans are basically innocent, at one with themselves and nature, and are corrupted by society. The French philosopher Jean Jacques Rousseau was a major proponent of this position. The opposite position is taken by those who view humans as primitive beasts, as did Freud and most of the early traditional psychoanalysts. Humans are seen as crude beasts who, without the civilizing influences of society, would rape, steal, and kill, attempting to satisfy all their impulses directly and immediately.

There is no satisfactory way to resolve this debate. Although there have been scattered reports in the scientific literature of *feral children* who have been abandoned in infancy and reared by animals, it is difficult to know how much socialization they had received before they were abandoned. Also unclear are the socialization effects of being reared by animals and the extent to which the deficiencies of the feral children were due to malnutrition and disease. Certainly, these feral children were not very "human" by typical standards; most of them did not walk erect, and none ever developed spoken language. About the only way in which this argument could be resolved would be to "hatch" fully mature humans, produced without either animal or human intervention, and observe their behavior. Obviously, this is an impossible task, and the ethics of psychological research would not permit such work to be done, even if it were possible.

It seems most sensible to recognize that the effects of socialization are so all-encompassing that no developing individuals can escape the socialization pressures of the cultures in which they are born. In our own society, parents who adopt a "permissive" posture, and attempt to avoid serving as agents of socialization, only surrender some of their potential influence to others. In addition, it is difficult if not impossible for parents to hide their own behavior from their children. Thus, parents automatically serve as agents of socialization by providing models for their children's behavior.

SECONDARY DRIVES AND MOTIVES

In Chapter 2 we defined drive primarily in terms of tension resulting from deprivation involving such need states as hunger, thirst and pain. At the same time we noted that most middle class adults rarely experience intense physiologically-based need states. Indeed, one of the most important goals of all human societies is to protect its members from these deprivations and discomforts. It is easy to forget, however, that this goal has not yet been met in many parts of the world, including some segments of our own so-called affluent society.

What motivates adult human behavior, in addition to physiological drives? There are a wide variety of acquired or **secondary drives** that serve to arouse and sustain behavior, and the acquisition of these drives is a critical part of the socialization process. Acquired drives reflect the dominant values of the society, and individuals who do not share these accepted values tend to be regarded with suspicion and are subject to negative sanctions. For example, consider the reaction of the middle class to those who do not share our society's concern for achievement, status, or affiliation. The hippie, the dropout, and the hermit are definitely not the folk heroes of the mainstream of Western society.

Although most psychologists emphasize the importance of acquired drives, there are a variety of views about their exact nature and number, and about the manner in which they are organized. Secondary drives tend to be combined and organized in patterns. For instance, the drives for money, achievement, and influence are often conceptualized as a more complex *need for power*. Such complex, organized patterns of secondary drives are usefully thought of as **motives.** While some psychologists use the terms drive and motive interchangeably, we believe that this distinction is a useful one.

The Development of Secondary Drives

Secondary reinforcement. There are a number of points of view about the ways in which secondary drives are established. Most discussions of this topic begin with the assumption that secondary drives are acquired through *conditioning* on the basis of the primary (physiological) drives and represent some modification of them. The concept of secondary drives is highly similar to the psychoanalytic view that underlying all motives is the libidinal drive.

In **secondary reinforcement,** a formerly neutral stimulus acquires reinforcing properties when it has been closely and repeatedly associated with a primary rewarding event. The behavior of chimpanzees in the token reward studies of Wolfe (1936) and Cowles (1937) is one example of the establishment of an acquired drive through secondary reinforcement. These studies showed that poker chips acquired reward value for the chimpanzees once they discovered that the chips could be exchanged for desirable food. In a sense, it could be said that the animals had acquired a poker-chip drive, much like the drive for money that is so important in our own society.

An important example of secondary reinforcement in child development involves the interaction between infant and mother. Because the mother is the principal source of primary reinforcement for the infant, providing satisfaction of all the infant's primary needs, the mere presence of the mother becomes reinforcing in its own right, a secondary reinforcer, creating a feeling of pleasure in the infant. The mother's approval and disapproval also acquire secondary drive properties through being associated with primary rewards and punishments. Later her approval or disapproval can help the child acquire new behaviors, such as doing well in school, saving money, and being neat and tidy.

The effects of secondary reinforcement have also been extensively studied in the animal laboratory. When a laboratory rat must learn to press a bar in order to obtain food, and the click of an electronic relay is always heard by the animal immediately before the food is delivered, the animal will come to press the bar just to hear the relay, even if no food is delivered. These clicks have become **secondary reinforcers** because of their association with the primary reinforcer, food.

Attachment. Recent research evidence suggests that the relationship between infant and mother involves not only the conditioning of pleasure to the mother's presence, but **attachment** as well. Attachment is defined as the predisposition of the infant to initiate reactions to the caretaker. Harlow and his colleagues (1959, 1966) conducted a series of studies on this topic with infant monkeys. These monkeys were reared in isolation, except for the presence of an artificial "mother" made of wire mesh, either covered with terry cloth or not covered at all. Both the terry cloth and wire mesh mother surrogates could provide the same amount and kind of food (through a nursing bottle), but when the infant monkeys were given a choice as to which mother they preferred, they almost always chose the terry cloth

Infant monkeys showed a stronger attachment to a cloth-mother surrogate than to a
wire one. They spent more time with the
terrycloth "mother" and ran to it for comfort
when frightened.

covered one, regardless of which one had fed them. Even if the terry cloth mother
never fed the infant, the baby monkey spent more time clinging to it than to the
wire mesh mother, leaving the terry cloth mother only in order to feed from the
wire mesh mother.

The terry cloth mother was also more effective than the wire mesh mother in
reducing the infant monkey's fear. When a strange and fear-evoking object was
presented, the initial reaction of the infants was to run and cling to the terry cloth
mother rather than the wire mesh mother. After a while the infant monkeys would
begin to explore the new stimulus if the terry cloth mother was present, but were
less likely to do so if only the wire mesh mother was present.

Harlow's research findings cannot be explained by secondary reinforcement, as
that interpretation would suggest that the infant should prefer the mother that had

reinforced the primary drive of hunger. Rather, his results suggest that there is an innate, unlearned clinging or grasping response that can be satisfied only by an object with certain characteristics, such as the natural mother or a terry cloth surrogate, and that this stimulus becomes the object of attachment for the infant.

Bowlby (1969) has attempted to demonstrate that attachment behavior is also present in human infants, and is the result of biologically encoded, inherited patterns. With certain modifications, this might be compared with *imprinting* in birds, a phenomenon that was first described by Konrad Lorenz in 1935. One example of imprinting is seen in the newborn duckling or chicken, as it typically follows the first moving object it encounters after hatching. Since, under natural conditions, the mother is that object, this response is highly functional to the survival of the organism. Similarly, the attachment of the human infant to the mother is seen by Bowlby as having a high degree of survival value.

In both secondary reinforcement and attachment phenomena, the importance of the mother's role in the development of motives is clearly indicated. The mother very quickly becomes an important stimulus to the infant, and by controlling her presence and absence, by offering and withholding her affection, she can have a lasting influence on the infant's behavior. The concepts of secondary reinforcement and attachment are much more complex than we have been able to portray here, but this introduction serves to give some indication of their important place in the socialization process.

Modeling. Modeling, or observational learning, is another important process in the establishment of secondary drives or motives. As we have already noted, the child is born into a society in which the most important values are omnipresent. Not only the parents but the remainder of society, too, plainly indicate the motives the individual is expected to adopt, the rewards for adopting them, and the sanctions for failing to adopt them. For example, the high regard that our society has for property—new and expensive possessions—is blatantly apparent in all the mass media to which a child is exposed. Children surely undergo many times more observational learning than would be necessary in order for them to develop a strong acquired drive to possess things. The importance of modeling in the learning of aggression and sex roles is discussed later in this chapter.

Conditioned fear. In Chapter 2 we pointed out how fear could be conditioned, as in the case of Albert and the white rat, and the topic will be further explored in Chapter 4. It is worthwhile to note here that fear is easily learned, quickly generalized, and difficult to extinguish, and some psychologists have suggested that learned fear accounts for the development of secondary motives. Brown (1961), for example, suggests that fear-avoidance is directly involved as a primary drive in money-seeking behavior. He notes that it is very easy to learn to be anxious or fearful about the absence of money; indeed, many dinner table conversations overheard by the young child center on this point. Getting money automatically reduces the fear, and thus is a powerful reinforcer. Fear can similarly be seen as responsible for avoiding a lack of power and lack of status, and in fact to account for most, if not all, acquired drives. Thus, Brown has suggested that conditioned fear could lie at the root of most of what are regarded as secondary drives and that the behaviors seen as drive-induced are better described as efforts to avoid fear.

Self-reinforcement. Another way in which secondary motives can be established, or at least maintained, is through **self-reinforcement.** Most parents continually and deliberately reinforce the behavior of children with verbal approval, material rewards, and other words and actions. The most effective parents also make explicit the basis for administering these reinforcers, the criteria for obtaining rewards: "Mary, you've done a nice job cleaning up your room," or "Steve, I'm glad to see that your report card is really improved this time." As children learn the criteria of adequate performance, they can then begin to reinforce themselves in much the same fashion. Frederick H. Kanfer and his colleagues (see Kanfer and Phillips, 1970) have demonstrated that research subjects accept the experimenter's criteria as their own and continuously monitor their own behavior, reinforcing themselves as they proceed. In this work, subjects reinforce themselves either through "points" or by acknowledging that they have done a "good job." Obviously, each of us has done much the same in a variety of real-life situations, as when we permit ourselves a cigarette or a snack after reading a certain number of pages in an assignment. According to Kanfer (1975), the effective use of positive self-reinforcement involves the following four steps: (1) selection of appropriate reinforcers; (2) selection of specific contingencies, or response-reinforcement relationships; (3) simple practice; and (4) checking and revising the procedure. We return to this process in Chapter 12.

Kanfer's work on self-reinforcement clearly illustrates the fact that we all learn a set of standards for a variety of socially important behaviors and incorporate these standards into our own value system, a process that Freud called **introjection.** This process has also been termed *internalization* or *incorporation.* We then regularly and routinely self-reinforce behaviors that meet these standards, thus bypassing, or at least reducing, the need for external reinforcements. Bandura (1977) has noted that these standards can be learned observationally or vicariously, so that self-reinforcement can affect behaviors that have never been practiced by the individual. In one of Bandura's experiments, children who watched a model play a miniature bowling game used the model's scores as their own criteria when they themselves were allowed to play. Also, the self-approving and self-criticizing remarks made by the model were imitated by the children.

The two important points to remember are that all of us learn, through the process of socialization, a set of standards against which to evaluate our behavior, and that we utilize these standards in a continual process of self-reinforcement (or self-sanctions) that has important effects on our behavior. Obviously it is vital to set realistic and appropriate standards for children so that their self-reinforcement processes will be as effective as possible.

We have posed a number of alternative explanations for the acquisition of drives. In a particular situation, any or all of them may indeed be operative. If we consider the case of money, for example, we may initially learn the value of these tokens via association, much as the chimpanzees did for the poker chips. This learning may be augmented by specific teaching by our parents on the wisdom of frugality and the dangers of reckless spending, coupled with a substantial dose of anxiety left over from their own penurious youth. Finally, these learning experiences occur in a culture where observational learning makes the accumulation of money a natural and desirable state of affairs. For most persons in our society, therefore, it is the constancy and simultaneous impact of these various pressures that leads to the acquisition of a strong drive for money.

The Number and Nature of Motives

How many motives are there, and how are these motives organized? A perusal of the psychological literature could easily give the impression that there are as many answers to these questions as there are investigators of motivation. Two well-known and long-standing attempts to list and categorize motives and their interrelationships with primary needs are those of Henry A. Murray (1938) and Abraham Maslow (1954). In addition to twelve "viscerogenic" or physiological needs, Murray has suggested twenty-eight "psychogenic" needs or motives, which he organized into six general categories. This scheme of psychogenic needs is presented in Table 3-2. Although it may appear overly elaborate, it does provide a reminder of the complexity of behavior that must be represented in any listing of human motives.

Maslow's system involves fewer motives than Murray's, and they are arranged in a five-level hierarchy, which also includes the primary drives or needs. **Maslow's hierarchy** is:

1. *Physiological needs:* basic bodily needs for food, sleep, stimulation, activity, and so on.
2. *Safety needs:* protection against bodily harm or injury, and security against threat.
3. *Belongingness and love needs:* acceptance, affection, approval, and warmth.
4. *Esteem needs:* adequacy, self-respect, status and worth.
5. *Self-actualization or fulfillment needs:* development of one's full individuality and realization of one's potential.

Other needs identified by Maslow are esthetic needs and cognitive needs, which he originally found difficult to fit into the hierarchical structure. Maslow further points out that the lower motives in the hierarchy are aroused through *deficiency* (D-motives), and are intense, urgent determiners of behavior when they are not satisfied. The motives at the upper end of the hierarchy, the *being* motives (B-

Table 3-2
Psychogenic Needs (or Secondary Motives)
According to Henry A. Murray (1938)

I. Needs Associated with Inanimate Objects
    1. Acquisition—gain property and possessions
    2. Conservation—collect, clean, repair, and preserve things
    3. Order—arrange, order, organize, and store things
    4. Retention—retain and hoard things; be frugal and miserly
    5. Construction—build and organize

II. Needs Associated with Ambition, Accomplishment, and Prestige
    6. Achievement—overcome obstacles, do something difficult
    7. Recognition—receive praise, commendation, respect
    8. Superiority—achievement and recognition combined
    9. Exhibition—self-dramatization; excite, amuse, stir others
   10. Inviolacy—preserve one's reputation; prevent loss of self-respect
   11. Avoidance of inferiority—avoid failure, humiliation, shame
   12. Defensiveness—defend oneself from blame; justify oneself
   13. Counteraction—overcome defeat by retaliating and restriving

III. Needs Associated with Human Power
   14. Dominance—influence and control others
   15. Similance—imitate and yield to others; agree and emulate
   16. Deference—admire, serve, and follow superiors
   17. Autonomy—maintain independence, resist others' influence
   18. Contrariness—be unique or different; take the opposite side

IV. Needs Associated with Injury
   19. Aggression—assault, injure, belittle, harm, or ridicule others
   20. Abasement—accept punishment, humiliation, depreciation
   21. Blame avoidance—avoid blame or punishment by inhibiting sanctioned
       behavior; be well-behaved

V. Needs Associated with Affection
   22. Affiliation—form friendships and associations
   23. Rejection—snub, ignore, exclude others
   24. Nurturance—nourish, protect, aid others
   25. Succorance—seek aid, protection, and sympathy from others

VI. Needs Otherwise Unclassified
   26. Play—amuse oneself, relax, and seek diversion
   27. Curiosity—explore, know, and understand the environment
   28. Exposition—explain, interpret, inform, and describe to others

motives), only operate when the D-motives are satisfied. In other words, in order for humans to develop their individuality and potential—to self-actualize—their more basic survival and safety needs must first be satisfied. A significant aspect to note in both Murray's and Maslow's classification of motives is the importance placed on "higher-order" motives as explanations for human behavior.

In another attempt to classify human motives, and specifically to explain such behavior as curiosity, adventure-seeking, and play, Robert W. White (1959) has suggested an inherent or unlearned human drive for *competence* or *effectance*. The concept of competence motivation, or desire for effective functioning and mastery of one's environment, provides a means of explaining a multitude of common human activities such as learning to walk, building toy towers, writing textbooks, and learning how to "do things," all of which are enjoyed for their own sake, satisfying "an intrinsic need to deal with the environment" (p. 319).

In contrast to the fairly complex and general schemes for classifying motives proposed by Maslow and Murray, some other psychologists have offered much simpler ones. B. F. Skinner (1953, 1974), for example, rejects all elaborate motivational schemes in favor of **conditioned generalized reinforcers.** As we have previously noted, any neutral event may become a secondary or conditioned reinforcer when regularly paired with a primary reinforcer. Conditioned reinforcers become *generalized* when they are paired with more than one primary reinforcer. The presence of the mother is a conditioned generalized reinforcer for most infants, as is money for adults, since both have been paired with the gratification of many primary needs. Skinner would prefer that psychologists consider the concept of conditioned generalized reinforcers a basic one, and examine the learning history of the particular individual to determine which stimuli serve as conditioned generalized reinforcers for that individual.

Skinner and many of his followers simply believe that efforts to identify and classify motives are a waste of time and that psychologists could more profitably devote their attention to studying the current, overt behavior of individuals and the reinforcement that sustains these behaviors. If, however, we view the efforts of Murray, Maslow, and others as attempts to list and categorize the reinforcers that are widespread and generalized in a particular culture, perhaps these views are not as different as they might initially seem.

Inferring Motives

Humans have always tended to explain their behavior in terms of some underlying motive, such as heroism, jealousy, love, ambition, hostility, pride, and sacrifice. Psychologists have accepted this view of behavior and have developed the concept of acquired drives—stimuli which now serve as drives although they fill no innate needs—to explain the development of motives. It should be clear by now to the reader that motives are usually inferred from behavior, and that most classifications of motives are really classifications of behaviors. Thus, ambition is inferred from consistent achievements, hostility from aggressive behavior, and heroism from courageous behavior.

Inferences of this kind are often quite unsatisfactory, however. An act of heroism may occur because the person was fearful of being seen as a coward, or was unaware of the dangers involved. To take an even more common example, a person may eat not out of hunger, but to avoid offending the friend who offers food. The process of attempting to perceive and assess the particular mechanism underlying any instance of human behavior is more thoroughly discussed in Chapter 10.

Let us note some of the problems involved in inferring the existence of acquired drives. First, the same behavior may reflect different motives. For example, a child may refuse to eat either to punish a parent or to please a parent. Second, the same motive may give rise to different behaviors. Thus, one child may become a rather talkative person in an effort to please a parent, while another may become quiet for the same motive. Also, motives may appear in rather "disguised" forms, so that hostile or aggressive behavior may represent a child's attempt to gain attention rather than to express hostility or anger. Finally, many behaviors have multiple motivations, so that writing a textbook may involve the expression of a creative need, the need for professional recognition, the need for money, and other motives besides. Hopefully, this discussion will help clarify some of the confusion that is frequently caused by the notion of acquired drives and will help the reader to understand why there is so much arbitrariness in the different listings of these drives, enabling each of us to infer whatever we wish about the factors that underly the behavior we observe.

Why have psychologists persisted with their emphasis on human motives? For one thing, it is difficult to avoid using concepts that are so much a part of the way human behavior is discussed by almost everybody else. By the same token, there is a long tradition in psychology of using the concept of motives, and this tradition is difficult to break. It may ultimately be possible and preferable for psychologists to abandon the concept of motives altogether, and to follow Skinner's emphasis on conditioned reinforcers, but we have not yet reached that point. In our ensuing discussions we shall make limited use of the concept of human motives, although we will spend considerable time analyzing the complex patterns of behavior which are usually regarded as being determined by secondary drives or motives. In these analyses we will search for the historical antecedents of these behaviors, and also for the contemporary reinforcers that sustain them.

Canalization

Before closing our discussion of the effects of socialization on drives and motives, it is important to note how socialization modifies and fixes the ways of satisfying

MILDRED! HARRY, JUNIOR, IS
CANALIZING ON GRASS!

many of the primary drives. While all humans experience hunger, the ways that are considered appropriate for reducing that hunger vary as a function of cultures. Thus, we may regard peanut butter and jelly sandwiches or steak and potatoes as the ideal way to satisfy our hunger, but in some cultures these would not even be regarded as edible. Similarly, roast dog or whale blubber are scarcely items on most of our menus, but they are clearly preferred in certain other cultures. The process of learning, through socialization, how to satisfy our primary drives through specific satisfiers, rather than through an entire class of satisfiers, has been termed **canalization** (Murphy, 1966).

Canalization means simply that individuals will prefer to satisfy their primary drives in known or familiar ways, and obviously, these satisfiers are learned in the process of socialization. Thus, socialization involves the development of preferences or *appetites* for certain satisfiers. Canalization can be noted in a number of areas— eating, drinking, sexuality—and is apparently not subject to extinction, since the response is satisfying by definition. Each time a canalized food is consumed, it reinforces the preference of the eater for that food. Although it is obviously possible for tastes to change—for the effects of canalization to be modified—the concept of canalization, that is, the socialization of primary drives, helps explain why it is difficult to eliminate tastes or appetites. And with experimentation, either deliberate or accidental, we can add newly acquired tastes to our existing ones.

THE AREAS OF SOCIALIZATION

The biological nature of human beings gives rise to universal socialization problems in which the unlearned natural responses of the infant must be changed into the adult responses that are prescribed by the culture. For example, all human infants suckle, but no human adults suckle. Similarly, all infants urinate and defecate whenever sphincter pressure increases, but all adults are expected to inhibit these responses. Although patterns of adult eating and toilet behavior vary from society to society, all cultures demand that the unlearned responses of infancy be supplanted with responses that are considered to be adult. It is to these universal socialization experiences that we now turn our attention.

We have divided our discussion of socialization into six areas: feeding, toilet training, sexuality, aggression, independence, and the development of prosocial behavior. In each of these areas of socialization, the child must learn to inhibit and control biological impulses, acquire new skills and competencies, and learn when and where it is appropriate to display various behaviors. All this learning takes place through the operation of an array of new secondary reinforcers which are themselves being acquired at the same time.

Let us repeat the reasons for our interest in socialization. We believe that these early experiences are very important in the shaping of adult behavior, not only because they are among the infant's first experiences, but also because the patterns of socialization, both on a cultural and a family level, reflect the dominant values and continuing concerns of that social group. Thus, the child who is born into a family or a society where "cleanliness is next to Godliness" will not only be subjected to strong socialization pressures in that direction during its early years, but will continue to experience these pressures throughout life.

Feeding

The feeding situation is perhaps the infant's first major experience in interacting with its environment. The hunger of the infant is an urgent, incessant and intense drive; there is a great deal of random activity and intense crying. And the infant cannot comfort or reinforce itself during these early weeks. It cannot say, "It's only a half-hour until dinner," or "I don't have to wait much longer." The only behavior through which the infant might make a difference to its environment is its crying; either the mother responds to the cries or she does not.

Let us examine some of the unplanned consequences of the mother's behavior. If she responds promptly to the infant's cries, then its behavior has indeed had some impact upon its environment. The infant thus learns to cry in order to signal its needs, because crying has been reinforced. What happens, however, if its cries are not answered? Perhaps the mother is always "too busy," or the infant is on a rigid feeding schedule. If the child is usually left to "cry itself out," it may learn that nothing it can do has any impact on its environment. In a manner of speaking, it learns to be apathetic. Indeed, it is quite possible that this is what happened in the case of the institutionalized infants cited in Chapter 2, who showed gross retardation in all aspects of their development. What if the mother intends to keep to a rigid, timed feeding schedule, but yields to the infant's cries when they become more and more violent? It is likely that the infant will learn to cry violently, since it is the violent crying that is reinforced. In this case, the mother is inadvertently teaching the child to overreact.

The child's initial success in dealing with the environment is represented by the way the mother reacts to its feeding demands, by the generalized and systematic way in which she responds to it. It is worth noting that several studies of the amount of psychological tension shown by the mother during feeding have indicated that this tension is communicated to the infant, and tends to result in a higher incidence of colic (spasmodic pain in the abdomen typically indicated by excessive crying) and other eating problems. Also, feeding is just one situation in which the mother responds to her child, and the same behavior patterns will be encountered by the child in many other areas of development. Thus, the mother who believes in a rigid feeding schedule is more likely to shape other areas of her child's behavior in ways which will conform to her expectations, rather than to respond spontaneously and flexibly to the child's needs as they occur.

There is now rather clear evidence on the behavioral consequences of learning that none of one's efforts are effective in producing any response from the environment. Under these conditions, people gradually minimize their efforts, and may eventually cease responding altogether (Seligman, 1975). This condition of **learned helplessness** may possibly have its beginnings in the failure of the mother to respond to the child's early crying. However, such experiences must be augmented by a continued pattern of nonresponsiveness.

Probably one of the important reasons for psychologists' strong interest in feeding is the impact of psychoanalytic theory. In that approach, it is assumed that there is an unlearned biological need for oral gratification, and that unless this need is adequately gratified during the "oral stage" of early infancy, there will be persistent problems throughout later life. Such persons are considered to be "fixated" at the oral stage, and will exhibit various patterns of adult behavior, depending upon when and how the fixation occurred. For example, children who are weaned early often tend to develop a low tolerance for frustration, impatience, and oral aggression.

The complexities of Freud's theory will not be explored here. Indeed, some psychoanalysts would insist that our empirical, behavioral approach is irrelevant to their theory, which is to some extent self-contained and thus difficult to verify in the usual scientific sense. Rather, we wish to emphasize the impetus that Freudian theory has given to the study of early experience and its general impact on our society.

As an example of this impact, let us examine the question of the need for oral gratification through suckling from the breast. Is the need for suckling an **instinct**—an unlearned, biological response—that requires gratification in order to ensure normal psychological development? The knowledge that is available to date seems to suggest that it is not. *Sucking* has been shown to occur even prior to birth, and most infants suck some object or other—nipples, fingers, blankets, or rattles. However, there is no evidence that sucking occurs more frequently or with greater vigor in infants who have had less opportunity to suckle from the breast. This is also true for infants who have been cup-fed from birth. There is no reason to deny the unlearned, "natural" nature of the suckling response, nor the infant's need for such oral gratification; indeed, it is almost impossible to prevent infants from engaging in this behavior. We do, however, question whether there are important negative consequences if there are no long periods of breast feeding. Similarly, there is no evidence to suggest that nonnutrient sucking, like thumb sucking, has negative consequences, either for the development of later personality or for the structure of the jaw.

There are two aspects of feeding training that should be distinguished. The first is the degree of *initial gratification* permitted in feeding—how long the infant is fed, how much love and care is involved in the feeding, and how late weaning occurs. In other words, this aspect refers to the amount of reinforcement that is permitted the child in feeding prior to socialization, before it is taught proper adult behavior. The second aspect involves the severity and suddenness of the weaning—the amount of *socialization anxiety*—that is involved. Whiting and Child (1953) have noted, in their analysis of more than fifty different cultures, that these two aspects of feeding training are pretty much independent of each other. Thus, they were able to identify certain societies with high initial gratification and yet also high socialization anxiety, other societies with high initial gratification and low socialization anxiety, and so on. Many theories of childhood development, including Freud's, fail to make this distinction, as did much of the original research in this area. The same distinction, between initial gratification and socialization anxiety, can also be applied to each of the other areas of socialization. We return to this analysis in Chapter 4.

The research studies that have attempted to investigate the relationship between early feeding practices and later behavior are neither consistent nor conclusive in their results (see Frank, 1965, for a review of much of this work). One important problem in this work that is not yet resolved involves the adequacy of methods for studying these behaviors. For example, mothers' retrospective reports of the way in which they dealt with infant feeding are very inconsistent and untrustworthy. On the other hand, long term longitudinal studies based on actual observations are difficult to carry out due to the time and expense involved. Also, many of the studies reported in the literature have attempted to study specific components of the behavior, such as demand feedings versus scheduled feedings, breast versus bottle feeding, and age of weaning, without recognizing the major importance of the overall psychological climate in the family. The mother who attempts to use a specific schedule of feedings, but who picks the child up and cuddles it when it cries before its scheduled feeding, is communicating a different message from the mother who simply lets her baby cry, although both of these mothers might be counted as using feeding schedules for the purpose of a research study. Because of our failure to produce research that is useful in a practical

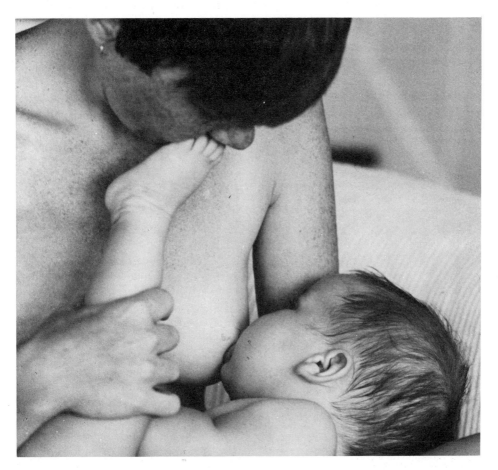

The feeding situation is one of the infant's first major experiences in dealing with its environment. The quality of the interaction between mother and child may reinforce patterns of behavior that will be repeated in other areas of development.

sense, we are forced to rely for a practical guide upon our general psychological analyses of the process of socialization, both in the case of feeding and in other areas of socialization as well.

Feeding not only provides the infant with its initial learning about the way in which the environment will respond to it, but it also provides information about ways in which it can control its environment. If the infant learns that its behavior can produce reinforcements from the environment, that its mother will respond to its cries, then the foundation is set for the development of competence in coping with the world. Clearly, the foundation can also be set for the development of some problematic behavior: the child might learn that it can best control its environment by refusing to eat, thus producing parental attention and concern. While these behaviors would certainly not carry over directly into adult life, it is easy to see how they could have long-term consequences. As the English poet William Wordsworth wrote, "The child is father of the man."

Toilet Training

All cultures have toilet-training procedures for their children. Since the products of human elimination, especially feces, contain dangerous bacteria, it is conceivable that those societies which did not toilet train simply died out through disease. On the other hand, since studies of animals show that other species also avoid their own waste, it is possible that the behavior is an unlearned avoidance reaction. Perhaps the distinctive odor of feces has an adaptive significance in this regard. Nevertheless, human infants have the same naive interest in their waste products that they have in their bodies and their environment. It is not unusual for mothers to find infants handling and playing with their feces. Such behavior leads to swift sanctions as soon as it is discovered, and children in our culture quickly learn not to do it. They also learn to attach considerable anxiety to all the cues involved in elimination, and it should come as no surprise to note that our slang words for bodily waste are used in expletives and curses.

The learning of toilet control is difficult to accomplish and is surrounded with anxiety. The initial response to sphincter pressure—elimination—must be inhibited, and a new, complex response must be substituted. Initially, the child must learn to maintain sphincter control and simultaneously inform the mother about the situation verbally. Later, the child must make the same inhibitory response, walk to the toilet, partially disrobe, and then eliminate to the cues provided by being seated on the toilet. Since Western society wraps its children in several layers of clothing and also provides a complex technological environment for elimination, the task of toilet training is much more difficult than it is in primitive cultures, where the unclad child simply leaves the hut and eliminates at the edge of the clearing.

Toilet training requires the inhibition of an unlearned response, and the substitution of a complex pattern of behavior which initially includes such verbalization as "Mommy, I gotta go!" Toilet training must ordinarily await speech development and adequate maturation of the nervous system, and is thus rarely successful at earlier then eighteen months of age. There are two primary techniques used in our culture for the teaching of toilet control: rewarding children for successful responses, and punishing them for "accidents," principally through anxiety, shame, and guilt. We have previously pointed out that reward is superior to punishment in producing effective learning, and toilet training is no exception to this rule.

Psychologists' interest in toilet training is also due in part to the impetus of Freudian theory. In the psychoanalytic approach, the second stage of psychosexual development is referred to as the anal stage; during this stage the main sources of gratification are through the expulsion and retention of feces, as children discover that they can also control their environment by voluntarily controlling elimination. As in the case of the oral stage, particular adult personalities are said to result from toilet training that is either too early or too strict—the so-called "anal character." Such people tend to be overly careful in their personal habits, neat and tidy to excess, obstinate, and thrifty.

Research studies of toilet training, both in our society and cross-culturally, do not support psychoanalytic theory in any consistent way. Most important is the finding that toilet training is strongly related to a number of other attitudes and behaviors on the part of the mother, including overrestrictiveness and high anxiety about cleanliness and sex. It thus comes as little surprise that four outcomes of severe toilet training are: (1) negative views of the mother and negative feelings about her; (2) development of maladaptive behaviors, such as enuresis (bed-wetting) or aggressiveness; (3) anxiety over sexuality; and (4) negative self-concepts on the part of children, as they begin to believe and overgeneralize the parents' negative reactions to their failure to achieve bladder and bowel control: "You're dirty," or "You're smelly," or "You're stupid."

Although we should not conclude that toilet training, taken alone, is critically important in shaping the individual's later personality or behavior, it does seem that this is one of several indices of the parents' relationship with the child which, when taken together, illustrate the parents' important and long lasting effects on the developing individual (Zigler and Child, 1973, p. 93).

Sex Training

One of the important findings of research in child development is the strong tendency on the part of mothers to treat toilet and sex training as a single phenomenon. Thus, when middle class American mothers were asked how they felt about modesty, a sex-training issue, the mothers tended to respond in terms of such behaviors as urinating outdoors. It appears that the foundation of sexual anxiety may develop during the learning of toilet control, and that the anxiety associated with each of these may enhance the anxiety attached to the other, creating a generalized tension and anxiety with regard to the genital area.

One important aspect of childhood sexuality is that our society views it as something to be completely suppressed. There are no substitute gratifications, as there are for weaning or toilet training. Sexual gratification is expected to be inhibited, at least until adolescence. The degree to which such suppression training is successful in our culture may be open to question, but there can be little doubt that complete inhibition is the goal. It is clear that the strong anxiety-based sanctions that are generally used in sex training lie at the root of the sexual problems and concerns so frequently found in adult life.

There appear to be four general goals of training to suppress sexuality in our culture: (1) to develop a strong taboo against incest (which may well be the only universal taboo); (2) to inhibit masturbation; (3) to prohibit sex play; and (4) to control information about sexuality as a way of postponing sexual activity and gratification. The principal incest taboo in our society involves the relationship between the child and the opposite-sex parent, called the *Oedipal* relationship in psychoanalysis. Psychoanalytic theorists believe that the resolution of this relationship, involving the boy's love for his mother and his sense of rivalry with his father for his mother's passion and affection, has a critical effect on the later development of the person. While a similar situation, the *Electra* complex, is presumed to exist for girls, this concept was not as carefully worked out by Freud, and it does not play a central role in psychoanalytic theory.

Research psychologists have attempted to check the accuracy of Freud's ideas about the Oedipal situation, and they have confirmed that the affection of the opposite-sex parent is generally more important to the child than the love of the parent of the same sex. Also, the affectional relationship between the child and the opposite-sex parent is different in nature from the relationship with the parent of the same sex. During later childhood, however, there very well may be some changes in the affectional ties, as, for example, the father begins to complain that the boy takes up too much of the mother's time, or that he is "too old" to sleep in the mother's bed. The mother may also begin to reject the child as his interest in her becomes more specifically sexual, a demand that is refused by almost all mothers in our society. Regardless of the specific events involved, however, it is clear that the incest taboo is a learned behavior and that it is a powerful one.

Earlier in this chapter we noted that the child has a naive interest in its own body and how it functions. In its efforts to learn about its body, the child discovers early that self-stimulation is both possible and pleasurable. Penile erection, for example, has been noted on a daily basis between the third and twentieth weeks of life. If unchecked, children soon learn to masturbate, an activity that arouses intense parental anxiety in our culture. This anxiety leads the parents to punish self-exploration, a behavior that was judged as "wrong" or "harmful" by about half of the mothers included in several studies of child rearing. Parents also have the same reaction to sex play and to the interest of children in sex generally, attempting to prevent interest and stimulation by dressing them in loose fitting, nonbinding clothes, observing modesty in the home, distracting them when they ask about sex, avoiding sexual words and using euphemisms instead, and generally steering clear of the subject altogether. At the same time, high anxiety sanctions are used when children transgress sexually, so that they are told that they are "filthy," that they can permanently damage their genitals by touching them, and that they will be "damned."

The notion that the way in which adults express their sexuality is heavily influenced by infantile experience is another of the legacies of Sigmund Freud. Freud's tendency to overlook psychosexual differences between men and women is seen in the fact that his theory of psychosexual development is couched in male terms. In psychoanalytic theory, the third stage of psychosexual development is the phallic, in which the genitals become the primary source of gratification, and masturbation and sexual curiosity abound. As discussed above, the Oedipal conflict occurs during this stage. Ultimately, the father's threat of castration as retribution for the boy's incestuous desires leads to the end of the phallic stage and the beginning of the next psychosexual stage, the latency period. Freud noted that it was difficult for most males to resolve the Oedipal conflict satisfactorily, and believed that these difficulties accounted for most of the neurotic conditions which characterize our society. The individual who is fixated at the phallic stage, with an unresolved Oedipal conflict, is seen as sexually inadequate and repressed, and as excessively moralistic.

Two aspects of the psychoanalytic approach to sexuality should be emphasized: the existence of infant sexuality, and the later consequences of the way in which infant sexuality is dealt with by the parents. Also, the reader should be aware that Freud used the term sexuality in two senses. First, it referred specifically to the development of an awareness of and an interest in the sexual organs, how they function, and how they may be used for pleasure. Second, Freud used the term to refer to the generalized source of energy, or libido, which he considered to underlie all behavior. In the psychoanalytic literature, the distinction between these two interpretations of sexuality is not always clear, and the social and learning factors which surround the development of sexuality are not emphasized.

There is one other important aspect of sex training, but we will postpone it until later in the chapter: sex role or sex typing. In Western culture there is a sharp differentiation between behaviors that are appropriate for the two sexes, and this differentiation begins at birth. We will discuss sex typing in the following section on roles, since sex typing serves as the most convenient and obvious example of the role aspect of socialization.

Aggression Training

All cultures are concerned with managing aggression, acts that may lead to damage or physical injury. The self-protective value of this concern is obvious. No society can survive for long without taboos against the destruction of life and property. It is necessary that these taboos exist and that they be internalized by adult members of the society, since there can never be enough policing or other kinds of external control to maintain the social order.

Aggression poses a special problem for the socialization process. As we have observed throughout this section, parents in their role as agents of socialization must continually and routinely interfere with, or *frustrate*, the behavior of their offspring. **Frustration** ordinarily has two meanings: the blocking of ongoing behavior, and the emotional reaction to this blocking. We will use the term frustration primarily in the sense of blocking, but it is obvious that emotional reactions are frequent occurrences in the socialization process.

The unlearned response to the frustration or blocking of behavior is to vigorously attack the source of blocking—in a sense, to attempt to move the block out of the way. This vigorous activity is often labeled **aggression,** particularly when it is directed at a

An important part of the socialization process is teaching children to express frustration and aggression in a socially acceptable way. Children must learn to control their aggressive impulses if they are to become well-functioning adults.

person. The vigorous crying of the infant is not usually seen as aggressive, and the child's early feeble attempts to strike out at the blocking mother may initially be regarded as "cute," but the parents' bemused attitude soon shifts once the child is capable of hurting.

In our society, parents generally teach their child to inhibit direct action against them, and they also try to ensure that the child accepts their standards as his or her own. This learning is generally accomplished by liberal dosings of anxiety, so that the child, when tempted to aggress against the parents, experiences sufficient anxiety to interfere with acting on the impulse. Thus, the child is taught that aggressive tendencies lead to anxiety, which blocks the expression of aggression and removes the child's freedom to act on impulse. "Nice little girls don't behave that way," or "If you ever hit your mother again something terrible will happen to you," are examples of frequent anxiety-arousing statements that are used to inhibit aggression.

There is a rather peculiar paradox in our aggression training. Parents often respond to their children's aggression by being aggressive themselves, by striking them, providing the children with an inappropriate model while at the same time labeling the children's behavior as unacceptable. Research on childhood aggression strongly suggests that the most aggressive children are those whose parents disapprove of aggression and, when it occurs, punish it with aggression of their own. The least aggressive children, on the other hand, are those who parents inhibit aggression by other means, such as by distracting them or threatening them with loss of love. These findings are consistent with principles discussed earlier, in which the observation of aggression would be expected to enhance the expression of aggression on the part of the observer.

We should not lose sight of the fact that it is frequently appropriate to make some vigorous response to blocking. We would not wish our children to respond to a stuck door or an initial failure to accomplish a goal with anxiety and passive withdrawal. The standards which parents set for frustration tolerance should be sufficiently high to allow for the vigorous pursuit of desirable goals, yet without frequent recourse to aggression. Teaching children to manage their aggressive impulses is a major part of the socialization process, and an appropriate balance between the extremes of inhibiting all aggression, on the one hand, and raw destructive behavior, on the other, is generally difficult to achieve.

Psychoanalytic theory places great importance on aggression; indeed, the expression of aggression is regarded as the other major problem of impulse control, along with sexuality. Psychoanalytic theory does not deal with aggression as a unitary phenomenon, however, but regards each psychosexual stage as having its own aggressive component. Thus, biting occurs in the oral stage, inappropriate releasing or withholding of feces in the anal stage, and hostility toward the same-sex parent in the phallic stage. Such a view tends to ignore the universality of frustration and aggression during the socialization process, and also tends to minimize the importance of the early socialization of aggressive tendencies.

Independence Training

In all cultures, infants are dependent upon their parents for the gratification of most of their needs. Adults, on the other hand, are independent in that they have skills and competencies not possessed by children. They are capable of feeding themselves, cleansing themselves, and arranging for the satisfaction of their desires and needs without the continual assistance of others. Further, adults in all societies have adopted or *introjected* the values of that society, and are thus more likely to behave in appropriate ways without continued surveillance by others. In addition, having accepted the values and standards of their society, adults are more capable of self-reinforcement, monitoring their own behavior, and periodically reinforcing those behaviors which meet society's expectations of adult conduct. Thus, in comparison with children, adults in all cultures are much more independent and self-directed in their behavior.

At the same time, we are very much aware that there can never be total independence of others, either in terms of emotional support or in terms of material goods and services that others provide (except perhaps for the mythical lone inhabitant of the desert island). However, the sharing and trading of resources or reinforcement that occur among adults are perhaps better regarded not as dependency, but as the interdependency of equals. Thus, the concept of dependency can perhaps be restricted to the reliance for affection, help, and support of a weaker subordinate on a stronger superior, both in terms of skills and emotional resources and stability. One of the important tasks of socialization is to develop in children the skills and competencies that free them of their early dependency on the skills of their parents, that enable them to develop close, supportive relationships with others, including peers, and that help them to learn how and when to reinforce themselves. In other words, independence training is the process by which parents systematically program themselves out of their initial role as their children's primary helpers and reinforcing agents.

Much of what we are calling independence training can be subsumed under the other areas of socialization that have been discussed above. The child who has been weaned, toilet trained, and taught to control its sexual and aggressive impulses is to some extent independent of its parents. In addition, however, independence training emphasizes the learning of such important behaviors as tying one's shoe laces, crossing a busy intersection, and complex vocational skills, all of which are critical aspects of competency development. Indeed, the more technologically sophisticated the culture, the more complicated and lengthy is the period of independence training, and the greater is the variety of skills that must be developed. Another basic area of independence training that is not covered in other areas of socialization involves the child's emotional dependence upon the parents and the manner in which this dependence is reduced.

There are obvious differences among children in the degree of dependence upon their parents. Research studies of children in our culture have shown that children who experienced consistent maternal reward but inconsistent punishment for dependent behavior, such as hanging on the mother's skirts, were more dependent than children who were consistently punished for dependency. Maternal reward and acceptance by itself, however, did not foster dependency, especially when the mother also valued and rewarded independence. Interestingly, the most dependent children of all were those whose mothers initially rejected their children's dependency but finally gave in to the children's repeated demands.

DON'T YOU THINK HE'S A LITTLE OLD FOR SEPARATION ANXIETY?

One interpretation of these findings is that mothers who permit initial dependency and provide consistent reinforcement produce rather secure children. Indeed, these are the children who are least likely to show **separation anxiety,** strong emotional reactions to the mother's leaving their presence. The continuity of warmth and reinforcement available from these mothers apparently develops a generalized sense of trust that allows the mother to absent herself from the immediate environment. Children who are either quite dominated by their mothers or rejected by them do show separation anxiety. A likely explanation of this clinging behavior is that it is learned on a partial reinforcement schedule in which the mother only occasionally rewards the child's clinging, making the behavior persistent and difficult to extinguish.

In traditional psychoanalytic theory, the development of independence is not dealt with as a separate concept, but dependence is treated as part of the oral stage. In the contemporary psychoanalytic writings of ego psychology, however, the development of competence and the freeing of emotional attachments to the parents do receive more specific attention.

DEVELOPMENT OF PROSOCIAL BEHAVIOR

Psychologists have traditionally shown more interest in the development of problem behavior and the foundations of psychological conflict than in the development of positive behavior and the foundations of superior adjustment. Thus, it is only in the last dozen years or so that developmental psychologists have begun to study extensively an area that is basic in any view of a well-adjusted person, namely, the development of caring, helping, and sharing, or **prosocial behavior.** This area has also been termed **moral development.**

What are the important factors in determining whether children will develop a strong prosocial or moral sense? According to Mussen and Eisenberg-Berg (1977), there are four important kinds of influences: biological factors, cultural factors, specific socialization experiences, and the child's particular level of cognitive maturity. In their view, the most important of these four is the child's socialization experiences. It should also be emphasized that children are capable of learning different prosocial behaviors at different age levels, so that the age at which a particular learning experience becomes available for the child is also important.

To date, what is known about the development of prosocial behavior? Mussen and Eisenberg-Berg summarize our current knowledge as follows. Prosocial behavior is most likely to be shown by children who are self-confident and active, whose parents show prosocial behavior, and who have been encouraged, early in life, to accept responsibility for others. Children are more likely to show prosocial behavior when they themselves feel happy or successful, when they are reinforced for helping others, and when they understand the reasons for helping. Thus, parents, teachers, and other educators are in a position to assist in the development of prosocial behaviors in children by themselves serving as models, by reasoning with their children, by rewarding prosocial behavior when it occurs, and by exposing children to varied portrayals of this behavior through such media as television and the school classroom.

We have now concluded our discussion of the six areas in which socialization is universal: feeding, toilet training, sexuality, aggression, and independence training. In each of these six areas we have observed how the developing individual learns to inhibit and control biological impulses and to acquire the skills and competencies expected of adults in that society. This learning occurs through the influence of a variety of acquired or secondary reinforcers, whose effects are also being simultaneously learned. Our discussion has been oriented toward the behavioral approach to adjustment with a heavy emphasis on the social and learning variables that are involved in socialization, and we have attempted to contrast this view with the classical psychoanalytic theory of Freud. It is important to understand the Freudian position since his was the first systematic attempt to describe the socialization process recognizing both the biological nature of human beings and the requirements of society to modify and control these biological needs. However, it is now generally recognized that Freud's theories are couched in the language of an earlier scientific age, and are somewhat less understandable today than they were during his lifetime. In addition, we are fortunate in now having fifty years of research findings in the psychology of learning and cultural anthropology available for our analysis of socialization. We are indebted to Freud for his pioneering work and for pointing up the significance of certain critical areas of socialization, but it is most appropriate for our purposes to treat his theories in a global sense, emphasizing the cultural and learning variables which are regarded as of primary importance by today's behavioral scientists.

ROLES

In each society there are coherent, organized patterns of behavior that are considered appropriate for different members of that society. As noted earlier, these **role** behaviors are mainly a function of one's sex and age, occupation, prestige position, and membership in certain groups. Socialization might well be viewed as the process through which people learn about these various roles in their own societies, and more specifically, as the process of learning one's own role. Thus, people can be said to be socialized when they know their "place" in their own society—when they behave in ways that are regarded as appropriate for a person of that sex, age, occupation, status, and group memberships.

The learning of roles frequently involves the inhibition of biological impulses and the acquisition of new skills and competencies under the control of secondary reinforcements, and might therefore be regarded simply as another aspect of socialization. However, role requirements and expectations are also important concepts in their own right, and it is informative to discuss them separately. We shall limit our discussion to sex and age roles, and deal with these only insofar as they enter into the socialization process.

Sex Typing

In our society it has been traditional to differentiate sharply between the behaviors appropriate for the two sexes, and this differentiation begins right at birth. The question that is most frequently asked first by the mother after giving birth is about the gender of her offspring. The parents are offended if a stranger misidentifies the gender of the infant, and later on, so is the child. There have traditionally been fixed expectations as to how boys and girls should behave. Brown (1965) has described them as follows: "In the United States, a *real* boy climbs trees, disdains girls, dirties his knees, plays with soldiers, and takes blue for his favorite color. A *real* girl dresses dolls, jumps rope, plays hopscotch, and takes pink for her favorite color" (p. 161). Clear gender differences in children's behavior have also been reported cross-culturally. After the age of three, in a number of different societies that were studied, boys were found to be more physically aggressive, more quarrelsome, and to enter into more fights than girls.

How do such clear differences in sex role develop? The fact that all societies prescribe different activities and attitudes for the sexes could suggest that they are based upon biological differences; and indeed there may be some biological basis, but the degree of diversity among cultures in sex roles strongly supports the notion that

(b)

(a)

Two deviations from the traditional sex-role stereotypes: (a) Former Los Angeles Rams player Roosevelt Greir works on a needlepoint project in his apartment. (b) A smiling Janet Guthrie accepts the congratulations of her pit crew for being the first woman to ever finish in the Indianapolis 500-mile Memorial Day Classic.

important social-learning factors are involved as well. At least four elements are involved in the acquisition of gender role: (1) the early and continual labeling of gender so that the child becomes highly aware of the array of differences between the sexes, both physical and behavioral; (2) observational learning, which includes modeling (particularly of the same-sex parent) and self-reinforcement; (3) direct reinforcement for appropriate sex-role behaviors when the child imitates the behavior of the same-sex parent; and (4) vicarious learning of the consequences of inappropriate gender behavior, as when another girl is observed being called a "tomboy" or a boy a "sissy." The net impact of these experiences is the production of strong gender roles in our society.

Research studies indicate that most of our sex-role learning occurs between the ages of three and seven, and that it tends to begin earlier in lower class families than in middle class families. Also, the sanctions used in lower class families are more severe for inappropriate gender behavior, and the gender differences are much clearer in these families. It is clear that the family plays a critical role in the development of sex typing; for example, fathers play rougher games with boys than with girls, while mothers play gentler games and play more with their girls than with their boys. Also, young boys in father-absent homes show much less aggressive behavior than in homes where the father is present.

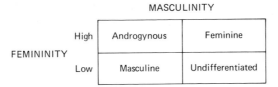

Figure 3-1. Scheme for defining the concept of androgyny.

Androgyny is a new concept for understanding the nature of sex roles. Traditionally, masculinity and femininity have been considered as opposite ends of a single dimension, with most males at the masculine end and most females at the feminine end. More recent theory and research (Bem, 1975; Spence and Helmreich, 1978) suggest that masculinity and femininity are two *independent* dimensions that describe human behavior. Masculinity involves such characteristics as mastery, competitiveness, and independence, while femininity involves such characteristics as emotionality, sensitivity, and concern for others. In this approach, persons can be high or low on *either* of these dimensions. As can be noted in Figure 3-1, persons high on feminine and low on masculine characteristics are best seen as traditionally feminine in their behavior and attitudes, and persons low on feminine and high on masculine characteristics are masculine in the traditional sense. Persons low on both dimensions are rather undifferentiated in their sex-role characteristics, showing relatively weak qualities ordinarily associated with either traditional masculinity or femininity. The androgynous person, however, shows above average development in both sets of characteristics. Spence and Helmreich have been able to show that androgynous persons are more successful both financially and interpersonally than persons who are traditionally either masculine or feminine.

Age Grading

Another set of roles that have important consequences for the process of socialization are those based upon age. Even before the ubiquitous Dr. Spock, certain behavior was "expected" as a function of the child's chronological age. The scientific research on child development and the popular books on child care have provided some factual information about the emergence of these behaviors, but the expectations that children will behave appropriately are very much part of the socialization process. Indeed, we can note that there are specific expectations for persons throughout the entire life span. The exhortation to "act your age" has clear implications for seven-year-olds and seventy-year-olds alike.

Parents make use of age roles in each of the areas of socialization. There is a "right" age for weaning, for toilet training, for knowing not to play with your genitals, for not hitting your siblings, and for tying your shoe laces. Although there are some cultural differences, so that weaning might occur at any time from the first to the sixth year, and some subcultural differences, so that middle class mothers in our society wean their children earlier than lower class mothers, each group views its age-role expectations for its children as the correct and natural way for children to grow up.

In each instance, the behavior to be eliminated is identified as that of a "baby," and the desirable behavior is called "grown up." The individual whose behavior is labeled in this fashion is thus made anxious, perhaps by the threat of loss of love, because being labeled as a "baby" is punishing while being called "grown up" is a reward. Implicit in this labeling process is the generalized cultural pressure toward independence, toward the achievement of competence and self-sufficiency.

One interesting difference between many primitive societies and our own is the use of formal rituals to mark the transition from one age role to another, especially from childhood to adulthood. These rituals clearly mark the end of one set of age-role expectations and the beginning of another, both for the individual and the rest of society; their clear and public nature greatly facilitates the change in expectations. In our own particular society, the period of independence training has been considerably lengthened by the influence of modern technology, and we have abandoned the use of these rituals because they serve little purpose. Clearly the thirteen-year-old Jewish male is not an adult, in terms of work role or sex role, after his Bar Mitzvah or confirmation, although this may have been the case in biblical times. Rather than attempt to develop more functional ways of signaling the movement from one age role to another, we have tended to give up such practices altogether. Although graduation from high school or college serves this function to some extent, its ritualistic significance is nowadays becoming blurred as education comes to be regarded as a lifelong activity. The identity crisis experienced by many adolescents in our culture may be traced to confusion over age-role expectations, over when they are to behave as obedient children and when they are to behave as self-reliant adults.

In our discussion of role determinants of behavior we have seen how each society expects individuals who have certain positions in that culture to behave in certain ways. Some kinds of behaviors are prescribed, some behaviors are optional and some behaviors are forbidden. These role expectations, because they are universally shared by members of a society, are powerful influences in the socialization process and throughout a person's entire life span.

TEMPERAMENT

Socialization might be regarded as the molding of the biological infant into the social adult. In our discussion of this molding process we have paid little attention to individual differences in the organism before socialization begins, or to the manner in which these differences could affect the socialization process. There are wide variations in the responsivity of the newborn infant to its environment, and these differences have important implications for what follows.

Biologically based differences in personality and behavior have been discussed in Chapter 1, together with certain "theories" of personality that emphasize such differences. The word **temperament** has often been used as a general term to refer to unlearned or congenital differences in the responsivity or activity level of the infant (Diamond, 1957). It is these characteristics that have led mothers to observe that their children were "different" from the first day. Psychologists at one time believed that all healthy infants were virtually identical in temperament, and that any differences among them were the product of different experiences; few now hold such extreme beliefs. One set of research studies, for example, reported that the average amount of time spent crying by infants ranged from less than one hour per day to over four hours per day. There appeared to be no clear reasons for these differences in responsivity other than some innate or biological differences in the infants.

Psychologists who study infant behavior have been able to identify five major kinds of temperamental differences in normal infants: (1) vigor of activity, including bodily movement, sucking and crying; (2) irritability, or readiness to cry or whine without apparent provocation; (3) social responsivity, or the degree to which infants respond to adult overtures; (4) stimulus satiability, or how quickly the infant looks away from an object introduced into its line of vision; and (5) perceptual sensitivity, or the capacity to respond to minimal changes in sensory stimulation, such as minor variations in light or sound. The reader can note the similarity between these five components and the Buss-Plomin framework discussed in Chapter 1. Although psychologists are not certain how long these initial differences in responsivity continue, it is obvious that mothers face very different problems in child rearing according to the temperamental nature of their infants. Hyper-irritable infants will constantly upset and bewilder their mothers, as they thwart any attempts to quiet them. At the other extreme are placid children who gurgle and coo, apparently delighted with their lot in life.

Another aspect of temperamental differences involves the match between the infant's temperament and the mother's customary modes of behavior. A slow moving, passive mother will respond rather differently when confronted by an active, vigorous infant than will an active, vigorous mother. The point to remember is that these initial differences in infant behavior call forth different reactions from the mothers, and that the mothers' reactions in turn modify the children's temperamental differences in ways that are not yet fully understood.

Mothers often tend to treat innate differences in infant temperament on a moralistic basis. The baby who is quiet and biologically regular, awakening every four hours for its feeding, is a "good" baby, while the child who awakens at irregular intervals and cries frequently poses a more difficult management problem for the mother, and is also regarded as a "bad" baby. It is obvious that to start life being labeled as "bad" is a disadvantage to a child under any circumstances. In this regard, it is interesting to note that mothers and other adults alike typically blame the mother for her failure to cope with a difficult infant. It is erroneously assumed that all children pose exactly the same problems of socialization for parents, and that the fault must therefore be the mother's—a belief which, hopefully, we have now modified in our readers.

SUMMARY

1. Socialization is the process by which the infant is continuously trained in the expected behaviors of its society. Parents, peers, other persons, and institutions all contribute in this process. Goals of socialization include: learning to inhibit and control biological impulses, acquisition of secondary drives representing the culturally approved values of the society, acquisition of the skills and competencies that permit participation in the company of adults, and learning what behaviors are appropriate and what behaviors are inappropriate for one's position in society.

2. Socialization can be regarded as a continuous process throughout life, although there is usually an emphasis on early childhood. In the traditional psychoanalytic view of socialization, the child develops through four psychosexual stages—oral, anal, phallic, and genital, which refer to the role of different parts of the body in gratifying basic drives. Philosophers have disagreed as to whether socialization is "natural" or whether it runs counter to basic human nature, but since socialization is universal and unavoidable, these arguments seem irrelevant.

3. The learning of prosocial behaviors is motivated by acquired or *secondary drives*, developed through their association with primary rewarding events. Also important is *attachment*, referring to the natural tendencies of the infant to initiate reactions towards its caretaker, usually the mother. Secondary drives or motives can also be maintained by self-reinforcement, in which children learn to tell themselves that they have transgressed or that they have done a good job.

4. Psychologists differ in their views of the number and the organization of acquired motives. Murray has listed twenty-eight "psychogenic" needs, organized into six categories; Maslow has suggested a hierarchy of five levels of needs, including the primary drives; Skinner has emphasized the concept of secondary or conditioned reinforcers that vary according to the individual's learning history. The learning of specific appetites is called canalization.

5. The process of socialization involves at least six important content areas, in which the child must learn to inhibit old behaviors and acquire new and sometimes complex skills: feeding, toilet training, sexuality, aggression, independence, and the development of prosocial behavior. The *feeding* situation is perhaps the child's first major experience in interacting with its environment, and the mother's behavior in

response to its urgent demands sets a pattern for what the child can expect from her and from the world in other interactions. Psychoanalytic theorists have placed great emphasis on early oral experiences, and believe that the basis for some important adult personality characteristics is set at that time.

6. All cultures have procedures for *toilet training* their children, and in Western society the responses to be learned are quite complex. Unfortunately, shame and guilt are typically used by parents in teaching toilet control, so that this area comes to be surrounded with anxiety and secrecy. Toilet training can be regarded as another of many indices of the parent–child relationship which, taken together, illustrate the important and long lasting effects of parental behavior on the child's development.

7. *Sex* training is another area that is associated with anxiety for most parents. In contrast to other socialization areas, where new skills are to be learned, the infant is expected to suppress its sexuality completely. This is done in four ways: development of a taboo against incest; inhibiting masturbation; prohibiting sex play; and controlling information about sexuality. Psychoanalytic theory has considered that the relationship between the child and the opposite-sex parent is one of the most critical factors in personality development, and that the important aspects of that relationship are sexual in nature. These views have gathered partial support from modern research.

8. All cultures train their children to control *aggressive* behaviors. Aggression is a natural response to the frustration or blocking of reinforceable behavior, and parents use anxiety here, too, as a means of teaching children not to act on their aggressive impulses. Parents often provide accidental models for children's aggression through their own aggressive behavior while attempting to decrease such behavior in the child. Another problem in aggression training is that successful adjustment does demand facility in expressing aggression at appropriate times.

9. A major goal of socialization training in general is to make children *independent* of their parents by teaching them adult skills and competencies. In addition to the areas discussed above, independence training involves a great variety of specific skills, such as self-help, job skills, and mastering the adult world.

10. For each person, the culture defines an appropriate *role,* on the basis of sex, age, occupation, prestige position, and group memberships. *Sex typing* begins right at birth, and there have traditionally been distinct expectations about the appropriate role behaviors for boys and for girls. Also important is *age grading,* and there are well defined "right" ages for weaning, toilet training, attending school, taking a job, and so on. The ritualistic ceremonies marking age progression that are of great importance in many primitive cultures exist only minimally in our own society, however.

11. Children are known to differ biologically in certain behavioral characteristics, and the word *temperament* is used to refer to such differences in responsivity or activity level in infants. Differences in children's temperaments interact with parents' expectations, and can create either happy or difficult experiences for all concerned.

KEY TERMS

agents of socialization

reality principle

pleasure principle

libido
psychosexual stages

oral

anal

phallic

genital

Oedipal

latency

psychosocial stages

secondary drives

motives

secondary reinforcement

secondary reinforcers

attachment

self-reinforcement

introjection

Maslow's hierarchy

conditioned generalized
  reinforcers

canalization

learned helplessness

instinct

frustration

aggression

separation anxiety

prosocial behavior

moral developement

role

androgyny

temperament

PART TWO

FOUNDATIONS OF MALADJUSTMENT: ANXIETY AND DEFENSES

FOUR

Anxiety

Anxiety is a universal phenomenon.

- Related terms are fear, worry, phobia, tension, stress, shame, and guilt.

A behavioral analysis of anxiety reveals three characteristics:

feelings of apprehension

physiological changes

interference with thinking

- It is not yet understood whether there is just one basic emotional state or many, nor is it known to what degree a low threshold of emotional arousal is hereditary.

Anxiety can be a learned response to almost any stimulus.

- Anxiety can, through conditioning, become attached to specific thoughts, a process that is heavily involved in teaching children to inhibit undesirable behaviors.

- The ways in which phobias are learned are not well understood.

Psychoanalytic theorists attribute a key role to anxiety in explaining psychological disturbance.

Humanistic theorists regard anxiety as a normal and inevitable part of human life.

ANXIETY IS A UNIVERSAL PHENOMENON OF MODERN CIVILIZATION, AND OUR times have been aptly described as the "age of anxiety." The noted historian Arthur J. Schlesinger, Jr., has made the observation that anxiety is the official emotion of our age, while psychoanalyst Karen Horney reflected the same sentiment in her well-known book, *The Neurotic Personality of our Time* (1937).

Anxiety is a common, everyday experience, familiar to virtually everyone. Who of us has not been anxious about an impending examination, an oral report that must be made or our dating and sex life? Indeed, those few persons who are unusually free of anxiety may constitute a special group—the psychopaths—who pose problems for themselves and society, problems that will be discussed in Chapter 7.

We have already seen that anxiety plays a critical role in the socialization process. Parents and other agents of socialization use anxiety systematically to inhibit behaviors that are regarded as culturally undesirable. Thus, when we "sin" or otherwise break cultural taboos, we experience anxiety, its extent depending on the seriousness of the transgression and the degree to which we have been socialized. Clearly, it is the avoidance of anxiety that is the major deterrent in preventing most of us from deviating from the standards set by our culture.

The role of anxiety is not necessarily an unadaptive one. As we have said in Chapter 3, anxiety acts as a drive and also serves to indicate the direction of new

behavior through its cue properties. Without some amount of anxiety, we would not be motivated to do many things that need to be done: get the car fixed, pay the rent, take care of bodily complaints, and study for exams. Referring again to the case of Adele in Chapter 1, it could perhaps be useful to Adele to have somewhat more anxiety about her life situation. On the other hand, the level of anxiety experienced by Frances clearly interferes with her ability to function effectively. In this chapter we are concerned with such dysfunctional anxiety, that is, anxiety which disrupts a person's normal functioning.

Anxiety has traditionally been closely connected with the concept of personal maladjustment, so much so that the two are often regarded as virtually synonymous. However, there are certain kinds of psychological disorders which do not appear to be based in anxiety. In addition, it is important to recognize that even well-adjusted persons experience significant amounts of anxiety in certain situations, but that the way they react to their anxiety and cope with it differs from the behavior of maladjusted persons. For these reasons, we must be careful of our terminology, and we should not consider anxiety and maladjustment to be the same, although there is clearly an important relationship between them.

It should be noted that there are two important criteria of adjustment to anxiety: (1) the degree of anxiety; and (2) the nature or quality of a person's attempts to cope with it. In general, the greater the degree of anxiety, the more difficult it is to manage. When someone is simply overwhelmed with feelings of tension, dread, and impending disaster, there seems to be no response that could be adequate. Also, as the following pages indicate, some responses are more effective than others in diminishing and controlling anxiety, and the effectiveness of our attempts to manage anxiety is determined to some extent by cultural factors. In our society, for instance, attempts to explain away or *rationalize* our concerns are more acceptable than heavy reliance on physical complaints.

Components of Anxiety

In view of the central position of anxiety in most of our current theories of behavior and personality development, it may be surprising to discover that there is less agreement about the specific nature of anxiety than there is about its significance. There is considerable disagreement among psychologists and psychiatrists about what exactly is meant by the term anxiety, and there are a number of other terms—fear, phobia, worry, emotion, stress, tension, shame, guilt—which are sometimes used interchangeably with anxiety, further confusing the issue. We will consider each of these terms in turn.

Fear and anxiety. Implied in our discussion of anxiety in Chapters 2 and 3 was the view that anxiety is an acquired or learned fear. There have been a number of attempts, however, to differentiate between the terms **fear** and **anxiety.** Some

An exaggerated fear of heights is a common phobia. There are a number of possible explanations as to how phobias are learned.

writers have used the term fear to refer to those instances in which the emotional reaction has a distinct and identifiable source, a consciously perceived object, such as a spider or a furry object. The term anxiety, on the other hand, has been reserved for those situations in which the individual cannot identify the stimuli that caused the emotional response, or where the identified stimulus has indirect or symbolic significance. When the stimulus cannot be identified, the emotional response is "free floating." In this use of the terms, fear has an identifiable source and anxiety does not. This distinction, however, is not widely made and we will use the two terms synonymously.

Phobia. Phobias are exaggerated fears of specific objects or events in situations where the actual possibility of harm to the individual is rather slight. Phobias can be extremely incapacitating, and can seriously interfere with an individual's functioning. Thus, people with a phobia about germs might avoid meeting other people, wash their hands many times each day, and perhaps even refuse to eat any food that they themselves had not prepared. Other phobias that could be quite incapacitating would include phobias about persons of the opposite sex, disease and illness,

high and enclosed places, daylight, and the dark. An elephant phobia, on the other hand, would give most of us little trouble.

Over half a century ago, G. Stanley Hall (1914), then a well-known psychologist, cataloged more than 130 different phobias, using the usual Greek derivative names such as *claustrophobia,* or fear of enclosed places, and *agoraphobia,* or fear of open places. This list could be endless since phobic reactions are thought to be learned and there are always new things to which individuals can become phobic. For instance, Hall did not include a phobia of flying in airplanes, a fairly common phobia today. Although it is nowadays recognized that the mere naming and cataloging of phobias serves no useful purpose, some of the Greek names are still in use.

It is important to recognize that the intensity of the emotional reaction in a phobia is disproportionate to the actual risk involved. In the case of a flying phobia, for example, airplanes do occasionally crash and there is some risk involved in flying. However, persons with this phobia experience a dread of flying that is so intense that not only are they unwilling to fly, but they often cannot even think of flying without experiencing anxiety; indeed, they are often unwilling even to watch airplanes take off or to read about airplanes. However, they do not show such a disproportionate reaction to driving an automobile, an experience that in reality is more risky than flying. The exact manner in which these intense and specific fears are acquired is not yet clearly understood, although a number of alternative explanations have been offered. We shall return to a discussion of phobias and their development later in the chapter.

Worry. Worry is a rather vague and poorly defined term, and most psychological textbooks do not even mention it. Yet worry is often an important factor in maladjustment, and most of us have had personal experience with something that we would call worry.

Let us define **worry** as the anxiety experienced by an individual thinking about a difficult personal situation, either actual or imagined, who can see no immediate solution to the problem. As the person's thoughts continually dwell on the difficulties, the person feels helpless and even hopeless about the final outcome of the situation. Worry often attaches to events that are unpredictable and unforeseeable—accidents which may befall the individual or significant other people in the individual's life, or catastrophes such as the loss of a house or a job. The worrier will constantly mull over these upsetting and nonfunctional thoughts, even though this can serve no useful purpose. The more individuals think about these rather unlikely events, the more anxious they become as they view their own inability to prevent them from occurring. Obviously, worrying can interfere a great deal with adaptive behavior, and it can pose significant mental health problems. For example, a client of one of the authors would constantly be concerned about a variety of possible matters whenever she went out of the house. She would worry constantly about having left a door or window unlocked, an iron still steaming, a water tap left running. These worries so preoccupied her that she was unable to give her attention to the movie she was attending or the conversation of her friends. This kind of intense and somewhat irrelevant worry is sometimes termed obsessional thinking.

A certain amount of worry is probably inevitable, and is a part of the complexity of everyday life. Since most of us feel that we are to some extent at the mercy of forces which we can neither control nor even completely understand, some degree of concern about an uncertain future seems inescapable. Worry can even be functional under some circumstances. Janis (1968), for instance, has reported that hospital patients who were unworried about their impending major surgery were less able to withstand the postoperative pain and other problems of recuperation than those patients who were moderately worried. Janis concluded that there is a "useful work of worrying" that prepares us for coping with actual future stress. Thus, a certain amount of worrying about actual situations might be helpful, although worrying about imaginary ones in generally nonadaptive. Obviously, however, it is not always possible to tell just how real a potential problem situation might be.

Tension. Tension is another term that is closely related to anxiety. In fact, it is often used as a synonym for anxiety, as when a person says, "I feel so tense that I could

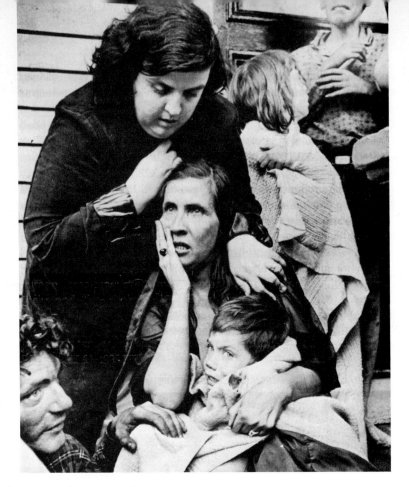

Stress and worry may be appropriate to a
particular situation. Here comfort is given
to a woman whose two-year-old grandson
perished in a tenement fire.

scream." Sometimes **tension** refers specifically to the increase in muscle tonus that is
part of the physiological changes involved in anxiety, and if it were reserved for this
use alone, it could be a useful concept. However, the concept of tension is generally
used in a rather vague manner, and appears to contribute little toward our understanding of anxiety; we shall not use it further.

Stress. Stress is yet another word used constantly in connection with anxiety. The
term is used in a number of different ways, and the user generally does not specify its

precise meaning. **Stress** can refer to: (1) certain characteristics of the environment, so that we might say individuals are under stress when taking an important examination; (2) the reactions of the individual without regard to the situation, so that we can say that people are experiencing stress without indicating whether they are about to take an examination or contemplating an abortion; (3) the characteristics of the situation *and* the particular responses of the individual, so that we might say that the patient was under considerable stress while being prepared for surgery; and (4) some characteristic or state of individuals that accounts for their behavior, so that we might "explain" someone's peculiar behavior as resulting from an ongoing stressful situation. The variety of uses of the term *stress* resembles very much the way in which the term *anxiety* itself is used, and in common parlance the terms are often used interchangeably. Thus, a stress, stressor, or stressful situation is one where it is expected that anxiety will be aroused; an individual who is "under stress" or "stressed" is in a stressful situation; and a "stress reaction" refers to those changes in individuals and their behavior that follow exposure to a stressful situation. In other words, situations that are stressful are anxiety arousing, and stress reactions are anxiety reactions.

One of the obvious ways in which we can account for differences among individuals in anxiety is to examine the ordinary or habitual level that different persons experience on a day-to-day basis. The business executive who is constantly pressured by the conflicting demands of his or her clients on the one hand, and his or her vice-president on the other, is functioning in a much more stressful environment than the traditional light-house keeper whose sole responsibility is to keep the light burning.

Shame and guilt. The terms shame and guilt are similar in some respects, as both refer to the anxiety aroused by violating a cultural standard or taboo. However, there are important differences between the two (Kagan, 1971). Their behavioral manifestations are different, with shame typically being accompanied by the lowering of the head and eyes and blushing, while guilt does not have a single, readily identifiable behavioral pattern of response.

The term **shame** is used to refer to the anxiety that is experienced when individuals recognize that other people will disapprove of their behavior, while **guilt** is the anxiety experienced when one disapproves of one's own behavior. Thus, guilt is a more individual and personal reaction, and indicates that the person has adopted or introjected the standards of society. Guilt refers to a process of self-judgment, while shame refers to anxiety prompted by actual or anticipated judgment by others. Both of these anxiety-based reactions, however, serve to prevent us from violating the cultural standards of the society into which we were socialized.

Now that we have reviewed some of the common concepts related to anxiety, the difficulties inherent in any simplistic definition of anxiety should be apparent. While previously we have simply defined anxiety as a learned fear, we have not yet elaborated on some of the complex issues involved in describing its nature and causes. Doing so forms the subject matter of the rest of the chapter.

The Experience of Anxiety

One way to approach the task of understanding the experience of anxiety is to examine the introspective reports and descriptions given by other persons, both in case history and literary form. The following is excerpted from John Updike's collection of short stories *Pigeon Feathers*.

. . . He had to go to the bathroom, and took a flashlight down through the wet grass to the outhouse. For once, his fear of spiders there felt trivial. He set the flashlight, burning, beside him, and an insect alighted on its lens, a tiny insect, a mosquito or flea, made so fine that the weak light projected its X-ray onto the wall boards; the faint rim of its wings, the blurred strokes, magnified, of its long hinged legs, the dark cone at the heart of its anatomy. The tremor must be its heart beating. Without warning, David was visited by an exact vision of death: a long hole in the ground, no wider than your body, down which you are drawn while the white faces above recede. You try to reach them but your arms are pinned. Shovels pour dirt into your face. There you will be forever, in an upright position, blind and silent, and in time no one will remember you, and you will never be called. As strata of rock shift, your fingers elongate, and your teeth are distended sideways in a great underground grimace indistinguishable from a strip of chalk. And the earth tumbles on, and the sun expires, and unaltering darkness reigns where once there were stars.

Sweat broke out on his back. His mind seemed to rebound off a solidness. Such extinction was not another threat, a graver sort of danger, a kind of pain; it was qualitatively different. It was not even a conception that could be voluntarily pictured; it entered him from the outside. His protesting nerves swarmed on its surface like lichen on a meteor. The skin of his chest was soaked with the effort of rejection. At the same time that the fear was dense and internal, it was dense and all around him; a tide of clay had swept up to the stars; space was crushed into a mass. When he stood up, automatically hunching his shoulders to keep his head away from the spider webs, it was with a numb sense of being cramped between two huge volumes of rigidity. That he had even this small freedom to move surprised him. In the narrow shelter of that rank shack, adjusting his pants, he felt — his first spark of comfort — too small to be crushed.

But in the open, as the beam of the flashlight skidded with frightened quickness across the remote surfaces of the barn and the grape arbor and the giant pine that stood by the path to the woods, the terror descended. He raced up through the clinging grass pursued, not by one of the wild animals the woods might hold, or one of the goblins his superstitious grandmother had communicated to his childhood, but by spectres out of science fiction, where gigantic cinder moons fill half the turquoise sky. As David ran, a gray planet rolled inches behind his neck. If he looked back, he would be buried. And in the momentum of his terror, hideous possibilities — the dilation of the sun, the triumph of the insects, the crabs on the shore in The Time Machine — wheeled out of the vacuum of make-believe and added their weight to his impending oblivion. . . .*

This literary excerpt illustrates the three primary characteristics which are recognized in any comprehensive account of anxiety: (1) a conscious feeling of fear or apprehension, in the absence of any immediate objective threat or danger; (2) a pattern of physiological arousal and physical distress that usually includes a variety of physical complaints; and (3) some disorganization of, and interference with, effective thinking and problem solving (Calhoun, Acocella, and Goodstein, 1977). Although different people tend to emphasize one or another of these aspects more than the rest in recounting their experiences of anxiety, all three aspects are recognized as being present. In the Updike excerpt, much more attention is paid to the conscious feelings of fear and dread than to the other two aspects, although both physical changes and the disorganization of thought are also definitely involved.

The fact that there are three rather distinct aspects to the experience of anxiety may help to explain why there is so much confusion among psychologists who work in this area. Not only are there differences among individuals in the relative emphasis which they give to the three aspects of their experience of anxiety, but these aspects may not be highly related. Thus, an individual might experience rather intense fears but without a marked disruption of thought or intense physiological changes. Also, many theorists and researchers tend to concentrate their efforts on one particular aspect of anxiety to the exclusion of the other two, with the result that they develop somewhat different understandings of the phenomenon. Some investigators devote their energies to the study of the conscious feelings of fear or apprehension, primarily through the analysis of interviews and self-report questionnaires, while others spend their time studying the physiological changes, either through direct observations or self-reports, and there tends to be little communication between workers across these fields of endeavor. Such fragmenting of the field leads to unnecessary misunderstanding and confusion.

We next explore the phenomenon of anxiety in some detail from a number of different points of view, starting with the social-learning approach and then contrasting it with the Freudian or psychodynamic approach and also with the approach of humanistic theorists.

A SOCIAL-LEARNING ANALYSIS OF ANXIETY

As we have said, the three key characteristics of anxiety are: feelings of fear and apprehension, physiological changes, and impairment of thought. We begin our analysis by considering each of these factors in turn.

**From Pigeon Feathers & Other Stories,* by John Updike, New York: Knopf, 1962. Reproduced by permission.

The Physiology of Anxiety

The physiological events which form part of the concept of anxiety are well known to all of us: A near crash on the expressway, a fall when climbing, or any other exposure to actual danger triggers the physiological components of anxiety. They involve the *respiratory* system, leading to breathlessness and feelings of suffocation; the *cardiovascular* system, producing heart palpitations, changes in blood pressure and pulse, and even fainting; and the *gastrointestinal* system, with loss of appetite, nausea, vomiting, and diarrhea. Other typical changes include perspiration, frequent urination, muscular tension, and sleeplessness. Although it would be very unusual for a person to experience all of these physical changes simultaneously, the occurrence of just a few of them is sufficient to cause great discomfort. Anxiety, with its accompanying discomfort, stimulates most people to activity directed at reducing the discomfort.

What are the origins of the physiological changes that we have just described? Basically, there is an increased secretion into the bloodstream of the hormones *adrenaline* and *noradrenaline,* which are produced by the adrenal medulla, a part of the adrenal gland. These secretions raise the blood sugar level through their action on the liver. The accelerated breathing rate increases the supply of oxygen to the blood, while the more rapid heartbeat speeds the distribution of these supplies of sugar and oxygen to the voluntary muscles. In addition, there is a decrease in the activity of the glands and smooth muscles, while the dilation of the pupil admits more light to the eyes.

Why do these changes occur? More than fifty years ago, the physiologist Walter B. Cannon proposed that these changes represented the body's preparation for an emergency situation, whether "flight" or "fight."

Many unusual feats of strength have been performed under emergency conditions which would not have been possible under ordinary circumstances. People have been known, for example, to enter burning buildings and carry out injured persons whose weight far exceeded what they could ordinarily carry. Obviously the innate physiological emergency reaction prepares for intense physical exertion and has clear adaptive significance, at least in those situations where fight or flight are adaptive responses. It is important to note that in order for this emergency reaction to be adaptive, it must be an anticipatory one, elicited by the threat of danger rather than by an actual, present danger so that the organism will be prepared to meet the threat in time.

It is ironic that in our modern civilization these emergency reactions are more often than not unadaptive, and often they actually interfere with responses that would be more functional. When confronted with a frightening situation today, the appropriate response would rarely involve either fight or flight. In asking one's boss for a raise, a situation that is frightening for many of us, a state of strong physiological arousal probably interferes with a person's ability to make a clear and forceful presentation of reasons for deserving the raise. And the role of physiological arousal in detracting from good performance on examinations is well known to most students. Sex is yet another area in which the physiological effects of anxiety almost certainly interfere with effective functioning, since anxiety interferes on the physiological level with maintaining an erection in males and with vaginal lubrication in females.

Although the physiological components of anxiety do not seem very useful to us today, they undoubtedly played a significant part in survival in primitive societies, where the major threats were physical and could best be met either by escaping as quickly as possible or by fighting back as fiercely as possible. It may be that emotional arousal evolved in humans as a natural or unconditioned response to physical pain, serving a direct survival function by enabling them to deal more effectively with threats to their physical well-being. All of us are familiar with reports of soldiers, athletes, and others who have not become aware of their serious injuries until after the stressful situation has been resolved. Thus, the greater energy and obliviousness to pain which are possible in an emergency reaction have certainly enabled both primitive peoples and their modern counterparts to survive drastic circumstances.

Syracuse University freshmen grimace in pain as they near the finish of a race. Emotional arousal may effectively spur the individual on to the limits of energy and endurance.

We previously noted that the emergency reaction must be anticipatory in order to be effective. How is this possible? The process of classical conditioning, or learning by association, is involved, and the emotional reaction initially made to the physical pain comes to be made to whatever cues were also present at the same time as the original pain. Since many of these cues are available prior to the onset of the pain, the emotional response can be made prior to the actual experience of pain. Indeed, if the emergency reaction operates effectively, the pain can be completely avoided, either by early flight or sufficient physical strength to overcome the threat. In addition, considerable learning of emergency reactions undoubtedly takes place through observation or modeling. Thus, the cave boy could well have observed his father responding quickly to the signs that a saber-toothed tiger was in the vicinity, and would therefore be able to model his behavior after his father's at a later appropriate time.

In discussing the physiology of anxiety, we have noted the occurrence of a number of bodily changes. These physiological changes are largely monitored or mediated by the autonomic nervous system, and they are often referred to by the general term **emotional arousal.** Emotional arousal generally involves increases in the individual's level of *activation,* and includes heightened activity of the cerebral cortex, as shown by changes in electroencephalogram (EEG) recordings; increased muscle tension, as shown by electromyogram (EMG) recordings; and increases in gross behavioral activity. A number of psychological theorists, including Duffy (1962), Malmo (1959), and Schachter (1966), have used the concept of emotional arousal as the basis for a theory of activation and behavior. These psychologists believe that all behavior involves some degree of emotional arousal, and that emotional arousal of a general kind is a necessary condition for alertness, coordination, and effective responses. While they agree that high levels of emotional arousal do interfere with effective behavior, they also believe that low levels of arousal result in decreased effectiveness. The impact of these theories is limited, however, by the fact that the mechanisms involved in emotional arousal—how our awareness or perception of an emergency is connected to the physiological response—are not yet clearly understood. Therefore, it is not yet possible to decide exactly how useful they are in our understanding of human behavior.

One emotion or many? In our discussion up to this point, we have implied that the same physiological reaction occurs whether the situation and subjective experience is anxiety, anger, or some other emotion. This is the viewpoint of the general activation theorists. Some psychologists, however, believe that the emotions of anxiety and anger have different physiological mechanisms and different observable signs, as well as different subjective experiences. Evidence in support of this view was reported by Wolf and Wolff (1947). These writers had the unusual opportunity to study the gastric responses of a patient who had severely damaged his esophagus at an early age by drinking very hot soup, so that it was necessary for him to feed himself through a permanent opening that was made directly into his stomach. After he had chewed the food it was put directly into his stomach through a tube which extended through the abdominal wall and the lining of the stomach. This opening provided Wolf and Wolff with an opportunity to observe the physiological changes in the stomach associated with emotional arousal. They reported that the stomach lining appeared to show two basic and different patterns of reaction to emotional conditions, one involving an increased blood supply and the other a decreased blood supply. Parallels were drawn between the subject's emotional reactions as observed on the face and in the stomach: increased blood supply was associated with rage or anger, while the pallor of decreased blood supply was associated with anxiety.

Other researchers have also tried to differentiate clearly between the physiological bases for anxiety and anger. One view is that the differences are due to corresponding differences in the secretion of adrenaline and noradrenaline. The research literature, however, shows that the differences, while real, are small and tend to be outweighed by the similarities. Also, as we have observed above, emotional reactions differ greatly from person to person, and they also differ within the same person when exposed to a series of similar situations at different times. Finally, a person's *thoughts* about the source of the emotional arousal play a very important part in the reaction to the arousal.

Let us emphasize again why it is so important to study and understand the physiological and cognitive aspects of anxiety arousal. In the vast majority of cases, they are *distressing* and *disruptive,* and interfere with effective performance. In other words, a chronically high level of arousal is acutely uncomfortable and it is also a distinct handicap in the performance of everyday activities.

Emotional arousal and heredity. In Chapter 1 we discussed the contributions of genetic factors to personality characteristics and to psychological maladjustment, and we concluded that there was little direct evidence for genetic influences. It is obvious,

however, that individuals do differ widely in their habitual degree of autonomic reactivity, that is, in the readiness with which they experience anxiety, and the question has been raised whether this characteristic might be at least partially genetically determined. In other words, are some people born with easily aroused autonomic nervous systems while others are born with less sensitive systems? There is little definitive research with humans in this area, although British psychologist Jeffrey Gray (1971) has summarized a number of studies done with laboratory rats. These studies led Gray to the conclusion that in rats, at least, susceptibility to emotional arousal, or fearfulness, does seem to have a significant genetic base. More recently, Buss and Plomin (1975) have provided some preliminary evidence that humans might also differ genetically to some extent in emotional arousal. A more complete answer to this question will enable significant advances to be made in the understanding of human behavior and the problems of adjustment.

The Learning of Anxiety

We have seen that the complex of physiological events that are an integral part of anxiety occur as natural responses to painful or aversive stimuli. These somatic changes are initially produced as a response to the pain, but through associative learning or classical conditioning they soon also come to be a response to other cues that were present when the pain was experienced. It is important to understand that any cue which is present at the time pain is experienced can later arouse the same emotional state that was aroused by the pain. These cues may include some that were present accidentally as well as those directly related to the pain arousal. Thus, through a process of conditioning we learn to be anxious in the presence of stimuli that previously were neutral. By such a process, virtually anything can become the stimulus for an acquired anxiety reaction, and we can now understand why there are so many different cues for anxiety in maladjusted persons.

All that is necessary for an individual to learn an anxiety reaction is for a sudden pain or other aversive stimulus to occur in the presence of a recognizable cue. Anxiety can also be intentionally taught, and, as we learned in the previous chapter, it plays an important role in the socialization process. Children who are spanked every time they stray beyond the front gate will become generally anxious whenever they are near the gate. Or, if they are consistently spanked for fondling their genitals, all stimuli associated with that behavior will come to arouse anxiety. Figure 4-1 illustrates the way in which anxiety is traditionally used in another important aspect of socialization, toilet training.

One of the earliest and clearest experimental attempts to demonstrate the process by which anxiety is acquired was that of Albert and the white rat (Watson and Rayner, 1920), and the process has been further demonstrated on innumerable occasions and with a variety of different subjects—infants, children, laboratory animals, and adult humans. A striking example of the conditioning of anxiety in adults was reported by

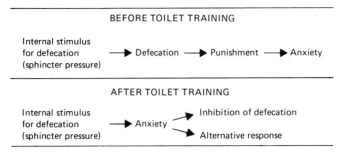

BEFORE TOILET TRAINING

Internal stimulus for defecation (sphincter pressure) ⟶ Defecation ⟶ Punishment ⟶ Anxiety

AFTER TOILET TRAINING

Internal stimulus for defecation (sphincter pressure) ⟶ Anxiety ⟶ Inhibition of defecation / Alternative response

Figure 4-1. How anxiety is traditionally used in toilet training. Initially the mother punishes the child, either physically or by threatening the loss of her love, for defecating freely in response to sphincter pressure. In order for the anxiety to affect the defecation response these events must occur rather close to each other in time. The anxiety becomes associated with the response of free defecation, so that, in time, this response is inhibited. Inhibiting the response of free defecation now permits the child to avoid the anxiety. Instead, the child makes an alternative response: either signaling that he or she must defecate, or going directly to the toilet and defecating there. The mother further enhances this learning by clearly specifying the desired alternative behaviors, and by positively reinforcing them when they occur. Thus, the learning of appropriate toilet behavior involves both anxiety avoidance and positive reinforcement.

Campbell, Sanderson, and Laverty (1964). These researchers were able to produce a very strong conditioned anxiety reaction to a simple auditory tone by pairing the tone with the onset of the effects of a powerful drug, scoline, which produced a momentary motor paralysis without loss of consciousness. The effects of scoline are quite traumatic, and can often produce a temporary interruption in breathing, so that the subject believes that he or she could be dying. The onset of this reaction was paired with the presentation of a tone, and the tone, when presented later by itself, elicited the same strong emotional reaction that had initially been stimulated by the effects of the drug. This fear reaction was quite long lasting, despite the fact that the drug and the resulting paralysis were only paired with the tone on a single occasion, a result which suggests that conditioned fears are both easily learned and difficult to extinguish.

The learning of phobias. Earlier in this chapter we defined phobias as exaggerated fears of specific objects or events, where the intensity of the fear is very much out of proportion to the actual risk involved. How are phobias learned? One possible mechanism would be through the direct conditioning of a fear reaction in the manner that has just been described. Indeed, the subjects who participated in the above experiment might be said to have learned a "tone phobia."

Many people who seek help with their phobias, however, report that they cannot recall any specific events that would account for their troublesome emotional reaction. Indeed, people often have strong phobic reactions to things with which they have had no prior experience at all. Many people, for example, have phobias about flying on airplanes, yet they have never been on an airplane, or even visited an airport. We must expand our notions about the acquisition of fear if we are to account for all instances of phobic reactions.

There are a number of possible explanations for the way in which phobias are learned, and all of them may be true to some degree and applicable in different instances. One possible explanation is simply forgetting the original experience. For example, it is quite possible that some of the subjects in the Campbell, Sanderson, and Laverty experiment would, over time, be unable to recall that they had ever taken part in the study, although they would probably still experience a twinge of fear whenever they heard the specific tone involved. Indeed, the unpleasant nature of the experience would be likely to hasten its being forgotten. Thus, in some cases, there could have been a specific situation in which the phobia was learned, but the individual involved may have forgotten the exact circumstances. We will return later to this concept of "motivated forgetting" in our discussion of the effects of anxiety on thinking.

We have discussed the importance of modeling or observational learning in a number of places in this book, and it is possible that some phobias are acquired through modeling. It is reasonable, for example, to suppose that modeling could account for some instances of phobias about snakes and airplanes, both of which involve situations with which the individual has usually had little direct, personal experience. These phobias could well be taught to children by their parents or other adults as part of the socialization process. One need only observe the television cartoon programs that are avidly watched by most small children to see many instances of the cultural transmission of fears.

Another view of the way in which phobias are developed involves the concept of the **displacement of anxiety.** Displacement of anxiety means that the feared object is not the real source of the anxiety, but represents the individual's defensive reaction to a situation that would otherwise be even more anxiety arousing or dangerous to that individual. Thus, a woman with a phobia about sharp knives might be displacing her fear of killing her husband, toward whom she has intense but unverbalized anger. Here, she makes the unconscious choice of fearing sharp knives rather than having to acknowledge her fear of "cutting his throat." Or a business man might develop a phobia of driving his car, leading to an inability to go to his failing business.

There is another explanation of the development of phobias that is similar to the concept involved in displacement. Some people experience strong, generalized fear reactions, or **"free-floating" anxiety**—a disabling state marked by a strong sense of impending doom, overwhelming but nameless fears, and a variety of somatic upsets. Under these circumstances people will often "choose" a convenient object that has some symbolic connection to the underlying problem, and use it to focus or "bind" the fear, in much the same fashion as displacement. Thus, a person with a strong sense of dread that is accompanied by the somatic reaction of heart palpitations might begin to believe that he is suffering from heart disease and that he might have a fatal heart attack. Consequently, he develops a phobia about leaving his house in case he needs to call his physician. Instead of experiencing a vague sense of doom and the unexplained physical changes of anxiety, the individual has now tidily isolated and "explained" his problem. Although this solution presents its own problems, a circumscribed or limited phobic reaction is more bearable, regardless of how much it may interfere with one's behavior, than an intense, diffuse anxiety reaction without any identifiable source.

The use of the concept of displacement to explain phobias is based mainly on subjective reports from clinical work with disturbed people, while those explanations that involve direct learning and modeling come primarily from laboratory research. The concept of displacement originated within psychoanalytic theory, in which phobias were always believed to stem from unexpressed sexual or aggressive impulses, and were held to be symbolic representations of an unresolved psychosexual conflict. In this view, the important consideration is the underlying or symbolic meaning of the phobia. Thus, a snake or airplane phobia is likely to be seen as symbolizing a sexual conflict, and not as a fear that was learned directly or through observation. Psychoanalytic theorists believe that a person can, in principle, never fully understand the symbolic or "real" significance of a phobia, because its true nature is buried or repressed as part of the defense against the anxiety surrounding those memories.

Many psychologists do not agree that the most important aspect of a phobia is its symbolic significance. However, it is obvious that phobias can serve to protect individuals from even more potent anxieties, help to preserve their sense of integrity, and otherwise make it easier for them to proceed with their lives, though at a substantial price.

There are two other explanations of phobias that merit our attention, involving the concepts of generalization and higher-order conditioning. Since both of these concepts are important, not only for our understanding of phobias but also for an understanding of the way in which acquired fears affect our behavior, we will examine each of them in turn.

Generalization of anxiety. The concept of generalization was introduced in Chapter 2. To repeat briefly, a response learned in the presence of one set of stimuli will tend to occur not only whenever these stimuli are present, but also in the presence of stimuli that are similar to the original ones. Thus, if a child encounters a situation that has some degree of similarity to a previous situation in which she experienced pain, resulting in a conditioned anxiety reaction, she will also be anxious in the "new" situation. Watson and Rayner (1920) reported that little Albert generalized his fear of the white rat to all furry animals, and a child who has been frightened by the large black dog next door is likely to generalize her fear to other dogs. In this sense, all phobias are generalized responses, since by definition they are exaggerated fear reactions to a *class* of stimuli rather than to a single stimulus or object. We still do not understand, though, why there is such an exaggerated level of anxiety. Clearly, it would be reasonable to be wary of dogs after a traumatic experience, and most observers would see this behavior as sensible and intelligent. But a phobia appears to be much more than this, for a person with a phobia of dogs not only avoids stray dogs, but might refuse to visit friends who own dogs, and might even become anxious at the sight of toy dogs or pictures of dogs.

The problem of how the intensity of the emotional distress involved in the original learning can be sufficient to account for the development of a phobic reaction is still unanswered. However, it is well understood that anxiety is both readily learned and easily generalized, and the significance of generalization in the maintenance of anxiety reactions cannot be overemphasized. To repeat, people react with habitual anxiety to situations which merely *resemble* the situation in which pain or discomfort was originally experienced, and it is completely impossible to keep track of all this conditioning. In other words, people almost universally become anxious in situations for reasons quite unknown to them. To be able to identify all our anxiety stimuli would seem to be quite beyond our capabilities.

As in the case of all generalized responses, the generalization of fear can be enhanced by labeling. For example, the mother who says to her child who has been frightened by the dog next door, "Well, you just have to be careful of strange animals," is facilitating the generalization of the fear reaction to animals other than dogs.

Higher-order conditioning of anxiety. We have seen how anxiety can be conditioned to a neutral cue, such as a tone or a furry object. What happens if we now pair an object that serves as a conditioned stimulus for fear with a new, neutral object? Suppose, for instance, that we now pair a flashing light with the tone that has become a conditioned stimulus for fear. Again, through the process of conditioning, the flashing light would also acquire fear-arousing properties. We call this process, by which neutral stimuli become conditioned stimuli through association with other conditioned stimuli, *higher-order conditioning.* In other words, the flashing light can acquire fear-arousing properties without ever having been directly associated with a pain-arousing situation. Of course, there is a limit to this process; as with any chain of associations, the response is likely to be somewhat weaker at each step. Thus, the emotional reaction to the flashing light will not be as strong as the initial reaction to the tone.

As a concrete example of how the process of higher-order conditioning may produce a strong conditioned fear, one of the authors once interviewed an eight-year-old boy who had a fear of red-haired women. A detailed examination of the history of this problem indicated that the child was extremely fearful of injections and had developed a conditioned fear of physicians, nurses, and anyone who wore white uniforms. The school dietitian, who wore white while at work, was red-haired and the child had reacted with terror when she once approached him to ask how he liked his lunch. Thus, despite the fact that the dietitian had never been directly associated with an injection, he reacted to her with a fear that had phobic intensity, and then developed further phobic reactions to other red-haired women.

Thinking and anxiety. For the moment, let us regard thinking as statements that are made in the privacy of our minds; or, to put it another way, let us view thinking as "subvocal" speech. This is much too simple a view for most purposes, of course, but it is useful for understanding the role of anxiety in thinking. The heart of the matter is that one kind of stimuli which are always present whenever pain is experienced are *thoughts*. These thoughts are every bit as much a part of the stimulus situation as are concrete observable objects, even though one cannot observe or measure them directly. To the child who was punished for venturing beyond the front gate, for example, the stimulus situation to which anxiety responses became conditioned included not only the sight of the gate, but also the *thought* of the gate. We can now understand how the occurrence of thoughts about going outside the gate can arouse anxiety, even when the child is nowhere near the gate. The majority of us likewise experience anxiety at the mere thought of aversive stimuli, for example, at the thought of having a tooth drilled by the dentist. And one well-known technique for increasing the effectiveness of punishment in suppressing undesired behavior is to make certain that a child is thinking about the misdeed while he or she is being punished.

Earlier in this chapter, in our discussion of the study in which a tone became a conditioned stimulus for anxiety, we noted that it was often difficult for people to recall the circumstances under which a given anxiety reaction was originally learned. Now we can see more clearly that one of the important reasons for this failure of recall is that memories of such experiences are themselves anxiety arousing, and are therefore very likely to be avoided. To ask people to recall the circumstances under which they experienced strong negative emotional arousal is to ask them to re-experience some of those same negative feelings. Just as people avoid objects that have proven to be painful, so too they avoid painful memories. The avoidance of painful thoughts is closely related to what Freud meant by the concept of *repression*, and it will play a major role in our discussion in Chapter 6 about ineffectual but persistent attempts to deal with anxiety. It is also an important factor in explaining how psychotherapy works, our topic in Chapter 11.

We have discussed the role of labeling and thinking in *mediating* the generalization of anxiety, and we have seen how very wide the range of conditioned stimuli that elicit anxiety can be, stemming in some cases from a single painful experience. The original painful or punishing event has been referred to as the natural or primary aversive stimulus, and we can refer to other stimuli that are present during or immediately preceding punishment, including thoughts, as **conditioned aversive stimuli.** If a parent says sternly, "Bad boy!" while spanking the child who has ventured beyond the gate, and repeats those words each time a spanking is administered, they soon become conditioned aversive stimuli. The child will come to react with anxiety to "Bad boy!" just as certainly as he will to the sight of the gate and to the sight of the parent's hand raised to spank. We can even observe children administering self-punishment, by saying "Bad boy!" aloud as they attempt to inhibit some previously punished act.

Let us reflect for a moment upon the enormous use that is made of words as conditioned aversive stimuli. By far the most common method of teaching children constraints, or socializing them in what is permissible, is the use of words as conditioned aversive stimuli. "Don't do that!" "Put it back!" are commands that are traditionally

Widespread use is made of words as conditioned aversive stimuli.

paired with sporadic natural or primary punishment. We have discussed in Chapter 2 the fact that punishment (or reinforcement) delivered on a partial or intermittent schedule is much more effective in establishing consistent and long-lasting behavior than punishment delivered on a continuous schedule. Once the words have become established as conditioned aversive stimuli, therefore, backing them up with actual punishment need be done only occasionally.

"Don't drive too fast," we say to ourselves, as we see another motorist being ticketed while we hover around the speed limit. "Speed kills!" says the billboard erected by the traffic safety council. "Don't be late for supper," says the mother to her adolescent son, who is thereby reminded of her anger whenever he does come home late. In the latter case, we would expect her admonishment to be most effective if she used exactly the same phrasing at such times, but paired with anger: "I told you this morning, don't be late for supper!"

Anxiety and avoidance behavior. So far we have seen how anxiety can come to be elicited by any cue, whether sensory or cognitive, that was present at the time of a painful event. A great variety of social-learning situations for both children and adults make deliberate use of this principle, using words as conditioned aversive stimuli. We are now ready to mention the second part of the anxiety reaction—what people do when they experience anxiety.

The immediate and universal response to any unpleasant event is to try to escape from it. Withdrawing your hand after touching a hot stove is a universal, reflexive event, as was running from a wild and ferocious animal for our early ancestors. Anxiety is also an aversive experience, and the natural response is to escape from it, and to avoid anxiety-arousing situations in general. In Chapter 2 we noted that any behavior that is successful in reducing noxious stimulation will be learned; that is, it will be more likely to be performed in similar situations in the future. To put it another way, anxiety reduction is reinforcing, just as certainly as pleasant events are reinforcing. The fact that any behavior which either prevents or reduces anxiety will be learned is a critical point in understanding what is typically regarded as *neurotic behavior*—behavior which is or was once anxiety reducing, but which has negative consequences in its own right. The topic of learned responses to anxiety will form the subject matter of Chapter 5.

Why anxiety is so persistent. The fact that anxiety avoidance is highly reinforcing helps to explain why anxiety, and behaviors that are learned in order to avoid anxiety, are so persistent. Since the avoidance of anxiety helps strengthen the behavior which led to its avoidance, the individual continues to avoid similar situations when, in fact, they are no longer dangerous, so there is no opportunity for extinction to occur. In other words, because the learned escape behaviors lead to an avoidance of anxiety, the person is prevented from learning that the feared object or situation is no longer dangerous, or that the danger can be conquered. Thus, people with a strong fear of elevators may never ride on them and therefore never discover that they no longer make them sick as they once did. The successful avoidance reaction leads to the continuation of both the anxiety and the anxiety-avoidance behavior, and not to extinction or unlearning of the fear. What is necessary for the unlearning of anxiety is a series of interactions with the anxiety-arousing situation *without* the experience of pain, but this is precisely what the avoidance reactions prevent. In order to extinguish the fear, someone with a fear of elevators would need to have a series of rides in elevators without getting sick, but the fact that such people have learned to avoid getting sick on elevators by walking up the stairs prevents the extinction process from occurring. Also, the fear of getting sick leads them to reject any suggestion that such a course of action might be helpful. It is for these reasons that anxiety is so persistent—

because avoidance behavior is so effective and because people avoid situations in which anxiety might be aroused.

Trait and State Anxiety

A moment's reflection will reveal that in colloquial usage, the term **anxiety** has two distinct meanings. Consider the statement: "John is an anxious person." There is little doubt that we are referring here to some stable characteristic, or **trait,** which describes John. We are indicating that anxiety is his typical reaction to a variety of situations, and we might contrast him with Margaret, who is typically relaxed and calm, seldom getting "worked up" or experiencing noticeable emotional arousal. Thus, when we refer to the trait aspect of anxiety, we are referring to a habitual aspect of behavior or personality, the base line or typical level of this characteristic.

The other commonsense meaning of anxiety refers to the fact that almost everyone reacts with anxiety to certain events—taking a difficult examination, the appearance of some obvious physical danger, or the threat of imminent punishment. This kind of momentary or temporary increase in anxiety level is called **state anxiety,** and it can be increased or decreased simply by presenting or removing the anxiety-arousing stimuli. State anxiety thus refers to anxiety arousal in some particular situation, while trait anxiety refers to the habitual or typical level of arousal.

The difference between state and trait anxiety is important both in understanding the way in which the concept of anxiety is used and in how anxiety is measured. The *trait* of anxiety is commonly assessed by self-report or written questionnaires, such as the Taylor Manifest Anxiety Scale. This instrument asks the individual to respond either *true* or *false* to statements about the frequency of behaviors that are usually associated with anxiety, for example, "I work under a great deal of tension," and "I tend to have trouble concentrating." The questions refer to rather stable behaviors, so that an individual's responses tend not to fluctuate very much over time and particular circumstances.

On the other hand, consider a group of volunteers who have been suddenly confronted with the possibility of a strong electric shock as part of their participation in an experiment. Regardless of their level of trait anxiety, they should show a sudden increase in *state* anxiety at that time. In this instance, the more appropriate measuring instruments would concentrate on tapping the immediate physiological changes, such as changes in heart rate or in electrical resistance of the skin.

One important question is whether the level of trait anxiety affects state anxiety. In other words, are persons who are chronically anxious—that is, who have high trait anxiety—more reactive to state anxiety? Do such people show relatively more physiological changes when under situational stress? The data are fairly clear (Spielberger, 1966, 1971): persons with high trait anxiety *are* more prone to show state anxiety than are individuals with low trait anxiety. Thus, people who report that they are anxious in general tend to show greater emotional arousal to specific stress than people who report that they are generally calm and nonanxious. The general distinction between trait and state anxiety can be thought of as one between habitual and temporary levels of anxiety.

FREUDIAN VIEWS OF ANXIETY

Let us now contrast the social-learning view of anxiety with that of psychoanalytic theory. Freud was very concerned with the phenomenon of anxiety, which he assigned a special and central role in his theoretical framework. Indeed, there are very few phenomena in the clinical mental health field that have been given as much attention as has anxiety. As might be expected, the views of anxiety held by most psychologists have been shaped primarily by the Freudian view, and it has only been rather recently that alternative approaches to anxiety have been offered. Of course Freud's work has also influenced social-learning theory concepts, including anxiety.

It is rather difficult to present any of Freud's concepts in a straightforward, simple fashion. First, as we have previously noted, they reflect the scientific approach of an earlier era, and their language does not mesh easily with our current ways of thinking and expression. Second, and equally important, Freud himself tended to be inconsistent in the way he wrote about various concepts, and this inconsistency is especially notable in his treatment of anxiety. Some degree of inconsistency is probably inevitable for such a prolific thinker as Freud, who produced twenty-five volumes in his life-time, but inconsistency was also central to Freud's style and method. Freud's theory was a growing and changing one, yet he rarely indicated that he had changed his opinion about an issue—he simply treated the subject differently. It is often possible, in the total context of Freud's writings, to find support for opposing points of view. The only way to understand these often subtle changes is to study psychoanalysis from a historical vantage point, and to observe the changes as they occurred. The interested reader will find Philip S. Holzman's *Psychoanalysis and Psychopathology* (1970) a brief and readable primer of psychoanalytic theory, written from a historical point of view. Or, best of all, read the original Freud.

Anxiety and repression. Freud offered two different views of anxiety at different times. In Freud's earlier view (1917), the cause of anxiety was "dammed-up" or repressed libido. As noted in Chapter 1, Freud regarded two basic instincts as the source of human energy: libido and aggression. The more important of these was the libido, or undifferentiated sexual energy of the organism. As we have already noted, the ways in which the libido can be gratified are considered to change as the individual develops through the various stages of psychosexual development. Direct gratification is usually not possible, or at least not completely possible, because libidinal impulses are generally not socially acceptable in their basic form. For instance, the child is not permitted to gratify fully its oral needs through sucking or biting, nor its anal needs through either the free expulsion or free retention of its feces. Some of the energy that would have been reduced through such gratification is discharged indirectly, and some is bottled or dammed up. Since a conscious awareness of many of these impulses would be unacceptable to the individual, thoughts about the impulses are also barred from consciousness. Freud labeled this process of barring impulses from consciousness **repression.**

The damming up of libidinal impulses was seen as creating a tension or pressure, in much the same way that damming up a stream creates pressure on the dam as the hydraulic force of the fluid presses from behind it. Freud saw these blocked forces as creating an internal pressure that was experienced by the person, and he originally regarded this pressure and experience as constituting anxiety.

Anxiety as a danger signal. Freud's later theory of anxiety is more detailed and complex than the earlier formulation that we have just described, and it is the later view that has been most widely accepted by psychoanalytic scholars and practitioners. The later theory differs quite markedly from the original view, and anxiety is given a much more important role in accounting for psychological distress. Indeed, in Freud's most complete formulation of his ideas about anxiety, *Inhibitions, Symptoms, and Anxiety* (1926), he makes the point that "anxiety would be the fundamental phe-

nomenon and the central problem of neurosis." This view of the central role of anxiety has been one of the most frequently used of all Freud's contributions to the study of psychological disorders.

In order to understand Freud's later theory of anxiety, we must introduce a number of additional concepts, including Freud's now famous three-part division of personality processes. First, there is the **id,** the unlearned source of libidinal energy, the storehouse or reservoir of primitive human biological impulses. The id, operating by the pleasure principle, demands immediate gratification for these impulses, and thus requires continuing control throughout life. Second, there is the **ego,** which develops over time, principally through the process which we today would call socialization. The ego, operating by the reality principle, represents the many realistic factors that need to be considered if impulses are to be justified in a socially appropriate manner. The ego represents that "portion of the personality" that monitors the interaction between people and the world in which they live. Without ego controls, the id would insist on immediate and constant gratification of its biological impulses, a state of affairs which would obviously be disastrous in any continuing interpersonal situation. Third, there is the **superego,** which represents the rigid moral taboos and constraints that the individual develops through the introjection of cultural values. While the ego operates on a pragmatic basis, continually assessing the realistic costs of gratifying the various needs, the superego attempts to control the gratification of impulses on the basis of rigid and absolute moral rules, through the mechanism of guilt. The child who does not steal an attractive toy through fear of being caught and punished would be operating according to ego controls, while the child who avoids stealing because it is "wrong" would be responding to superego controls.

Each of these elements is said to be in conflict with each of the other elements. For example, there is strong conflict between the id, ever demanding impulse gratification, and the superego, which prohibits direct gratification and which attaches guilt even to thoughts about the impulses. In this struggle the ego, which serves a kind of executive function, continually attempts to monitor these conflicts. Both the ego and the superego can be regarded as learned components of the personality structure, while the id is unlearned. The adult who has progressed adequately through the several stages of psychosexual development has developed a reasonable balance among these three conflicting forces, and so can gratify a reasonable number of impulse needs without unnecessary delays and without experiencing incapacitating guilt for that gratification. It should be remembered that all three of these conflicting forces operate on the unconscious level; that is, the person has no awareness of the underlying personality structure, and is not aware that the three elements are in continual conflict.

It is when the unacceptable libidinal impulses of the id threaten to overwhelm the rational constraints of the ego that neurotic anxiety is aroused. This anxiety serves as a danger signal that the unconscious and unacceptable id impulses are threatening to overwhelm the repressing forces that serve to keep these impulses and the entire psychic structure away from the person's awareness. The danger signals indicate that

some additional defenses are necessary in order to strengthen the repressions and thus continue to protect the individual from consciously having to deal with unacceptable matters. Once the ego has increased the strength of the repression, the anxiety diminishes. In Freud's later theory of anxiety, then, repression is regarded as the *result* rather than the cause of anxiety, and indeed, repression serves an anxiety-*reducing* function. To summarize, when unconscious, unacceptable impulses threaten to break into consciousness, the person experiences anxiety. This anxiety serves as a danger signal to which the person responds by bringing into operation a **defense mechanism,** a minor distortion of reality which helps control the threatening impulse and force it back into unconsciousness. Once the impulse is repressed, barred from awareness, the anxiety disappears.

Freud's later concept of anxiety has been an important and influential one in mental health fields. Not only did it focus on anxiety as the central problem underlying neurotic behavior, but it also introduced the notion of defense mechanisms, or responses to anxiety, a topic to which we will return in Chapters 5 and 6. One additional point about Freud's later theory should be made now, however. We are referring to Freud's view that anxiety was primarily a signal or a symptom of some underlying serious problem, rather than a separate problem by itself. This aspect of Freud's approach to anxiety reflects his own medical training, and it remains today a prevalent view in psychiatric circles, once again reflecting the medical training and medical orientation of psychiatrists. In this view, neurotic anxiety is a signal of an underlying psychic problem, much like fever or pain is a signal of some underlying medical problem. The physician's task is to uncover the "underlying" cause of the fever or pain—the "true" problem—and the psychiatrist's task is seen analogously as that of uncovering the underlying cause of the anxiety. In this view anxiety is never the basic problem, and is never directly learned in the manner outlined in the earlier part of this chapter. Rather, the causes of the anxiety are always hidden, even to the individual who experiences the anxiety, and it is only the trained psychoanalyst who can uncover the unconscious sources of this "psychic pain."

It should be clear to the reader that this view of anxiety as only a signal or symptom of some underlying problem is not consistent with the social-learning viewpoint. Although we agree that it is possible for anxiety to be displaced, as discussed earlier in regard to the case of the woman with the knife phobia, it is also common for anxiety to be learned directly, and in these cases the anxiety is the actual problem, and not simply a signal or a symptom of some other underlying condition.

HUMANISTIC VIEWS OF ANXIETY

Of the several humanistic views of adjustment, the one that has dealt most directly with the problem of anxiety is existentialism. As we saw in Chapter 1, existentialism is a philosophical position concerned with human nature, people's understanding of themselves, and the nature of human existence. The existentialist treatment of anxiety is rather different from that of either of the two positions we have just discussed. The concept of anxiety, couched in philosophical terms, is basic to the existentialists' views

of human nature. It is virtually impossible to present any simple definition of existential anxiety, and especially any operational definition, since the concept of operational definition has no place in existentialism. Existentialists emphasize that it is necessary to *experience* anxiety personally to understand it, so that real understanding can never be communicated by the printed word.

One central theme of the existential philosophy is people's freedom to choose their own destiny. This theme is exemplified in the writings of two of the European philosophers who did much to shape this movement, Soren Kierkegaard (1944) and Martin Heidegger (1963). For Kierkegaard in particular, freedom involves the growing awareness that freedom is indeed possible, and brings with it an awareness also of the responsibility that is inherent in the possession of freedom. In Kierkegaard's view, human freedom is freedom to conceptualize the choices open in life, to choose among them and to actualize or realize fully what is chosen. **Anxiety,** in this view, comes from the awareness of the gap between what is possible and what has been achieved. Anxiety arises with the awareness of freedom—when humans fully understand that they are free agents and that they must bear full responsibility for the choices they make, although they have no complete understanding of how the choices will work out.

Existentialists stress that individuals must develop insight into their own self-relatedness, their own sense of freedom and choice, and their relationships with the world around them. Both the self-awareness and the understanding of their relationships with the world become ever more difficult to obtain because of the human rootlessness that is a part of modern technological society. As the American psychotherapist Rollo May, another influential person in the existential movement, has noted: "The will is left to act in a vast, lonely meaningless vacuum where, like a moth trapped by a window at night, the only sound breaking the silence is the echo of its own mute and helpless struggle" (1969, p. 90).

As viewed by May (1950) and also by J. F. T. Bugental (1978), another existentially oriented American psychologist, anxiety is an inevitable aspect of human life experience. According to Bugental, there are a number of sources of basic, or universal, or existential, anxiety which we must all confront and come to terms with at various points in our lives. The most important kind of existential anxiety, for example, involves our awareness and recognition of our ultimate fate, death. All of us must come to grips with our knowledge of our own finiteness. Such existential anxieties are not only common, but they are inescapable. According to existential theorists, people who try to avoid confronting these basic existential issues develop neurotic anxiety and conflicts. Individuals who chronically avoid dealing with their own mortality, for example, develop neurotic anxiety over their experienced sense of powerlessness, and respond to it with neurotic resignation and apathy. The psychologically adaptive response to anxiety over life and death is to recognize and accept it as a natural part of human existence, and to face realistically the fact that life is unpredictable and always, in some measure, both unknown and unknowable.

The position that existential anxiety is natural and should be regarded as a sign of strength rather than maladjustment is also taken by the American personality psychologist Salvadore Maddi (1967): "When you are in a rather continual process of change you cannot predict what the existential outcome will be. . . . Existential anxiety is a necessary concomitant of the ideal identity" (p. 321).

The views of psychoanalyst Karen Horney on anxiety, although not existential, are also of a philosophical nature. In direct contrast to the existential view, however, Horney regards anxiety as an undesirable state of affairs that interferes with good psychological adjustment. According to Horney, if a child does not develop a secure sense of "belonging," if it does not experience adequate warmth and security, it develops what Horney (1950) calls *basic anxiety*, a feeling of profound insecurity, isolation, and vague apprehensiveness, ". . . of being isolated and helpless in a world conceived as potentially hostile" (p. 18). The pressure of a child's basic anxiety prevents it from experiencing the natural spontaneity of its feelings, and forces it to become preoccupied with ways of dealing with the anxiety. Horney's views are appealing to many people, but are too vague and nonoperational to serve as the basis of a scientific approach to the understanding of anxiety and its role in human maladjustment.

SUMMARY

1. Anxiety is a universal human phenomenon, and we have previously discussed its critical role in the socialization process. Anxiety is not synonymous with psychological maladjustment, although the two have always been seen as closely related. Related terms include: *fear,* synonymous with anxiety; *phobias,* intense, irrational anxieties about specific objects or events; *worry,* the anxiety experienced while thinking about a difficult personal situation, where no solution is apparent; *tension,* referring to muscle tonus, not to anxiety; *stress,* interchangeable with anxiety; and *shame* and *guilt,* which refer to anxiety over moral transgressions.

2. A comprehensive view of anxiety recognizes three primary characteristics: a feeling of apprehension in the absence of real danger; physiological changes; and interference with effective problem solving. Much confusion has been generated by researchers who concentrate on the study of just one of these aspects and claim that theirs is the "real" study of anxiety.

3. The physiological changes related to anxiety include respiratory, cardiovascular, and gastrointestinal effects; perspiration; muscular tension; sleeplessness; and frequent urination; with different effects being predominant in different individuals. These changes result from increases in the secretion of the hormones adrenaline and noradrenaline, and it has been theorized that their traditional function has been to prepare the body for "fight or flight" as a response to impending physical danger. However, in modern society they often interfere with adaptive functioning since physical actions as a response to threat are often inappropriate.

4. Some psychologists have proposed a general theory of activation or emotional arousal, in which a certain degree of general physiological activation is necessary for the occurrence of any effective behavior. It is believed that there is just one basic emotional state, whether a person's subjective experience is anxiety, anger, or euphoria. The research evidence on this hypothesis is conflicting, although it is known that the physiological differences between the various states are not as great as the subjective differences. Another fascinating but unanswered question concerns the degree to which autonomic reactivity is a hereditary characteristic.

5. Anxiety can be a learned response to just about any stimulus, since all that is necessary is for the stimulus to have been present at the time pain or strong anxiety was experienced. In some cases a single pairing of the two events is sufficient. The mechanism by which *phobias* are learned presents a fascinating problem, because the intensity of the phobic anxiety reaction often appears to be greater than that accompanying the original learning experience, which sometimes cannot be identified at all. It is possible that there is a simple forgetting (repression) of the original experience; another possible explanation involves the modeling of adult fears on parents, television programs, or other stimuli. Phobias could also involve the displacement of anxiety, in which the phobic stimulus is not the actual source of the anxiety, but one which represents a defensive reaction in the Freudian sense. Thus, the individual would never understand the "real" significance of the phobia, which would always be simply "symbolic" of the original feared situation or object. It is also possible that phobias could involve the generalization of anxiety from the original stimulus to similar stimuli. Also involved could be higher-order conditioning, in which a new stimulus can acquire fear-arousing properties through association with another conditioned fear stimulus, without ever being associated directly with a pain-arousing situation.

6. Thoughts can function as conditioned stimuli for anxiety, and since thoughts are almost always present during a painful experience, they are widely used by parents in teaching children to inhibit undesirable acts. Our adult behavior is constantly being controlled by thoughts and words to which anxiety has been conditioned. The immediate and universal response to anxiety is to try to escape from it, and everyone has a wide variety of learned behaviors that are reinforced by anxiety reduction. Since anxiety reduction is highly reinforcing, these behaviors are thoroughly learned, and the more successful they are in avoiding the feared stimulus, the less opportunity the individual has to confront it and learn that it need not now be feared. Thus, effective avoidance behavior tends to be self-perpetuating, and anxiety in such instances is extremely persistent.

7. The term anxiety is used colloquially in two distinct ways: to refer to a *trait*, or stable characteristic of a person, and to refer to a *state*, or temporary condition brought about by some environmental stimulus such as an impending exam.

8. Psychoanalytic theory gives the concept of anxiety a central role in its explanations of psychological disturbance. Freud originally regarded anxiety as the feeling that

resulted from the forces of repression. In his later and more widely recognized theory, anxiety was seen as a danger signal indicating that unacceptable libidinal impulses are threatening to overwhelm the ego. The individual responds by bringing into operation an ego defense mechanism, by which the threatening impulse is barred from consciousness, and the anxiety disappears. Thus, in the Freudian view, anxiety is not the problem, but is a signal of a more basic problem, in much the same way as pain is usually a signal of a basic medical or physical problem.

9. Humanistic thinkers define anxiety in a philosophical manner that cannot be adequately translated into the language of science. In this view, anxiety is regarded as an inevitable part of existence, and failure to recognize and confront it leads to various psychological disorders, such as apathy and resignation.

KEY TERMS

fear	"free-floating" anxiety
anxiety	conditioned aversive stimuli
phobias	trait
worry	state anxiety
tension	repression
stress	id
shame	ego
guilt	superego
emotional arousal	defense mechanism
displacement of anxiety	anxiety

FIVE

The Process
of Adjustment

The process of adjustment refers to the continuous arousal and satisfaction of physiological and psychological needs.

- The effectiveness of a person's adjustment depends on a variety of factors.
- Adjustment involves both the individual and the environment.
- Each conflict situation is different, and must be handled differently.
- There can be no meaningful criteria for "perfect" adjustment.

Frustration refers to the blocking of goal-directed behavior.

- A common response to frustration is to make the same response with increased vigor.
- There is disagreement as to whether this increased vigor represents a "natural" drive of aggression.
- Another common response to frustration is scapegoating.

A conflict situation exists when there are incompatible response tendencies.

- Approach-approach conflicts are easily resolved.
- Approach-avoidance and avoidance-avoidance conflicts usually result in indecision.

LET US PAUSE BRIEFLY TO PUT INTO PERSPECTIVE WHAT WE HAVE LEARNED SO far in our study of human psychological adjustment, and to give a preview of what is to come. In the first part of Chapter 1 we introduced the concept of adjustment, and presented three approaches to the study of this area of psychology: the moral, the humanistic, and the social-learning approach. We indicated that this text would emphasize the social-learning approach, using it as a central viewpoint from which to discuss the other approaches.

The remainder of Chapter 1 and Chapters 2 through 4 presented the scientific foundations that are necessary for an adequate understanding of adjustment. Included were discussions of biological factors in personality and development, basic learning theory, the process of socialization, and the nature of anxiety.

The bulk of the basic scientific material has now been presented, and it is time for us to ask once again "What is adjustment?" and to spend time regrouping our thoughts, as we prepare to *apply* the scientific foundations in answering this question throughout the remainder of the book. We expect that the reader has gained considerably in sophistication through having read Chapters 1 through 4, so that our inquiry into the nature of psychological adjustment can now take on a broader and deeper meaning. Chapter 5 is intended to orient the reader to the full nature and implications of the question "What is adjustment?" while Chapters 6 through 12 present a detailed and systematic answer to this question.

WHAT IS ADJUSTMENT?

All of our **behavior**—conscious or unconscious, voluntary or automatic, planned or unplanned, wise or foolish—represents our attempts to meet our needs of the moment, or at least to meet these needs as we understand them. The simplest of our needs are physiological in nature, based upon primary, biological demands such as those for food, water, and oxygen. Through the process of socialization, however, we develop a variety of secondary psychological requirements—for affection, affiliation, status, recognition, and so on—as discussed in Chapter 3. Throughout life, our physiological and psychological needs are continually being aroused, and we engage in behavior that reduces or satisfies our needs. This constant cycle of need arousal and satisfaction, in a broad sense, is the process of adjustment.

Our existence would indeed be simple if all our needs could be satisfied directly and promptly. Obviously, however, this is not the case; there are a multitude of factors, both internal and external, that prevent us from routinely satisfying all our needs. Perhaps we wish to eat, but there is no food available; or the food that is available might not be appetizing to us; or we might be on a diet. We all desire approval and recognition, but others often criticize what we have done. We desire adequate sexual satisfaction, but we have learned that many of the desired behaviors are culturally forbidden, or that our attempts at satisfaction make us feel guilty or anxious. Sometimes our needs are themselves contradictory, and thus are impossible to fulfill directly, as when we simultaneously desire privacy and solitude on the other hand and love and support on the other. Further, many of our needs are themselves anxiety arousing, as noted in Chapter 4, and this interferes both with our attempts to understand the needs and with attempts to satisfy them. In this chapter we analyze and discuss the issues and problems that are involved in our efforts to satisfy our needs.

In the study of psychological adjustment, we concentrate our attention on the learned or social needs as distinct from physiological needs. As we have said previously, one of the important characteristics of our technological society is that it is possible for the majority of us to have our physiological needs met rather routinely. For most middle class people, hunger, thirst, oxygen deprivation, and other intense physiological deprivational states are relatively rare events, and when they do occur, they usually result from accidental circumstances. Satisfying our secondary or psychological needs, however, is a far more difficult proposition. While Western civilization may have been successful in reducing the problems involved in the satisfaction of physical needs, it has created considerable difficulties in the satisfaction of psychological needs. As our culture has become more complex, as the traditional patterns of family living have changed, as a variety of moral and ethical imperatives have been questioned or abandoned, as life expectancy has been lengthened, so have the problems of meeting our psychological needs increased.

Physiological and psychological needs are different in another important respect. If we do not satisfy our demands for oxygen, food, or water, no compromise is possible and the inevitable outcome is death. But if our psychological needs are not met, life goes on nevertheless. One can exist without recognition, status, or affiliation—without any of one's innumerable psychological needs being met. Although failures of the adjustment process certainly lead to much unhappiness, they do not usually lead to death.

Some psychologists believe that there is an innate psychological need for love that simply must be met. These psychologists point to the work of researchers such as Bowlby (1969) and Harlow and Harlow (1966), which we have discussed in Chapter 3, and Spitz (1945), discussed in Chapter 2, who found that some of the infants who were consistently denied the tactile stimulation usually associated with maternal love actually died. It is not clear whether the important variable in this process is simple physical stimulation or whether a broader concept such as mother love is involved. As far as adults are concerned, however, it is clear that one can indeed live with unrequited love, despite the poets' claim to the contrary.

Factors Determining Adjustment

We have defined adjustment as the process through which we deal with the needs of everyday living; **psychological adjustment,** therefore, is the process by which we attempt to satisfy our psychological, learned, or social needs. Yet, as we have already stated, these needs are often difficult to meet in today's society, and for the majority of us, many psychological needs are not routinely satisfied. Since most of us have unmet psychological needs, are we to conclude that we are therefore poorly adjusted psychologically? Most psychologists would not accept this conclusion, because it offers little for our understanding of the process of adjustment, and it is an unnecessarily pessimistic view of humans and their experiences.

It is more appropriate to recognize that the quality of an individual's adjustment is determined not only by the degree to which psychological needs are satisfied, but also by a number of other factors. Included among those factors are: (a) the capacity to tolerate delay in having needs satisfied; (b) the degree to which a person continues striving to satisfy needs when they are not immediately satisfied; (c) the ability to substitute a new or different set of satisfactions for those originally sought; and (d) the extent to which the needs are regarded as legitimate by society. We will examine each of these considerations in turn, recognizing that there are no firm or absolute guidelines for evaluating the quality of an individual's adjustment, and that all of these factors must be considered in reaching a final judgment about how effective or ineffective the adjustment of any person may be.

Toleration of delay. Effectively adjusted individuals are able to tolerate some delay in the satisfaction of their needs. The infant, with its primitive adjustment skills, demands instant gratification of its needs. The adult, however, understands and accepts the idea that satisfactory need gratification can only occur over a period of time. Psychoanalytic writers have used the term *pleasure principle* to characterize the infant's behavior, while the adult, with a capacity for delaying the gratification of needs, is said to operate by the *reality principle*. As adults, we are usually willing to wait to eat until it is "time," and we routinely wait until the end of the week or the month to receive our paychecks. Indeed, a moment's thought will reveal that most adult behavior is programmed to function under quite lengthy delays of reward. University study, with grades at the end of the semester or quarter, and with a degree at the completion of several years of study, is another good example of a long-delayed reward. Mature adults are expected to accept these delays in the gratification of their needs, and those persons who cannot tolerate delay of reward fit rather poorly into modern society. It is interesting to note that certain religions offer the salvation of heaven as a final reward, thereby stretching human capacity for delay in need gratification to its ultimate limit. It is important to understand that human capacity for delayed gratification, the ability to function according to the reality principle, develops as part of the socialization process. We shall examine later the way in which one learns to accept delayed gratification.

Persistence. Not only must humans learn to delay gratification of their needs, but they must also learn to continue striving to have their needs gratified. Obviously, if we were to abandon our efforts and give up our goals every time we encountered

an obstacle to our striving for need gratification, we would accomplish little. Most of the heroic figures in Western history are people who have persevered in spite of many substantial obstacles. Inventors who continue to work despite innumerable failures, writers who submit manuscripts despite many rejections, artists who continue to paint although their work is condemned, and politicians who run for office though repeatedly defeated are all prevalent in our society.

On the other hand, when *should* an obstacle be taken as sufficient reason to abandon a course of action? How much discouragement is required before an inventor, a writer, an artist, or a politician should seriously consider that the goal is not attainable? Obviously there is no simple answer to this question. It is extremely difficult to make a judgment about the adequacy of the adjustment of individuals who persist in their efforts even though they receive constant rebuffs. It is simple to say that a person should continue the initially unsuccessful efforts until it is apparent that these efforts are doomed to failure; the point at which failure becomes apparent, however, is not the same for everyone, and is not always easy to determine. Judging the adequacy of psychological adjustment in these circumstances is a highly complex task, and there is often little agreement even among experts.

Substitute satisfactions. Another characteristic of effective adjustment is the person's capacity to change or shift the sources of satisfaction. Those who recognize that they will not receive the acclaim and status they desire through athletic competition can attempt to secure recognition by scholarship, by artistic endeavors, or by assuming group leadership roles. Human psychological needs are quite complex and difficult to catalogue, and we are frequently uncertain what needs are being gratified by different behaviors. But it is clear that there are many avenues open to us for need gratification in our complex society and that well-adjusted people are flexible in finding ways to meet their needs.

Legitimacy of needs. Lastly, it should be emphasized that all need gratification, and particularly the gratification of our psychological needs, occurs within a social context. The people with whom we live and work are closely involved with our needs and the ways in which we gratify them, and they continually evaluate the legitimacy of our needs and behaviors. Obviously, the standards by which needs and avenues of gratification are evaluated tend to change over time, and are different for different subgroups within a society, but it is a fact of life that other people continually pass judgment on them. Some needs, such as achievement and nurturance (caring), are positively regarded; others, such as narcissism (excessive self-admiration) and sadism (getting pleasure by hurting others) are viewed negatively. Those needs that are regarded positively are not only easier to gratify but their gratification frequently brings further satisfactions, so that gratifying one's needs for achievement may also bring recognition, status, power, and wealth. On the other hand, those needs that are negatively valued are more difficult to gratify and often have long-term negative consequences. Thus, gratification for a sadistic need is not only difficult to obtain, but may involve serious social and legal consequences.

Some behaviors have complex consequences. It is clearly possible to gratify our needs by engaging in behavior that meets the needs in question but also has some long-term negative effects. Individuals who "act up" at a party to satisfy their needs for attention may not be invited again, and the person who is sexually promiscuous in order to satisfy needs for affection may not be regarded as a suitable marriage partner. Thus, an important consideration in judging the effectiveness of an individual's adjustment involves not only the degree of immediate success but also the longer-term consequences of the methods of need gratification. Situations in which a person suffers negative effects because of failure to consider these longer-term consequences have been termed social traps (Platt, 1973), and are further elaborated in Chapter 12.

Obviously, the way in which one's needs are evaluated socially is an important factor in determining the consequences of need gratification. Thus, it is difficult to find ways in which some needs, like abasement, sadism, or masochism, can be satisfied without negative consequences. Usually, however, it is not the nature of the needs that raises a problem for the individual but rather the mode of gratifying them. Recognition or status can be achieved either in ways that society regards favorably, such as election or appointment to leadership roles, or in ways that are negatively valued, such as the usurpation of power and the disregard of legitimately constituted authority. To cite a more clinical example, walking down the main street of one's town completely unclad will certainly bring attention, but there will also be some direct negative consequences.

One of the major assumptions of social-learning theory is that any behavior that is persistent is bringing reinforcement to the individual in some way; that is, in terms of our present discussion, the behavior is gratifying certain needs. Why, then, does an individual engage in behaviors that seem self-punishing or even self-destructive? Such behaviors, often called **persistent unadaptive reactions,** are responses that meet the individual's immediate needs to some extent, and are reinforcing in terms of a particular learning history, but which also have longer-term negative consequences. For example, a child may throw severe temper tantrums which usually lead to spankings, but will continue in this behavior if its need for attention is greater than its fear of spanking. Similarly, a student with a strong need for order and symmetry may continue to need to arrange the desk perfectionistically throughout all his or her examinations even though valuable time is wasted.

Adjustment as a Process

Psychological adjustment can be viewed as a process—a dynamic, complex, continuing process—through which individuals respond to their everchanging needs and desires with a variety of behaviors. While much of an individual's total behavior represents efforts to adjust, all of these efforts are not in fact adjustive; as we have seen, some behaviors are adjustive in the short run, but have negative consequences in the long run.

The process of adjustment can be described in terms of two factors: (1) the *individual* and his or her characteristics, including needs and desires as well as the competencies and skills that enable persons to fill their needs; and (2) the *situation* in which individuals find themselves and the demands placed upon them by that situation. As previously noted in our analysis of the socialization process, each of us is born with a set of innate biological needs and a repertoire of behaviors by which these needs can be satisfied. The hungry infant can cry to signal its hunger, and can consume and digest the food which is then offered. As socialization progresses, a variety of other needs, psychological and social, are learned, together with the responses by which these newly learned needs can be gratified. Thus, the child learns to need or desire the approval of its parents and its peers, and also comes to learn the behaviors that will lead to approval: acquiring self-care skills, developing motor skills, and becoming what is regarded as a useful member of society. Both the learning of new needs and the learning of the skills and competencies to gratify those needs are dependent on the previous experiences of the individual, so the process of adjustment can be seen as a continuous one, best understood in a developmental context as the individual progresses through life.

Whenever people encounter a new situation, they bring to it their own unique developmental history of experienced needs and need gratifications, plus the competencies and skills which they may be able to exercise in this new situation. They respond to the new situation not as passive observers but as active participants, deciding whether or not to get involved in it, deciding what elements they will respond to, wondering what might be expected of them both by themselves and by others, and wondering which of their needs, if any, might be relevant in the situation and how these needs might be gratified. Students entering college for the first time, for example, come with the array of psychological needs that are a result of their experiential histories. They are aware of these needs, at least to some extent, and know how they have been satisfied in the past and how they might be satisfied in this new situation. On the basis of their appraisal of themselves and of the situation, they evaluate this new experience in terms of its opportunities and challenges. The high school athlete who enrolls at a large state university on a football scholarship has a different set of needs and expectations from the high school valedictorian who enrolls in a small, elite liberal arts college. Not only are these two people quite different in their needs and expectations, but the situation of entering college, as they perceive it, is different for each. The demands upon them are different, and their different skills and competencies will lead to quite different ways of having their needs met. The same would be true, of course, even if they had enrolled in the same university.

Most people tend to have a reasonable idea of the nature of their own needs and of the best ways of meeting them. They tend to respond to those elements of a new situation that appear most likely to be rewarding, most likely to provide them with need satisfaction. There will usually be a certain amount of trial-and-error, or risk-taking behavior, where the person tries out new responses in order to see whether they will result in gratification, but it is most unlikely that this behavior will continue if no gratification is forthcoming.

Most of us develop a fair degree of competence in arranging to have our psychological needs gratified. When we enter new situations, we tend to search for those elements which permit us to exercise our own particular skills in an effort to maintain our patterns of need gratification. Since many of these skills, particularly interpersonal skills, are quite transferable and can provide rewards in a variety of situations, we are seldom disappointed. And, of course, we also try as far as possible to select our new situations on the basis of the opportunities that they provide for us to meet our needs.

There are times, however, when we are faced with situations in which the demands upon us are high and we lack the competence to deal effectively with them. These situations often involve new and unusual demands—accidents, a death in the family, failure of a business, natural disasters, war—for which the

It appears that the ability to perform high-stress jobs routinely and effectively is acquired under normal childhood circumstances, rather than by continued exposure to stressful situations.

necessary coping skills have simply not been developed in previous circumstances. Such situations, where there are unusual stresses upon the individual and where resources to meet the situational demands are limited, can be termed **psychological crises.** As Lazarus (1966) has pointed out, "Crisis seems to imply a limited period in which an individual or group is exposed to . . . demands which are at or near the limits of their resources to cope. . . . in crisis, the focus is on a period of the person's or group's life in which major threats and frustrations that tax adaptation are prominent" (pp. 407-408). It is quite possible for all of us to be confronted by crises in which our resources for continuing to meet our own needs and also the demands of the situation might not be adequate. Since crises are rare events, it is difficult to predict how any given individual will respond to them.

Psychologists still know very little about the best ways of preparing people to deal with high stress situations, and of teaching complex skills and competencies in such a way that they will not be disrupted by situational stresses. We do know, however, that people who are able to perform high stress jobs routinely, such as astronauts, test pilots, air traffic controllers, and submariners, generally come from stable middle class families and have had ordinary, uneventful childhoods. It appears that the adjustive skills that are necessary to withstand high stress and to perform adequately under such conditions are acquired under fairly normal and traditional childhood circumstances, and not by continual exposure to stress or unusual experiences.

At any moment in time, an individual with needs and customary modes of gratifying them will find that the environment is also making demands. The effectiveness with which people continue to meet their own needs and also respond to the demands of the situation provides one important index of the effectiveness of their psychological adjustment. When the demands of the situation are congruent with the person's needs, there is very little at issue. The scholar who is asked to prepare a new manuscript, the musician facing a new audience, and the tennis player about to begin a match will all usually perform competently in simultaneously satisfying their own needs and meeting the demands of the situation. However, when there is a conflict between the person's needs and the demands of the situation, the effectiveness of his or her adjustment is put to the test. The degree to which individuals should put their own needs first, on the one hand, or meet the demands of the situation, on the other, cannot be determined by any general rules. The folktale that Nero fiddled while Rome burned implies that Nero was inappropriately placing his own needs above the demands of the situation. On the other hand, the adage that "the show must go on" implies that one must respond to situational demands, and this may not always be appropriate either.

Effective psychological adjustment, or coping, certainly does not mean blind conformity to the demands of the situation without consideration of the legitimacy of those demands of one's personal resources to meet them: there is no merit in trying to stop a rolling locomotive with one's bare hands. Effective adjustment involves an awareness of the situation and its implicit and explicit demands, a weighing of those demands based upon an understanding of one's own needs and resources, and a decision as to which (if any) of the demands one is willing to accept. Thus, coping involves maintaining a continual balance between personal needs and those of the situation.

An important theoretical question is whether an actual act of decision is in fact ever involved in such situations. The strict deterministic view would hold that people's responses to any new situation are automatic outcomes of their social-learning history. Although we might believe that we are making active and free decisions, the strict determinist would insist that the choices are already determined by the circumstances of our lives.

The position taken in this book is not a rigidly deterministic one. Human behavior is assumed to be at least in part a function of active decision making, of higher mental processes, on the part of the behaving person. There can be no question that higher mental processes, or thinking, or *cognitive mediational responses*, do influence human behavior (see, for example, Dollard and Miller, 1950; Meichenbaum, 1977). Obviously, since adjustment is a continuous process, our needs at any moment of time, our level of need gratification, resources to meet new situations, and perceptions of new situations are all determined by what has gone before. But we also think about these factors, and talk about them with others; and our thoughts, or mediational responses, also have an important influence on our subsequent behavior. In analyzing or thinking through any new situation we might well reassess our needs and ways of meeting them, or we may decide that the new situation, which originally seemed attractive, has dangers of which we were initially unaware. Careful thought might lead us to the conclusion that our resources are adequate to meet the challenge of the new situation, or we may decide that they are not adequate.

It can be argued, of course, that our thoughts are themselves predetermined, that the ways in which we customarily think about and understand situations are also a product of our experience. If, for example, our experience has taught us that we ordinarily fail at new undertakings, so that we tend to think about new situations with an expectation of failure, then this will surely be an important factor in determining how we respond to new situations. If, on the other hand, we tend to think of ourselves as risk-takers, and particularly as successful risk-takers, then we will come to different decisions about ways of facing new demands. Thinking about a problem can also result in "insight," and in novel responses, that is, behaviors that have never before been performed by the person but which are specifically suited for meeting the demands at hand. Obviously the question of thinking and how it affects behavior is a complex one, and cannot be developed in detail here. We shall return later to another aspect of the role of thinking in the adjustment process when we discuss the inhibiting role of anxiety on thinking and personal problem solving.

EVALUATING HUMAN ADJUSTMENT

So far in this chapter, we have emphasized that adjustment is a continuous process, in which one's social-learning experiences create psychological needs and also enable the acquisition of the competencies and skills through which they can be satisfied. How can the effectiveness of this process be evaluated? How is it possible to assess the adequacy of a person's psychological adjustment?

Obviously, it would be extremely difficult and impractical to evaluate the adequacy of a person's entire adjustment process, since this would mean trying to evaluate the quality of an entire lifetime. We would be asking to what extent the person had met the myriad challenges and opportunities encountered, how adequately the person's own needs had been gratified, and, in general, how "satisfactory" he or she was as a person. The labor that would be involved in performing such a task routinely staggers the imagination; imagining the amount of work involved in preparing a complete biography of one person will give some idea of the effort that would be necessary.

There are also some complex value considerations involved. Is a person whose needs are simple and easily gratified—who either has never been in challenging or demanding situations or who has made no effort to meet such challenges—more effectively adjusted than the person with more complex needs that are less easily gratified, the person who has seized upon the many opportunities and responded to the many challenges of life, but often unsuccessfully? For example, is a rural worker, who leads a simple, unchallenging existence where it is relatively easy to gratify personal needs and where there are few situational demands, more effectively adjusted than a harried young professional, who consistently but rather unsuccessfully attempts to create a better urban society? There is no easy answer to this question, although perhaps it is reasonable to assume that the former person would be regarded objectively as better adjusted, while the latter may feel more personally satisfied and fulfilled.

If it is impractical to attempt an evaluation of a person's entire adjustment process, what alternatives are there? Usually an assessment is made of a person's adjustment *at a given point of time*, and with a specific purpose in mind. This simplification of the problem has several advantages. First, we can assess the effectiveness of a person's adjustment with regard to a specific situation. We observe, as objectively as possible, the situation and its demands and how the person is responding to that situation in terms of personal needs and competencies. To evaluate a lifelong process of adjustment would involve a lengthy series of such analyses for countless different situations, plus a lengthy integration of these complex data. Obviously, it makes much more sense simply to consider a particular situation at a particular time.

There is a further general point to be noted in evaluating psychological adjustment. We are referring to the natural tendency for psychologists to allow their own personal values to intrude into an evaluation. Although most psychologists would insist that they are objective in their work, there is strong evidence to suggest that this is not the case. In a now classic study, Broverman and her colleagues (1970) found that mental health professionals described psychologically well-adjusted women in terms rather different from those used to describe psychologically well-adjusted men. The qualities of the well-adjusted women differed from those of the men in being more submissive, dependent, open to influence, and easily hurt, and less adventurous, aggressive, and competitive. Clearly these data include the intrusion of personal values and biases, and place in serious question the very possibility of total objectivity.

Psychologists frequently are asked to evaluate the potential of an individual to respond effectively to a new situation, one which the individual has not yet encountered. For example, psychologists have played an important role in selecting people to serve as Peace Corps volunteers, astronauts, police, missionaries, and business executives, all of which involve situations to which the applicants have not yet been exposed. Typically, the psychologist makes a careful evaluation of the situation and the demands that are likely to be placed upon the person, although this is often difficult because reliable data are not always available. For instance, who knows what demands will be made in a year-long interplanetary space flight? Or in a war-time spying assignment? The psychologist must nevertheless formulate a judgment regarding the demands of the situation, and then attempt to assess the competencies of the individual to meet them, including the potential hazards, adversities, frustrations, and failures that may arise. In making these evaluations the psychologist recognizes that the individual's adjustive abilities are often best under-stood in terms of previous life experiences, and tends to look for clear evidence of demonstrated competence in dealing with similar situations in the past. Another valuable and important source of information comes from standardized assessment procedures, or psychological tests of all kinds. We will return in Chapter 10 to a further examination of the way in which psychologists go about their professional task of evaluating an individual's personal characteristics and potentialities.

It is often helpful to think of quality of psychological adjustment in terms of a broad continuum, with effective and ineffective adjustment at the two extremes. As we have implied in our previous discussion, even the most effectively adjusted person has unfilled needs, limitations in competency and skill, and anxieties. There is no such thing as an ideally adjusted person. Indeed, there is little possibility of agreement as to what such a person would be like. Certainly any absolute definition of ideal adjustment would be highly dependent upon cultural and social class values, and would tend to be limited in its usefulness. It is possible and useful, however, to talk about a range of psychological adjustment as a broad dimension, with competency and highly adaptive behavior at one end and helplessness and inflexible behavior at the other end. As with most dimensions of human characteristics, we would expect that most people would fall somewhere near the middle of the dimension. It might also be borne in mind that the quality of adjustment varies from time to time and from situation to situation, so that there are periods in the lives of most of us when we function less adequately than at other times.

Toward the "effective" end of the adjustment dimension would be those people who, by virtue of their superior biological endowment, the competencies and skills which they have acquired, and the situations they have been in, are now able to function successfully nearly all the time in simultaneously meeting their own needs and the demands of the immediate situation. Such individuals are not without limitations, particularly in our complex society, but they seem able to handle them comfortably, or at least they appear not to be unduly troubled by them. Such people are quite self-aware, and this includes an accurate awareness of their own limitations. They also have the ability to establish strong affectionate relationships and also to be productive in their work and careers. It is significant that Freud emphasized the roles of love and work in establishing and maintaining an effective level of adjustment. These are values that are certainly very much part of our culture, and they are also important aspects of our criteria for adjustment and mental health.

A colleague of the authors is a reasonably successful professional person who feels comfortable in his achievements and who is highly regarded by members of the professional community. He has a close-knit family life, and people comment about the obvious affection that exists among members of the family. While once a promising musician, he does not regret that he gave up developing this potential in order to devote himself more fully to his chosen profession. He recognizes that he is unlikely to achieve the professional recognition that many crave, but is comfortable in his well-deserved sense of competence. He is able to accept the achievements of his colleagues with genuine pleasure and does not put them down if they are more successful than he.

Toward the other extreme of the adjustment dimension would be those persons who have few skills or resources to meet the demands of living even rather sheltered, unchallenged lives. They often seem to be overwhelmed by their limitations and unaware of their needs and their problems. At the most extreme are the many persons who lack the necessary biological equipment to deal successfully with stress and whose failures to cope are to some extent a consequence of hereditary inadequacies, as we discussed in Chapter 1. This would appear to be especially true of those severely disturbed persons who are virtually unable to cope with even minimal demands of ordinary everyday living—those who are called *psychotic*. An example of such a person is Carl, described in Chapter 1, a twenty-six-year-old man who has been frequently hospitalized over the last ten years and who has few skills for dealing with even the simplest challenges of life. Chapter 7 will deal in detail with these severe failures of the adjustment process, but we can note in passing that they are usually people who have failed at both love and work, being able neither to establish close affectional ties with others nor to maintain productive lives.

Sometimes the view is advanced that certain creative persons, like the famous artists van Gogh or Gauguin, were productive precisely because of their psychological problems and difficulties. It is known, however, that the most productive periods for these two men were when they were least disturbed, and that they were unproductive during their most severe periods of disturbance. Nevertheless, it must be admitted that we know very little about the effects of psychological disturbance on either the content or the flow of artistic productivity. It is certainly not beyond the realm of possibility that the experience of undergoing and conquering personal disturbances could give some artists a special sensitivity and awareness that heightens the quality and meaningfulness of their work. The British psychiatrist R. D. Laing (1967) has taken the extreme position that an enhancement of life following personal disturbance occurs not only for artistic and creative persons but is possible for all of us. It is perhaps safest to conclude, however, that although there occasionally may be people who can make use of their problem experiences in this manner, the majority of such people continue to lead rather ineffectual and unproductive lives.

PERSONALITY AND ADJUSTMENT

In our discussion of the process of adjustment, we have introduced a wide variety of psychological concepts: behavior, responses, competency, needs, and gratification, to name a few. However, we have not emphasized the term *personality*. Although this concept has always been a central one in human psychology, it is at

the same time ambiguous and elusive. At this point, we need to explore this term more fully and to distinguish it from the concept of psychological adjustment.

In common nonscientific usage, personality often refers to social poise and interpersonal effectiveness, as in the statement, "Jeanie has a lot of personality." By the same token, people who lack social poise and interpersonal effectiveness are often said to have "no personality" or to have a "weak personality." Another popular usage of the word refers to an individual's most distinctive interpersonal characteristic. This is what is usually meant by saying, "Mary has a dominant personality" or "Bob has a neurotic personality."

Psychologists have traditionally thought of personality as some internal process or structure within the individual which can be used to explain or account for the observable behavior. The exact nature of whatever is inside the individual, however, has been the subject of an enormous amount of conflicting theory and argument for many years. In a classic review of the various efforts to define personality, Allport (1937) was able to identify more than fifty different definitions. He concluded his survey by offering his own: "the dynamic organization within the individual of those psychophysical systems that determine his unique adjustment to his environment" (p. 48). According to Guilford (1959), personality is "the individual's unique pattern of traits" (p. 5). More recently, Hilgard and Atkinson (1967) defined it as "the arrangement, or configuration, of individual characteristics and ways of behaving which account for an individual's unique adjustment to his total environment" (p. 462), while Mischel (1976) defined it as "the distinctive patterns of behavior (including thoughts and emotions) that characterize each individual's adaptation to the situations of his or her life" (p. 2).

There are some distinct differences among these definitions (and we could add other definitions that are even more divergent), but there are also some basic similarities. Implicit in all of them is the notion that individual personality is an abstraction that is based upon, or inferred from, observable behavior. All of these definitions suggest that our understanding of the personality of another individual is gained by observing overt behavior and then making inferences about underlying factors that might account for what we have observed. In this sense, then, the study of personality is synonymous with the study of behavior. Indeed, Hall and Lindzey (1970) have noted that personality refers to an area of inquiry within psychology as a discipline rather than to a distinct attribute of the individual.

Another similarity among these definitions of personality is their emphasis upon behaviors that relate to the adjustment of individuals to their environment. It should be obvious to the reader by now, however, that virtually all of a person's behavior is directly or indirectly relevant to efforts to adjust to the environment. In this respect too, then, personality can be regarded as encompassing all or nearly all of human behavior.

The behavior of the developing individual increases gradually in scope and complexity through the process of socialization, and by the time of adulthood, a fairly

FRIENDLINESS TOWARD MY FRIENDS
SEEMS TO BE ONE OF HIS
ENDURING CHARACTERISTICS!

stable set of interpersonal behaviors has been learned. While changes in these behaviors are certainly possible, especially if there are significant changes in the person's habitual environment, it is usual for relatively little change to occur, and in fact most of us resist major changes in our environments for the very reason that we wish to avoid having to make major changes in ourselves. Within a person's stable pattern of behaviors, certain responses are more prominent than others, particularly in interpersonal relationships, and it is by means of these behaviors that a person comes to be understood and characterized by others. Let us therefore define **personality** as *the enduring characteristics which we infer about a person that are significant for interpersonal behavior.*

Our own definition of personality, like those presented above, regards personality as an abstraction, as a set of inferred characteristics of the individual. It refers to those stable and salient aspects of the individual's behavior that tend to characterize interpersonal interactions. Our definition thus has much in common with the second popular usage of the term, in that it refers to the most easily observed aspects of the individual, especially interpersonal behavior.

In contrast with several of the other definitions cited above, our definition does not emphasize the role of personality in accounting for the uniqueness of individual adjustment to the environment. While the idea that we are each unique is rather comforting to most of us, it does not seem to add anything to a definition of personality. Also, our definition does not assign any explicit role to personality in determining or controlling an individual's adjustment. It can be taken for granted that those characteristics of an individual that are both stable and interpersonally significant must play a fairly central role in the adjustment of the individual. To summarize, the term personality is best used to refer to stable or habitual interpersonal behaviors, whereas adjustment has to do with the continuous process of gratifying needs in the context of environmental demands.

FRUSTRATION

Human existence would be rather simple if all our needs could be satisfied promptly and routinely. But this can never be the case. As we have emphasized, humans constantly experience both internal and external barriers that prevent need satisfaction. In this section we systematically examine the concept of **frustration,** which can be defined as the blocking of goal-directed behavior.

The problems created by frustration have long interested psychologists, particularly those concerned with the process of adjustment. Aware of the deep unhappiness experienced by many people and their inability to cope with the

adversity they encounter, and recognizing that maladaptive responses often seem to follow adversity, many psychologists have viewed frustration as a key concept in understanding the complexities of the adjustment process.

Frustration is a daily occurrence for all of us. A smoker is out of cigarettes and all the shops are closed; a letter which we are expecting day after day does not arrive; a high school boy finds that he is not tall enough to play on the school basketball team; a parent refuses a child permission to use the family car. All of these situations involve the blocking of an anticipated goal and are therefore examples of frustration.

There are innumerable causes of frustration. There may be a physical barrier, as when our key breaks off in the lock or we discover that we cannot reach a high shelf. There can be social barriers, as when someone fails to get a desired job, or when parents refuse their children permission to stay out late. One important aspect of our reaction to frustration is the way in which we think about or analyze the situation, and the labels we use. If we identify the barrier as internal—as some sort of a personal limitation or lack of competence—then our reaction to the thwarting is usually more intense. Thus, if we flunk an examination and conclude that the reason was our own incompetence or stupidity, our reaction is likely to be much more painful than if we were to regard the exam as unfair or the teacher as

prejudiced against us. The interpretations that we habitually place upon frustrating situations are important determinants of the quality of our adjustment. We shall discuss thought processes more fully in the next chapter; for now, the important points are that we all habitually respond to frustration with our own interpretations of the event, and that these thoughts are important determinants of our further reactions to frustration.

One's first reaction after making a response that is thwarted, or does not yield the expected outcome, is usually to repeat the same response. And repeated efforts in some situations, such as forcing open a jammed door or wheedling the family car from a reluctant parent, will often pay off. The old adage, "If at first you don't succeed, try, try again," does have some wisdom. Frustration not only leads most often to a repetition of the response, but it also leads to an increase in the *vigor* of the response. Years of psychological research, with both animals and humans, have clearly demonstrated that the responses made after frustration are usually more vigorous than the responses first made in the situation. Experimental rats in the laboratory runway run faster, children push their laboratory levers with greater force, and problem-solving behavior in the laboratory group is resumed with increased vocal intensity if anticipated rewards are suddenly withdrawn. The increase in vigor is usually taken to indicate that the frustration has led to an increase in emotional arousal or drive. In other words, frustration seems to have the effect of increasing the strength of the needs that were already operating in the situation. One could also explain the increased vigor of response following frustration by saying that the organism has simply learned that vigorous responses are more likely to be successful in leading to need gratification following initial frustration.

The vigor of the response after frustration is related to distance from the goal— the closer the organism is to the goal, the greater the vigor of the response. Thus, we might say that the level of frustration appears to be higher when we are thwarted close to attaining our goal. Barely missing the train or having the telephone stop ringing just as we are ready to pick up the receiver after rushing downstairs to answer it are more frustrating than missing the train or the phone by a large margin. One way of explaining this heightened frustration is in terms of the expectations that we have developed in these situations. Seeing the train in the station as we hurry toward it, and continuing to hear the phone as we race downstairs, lead us to expect that we will attain our goal, even though we recognize that we may be "cutting it close." When we have raised our expectations only to have them dashed, the frustration is particularly intense.

Level of frustration is also higher when the response that is thwarted is an overlearned or highly habitual one. When our hitherto trusty car refuses to start, when the gum machine which has always dispensed our favorite brand does not deliver, when our favorite teacher downgrades us, we experience a higher level of frustration than when the same thwarting is produced by situations in which we have not had the same long history of reliable experience. This effect also can be explained in terms of heightened expectations built up by experience. Thus it would appear that expectations, created by experience, by proximity to the goal, or perhaps in other ways, are important determinants of the level of frustration.

What further consequences of frustration are there? One answer is found in the **frustration-aggression hypothesis** of Dollard and his colleagues (1939), which states that frustration tends to increase the probability of *aggression*, defined as an act where the goal is injury to a person or object. According to this hypothesis, the higher the level of frustration, the higher the probability of aggression against the thwarting agent. The level of frustration is said to be a function of: (1) the strength of the original drive being thwarted; (2) the degree of interference involved, that is, the extent to which alternative responses are also thwarted; and (3) the number of times the thwarting occurs. From our preceding discussion we would add the two factors of proximity to the goal and degree of overlearning of the response. According to the frustration-aggression hypothesis, the tendency to aggress against the blocking agent is natural, automatic, and unlearned.

This view of aggression as a natural response to frustration is consistent with the psychoanalytic view of aggression as the other basic human drive, beside sex. The same view of aggression has also been taken by the ethologist Konrad Lorenz (1966), who sees aggression as a natural instinct, or unlearned response, of all mammals, including humans, to fight their own kind. But it is not necessary to view aggression as instinctive in order to see how it might be a normal response to frustration. The frustrated organism is likely to attempt vigorously to set aside whatever is blocking its goal-directed behavior. And the more frustration involved, the more likely is such a response. Any vigorous activity that is directed either at a specific object, such as a stuck door, a malfunctioning cigarette machine, or a reproving parent, is very likely to be labeled as aggression. If we define aggression in terms of vigor rather than intent to injure, then we are simply restating the frustration-aggression hypothesis: the frustrated organism will vigorously attempt to counter whatever is thwarting or blocking its behavior.

Dollard and his coworkers assumed that virtually all aggressive behavior came about as a response to frustration. Recent experimental work, however, leads us to question that assumption. Research on the psychological learning process of modeling (Bandura, 1977), for example, indicates that simple observation of aggressive behavior is often sufficient to arouse similar aggressive behavior on the part of the observer. Also, it is clear that the frequency and nature of aggressive behavior can be powerfully influenced by reinforcement. For instance, children who saw models being rewarded for aggressive behavior showed much more aggressive behavior themselves than those who observed models being punished following aggression (Bandura, 1977). Thus, we must conclude that the frustration-aggression hypothesis provides only a partial answer to our question as to the consequences of frustration.

Frustration is said to lead to increased vigor
of response, to regression, and to aggression.
Most theorists would agree that one common
aspect is increased emotional arousal.

Some psychological theories have suggested that another important consequence
of frustration is **regression,** or a return to earlier and more childish forms of behavior.
The idea that regression should be an expected response to frustration comes from
psychoanalytic theory, and would be exemplified by an older child or an adult showing behavior such as temper tantrums or thumb sucking in response to the blocking of
a desired goal. Let us examine a famous experiment conducted by Barker, Dembo,
and Lewin (1941), which is often cited in support of the view that regression is a
natural consequence of frustration. A group of young children, aged two to five, were
observed while playing with a standard set of toys, and their age-level of play was
rated by a team of trained observers on a scale of "constructiveness." Then the

children were allowed to play with a new and highly attractive set of toys, which previously had been hidden from their view. Next, the more attractive toys were taken away and placed behind a wire mesh screen where they could be seen but not used. All that remained were the less attractive, standard set of toys that had been used initially. The "constructiveness" of the children's play with the standard toys was rated a second time in the post-frustration period, and was found to be much lower; in fact, the average age-level of play decreased about one and a half years.

It was concluded from these results that regression is a natural consequence of frustration, but this interpretation of the Barker, Dembo, and Lewin study is not the only one possible. It is obvious that the children became much less interested in playing with the standard set of toys after they had been allowed to play with the more attractive toys. And they did indeed spend much of their post-frustration time both attacking the wire mesh barrier and looking at the toys behind the barrier, all of which contributed to lower "constructiveness" ratings of their play. But it is not at all certain that their interest in the more attractive toys or in breaking down the barrier should be interpreted as regressive or more childish behavior. Indeed, it could also be argued that ignoring the newer and more attractive toys might be more appropriately called regressive than the behavior that was shown.

Perhaps what emerges most clearly from the research and theorizing based on the frustration-aggression hypothesis and the psychoanalytic notion of regression following frustration is that frustration causes an interruption in the smooth flow of behavior and usually results in increased emotional arousal. People differ widely in their responses to this disruption and emotional arousal, so that the question as to the consequences of frustration can have no single answer. We have pointed to some consistencies, such as increased vigor of responding; other consequences of frustration are determined by the socialization experiences of the individual, and will consequently vary from person to person and from culture to culture.

Learned Responses to Frustration

Although the frustration-aggression hypothesis is incomplete at best, it can serve as a starting place for examining a number of important points about aggression and its control. According to the original frustration-aggression hypothesis, aggression should be directed at the source of the frustration. But it is often difficult or impossible to identify the frustrating agent clearly, particularly in complex social situations. For example, during the depression of the 1930s it was not customary for those who were out of work to identify the causes of their frustration within the complicated political, economic, and social conditions of the time, and to react to these causes directly. Rather, they tended to blame themselves for their difficulties, a response that is usually low in our hierarchy of preferences. Today, people are much more likely to blame the "establishment" for frustrating conditions, and to respond with the various forms of open social unrest that we saw in our major cities during the 1960s, including actual riots. The effectiveness of these aggressive responses in changing the frustrating conditions is still an open question.

The problems involved in adequately identifying the causes of frustration also give rise to the displacement of aggression, or **scapegoating.** A convenient but often innocent person is blamed for the frustration, and becomes the object of aggression. One important factor in choosing a scapegoat is the inability of the victim to retaliate against the displaced aggression. For instance, Dollard and his colleagues point out that over the years 1882–1930 the price of cotton in the United States was negatively correlated with the number of lynchings in the South; the lower the price of cotton, the higher the number of lynchings. The conclusion drawn by these researchers was that the greater the economic frustration, the greater was the displaced aggression against the blacks, who served as scapegoats even though they obviously were not responsible for the price of cotton.

During the child's first few years of life, the parents are the primary source of frustration. The process of socialization requires that parents regularly interfere with the child's goal-directed behavior in order to teach new responses. Why then do children not display much more direct aggression against parents, who are continually frustrating their important, intense drives? The answer lies in children's learning about aggression; as discussed in Chapter 3 on socialization, children's angry responses, and particularly those directed against parents, are systematically punished, and anxiety is attached not only to aggressive behavior, but also to aggressive impulses and thoughts.

This inhibition of direct aggression toward parents and other powerful figures who might punish aggressive responses leads to displacement and scapegoating. Thus, when children are thwarted by a parent, they may displace their aggression toward a younger sibling, a family pet, or even a doll. Similarly, when we are frustrated by a boss at work we may either vent our anger at a subordinate or wait until we return home and "take it out" on our unsuspecting roommate, spouse, or children. While displaced aggression may provide temporary relief to the aggressor, it does nothing to change the frustrating conditions which lie at the source of the problem.

Is displacement of aggression or scapegoating inevitable? There are two possible answers to this question, depending upon one's theoretical view of the nature of aggression. If aggression is seen as a basic impulse or drive, as it is by psychoanalysts, then unexpressed aggression forms an increasing reservoir of pent-up energy that must somehow be discharged. If direct discharge is inhibited, then the energy must be released indirectly through displacement and scapegoating, or perhaps even more indirectly through fantasy. Once this energy is released, directly or indirectly, the drive is diminished and the likelihood of further aggression occurring is reduced for the time being. This discharge of energy, or **catharsis,** is regarded as therapeutic or healthy for the person with the aggressive drive.

Quite the opposite answer is obtained when the question is analyzed from a social-learning viewpoint. In this view, any aggressive behavior that is rewarded (and perhaps all aggression that does not result in punishment) is likely to increase the probability of further aggression. Thus, rather than predicting catharsis and a reduced probability of aggression, the social-learning point of view leads us to conclude that aggression will be followed by more aggression.

The research evidence on this extremely important question is inconclusive to date. While some studies have concluded that the catharsis theory is correct, others have found that aggression leads to further aggression. An examination of the differences in the details of these experiments tends to suggest that both consequences of aggression can sometimes occur, depending upon the particular characteristics of the situation and of the individuals involved. It can be said with more certainty, however, that a critical factor in determining how aggressive people will be is their social-learning history—what they have learned to do in response to frustration and aggressive impulses.

There is ample research illustrating the fact that a variety of different behaviors can be learned as responses to frustration. In one experiment, Davitz (1952) used children in a summer camp who were systematically trained either in aggressive, competitive responses, or in collaborative, problem-solving responses. When the children were then frustrated by being deprived of an expected reward, there were clear differences in their responses in a free-play situation. Those children who had spent most of their time in camp engaging in aggressive, competitive activity behaved in an extremely aggressive manner both toward their environment and toward each other, while those who had been involved in cooperative, problem-solving behavior were much less aggressive, and spent their time in attempting to find ways of circumventing the frustration.

Learning can also affect an individual's willingness to tolerate frustration; that is, to wait for a delayed reward or future gratification. In an important series of studies, Mischel (1966) demonstrated that children who chose smaller, immediate rewards rather than larger, delayed rewards, selecting a smaller piece of candy immediately rather than a large piece of candy for one week later, were more likely to be younger, to come from lower socioeconomic class homes, and not to have a father present in the home. Mischel's findings have been replicated in other settings and cultures, and indicate that ability to delay gratification, or to tolerate frustration, is learned as part of a general pattern of social responsibility, which includes self-control, orientation toward the future, and reliance on planning. This pattern appears to be an aspect of middle class societal values, and to depend to some extent on the presence of the father in the home for its effective transmission to the children.

We have emphasized that a person's responses to frustration are primarily learned, so it is obviously very important for parents and teachers to provide opportunities for a child to learn these reactions as part of the socialization process. The child needs to learn a variety of responses depending on the circumstances: to attack some blocks vigorously, to find alternative ways of circumventing other blocks, to find new goals when neither vigorous responses nor alternative behaviors will lead to the removal of the block, and a capacity to wait out some frustrations. Clearly a central part of this training involves the discrimination of the specific circumstances under which each of these several courses of action is the most likely to be effective.

CONFLICT

Problems in psychological adjustment often arise in situations where two or more incompatible needs are aroused at the same time. We might want to study in order to do well on our examination tomorrow morning, but tonight might also be the last opportunity for a film that we very much want to see. We might be committed to a major in Romance Languages, but find ourselves developing a strong interest in mathematics. Two conflicting impulses do not cancel each other out, but rather result in a state of increased drive and subjective tension, and the result is an increase in restlessness and seemingly random activity. Conflict involves the simultaneous arousal of two or more incompatible response tendencies, in a situation where one response or the other must be made. In the conflict situations of concern in psychological adjustment, it is the unattractive aspects of the response possibilities that create the greatest difficulties in making the final choice.

The theoretical analysis of conflict stems from the work of the psychologist Kurt Lewin (1935), who hypothesized that all aspects of our environment, both objects and people, have either positive or negative "valences." Positive valences—perhaps elicited by rock music, football weekends, and pizza—produce *approach* tendencies or behaviors; while negative valences—perhaps produced by college examinations, being poor, or having to use the city bus system—produce *avoidance* tendencies. These particular valences are rather idiosyncratic and are a product of the unique life experiences and learning of the individual; valences of other situations or events, such as money or electric shock, are close to universal.

Positive and negative valences can result in three kinds of conflict: (1) approach-approach conflicts, where there are incompatible tendencies to approach two objects with positive valences that lie in opposite directions; (2) avoidance-avoidance conflicts, in which two objects with negative valences are so arranged that escape from one would force the person closer to the other; and (3) approach-avoidance conflicts, in which there is a simultaneous arousal of both approach and avoidance tendencies by a single goal or object that has both positive and negative valences.

Approach-Approach Conflict

When we have to choose between two equally desirable goals, such as two of our favorite desserts or two films that we wish to see, we face an **approach-approach conflict.** In general, approach-approach conflicts tend to be easily solved and rarely cause us much distress. This is because any small fluctuation in the valences of two desirable goals that renders one goal more attractive will move us closer to that goal, psychologically speaking, and this movement will simultaneously weaken the valence of the other goal. Thus, decisions between two desirable goals are made easily, and sometimes on rather arbitrary grounds. One film might be selected over the other because it is preferred by a friend, requires a shorter walk, or finishes at a more convenient time; one dessert might be selected because it is closer at hand or is a preferred color.

It is important to emphasize that many rather complex and involved conflicts are initially seen as simple approach-approach conflicts, although closer examination proves them to be much more complicated. Perhaps a student is trying to choose between two equally attractive graduate schools, or a young professional is unable to make a

Approach-avoidance conflicts involve goals
with both positive and negative aspects.
Cigarettes may taste delicious, but how does
this compare with the consequences to your
health?

choice between two equally attractive job offers. In each case the person is experiencing genuine distress and is unable to make a choice. In such a situation, each of the apparently positive goals usually also has a hidden negative valence that prevents the person from resolving the conflict easily. Rather than facing a simple approach-approach situation, the people involved are really confronting a double approach-avoidance conflict in which they are attempting to choose between two goals with both positive and negative valences—a much more difficult task, as we shall see below.

Avoidance-Avoidance Conflict

When we talk about being caught between the frying pan and the fire, between the devil and the deep blue sea, between the rock and the hard place, we are usually referring to an **avoidance-avoidance conflict.** Shall we continue to study for this terribly boring course or shall we risk failing it? Shall we confront our boss about sarcastic remarks and risk getting fired, or shall we suffer on in silence? These are but two common examples of this very frequent conflict situation.

In contrast to approach-approach conflicts, in which any movement at all toward either goal resolves the conflict, any move closer to either of the two negatively valued goals involved in an avoidance-avoidance conflict simply intensifies our discomfort and we tend to retreat immediately. This retreat brings us closer to the other negative

goal, causing us to retreat in the opposite direction. Thus, vacillation and indecision are the hallmarks of avoidance-avoidance conflicts: as we approach one goal, find it is punishing, retreat to the other goal, find that it is equally punishing, and continue to shuttle back and forth unhappily, very much on the "horns of a dilemma."

When a person is confronted with an avoidance-avoidance conflict, a frequent attractive solution is to *leave the field;* that is, to find an alternative response that avoids both of the goals with negative valences. We might put off studying the boring subject, and concentrate on trying to figure out how we can drop the course and still graduate. Or, we might begin to look for a new job with a different boss. In these solutions, we try to resolve the avoidance-avoidance conflict by finding a "way out" of our dilemma; we try to avoid having to make the choice between the two equally undesirable goals. Many times, of course, it is simply not possible to leave the field, and our conflict remains unresolved. The exam in the dull course is still tomorrow morning and the deadline for dropping courses without penalty has passed; or nobody else seems to need someone with our exact qualifications at our salary. It is these unavoidable and seemingly insoluble conflicts that lead to a variety of nonadjustive responses, such as diffuse anxiety, the development of physical ailments such as headaches, intense restlessness and sleeplessness, or psychological withdrawal from the situation if complete physical withdrawal is not possible.

Approach-Avoidance Conflict

We tend to regard most goal objects in our environment with an ambivalent attitude. As stated above, most goal objects simultaneously exert both a positive and a negative valence, eliciting both approach and avoidance responses. We enjoy smoking but recognize that it increases the risk of lung disease; we would like to get married but we do not want to surrender our freedom and independence. It is important to understand fully the nature of approach-avoidance conflicts, since they are involved in our daily attempts to deal with goals toward which we have mixed feelings.

The concept of **goal gradients** (Figure 5-1) is useful in understanding conflicts, particularly approach-avoidance conflicts. A goal gradient reflects the strength of the approach or avoidance tendency at various distances from the goal object. As we move toward a goal object having a positive valence, the strength of our tendency to approach the goal becomes stronger; likewise, as we approach a goal with a negative valence, our tendency to avoid the goal increases. In research with laboratory rats, Brown (1948) actually measured these goal gradients by attaching a special harness to the animals and measuring the amount of pull which they exerted while either approaching a positive goal (food) or avoiding a negative goal (electric shock) at different degrees of closeness to the goal. The animals consistently increased their pulling force when they were closer to the goal—pulling harder toward it as they approached a place where they previously had been fed; and pulling harder to get away, the closer they were to a place where they had been previously shocked.

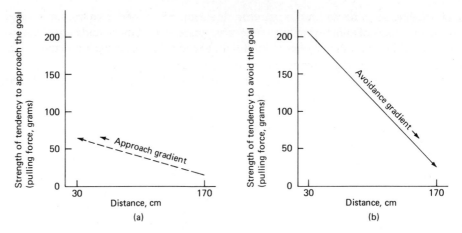

Figure 5-1. Slopes of (a) approach and (b) avoidance gradients, based on the findings of Brown (1948).

The most important finding of Brown's study, however, was that as the animals were tested closer and closer to the goal area, the force exerted in avoiding the shock increased at a faster rate than did the force exerted in approaching the food. Similar but somewhat weaker findings have been recently reported for humans by Losco and Epstein (1977). These findings illustrate the central point that avoidance gradients have steeper slopes than approach gradients.

What are the implications of these differences in the slopes of the approach and avoidance gradients? As long as we maintain some distance from the ambivalent goal object the approach tendency will be stronger than the avoidance tendency. Thus, the net tendency will be a positive one and we will tend to approach the goal object. As we near the goal, however, the avoidance tendency, because its slope is greater than that of the approach tendency, more than balances it out, so that the net tendency is negative rather than positive and we begin to retreat. As we withdraw, we reach a point where the net tendency is once again positive—where the approach tendency is higher than the avoidance tendency—and we turn again and begin to approach the goal until the avoidance tendencies once again become stronger. Thus our behavior will be characterized by vacillation and indecision, and this is characteristic of all dealings with ambivalent goal objects. When we go to our boss's office to ask for a raise, an ambivalent goal since we want the money but are fearful of being refused, we approach the office resolutely, but as we get closer to the door, we hesitate and turn, perhaps stopping for a drink of water. We then turn back to the office, but hesitate once again; and we may repeat this sequence several times until the situation is resolved for us, either by the boss's stepping out of the office as we approach, or by our being called back to our own desk. Approaching an ambivalent goal object can be a time-related as well as space-related behavior, and so we can also understand why many ambivalent goal objects, like weddings or optional surgery, are frequently post-poned. As the date for the ambivalent goal approaches, the avoidance tendency becomes higher than the approach tendency, and the date is set back to a time in the future for which the approach tendency is again higher. As the date again nears, we again wish to set it back. Eventually, however, this behavior must come to an end, because the act of postponement itself carries a negative valence, and we find it easier to go ahead with the ambivalent goal.

We noted earlier that many conflicts that are initially identified as approach-approach, turn out to be double approach-avoidance conflicts upon closer examination. In these situations we must choose between *two* ambivalent goals, and the vacil-lation again follows the pattern that is determined by the relative strengths of the approach and avoidance tendencies. We first approach one goal in response to its net attractiveness, until we reach that point where the avoidance tendency is stronger than the approach tendency; then we switch to the other goal until a similar point is reached, and we once again reverse our behavior.

In a clinical example of a double approach-avoidance conflict, a young woman sought counseling help because she was unable to choose between two men who were eager to marry her. Initially she was able to say only how very attractive and desirable they both were, but she eventually came to admit that each had negative valences also. One was rather conservative and was likely to insist that she should play the role of the typical middle class housewife, a role which she did not find particularly appealing. The other was much less traditional, and was insisting on an "open mar-riage," which also aroused considerable anxiety because she was not sure that she would be able to hold his affection in such a situation. Only when these negative valences, which she had previously been unable or unwilling to examine, were brought out and fully explored was she able to make a choice. In double approach-avoidance situations it is often a matter of having to choose the lesser of two undesirable alternatives, and this is the reason that we often tend to gloss over the negative valences in our own analyses of the alternatives, lest we should find both choices unacceptable.

In the case of simple approach-avoidance conflicts, where we are faced with a single ambivalent goal object, we often find that the conflict is between a behavior and the learned anxiety that has been attached to that behavior. It is not necessary to accept the Freudian view that the two basic human drives are sex and aggression in order to appreciate that sexual and aggressive behaviors are the most strongly inhibited in our society, and that many ways of expressing these behaviors are strongly anxiety arousing for the majority of us. Again, without accepting the psychoanalytic view that conflicts are either between id and superego or id and ego, we can readily see that most of our conflicts are between impulse expression on the one hand and impulse inhibition on the other, usually involving sexual or aggressive impulses.

Because of the ethics of human experimentation, there have been few human experiments involving intense conflicts. The experimental work of Masserman (1961)

with animals is very informative. Using both cats and monkeys as subjects, Masserman initially trained these animals to respond to a signal by approaching and opening the lid of a food dish in order to obtain food. Once this response had been learned, a noxious stimulus was presented each time the animal approached the food dish, a blast of air in the face of the cats and a toy snake for the monkeys. Within a very few trials a strong conflict was established between approach tendencies in order to gratify hunger and avoidance tendencies for the noxious stimuli. The animals showed strong behavioral disturbances—crouching, trembling, pilar erection, pupil dilation, rapid and shallow breathing, irregular pulse, and increases in blood pressure—all the classic signs of anxiety. They also showed an increased startle response and a number of phobic reactions. Some animals even began to refuse food when it was offered outside the experimental situation. Interestingly enough, the monkeys showed more intense behavioral disturbances than the cats, including a loss of sexual functioning, stereotyped pacing back and forth in their cages, and somatic disorders such as diarrhea.

Masserman's results are closely parallel to clinical evidence obtained from humans suffering strong approach-avoidance conflicts in real life. For example, a young homosexual man described his experience as follows. If he had not engaged in any sexual activity for a time, he would find himself increasingly attracted to other men and would notice himself making covert sexual signals. At the first sign of a response from them, however, his anxiety level would increase markedly, and he would become acutely aware of thoughts about the social unacceptability of this behavior and about his own aversion to it. With the further passage of time, his desire for homosexual interaction would become even stronger, and he would begin accepting sexual invitations from other men, only to break off the interaction before the occurrence of any physical activity because of his increasing anxiety. Eventually he would continue to the extent of a physical homosexual act, and immediately he would become overwhelmed by feelings of anxiety, guilt, and shame, and would vow never to do such a disgusting thing again. He had repeated this pattern of behavior for a number of years.

In this example, the goal object once again had both strong positive and negative valences. With the passage of time, the approach drive increased to the point where, despite very high anxiety, the approach behavior would be performed and the impulse gratified. Once having reduced the approach drive, the avoidance tendency would immediately force the young men far away from the goal. It is reasonable to assume that this situation represented one half of a double approach–avoidance conflict in which the other ambivalent goal involved sexual interaction with women, and that the avoidance tendencies for that goal were far stronger than for the homosexual goal.

SUMMARY

1.   Chapters 1 through 4 have discussed the scientific basis for studying psychological adjustment, and Chapter 5 explores the concept of adjustment in depth. Human adjustment refers to the ongoing practical problems of everyday life, and the process of adjustment is the continuing process of the arousal and satisfaction of needs, both primary (physiological) and secondary (psychological). For most people in our society, physiological needs are met rather routinely, but the satisfaction of psychological needs, which is the focus of this book, is a much more difficult task.

2.   The effectiveness of a person's psychological adjustment is determined not only by the degree to which psychological needs are satisfied, but also by a number of other factors: capacity to tolerate delay in need satisfaction, the degree of persistence after initial failure, ability to be flexible in accepting substitute sources of need satisfaction, and the extent to which needs and methods of satisfying them are regarded as legitimate by the society in which the person lives. Some people appear to gratify their needs by engaging in behavior that meets the needs in question but also has long-term negative consequences. Behavior that appears to be persistently unadaptive for an individual can often be explained in this manner.

3.   Psychological adjustment can be viewed as a continuous, dynamic process, involving two factors: individuals and their needs and skills, and the situation and its demands. Each of us views a new situation in different ways, perceiving different demands and different possibilities for need satisfaction. Most of us are reasonably aware of our own needs, and know how to respond optimally in most situations. Also, we try to select situations in which we will be able to maintain our accustomed patterns of need gratification. In situations which are so infrequent that we have had little or no opportunity to learn adaptive ways of responding, such as accidents and other crises, it is impossible to predict how a given person will react. It is known, however, that people who successfully handle high stress occupations have generally come from uneventful backgrounds. Adjustment problems arise when there is a conflict between meeting one's own needs and the demands of the situation. There are no general rules to aid in resolving such conflicts, but the effectively adjusted person tries to be fully aware of all relevant factors and to give each the proper weight in the decision. A strict deterministic position would hold that all decisions are predetermined by a person's social-learning history; such a view, however, fails to consider the important role of thinking in determining behavior.

4. To assess someone's psychological adjustment over an entire life period would be an enormous task, and is rarely attempted except by professional biographers. It makes more sense to confine evaluations to specific points in time or to a person's adjustment in regard to a specific situation, such as suitability for a particular kind of employment. Psychologists tend to look for evidence of satisfactory adjustment in similar situations in the past, and try to maintain objectivity despite their own personal values. Although it would be meaningless to attempt to set up absolute criteria for "perfect" adjustment, it is often useful to think in terms of a broad continuum ranging from effective adjustment toward one extreme and poor adjustment toward the other. Effective adjustment involves a wide variety of skills and competencies, awareness of limitations, close affectional ties, and successful vocational experiences. The view that a certain amount of psychological disturbance is necessary in order for creative persons such as artists and writers to be at their most productive is not borne out by observation, although it might be true of an occasional person.

5. We distinguish between the process of adjustment and the term personality, a concept that we have not emphasized to date. In popular usage, personality refers to the enduring characteristics of the person that are significant for interpersonal behavior. This definition includes no direct reference to adjustment, the continuous process of satisfying one's needs within the context of environmental demands, although it is obvious that one's enduring interpersonal characteristics must play a central role in this process.

6. The consequences of frustration, or the blocking of goal-directed behavior, have long been of interest to psychologists. A common response to frustration is to continue the same behavior but with increased vigor, the degree of which appears to be related to the organism's expectations of success. Further factors are postulated in the frustration-aggression hypothesis put forward by Dollard and his colleagues. There is theoretical disagreement as to whether the increased vigor represents a natural drive of aggression or whether it is used simply because it often leads to reinforcement. It has also been suggested that frustration is naturally followed by behavior that is developmentally regressive. What is most clear experimentally is that frustration causes a disruption in the smooth flow of behavior, to which the individual responds with emotional arousal plus any of a wide variety of other responses, depending on what has been learned during socialization.

7. One response to frustration, particularly if the causes are not easily identified, is the displacement of aggression, as by scapegoating, in which an innocent victim becomes the object of the aggression. There is evidence that a variety of responses can be learned to frustration, and that one important aspect of the socialization process is to teach children tolerance for frustration, or for delay of gratification as an aspect of self-control.

8. Conflict involves the simultaneous arousal of two or more incompatible response tendencies, in a situation where one response or the other must be made.

Approach-approach conflicts, in which a choice must be made between two desirable goals, ordinarily pose little problem. At times such conflict situations also involve hidden avoidance tendencies, however. *Avoidance-avoidance* conflicts result in vacillation and indecision, since any move away from one feared goal moves us closer to the other. A frequent response in this situation is to "leave the field" entirely. *Approach-avoidance* conflicts involve incompatible response tendencies toward the same goal. It has been shown that both the approach and avoidance tendencies increase in strength the closer one is to the goal, but that the avoidance gradient is steeper than the approach gradient. This results in vacillation at a point some distance from the goal. Double approach-avoidance conflicts are especially common and particularly difficult to resolve.

KEY TERMS

behavior

psychological adjustment

persistent unadaptive
 reactions

psychological crises

personality

frustration

frustration-aggression
 hypothesis

regression

scapegoating

catharsis

approach-approach conflict

avoidance-avoidance
 conflict

goal gradients

SIX

The Management of Anxiety: The Adjustment Mechanisms

Adjustment problems involving anxiety are often handled by avoiding the anxiety in one way or another.

- In the psychodynamic framework, these avoidances are called defense mechanisms.

- The basic concept underlying the defense mechanisms is repression.

- In social-learning terms, repression refers to the automatic avoidance of anxiety-producing thoughts.

- Common defense mechanisms based directly on repression are rationalization, projection, and reaction formation.

- Anxiety may also be avoided through the mechanisms of compensation, sublimation, fantasy, and withdrawal.

Self-concept refers to one's view of one's own behavior.

- An important aspect of self-concept is self-esteem, one's judgment of one's own worth.

Direct control of anxiety can be achieved by certain drugs, and also possibly through autonomic conditioning.

THE PROCESS OF ADJUSTMENT INVOLVES THE SATISFACTION OF MOTIVES AND
needs, the resolution of frustration and conflict, and the reduction of drives or
tensions. We recall from Chapter 5 that anxiety is a strong, disruptive emotional
reaction that interferes with the flow of behavior and thus can disrupt the process
of adjustment. A central issue in adjustment is how we attempt to manage or control anxiety in order to reduce its interfering effects. Most of the strategies that adult
humans use for the management of anxiety are cognitive in nature, involving systematic changes in *the way we think* about the problem situation. These cognitive
strategies for handling anxiety are what Sigmund Freud referred to as **defense
mechanisms.** Freud's description of the processes underlying the defense mechanisms can only be understood within the context of psychoanalytic theory. In this

chapter, we reformulate these processes using the language and concepts of social-learning theory.

Although our primary interest in this chapter is in the ways people handle problems in adjustment that involve anxiety, it is important to recognize that there are some failures of the adjustment process in which anxiety is not the key factor. Such failures to achieve need satisfaction arise through the prior learning of responses that are inadequate, either by direct reinforcement or through the presence of inadequate models. Thus, children may learn to avoid close interpersonal relations not because anxiety is involved, but because other behaviors such as reading or listening to music alone have been positively rewarded by their parents. Or, the children may never have had the opportunity to observe adequate models of close interpersonal behavior. And it is not uncommon to find that problem behaviors for which children are brought to guidance clinics are being unwittingly maintained through positive reinforcement by the parents. Thus, not all human adjustment problems are anxiety based.

As an example of a problem that is maintained by positive reinforcement, consider the case of two-year-old Tommy, who is brought to the guidance clinic by his parents. Tommy has temper tantrums whenever he is required to do something he would rather not do, such as to come in from outside in order to eat his lunch. Tommy's parents almost always give in to him because his loud shrieks and his head banging terrify them. Their attention and compliance with his wishes serve as unwitting but clear reinforcement for his tantrums.

The cognitive behaviors called defense mechanisms are, of course, learned in the same way as any other set of complex behaviors. Further, the more successful these responses are in helping people manage their difficulties in adjustment, the more they will be repeated over and over again. The concept of defense mechanisms originally referred to processes for keeping anxiety out of the person's awareness, but it has now taken on the more general meaning of defending or protecting the individual's sense of self-worth or self-esteem, in addition to reducing anxiety.

The case of Ed. Ed, the young college graduate whose case was briefly presented in Chapter 1, puts to use several of the defense mechanisms or cognitive distortions in the process of adjustment. To repeat briefly, Ed, who has been living in a commune, is seeking psychological help because he is not altogether satisfied with his current life. In counseling, it is learned that Ed's parents have always been careful to tell him that they would emotionally support him in whatever ways he might choose to fulfill himself in life. Yet he is troubled with the very strong feeling that he is letting them down. Patient exploration by the therapist begins to reveal that the parents' actual behavior has suggested a much stronger commitment to rather traditional occupational roles and a definite unwillingness to consider real alternatives. When Ed's parents have talked about the children of others, they have only respected those who have accomplished much in rather traditional avenues, the very options that they have insisted they do not demand from him. These discrepancies are readily apparent to the therapist, but not to Ed. With the emotional support of the therapist, however, Ed is gradually able to change his distorted patterns of thinking about the situation. The most important step is for him to recognize that the true source of his anxieties is that he could never live up to his parents' role expectations. We will examine aspects of Ed's thinking processes and other aspects of his behavior as we proceed in the chapter.

The capacity to think—to say things to ourselves and to analyze situations in ways that enable us to make sense of our circumstances—and to understand what is happening to us are among the most basic characteristics of humans. In the case of defense mechanisms, the cognitive activities that are involved usually consist of self-justification and almost always involve some kind of *self-deception,* or cognitive distortion. This self-deception may take either of two forms, **denial** or **disguise.** It is a common human practice, whenever anxiety is aroused in the context of some particular behaviors, to "reappraise" the situation in order to cope better with the anxiety and the behavior.

Let us first consider the self-deception mechanism of denial. When denial is used, it is usually in situations where the behavior engaged in does not meet either the person's own standards or others' expectations. Thus, when a boy who has broken a lamp in his room is asked how it became broken, he might say, "I didn't do it!" Or, a husband who has beaten his wife in a fit of rage might later have *amnesia,* or temporary loss of memory of the incident. How can we know that such people are not simply lying to avoid punishment for their behavior? The answer is that denial is usually considered to involve self-deception as well as the deception of others. We would know that someone was practicing self-deception if we were able to recover these memories through the use of hypnosis or certain drugs (such as sodium pentathol) which reduce the individual's level of anxiety. This would show us that the individual had not been able to recall the experience voluntarily, and we would conclude that the material was anxiety arousing. The exclusion of anxiety-arousing material from awareness is referred to as **repression,** which is a central concept in understanding the problems involved in the management of anxiety.

REPRESSION

Repression can perhaps be best understood if we first discuss a similar and related process, **suppression,** which is more familiar in our everyday experience. Consider a group of people discussing a friend who has been ill or who has recently undergone surgery. The conversation gradually moves into a general discussion of disease and perhaps even death. As the discussion becomes more and more morbid, the general anxiety level of the group increases. Under these circumstances, it is likely that somebody will say, "Why are we on this gruesome topic? Let's discuss

something else!" The immediate reduction of anxiety in the group following the change in subject matter would be evident to all present, and it would be clear that the anxiety-arousing material had been deliberately avoided, or suppressed.

Of course, the response to an anxiety-arousing conversation is not always one of suppression. We sometimes find that in discussing the misfortunes of others, however distressing they might be, we can enhance our own self esteem. For example, we might relish hearing that some rival has a serious illness that will keep her or him out of action for some time. In this case, the positive reinforcement obtained from such comparisons would be stronger than the anxiety aroused, and the approach–avoidance conflict would be resolved by approach. Also, certain discussions of anxiety-arousing events might be motivated by the expression of indirect aggression, as when we discuss how we might torture some hated enemy. Usually, however, we tend toward the deliberate avoidance of anxiety-arousing subjects in our conversations. It is also common to avoid topics that might be anxiety arousing for somebody else, like divorce, or the alienation of a child from its parents, or failure in school.

Suppression can also occur on the individual level, so that, for example, we might decide to go to the movies or to a ball game when we are tense or worried. We hope that the impact of these events will crowd out the anxieties that would otherwise be the center of our attention. Similarly, we might read a book or watch television at night to help us to sleep if we are upset, in the hope that the thoughts about what we have read or seen will interfere with anxiety arousal. Sometimes, of course, the reverse may occur, and we find that the anxiety is so strong that we cannot concentrate on the book or the television program.

Repression, which also refers to the avoidance of anxiety-arousing thoughts, is similar to the process of suppression, but there are two important differences. First, the level of anxiety involved is usually more intense. Second and more important, the process is automatic; that is, one does not make the decision to avoid a certain thought, but the avoidance occurs in the same way that one would automatically avoid a hot stove on which one had been burned. There might be a strong positive drive to approach a forbidden thought or memory, and as would be true of any approach-avoidance conflict, the closer one approaches, the more intense the anxiety.

The existence of repression, which has also been termed *cognitive avoidance* (Mischel, 1976), is widely accepted and there would be few psychologists who doubt that thoughts can be automatically inhibited. On the other hand, the explanation that we are offering for repression differs rather markedly from the traditional psychoanalytic view of this concept, which occupies a central place in Freudian theory. In that view, repression involves the rejection by the conscious mind of memories and impulses that are unacceptable because they threaten to overwhelm the individual or threaten loss of control. Except for the emphasis upon the conscious mind, this aspect of the theory is very much like our own. The next aspect contains an important difference, however; in the Freudian view, repression forces these unacceptable materials into the unconscious mind. The concept of an unconscious mind as a memory bank of all of the unacceptable thoughts and impulses that press for release is clearly not part of our understanding of how the human mind operates. Rather than distinguishing between conscious and unconscious parts of the mind, most psychologists now feel that it is simpler and more direct to take the view that certain thoughts and memories can be anxiety arousing when they are the focus of one's awareness or attention. In order to avoid the anxiety, we avoid thinking such thoughts. In other words, repression is the response of avoiding certain thoughts, a response which is reinforced by the relief of anxiety avoidance.

If repressed memories are not stored in an "unconscious mind," where are they? First, we can note that most psychologists nowadays do not talk of the mind, either conscious or unconscious, although psychologists of all persuasions recognize the importance of *memory*. Indeed, the psychology of learning, a field of major importance, is specifically concerned with how and what we remember. Second, while we all have a large store of memories, practically none of them are in our immediate awareness; rather, we must recall or remember them—retrieve them from storage. There are a number of factors that determine how readily we can remember something, including the strength of the impression originally made by the event, how long ago the event occurred, and the current presence of cues that were involved in the original event. Another factor that determines how easily a memory can be brought into awareness is the amount of anxiety attached to the memory. Thus, repression simply refers to the fact that anxiety-arousing memories will be brought into awareness less readily than neutral or positive memories, as individuals attempt to protect themselves from the discomfort of the anxiety. In other words, if a person has two thoughts that are of equal strength, and one of them is highly anxiety arousing while the other is neutral, the neutral thought will be more readily available.

The retrieval of some memories is made easier by certain procedures that are well known to mental health professionals—free association, hypnosis, imagery and other techniques. There are two possible explanations for the effectiveness of these procedures in improving recall. First, they often involve very deep and complete levels of bodily relaxation which block out interfering sounds, feelings, and thoughts, enabling the individual to focus attention fully on the recall task at hand. The other possible explanation is that in these procedures, the psychologist provides structure, feedback, and help in searching for the memory fragments. For example, in helping an individual to overcome chronic distress that originated from a traumatic experience, the therapist might ask for specific descriptions of a variety of details concerning the event, such as the physical surroundings, the other persons involved, the clothes worn, the time of day, and the weather. In this way a memory framework is developed that facilitates the recall of other more obscure memory fragments.

If repression serves as a safety device to guard the person from experiencing anxiety, why should it pose a problem for psychological adjustment? In the Freudian view, a certain amount of energy is required to maintain painful and anxiety-provoking materials in the unconscious mind. That is, repression produces a drain on the individual's store of psychic power, leaving fewer resources for dealing with other problems. Also, and equally important, the repressed material is still active in the unconscious, and it continually presses for release into consciousness. Since repression is never quite complete, some of the unconscious material slips out. Slips of the tongue ("I'm so sorry that you invited me to dinner"), jokes, random thoughts, and dreams are all regarded by psychoanalysts as involving unconscious material which has gotten by the part of the mind responsible for maintaining the repression. Again, because repression is imperfect an occasional person might resort to even more extreme measures to prevent the repressed material from coming into consciousness, such as the development of a **conversion reaction,** or **hysteria.** In the Freudian view, these disorders (such as the loss of vision or hearing without any physical reason) represent an extreme attempt by the individual to avoid seeing or hearing the unacceptable material which has broken through into consciousness due to a failure of repression. While a certain amount of repression is regarded as normal for all of us, the less repression we engage in the better adjusted we are, and in general it is not desirable to handle anxieties by repressing them.

A similarly negative view of repression is also held by most social-learning theorists, although for slightly different reasons. In our understanding of how repression is learned it is important to note that anxiety is attached not only to behavior, but to thoughts as well. The child who is angry at its mother is told not only that striking back is forbidden, but that "nice children" would not even *think* of hitting a parent. In other words, not only is the behavior labeled as "bad" but the thoughts or impulses which precede the behavior are also labeled as unacceptable. In such a fashion anxiety is attached to the thought as well as the deed.

Our inability even to think certain thoughts produces a set of gaps in our thinking. In the case of Ed, he was unable to think about disappointing his parents. In order to confront this topic, he would have had to examine his own resources and his willingness to use these resources to live up to his parents' expectations. Because he seriously doubted his capacity to live up to their very high implicit expectations, any thoughts about this area generated strong anxiety and were systematically repressed.

As we emphasized in our discussion of the socialization process in Chapter 3, anxiety plays a very important part in learning the taboos and values of the society in which we are reared, and it is considered important that this learning be full and complete. In this context it is worthwhile noting that children are often rather obvious in their behavioral intentions. The child eying a box of candy is usually thinking of taking a piece, and the child who is resentfully watching a younger sibling play with a new toy can be assumed to be thinking about appropriating the toy for personal use. When the parent observes these signs and tells the child that it should not be thinking such thoughts "if you know what's good for you," it is difficult for the child not to conclude that the parent is indeed capable of mind-reading, and that such thoughts should be banished. In other words, parents, because of their superior experience and understanding, can often infer the presence of a thought in the child and punish it directly. The process of generalization can also be involved, of course, in learning to attach anxiety to thoughts. Once the behavior is punished, the anxiety will also become attached to whatever thoughts are present at the time of punishment.

Displacement

If anxiety is attached to a particular thought, we must expect to have difficulty in identifying the source of the anxiety, since the process of repression, or motivated thought-avoidance, will often prevent us from making an adequate examination of the thought. As a consequence we will often *mislabel* the source of our anxiety, a process that Freud originally called **displacement.** In our example, Ed related his anxiety to his unwillingness to adopt the "materialistic" values of American society, or the "imperialistic warmongers" of Wall Street. As he is later to understand, the real cues triggering his anxiety are to be found in his parents' underlying expectations, and not in these more generalized social concerns. We expect that any time he moved close to thinking about his relationships with his parents and how troublesome this area was for him, he would immediately switch his thoughts about more global political issues. When the therapist noticed the consistency of this behavior, it was possible to point out to Ed his problem of displacement.

In Chapter 5 we discussed the displacement of aggression, referring to the release of aggressive behavior toward a scapegoat, a target less likely to retaliate than the frustrating agent. Displacement of anxiety has a rather similar meaning, and refers to the

process of misidentifying the source of anxiety as some object, person, or situation that is less threatening than the correct source. Freud's case of "Little Hans," a boy with many fears, is a very famous but rather complex example of displacement. Freud concluded that Hans's fear that a horse would bite him represented a displacement of intense fear that his father would harm him physically. To Hans, the fear of horses was an acceptable fear, and one that could be tolerated, while the thought of being harmed by his father was so intolerable that it had to be repressed. The important point to remember about displacement is that it refers to misidentification of the source of anxiety, due to the strong anxiety that would be aroused if the source were correctly perceived and labeled.

It has always been regarded as very important to be able to correctly perceive the source of one's anxiety, for only when we have identified the source can we embark on a process of anxiety reduction. In treatment by psychoanalysis, this problem is approached by attempting to identify the original or early learning conditions for the anxiety—that is, the early and threatening experiences of the childhood socialization process. A task of this magnitude demands very high motivation, good verbal skills, and a great deal of time, so that the treatment of an adjustment problem by psycho-analytic psychotherapy is normally a major undertaking. Psychologists nowadays believe that it is not always necessary to know the original learning conditions of an anxiety in order to eliminate it, but that it is usually sufficient to be able to identify current situations in which the anxiety is aroused.

In displacement, what determines the choice of the particular object or situation that is misidentified as the source of the anxiety? According to psychoanalytic theory, the

Other strong feelings besides anxiety can also be displaced. This little boy harbors intense feelings of rage toward his newly arrived baby brother, and is handling them in an acceptable manner by displacing them onto a stuffed animal.

displaced source usually bears some symbolic relationship to the true source, so that anxiety about dirt might represent anxiety about feces, and tunnels might represent the female genitalia. It is useful to regard displacement as a special case of *generalization*, a concept that we introduced in Chapter 2. In the present context, generalization refers to the fact that the symbolic or generalized cue for anxiety has certain elements in common with the original cue, and it is these common elements that permit the individual to "recognize" the generalized cue as an anxiety source. It should be emphasized, however, that many persons with adjustment problems involving anxiety do not identify any source at all for their anxiety, even a displaced or generalized one.

Repression refers to the avoidance of certain thoughts because they are anxiety arousing. Avoidance of certain thoughts can often make people appear rather stupid, when it might prevent them from understanding things that are rather obvious to others. For instance, a young female patient complained bitterly about being the frequent object of seduction attempts by different men. These complaints were initially surprising to the therapist, since her overt behavior would have been regarded as sexually provocative by just about any objective observer. She dressed carefully and modishly in clothing that accentuated her ample breasts, and she often left open the top buttons on her blouse. Her nonverbal behavior was quite provocative: she frequently stretched herself, thrusting out her breasts, and in conversation she would stand much closer to the male listener than was necessary. In extended discussions, however, it became clear that she had been taught from an early age that "nice girls" are not interested in sex, and all her sexual thoughts and feelings were obviously repressed. She had also been taught to be very fussy about her appearance and dress. As a result of this combination of teachings, she was quite unable to see that her own behavior was a basic element in eliciting the sexual interest of men. As might be expected, this behavior caused a variety of difficulties for her, since most of her male acquaintances assumed that she was fully aware of her impact and willing to deal with the consequences. As a result of psychotherapy, in which she received feedback about her effect on others and a consequent lessening of the repression, she was able to modify her behavior in ways that reduced the frequency of sexual overtures by men and enabled her to deal with them in a more effective manner.

Unconscious Behavior

Many observers, especially those with a psychoanalytic orientation, would conclude that this patient had an "unconscious" desire or need to seduce men. Before we continue our analysis of the process of repression, let us see whether this kind of conclusion is a useful one, and whether it leads to an improved understanding of the patient's behavior. We have already said that we do not consider it useful to speak of an unconscious mind, where such a desire might lurk. What, then, can be meant by **unconscious behavior?**

Let us answer this question by examining yet another example. A young boy must pass a particular house on his way to and from school. In this house lives a large, ferocious dog which spends most of its time in the yard. When the boy passes the yard, the dog follows him, growling and lunging at the fence which separates it from the boy. The boy, in sharp contrast to his usual leisurely pace, runs past and sometimes crosses the street to walk on the other side. At times he even takes an alternative, longer path to his home. However, when we ask the boy whether there is any special reason that might account for his behavior in the area of this house, he steadfastly denies it.

There are at least two straightforward explanations that could account for the boy's statement. First, the boy could be perfectly well aware that he is afraid of the dog, but unwilling to admit this fear either because he is ashamed of it or is fearful of how we might react to his admission. The extent to which any person is deliberately lying in such a situation is often very difficult to determine, and can only be guessed at. A second and equally likely alternative would be that the boy has repressed the thoughts associated with his behavior, and has not labeled it as "fearful," most probably because admitting to being frightened is often punished with ridicule. Thus, while other observers would not hesitate to identify the boy's pattern of behavior as involving fear, he himself might not identify it in that way.

The conclusion to be drawn from these examples is that behavior is usually called unconscious when the reasons given for it by the individual involved do not agree with those given by other observers. Thus, in the example just described of the female patient, she had not identified her own behavior as seductive, but most observers had labeled her behavior seductive.

How does one decide when other people's labeling of their own behavior is incorrect or inadequate? Obviously, such interpretations should be made only by trained professionals, and should always be advanced rather tentatively. In most cases, they should be regarded simply as alternative ways of explaining the behavior that may or may not enhance our understanding of it. There is rarely a single correct way of understanding the complexity of a person's actions; rather, there are usually a variety of possible explanations for a given aspect of behavior and the factors which underly it, and some of these explanations are more likely to enable us to alter the behavior than others. From a practical standpoint, the usefulness of different ways of explaining an individual's problem behavior depends on the extent to which they lead to meaningful differences in the behaving person—such as changes in anxiety—and not whether one interpretation is more "accurate" than another. The point to remember is that unconscious behavior is best regarded as behavior which is understood differently by the individual involved and by others who observe the behavior in situations when this difference has important negative consequences for the individual.

What Is Repressed?

There appear to be at least three ways in which repression can affect behavior. First, anxiety can lead to a failure to provide adequate labels for one's thoughts or behaviors. In our last two examples of repression, the behavior was present but not identified. The young woman behaved provocatively, and the boy avoided the dog, even though neither could identify the behaviors as such. Second, repression can involve the actual inhibition of the behavior itself. The clearest example of this kind of repression can be seen in sexual behavior in males, whose typical response to sexually arousing materials is penile erection. However, if the male is made strongly anxious, then the erection will disappear. The attachment of strong anxiety to what are ordinarily sexually arousing materials can thus lead to an inhibition of the usual sexual response. As we will point out in Chapter 8, the problem of impotence, describing men who are not able to maintain an erection that is adequate for successful intercourse, is usually a result of this kind of repression.

The third kind of repression involves the inhibition of mediational responses that ordinarily lead to the behavior. It is as though the anxiety-arousing cues did not exist at all. For example, if we recognize that a person is insulting us, and in addition, that it appears to be deliberate, then we are faced with the challenge of having to deal directly with this threat. However, if we do not identify the behavior of the other person as deliberately aggressive, then we do not have to consider what our response must be. Thus, we are protected from experiencing any anxiety that might be associated with the receipt or performance of aggression, or with thoughts about it.

There is an important difference between the first kind of repression and the other two kinds. In the second and third kinds, the drive appears to be weakened by the repression and the behavior is inhibited. Such people are likely to be seen as tense and inhibited, and are often described as shy and lacking in social awareness. In the first kind of repression, the drive and the behavior are fully developed, although they are unidentified and unlabeled. Such people are likely to be seen as active, impulsive individuals with little or no understanding of their social impact on others. Yet in all three types of repression, the same basic mechanism is involved—the inhibition of thinking by anxiety.

The Research Evidence for Repression

A considerable amount of research has been conducted in an attempt to provide scientific demonstrations of the phenomenon that Freud called repression. In early studies conducted some forty years ago, researchers explored differences in the recall of pleasant and unpleasant experiences, with the expectation that memory would be poorer for unpleasant experiences. Such studies are inadequate as proof of repression, however, since mere unpleasantness is not the same as the strong anxiety arousal that is said to be involved in repression. Also, it is extremely difficult to control the exact nature and strength of the subjects' pleasant and unpleasant experiences, so that it is not possible to know for certain whether a subject's superior recall of pleasant experiences might not be due simply to greater exposure to pleasant experiences.

More recently, there have been a number of careful studies (D'Zurilla, 1965; Zeller, 1950a, 1950b) that have attempted to create and study repression in a structured laboratory setting. In a typical study, two groups of subjects would be equated on a standardized memory task, and then one group would be exposed to an anxiety-arousing situation. They would be told, for example, that they had performed poorly on some task or that they had shown some "homosexual signs." These studies usually found that the threatened group did indeed recall less well than the control group, but once again (aside from the ethical problems raised in treating subjects in such a manner), it is questionable whether such laboratory situations are basically analogous to those considered by Freud to be responsible for repression. Also, it is quite possible that the results could have come about through the threat interfering directly with learning.

Some evidence bearing on the phenomenon of repression is found in the careful clinical studies of combat neuroses reported by Grinker and Spiegel (1945), who studied men with amnesia for their combat experiences. Since highly anxious experiences could generally be recalled by the men after their anxiety had been reduced through the use of hypnosis or sodium pentathol, it was clear that the memory loss was not due to an organic cause such as an injury to the brain.

In a controlled laboratory experiment, Levitt et al. (1961) aroused strong anxiety in a group of normal subjects through hypnosis. These subjects were also told, as part of the post-hypnotic suggestion, that they would not be able to recall participating in the experiment. They were later asked to participate in a second study which was similar to the first. Although the subjects were not able to recall the first experiment, a variety of psychophysiological measures obtained at the beginning of the second experiment clearly showed a high level of anxiety. These anxiety indicators were not present in a control group of subjects who did not participate in the first experiment. Thus it was clearly demonstrated that conscious awareness of the anxiety-arousing event—the original experiment—was not necessary in order for it to continue arousing anxiety.

What, then, can we conclude about the evidence for repression? Let us be clear in distinguishing Freud's use of the term repression, referring to the memories of intensely traumatic childhood experiences that have been forced into unconsciousness, from the social-learning use of this term, referring to the effects of strong emotions, particularly anxiety, in inhibiting the recall of memories. It is probably correct to say that Freud's original notion has never been experimentally studied, as it would seem to be too complex ever to be approached scientifically. The research that has claimed to study it has failed to include critical factors; for example, it has usually had nothing to do with traumatic childhood experiences.

There is, however, satisfactory research evidence to support the reality of the social-learning definition of repression, referring to any failure of memory or awareness that is motivated by the avoidance of anxiety. Basically this means that people have the ability to avoid anxiety-arousing thoughts in an automatic and unthinking fashion, just as we automatically and unthinkingly avoid the hot radiator, the sharp blade of a knife, or the edge of a cliff. Thoughts, memories, and images that arouse other strong negative emotions are also avoided automatically, and their avoidance is reinforcing—and therefore is learned—because it eliminates the unpleasant emotion. On the other hand, thoughts that arouse positive emotions and enhance our sense of self-worth will be easy to recall, because their presence constitutes a pleasant state of affairs.

This activity stimulates thoughts of danger and injury in many of us, arousing fear and avoidance. People who respond enthusiastically to its excitement have learned to systematically repress these anxiety-arousing thoughts, enabling them to experience fully the exhilaration and the challenge.

THE MECHANISMS OF DISGUISE

We have described the way anxiety can inhibit our awareness of our thoughts and even awareness of our own overt behavior. Yet we live in a culture which assumes that humans are rational and expects adults to understand what they do and why they do it. In other words, we are expected to label our own actions accurately and to explain to others what underlies these actions. Everybody has been asked on many occasions, "Why did you do *that?*" and our answer is expected to demonstrate that we have behaved in a reasonable fashion and on the basis of acceptable motives, needs, or thoughts. Since a considerable amount of our behavior is triggered by thoughts, needs, and motives that we are not able to identify precisely because they are not acceptable, either to ourselves or others, such questions pose quite a dilemma. To deal with them, all of us have developed a variety of ways of responding which disguise both our behavior and the motives or thoughts underlying it. These disguises are what Freud called *defense mechanisms,* or learned cognitive mechanisms of protecting ourselves against anxiety and conflict.

It should be emphasized that these disguises are taught to us specifically, although not deliberately, as part of the socialization process. If a little boy hits his sister in a fit of anger, and when asked why, claims that he hates her, he will be severely punished for the hitting and also for the explanation. "Nice children don't hate their brothers and sisters, and if you ever hit her again, you'll wish you were dead!" Such punishment is scarcely likely to lead to understanding and acceptance of one's angry feelings. It is far better from the child's point of view to insist that he never hit her, or that she hit him first, or that it was an accident. In such a fashion each of us learns to disguise many of our thoughts and motives, if not the actual behavior, initially hiding it from others and ultimately from ourselves.

One of America's leading child psychologists, the late Haim Ginott, has offered an alternative strategy for parents under these circumstances. Ginott recommended that, instead of punishing the thoughts, parents should help the child to acknowledge the impulse but inhibit the behavior. Thus, a parent might say, "I know you're very angry with me, but we don't hit each other in this house."

Let us stress that the disguising of thoughts and motives is present in everyone's behavior, and is a *normal* consequence of how we have been socialized. These are necessary and important ways of coping with the demands of everyday living and, when used in moderation, they enable us to enhance the satisfaction that we get out of life. However, when these mechanisms are so overused that the person's self-awareness is grossly different from the view held by others, then they must be regarded as part of a pattern of psychological maladjustment. It should be stressed that there is no single correct way to classify the mechanisms of disguise, but that the traditional categories such as rationalization and projection were developed by psychoanalysts in the hope of isolating mental disorders in a parallel sense to physical disorders. For convenience we continue to use the same labels. It should be clear that identifying the use of a particular mechanism does nothing to explain the behavior involved. What is needed for an adequate explanation is a complete account of the situation and of the thoughts and behaviors that are being disguised. Table 6-1 presents hypothetical examples of some of the mechanisms of disguise that will be discussed in the following pages.

Table 6-1
Quotations from a Hypothetical Adolescent Girl Illustrating
Various Defenses to Avoid the Recognition of Sexual Needs

Defense	Illustration
Denial	"I have no sexual desires of any kind."
Rationalization	"I spend a lot of time with Jack simply because we happen to be taking the same courses."
Projection: Similar	"I'm appalled at the degraded morality of practically all the students here except me."
Projection: Complementary	"Although they never mention it, all the guys in this building are obsessed with trying to get me into bed."
Reaction Formation	"There's a strong need for nuns these days, and I'm thinking seriously about it."
Intellectualization	"The scientific study of sex sounds like a really fascinating subject."
Fantasy	"I daydream a lot about sex."

Rationalization

Rationalization refers to giving convenient "logical" reasons for our actions, and is probably the most commonly used defensive procedure. Since most of us want our actions to appear reasonable and to be based upon acceptable thoughts and motives, we tend to respond to questions about our behavior in a manner that will give that impression to both ourselves and others. Even as adults we are systematically reinforced for "rational" analyses of our actions, while vague statements of our motives, "just because," or answers that indicate that our motives are socially unacceptable, tend to be punished.

Thus, when confronted with the need to explain ourselves, we often search for acceptable reasons rather than the "real" reasons. Rationalization is said to occur if the reasons that we offer are actually involved, but give a misleading or incomplete impression. In other words, a rationalization does not include the socially unacceptable aspects that we are attempting to hide from others and from ourselves. For example, when we are late for an appointment that we did not really wish to keep, we might acknowledge that our alarm failed to go off (but not that we failed to set it) or that the traffic was unusually heavy (although it is always heavy at that time of day). The unpalatable alternative would be the admission that we simply did not want to keep the appointment but that we could not accept this cowardice in ourselves.

An interesting cultural example of rationalization is found when we ask people to explain why it is "bad luck" to walk under ladders. The usual answer is that the ladder might fall on you or that something might drop down from the ladder, both of which are certainly possible, but scarcely suggest bad luck. This superstition arose in the Middle Ages, when it was believed that walking under a ladder disturbed the Holy Trinity, which was represented by the triangle formed by the wall, the ground, and the ladder, and that the person's soul could be trapped by the devil at that moment. Although the original rationale for this belief is no longer taken seriously, the behavior persists, and we try to account for our superstitious behavior by offering a reason that seems plausible.

Another example of rationalization that demonstrates the lack of awareness often involved is found in a report by Hilgard (1965), who hypnotized a subject and gave the post-hypnotic suggestion that, when the hypnotist took out his handkerchief, the subject would open the window. Further, the subject was told that he would not be able to recall the hynotist's instructions. Shortly after the subject awoke from his trance, the hypnotist took out his handkerchief and the subject did indeed open the window. When the subject was asked to explain his behavior, he indicated that he had found the room stuffy. It should be noted that the "correct" reason for the subject's behavior was that he was following the hypnotist's suggestion, but that that reason was not easily recalled. Thus, the subject used a plausible but incomplete answer to justify his behavior, and was thereby able to demonstrate that he was a rational, reasonable person.

We all similarly attempt to justify our behavior by attributing logical and acceptable, if not admirable, motives to our actions. We explain that our actions are *necessary* (I did not want to be chosen as president of the organization but there was nobody else available; or, I really needed the new car because our old one would have required both a mechanical overhaul and new tires); we blame *circumstances* (there just wasn't enough time to complete the job; or, I didn't have the right tools); we blame *others* (we would have been on time but my husband is always so slow; or, I didn't start it, he did); and we try to *justify* our actions (everybody cheats in that course and I'd be a sucker not to); all in an effort to provide our actions with an acceptable veneer.

We also attempt to cushion the blow of our failures and frustrations with a similar set of cognitive reinterpretations. The most common of these is the *sour grapes* rationalization, labeled from Aesop's fable of the fox who, because it was unable to reach the grapes that it wanted, decided that they were sour anyway. The converse is the *sweet lemon* rationalization—that whatever we do have is worthwhile. This would apply, for example, to the person who claims to be glad to have been elected vice-president rather than president, because there is just as much glory but less work.

Rationalizations are complex attempts to protect ourselves by managing our "cognitive environment," and since they contain elements that are plausible and partially true, they are often difficult to detect. In the case of Ed, his efforts to account for his problem in terms of his dissatisfaction with contemporary American society can also be seen as a rationalization. While there certainly are legitimate reasons for dissatisfaction with some aspects of American society, Ed was not able to see how his preoccupation with these matters protected him from recognizing his conflicts with his parents.

We should be willing to recognize that rationalization is probably involved wherever we are not able to see inconsistencies in ourselves that others have pointed out, or if we become overly emotional or defensive when our motives are questioned or when alternative explanations are suggested to explain our behavior. The price of rationalization is self-deception and an inability to accept elements of ourselves that are really very much a part of us, at least as others see us.

Projection

One form of rationalization involves blaming others for our own unacceptable behavior. **Projection** is a term that refers to an extreme form of this tendency, in which we attempt to protect ourselves from an awareness of our own undesirable thoughts or motives by finding them in others, often to an exaggerated degree. Thus, an accountant's excessive concern over the honesty of the accounts which are being audited might well be protection against awareness of personal dishonest thoughts.

Projection seems to be found more readily among persons who have undergone a strict moral upbringing. The rigid moral code in which they have been socialized makes it highly threatening for them to recognize thoughts or needs in themselves that deviate from this code. At the same time, their rigid social-learning experiences have also made them extremely sensitive to any deviations from morality, and in order to avoid attending to the threatening evidence for their own fallibility, they concentrate this sensitivity on others. Thus, they are certain that they can find evidence of impure, improper, sinful, or destructive thoughts and motives in others, while they themselves are blameless. The sexually "pure" woman complains that she is constantly the target of improper advances, while the man with unrecognized homosexual feelings may claim that he is surrounded by men who are trying to seduce him. Such behavior is best understood as an effort that is made by these persons to avoid the recognition of needs and thoughts they consider unacceptable.

The above illustrations involve two different kinds of projection; in one, the characteristics observed in others are the same as those that are providing the threat, while in the other, the actions of other people are perceived as forcing us into an undesirable act. In the first, **similar projection,** others are dishonest or homosexual, while in **complementary projection,** others are trying to involve us in their illegitimate schemes or trying to seduce us by their homosexual behavior. In a recent study, Halpern (1977) was able to demonstrate clearly that similar projection occurred when persons with high sexual anxiety were exposed to sexually explicit materials. The higher their sexual anxiety, the more they denied being sexually aroused but the more they perceived and unfavorably rated other persons as being lustful. This and other experimental evidence adds support to the concept of projection as a widely noted and clinically common phenomenon.

Reaction Formation

In **reaction formation,** the individual guards against unacceptable thoughts and motives by developing strong conscious attitudes and behaviors that are their direct opposite. Since the unacceptable need creates an approach-avoidance conflict situation for the individual, the strengthening of the avoidance tendency by an overt and opposite act is one way of resolving the conflict. Thus, parents who resent their newborn infant may become overly protective and concerned about the child's welfare, in an effort to disguise their unacceptable negative feelings toward the child. A variety of other examples can be given: the small boy who whistles while passing the graveyard, the old maid who peers under her bed, and the exaggerated joking and laughing among medical students as they prepare for their first experience in dissecting a human corpse. In such cases, reaction formation helps prevent the individual from acknowledging unacceptable feelings by generating thoughts, feelings, and situations that are the opposite.

Of some serious concern to society is the fact that reaction formation is often present in those individuals who initiate crusades to defend public morality by attacking pornography, drugs, sexual misconduct, and other "vices." The crusaders are often fascinated by their material, and spend much of their time studying it, but always in the interest of "public morality." At the same time, their obsessive fight protects the crusaders from becoming aware of their own fascination.

We do not mean to imply that the motives of people interested in reform can never be taken at face value; not all reformers are motivated by factors of which they are unaware, and there are certainly many problems in our society that need the attention of concerned citizens. What we are suggesting is that an overconcern, especially with sexual and aggressive behavior in others (the areas in which most of us have received our strictest socialization) is likely to involve more than mere reform. Trevor-Roper (1969) has presented a fascinating account of the witch-hunts during the Middle Ages, and he clearly demonstrates that most of the judges and prosecutors in these cases were extremely "repressed" individuals who, through their program of persecution, were able to satisfy their forbidden needs without contradicting their own self-concepts, and even gained public support and praise for their behavior.

Some Comments on the Repressive Defenses

We began our discussion of the management of anxiety with an analysis of repression—the learned avoidance of anxiety-arousing thoughts—and we then discussed three common ways of maintaining or facilitating repression: rationalization, projection, and reaction formation. These three mechanisms involve some restructuring of the way individuals perceive a situation, which serves to protect them from having to deal with the anxiety-arousing material. The fact that these mechanisms result in the avoidance or reduction of anxiety explains why they are so commonly used by all of us in our daily lives. If there are no undesirable long-term consequences of its use, a defense is regarded as "successful" or "adaptive"; if it does have significant undesirable future consequences, it is said to have failed. But because we tend to respond to the immediate rather than the long-range consequences of an action, many of us continue to employ unadaptive defenses despite their negative effects.

Compensations and Substitutions

There are a number of other behavioral patterns that are also regarded as defenses, in that they are attempts by a person to protect self-esteem, but are not as directly related to repression as are rationalization, projection, and reaction formation. These are common responses to failure and frustration, or the anticipation of failure or frustration, and they tend to involve a much more obvious pattern of behavioral change than the first three defense mechanisms. Rather than simple thought-avoidance or cognitive-rearrangement of the individual's view of the world, these behavioral patterns frequently involve basic changes in the person's overt responses.

As we noted in Chapter 5, frustration is a common experience for all of us, since we are frequently unable to reach the goals that we desire. One obvious type of response to frustration would be to find alternative ways of reaching the goal or to change to a highly similar goal. Consider the boy who learns that he is poorly coordinated and will not excel at athletics, one of his desired goals. He might instead use his social skills and interpersonal maturity to become a student leader. It is not clear whether he has changed his basic goal, or whether he has simply found another way to satisfy it, and it is impossible to determine whether his basic goal was athletic achievement or recognition by other people. In any event, if he receives satisfaction from his substitute goal and has no sense of regret for what might have been, we can conclude that his behavior was a useful way of dealing with frustration and avoiding damage to his sense of self-esteem.

In **compensation,** or **substitution,** then, the behavior involved leads to satisfactions that are close to those that were frustrated, and the original need is at least satisfied. Because these behaviors serve to protect the individual from failure or lowered self-esteem, and thereby from anxiety, they can be regarded as defense mechanisms. Rationalization may at times be involved, as when students point out that it is really better to be involved in student politics than athletics, because it will help them get into law school, or that they were never really interested in athletics anyway. The use of rationalization probably indicates that the substitute goal is still an ambivalent one, and this amount of self-deceit suggests that the mechanism of compensation is not completely effective in the situation.

Overcompensation. Overcompensation is a special form of compensation in which the individual attempts to cope with what is seen as a weakness by excelling in that very behavior. The weakness serves as an impetus to concentrated effort, and in the case of overcompensation, to superior performance. A common example of overcompensation is the physically weak boy who is determined to excel in sports and involves himself in an intense program of exercise and muscle building. Alfred Adler, one of Freud's colleagues, utilized overcompensation as one of the central concepts in his system after he broke away from Freud to develop his own theories. According to Adler, each of us has some kind of *organ inferiority,* and we spend most of our lives trying to overcompensate for our particular inferiority. In this theory, such men as Napoleon, Hitler, and Stalin were overcompensating for their sense of powerlessness which resulted from their short stature. More common clinical examples of overcompensation involve the development of bullying behavior on the part of weak or frail children, or excessive amounts of time spent in studying by some students with limited intellectual capabilities. While overcompensation might be seen as an admirable attempt to overcome one's limitations, in all too many cases the goal is still not obtained and serious psychological problems then arise. Most of the anecdotal reports of overcompensation tend to glorify the successes rather than recount the difficulties of those who tried, tried again—and failed.

Sublimation. When socially unacceptable impulses are transformed into socially acceptable behavior, **sublimation** is said to have occurred. This concept is based in classical Freudian theory and refers to one of the ways in which repressed impulses come into consciousness in disguised form. For example, strong repressed hostility and anger could be sublimated by the choice of dentistry or boxing as a career, since these professions permit the hurting of others without negative sanctions. Similarly, persons fixated at the anal stage of psychosexual development could gratify their unconscious anal impulses by becoming artists and smearing paint rather than feces.

It is not clear how useful the concept of sublimation is in the explanation of human behavior. As we noted earlier, it is difficult to determine what fundamental needs are operating in any particular situation. In the case of the classical notion of sublimation, the way in which infantile needs may become modified and relevant to adult life is extremely difficult to understand.

Remote compensation. Since we are often still frustrated, despite our best efforts, we sometimes try to develop a sense of satisfaction through the successes of others that we count as our own. This process is known as **remote compensation,** and is most obvious in the satisfaction sought by parents through the accomplishments and activities of their children. Many parents, particularly those with a strong sense of frustration in a particular area, often urge their children to enter that area, usually without any awareness that they are attempting to make up for their own failure or lack of

opportunity. Thus, the father who was never as good a football player as he wanted to be might push his son into football with excessive zeal, and take an inordinate amount of pride in his son's accomplishments; or, more seriously from the son's point of view, push him in ways that are contrary to his particular talents and interests.

Another frequent kind of remote compensation is through identification with the achievement of another person or group, although in this case not a child. We take pride in the success of our college or hometown teams, and we experience a sense of satisfaction when our company's bowling team wins the championship even though we ourselves are not members. Clearly, this is one of the important aspects of a sense of membership in organizations and groups. It is interesting to note the work of Cialdini and his colleagues (1976), who clearly demonstrated that undergraduates more often wore apparel with University emblems on the Monday following a victory for the school football team than after a defeat. In addition, students used the pronoun "we" more often when describing a victory than a defeat of their school's football team.

A problem arises for one's psychological adjustment when such successes must substitute for actual successes in one's own life. In a case known to the authors, a teenage boy was brought to the clinic by his parents who were concerned because he spent almost all his waking hours pursuing his interest in the hometown baseball team. He listened to all the games, collected pictures and articles about the team, and compiled his own statistics, to the exclusion of any other activity except those necessary for life. When the team lost a game, he would become morose and would withdraw from contact with other people, and when they won, he would be as elated as though he had been personally responsible for their success. Such a degree of remote compensation would usually require professional attention.

Fantasy

Yet another way to attain some of the satisfactions denied us is through **fantasy,** the imaginary representation of desired events. Since fantasy is easy to produce and requires little effort, we should not be surprised to find that it is one of the most frequently used defense mechanisms. The play activities that occupy a great deal of the free time of children during the elementary school years are based largely upon fantasy, and it is obvious that much of this fantasy involves the production of satisfactions unobtainable by any other means. Thus, "playing house" and playing with soldiers permits children an opportunity for satisfying some of their needs for doing what adults do. As children grow older, fantasy is negatively sanctioned as immature and "childish." By this time, however, fantasy is well learned as a way of gaining satisfactions and avoiding anxieties, and we simply learn not to share or discuss our fantasies.

Daydreaming is very common, in adults as well as children, and its psychological importance is probably underestimated by most current researchers. Two common kinds of daydream are the "conquering hero" and the "suffering martyr," both of which involve need satisfaction, although not of exactly the same kind. In the conquering hero daydream, the individuals imagine themselves to be persons of power and renown, such as an athletic star, government leader, or the richest person in the world, and in this way they obtain satisfactions that are not available in their real lives. James Thurber, the famous American satirist, illustrated this theme in *The Secret Life of Walter Mitty,* in which he described a meek, ineffectual man who used his fantasies to accomplish what he was unable to do in the real world.

In the suffering martyr daydream the individual suffers great injury, hurt, and neglect. When others recognize what has happened, they deeply regret that they have not given enough understanding, love, or care. The child who imagines running away from home and being killed while crossing the road receives satisfaction not from the thought of death, but from the hurt and despair that the parents will experience when they learn of the child's death. The suffering martyr daydream provides a good example of behaviors which seem at first glance to be anxiety arousing, but which, upon more careful analysis, turn out to be positively reinforcing.

It is also possible to "borrow" fantasy—from films, television, and books. When the hero of the television program conquers obstacles and wins a just reward, we too experience a sense of satisfaction for the accomplishment. Borrowed fantasy is similar to identification and to remote compensation, and this similarity illustrates the ambiguities that occur when one attempts to catalogue the various defense mechanisms. However, the basic point is that the fantasy involved in various forms of entertainment can provide some persons with a source of satisfaction that is not otherwise available to them.

When does the use of fantasy create adjustment problems? Involvement in fantasy is time consuming and removes the person from the necessity of involvement in the

When a person is confronted with an insoluble conflict, one solution is to withdraw completely from the situation.

pursuit of real-life satisfactions. Thus, it is when the person relies on fantasy for most satisfactions, and prefers to seek out fantasy satisfactions rather than real-life ones, that adjustment problems may be present. Obviously, in many cases it is difficult to decide exactly when that point has been reached.

Need satisfaction occurs in night dreams as well as daydreams. Freud originally theorized that night dreams were one way in which repressed wishes, desires, and fantasies could find expression, and it is these early views that account for the importance psychoanalysts place on dream interpretation. Scientific research on night dreams provides strong evidence that dreaming is an important part of the sleep cycle. Research subjects who have been deprived of their dreams (by being awakened at every occurrence of the rapid eye movements that are usually associated with dreaming) become much more tense and irritable than control subjects who have been awakened the same number of times, but when they were not dreaming. Also, it has been shown that the control subjects tend to express feelings and impulses that are not expressed by subjects who have been dream deprived for several days (Cartwright, 1978).

It is easy to point out the nonadjustive implications of fantasy: it occupies time that could be spent in real accomplishments, it provides tension reduction without real accomplishment, and it sets unrealistic expectations that cannot be met in real life. However, psychologists are now beginning to note that there are also powerful adjustive implications for fantasy. Jones (1968), for example, has noted that fantasy plays an important role in creativity, and that to enhance creativity the use of fantasy should be encouraged in education processes. The extensive use of fantasy in desensitization, one form of behavioral psychotherapy (see Chapter 11), and in self-exploration exercises for personal growth (see Chapter 12) provide further examples of the powerful adjustive implications of the constructive use of fantasy.

Withdrawal

In discussing conflict in Chapter 5, we noted that whenever a person is confronted by an insoluble avoidance–avoidance conflict, one solution is to leave the situation altogether. This behavior, of handling conflict situations by leaving them altogether to avoid anxiety, can be identified with the defense mechanism of **withdrawal.** Withdrawal is often closely related to fantasy, since when we withdraw from problems, conflicts, or frustrations in real life, we frequently engage in fantasies about ways in which we could solve them. The combined use of withdrawal and fantasy is sometimes called **escapism,** especially when it involves a heavy use of borrowed fantasy. Escapism is more common than may be initially apparent, since the kind of shy retiring people who engage in it are often overlooked, and are not recognized as having the problems from which their withdrawal constitutes an escape.

There are a number of different ways in which withdrawal can occur. The most direct way is for the person to avoid entering those situations in which anxiety, conflict, or frustration would be involved. Some psychologists believe that schizophrenia, a severe form of psychological maladjustment which we will discuss in greater detail in the next chapter, is simply a state in which people have trained themselves to rely very heavily on withdrawal and fantasy as the major way of coping with anxieties. These behaviors eventually become so perfected that the schizophrenic is at times unable to differentiate between reality and fantasy.

Emotional isolation. Another form of withdrawal is **emotional isolation,** in which the individual is physically present in the situation but blocks any emotional reaction from occurring. Most of the time our overt actions and our emotions are parallel to each other. We are thwarted and we feel hurt; we are angry and we strike back; we feel affectionate and we reach out. However, we have all learned that in certain situations it is more appropriate to inhibit our emotional reactions. We are careful not to celebrate prematurely, we sometimes have difficulty in reacting to "good fortune," and many people find it difficult to react immediately to the news of the death of a loved one. Emotional isolation of this nature can be adaptive, as it permits us to attend to the tasks at hand without interference from our emotional reactions.

Emotional isolation can take very extreme forms, however, as when an individual is apathetic or indifferent and *never* makes an emotional reaction to the situation. Apathy can result from prolonged, intense frustration, and has been found in long-term prisoners, concentration camp victims, and persons who have been unemployed for long periods of time. It can also be present in persons who have been systematically taught to ignore their feelings and the thoughts associated with them. Emotionally isolated individuals have thus withdrawn psychologically from the situation, although they might still be physically present and fulfilling a particular role. We have previously discussed in Chapter 3 the condition of *learned helplessness*, in which individuals learn that none of their efforts are effective in eliciting any response from the environment, leading to low levels of activity and interference with new learning. Clearly, emotional isolation is one of the important elements of learned helplessness (Seligman, 1975).

Emotional isolation of the kind described above is also called **dissociation,** because the feelings are dissociated or split off from the behaviors. Most people would find it impossible to overlook their feelings, and dissociation often involves a number of other behaviors that facilitate the process. One of these is compulsive behavior or ritualized behaviors that engage the person's attention and thus inhibit awareness of the emotion. Such people feel compelled to count all the tiles or window panes in the room, or touch all of their buttons. Since compulsive behaviors serve to divert attention from anxiety or other negative emotions, and to inhibit one's awareness of them, these behaviors are strongly reinforcing. The strength of the reinforcement can be seen when we attempt to interfere with the person's compulsive behaviors, and witness both an emotional reaction to the interference and the lengths to which the person will go to make certain that the behaviors can continue to be performed.

Intellectualization. This refers to excessive theorizing, or a kind of excessive rationalization, and is similar to emotional isolation. To avoid the emotional reactions that would be expected in a particular situation, the person concentrates on finding reasons to explain or justify what has happened. Rather than experience directly the sense of loss that follows the death of a loved one, for example, intellectualization would lead us to point out how little suffering had been involved, or how difficult it would have been for the person to have lived with the illness, or that one should not quarrel with the "will of God." By rehearsing these explanations, both to oneself and with others, the person can use intellectualization to minimize the painful emotion of the situation.

As with the other mechanisms, intellectualization can be overused and become a way of life. For example, when asked how she feels about her husband, a woman might enter into a long discourse about the difficulties involved in defining love or might point out how very well matched they are. Such people often report that they can never "feel" anything, which should not surprise us, since they insist on looking at situations only from a logical viewpoint, and they tend to regard emotions, particularly any open display of emotions, as inappropriate and bothersome. Either they have never learned to attend to their emotional reactions, or they have been deliberately reinforced for not attending, and for being "cool" and "logical." Intellectualization is not simply an attempt to avoid unpleasant emotions, but rather can become a lifestyle in which all emotional arousal is avoided. Under prolonged stress, such persons at times develop psychologically based physical disorders, such as ulcers, headaches, and functional heart conditions.

Obviously, emotional isolation is occasionally necessary for all of us. There are times when circumstances require that we overlook our emotions and "carry on" regardless. But continued isolation, facilitated by the use of compulsions, intellectualization, or other defensive behaviors, does interfere with normal emotional development and prevents full participation in human relationships. We will return to this point in Chapter 9.

THE DEFENSE MECHANISMS AND ADJUSTMENT

We have seen that humans are capable of rational problem solving, but we have also seen that our defensive behaviors often get in the way of effective problem solving, because we deny or disguise both our actions and the circumstances underlying them. Thus, a basic problem caused by the use of defense mechanisms is that they prevent the full use of our decision-making and problem-solving capabilities. To put it more bluntly, the use of defense mechanisms often makes us look foolish. In the case of the seductive woman described above, her inability to recognize and understand her own behavior often led other people to conclude that she was rather stupid. Similarly, students who rationalize or deny poor academic performance may deceive themselves, but other people wonder why they persist in being so unrealistic.

Although we have emphasized the negative aspects of defensive behavior, there obviously are also some positive elements. If these behaviors were not so reinforcing for the individual (through the operation of anxiety reduction), they would not be so persistent. Kroeber (1963) has suggested that, in addition to anxiety avoidance, each of the defense mechanisms should be viewed in the context of its adaptive aspects. He has emphasized that each of these mechanisms has both a positive or *coping* aspect and a negative or *defensive* aspect, and that it is wise to determine in each situation which aspect is in use. A summary of Kroeber's scheme is set out in Table 6-2. He points out, for example, that impulse inhibition or denial involves both repression, the defensive total inhibition of a thought or feeling, and suppression or concentration, the setting aside of the thoughts or feelings until the proper time arises for their expression, thus freeing the individual to deal effectively with the task at hand. As another example, in regard to the mechanism that Kroeber has called "time reversal," the defensive form is regression, the reversion to inappropriate earlier age responses to protect oneself from having to accept an unwanted adult responsibility, while the coping form would be playfulness. Kroeber's scheme would permit a recognition of the creative use of fantasy as one of the coping aspects of time reversal, while still recognizing its potentially dangerous consequences through regression. Thus, according to Kroeber's analysis, the use of these mechanisms does not necessarily create poor adjustment; rather, a person's overall level of adjustment would depend on the degree to which the coping rather than the defensive aspects were used.

In sum, we have seen that what are commonly referred to as defense mechanisms are learned ways of handling anxiety, and that the primary motivation involved in acquiring these behaviors is anxiety reduction. Although it is usually anxiety that accounts for their persistence, the adaptive value of these behaviors must be measured by their long-term consequences. Those mechanisms that lead to socially desirable consequences are regarded as successful, while those that lead to socially undesirable consequences are considered to have failed.

Table 6-2
The Defensive and Coping Aspects of the Mechanisms

Mechanism	Defensive aspect	Coping aspect
Discrimination—The separation of ideas and feelings.	*Dissociation*—The separation of ideas and feelings that belong together.	*Objectivity*—The separation of ideas and feelings to achieve a necessary rational judgment.
Means-end symbolization—The analysis of experience, anticipation of outcomes, and consideration of alternative choices.	*Rationalization*—The use of apparently plausible explanations to conceal the underlying impulse.	*Logical analysis*—The analysis of the complex causal aspects of the situation.
Selective awareness—Differential focus of attention.	*Denial*—The refusal to face painful feelings or thoughts.	*Concentration*—The temporary setting aside of painful thoughts in order to accomplish a task.
Sensitivity—The understanding of others' unexpressed feelings.	*Projection*—The self-protective attribution of one's own unacceptable impulses to others.	*Empathy*—Putting oneself in another's place to understand how the other feels.
Time reversal—The recapturing of ideas and feelings from the past.	*Regression*—The use of age-inappropriate behavior to avoid taking an adult role.	*Playfulness*—The use of feelings and ideas from the past to add to the enjoyment of life.
Impulse modification—The changing of the goal or object of an impulse.	*Displacement*—The temporary use of an inappropriate target to help repress an unacceptable impulse.	*Substitution*—The use of alternative, socially acceptable ways of satisfying primitive impulses.
Impulse inhibition—The controlling of impulses to prevent expression.	*Repression*—The total inhibition of ideas and feelings.	*Suppression*—The temporary inhibition of impulses until an appropriate time and target are available.

Adapted from Kroeber (1963).

Occasionally a person engages directly in highly forbidden behavior. Called **acting-out,** or **externalization,** such behavior may occur when the person has only a limited repertoire of mechanisms to use, and when external circumstances provide strong cues, or when the person has strong internal cues through highly unusual and pathological thought processes. For instance, a man who has consistently repressed his hostility and anger may suddenly lash out in a series of destructive acts when he is highly frustrated, although the particular event that triggers the acting-out may appear rather insignificant to others. Typical examples are found in the frequent newspaper reports of apparently mild-mannered individuals who, for no obvious reason, murder a number of people or destroy large amounts of property. The term "acting-out" is usually reserved for the expression of behaviors that have serious negative consequences and that are in direct contrast to the person's usual way of behaving. Acting-out is usually taken as a sign that people's stable patterns of coping and defensive behavior have not adequately met their needs.

THE SELF-CONCEPT

We have indicated a number of times throughout this chapter that defense mechanisms are important to the individual in maintaining a sense of self-esteem or self-worth. Let us now examine the notion of the **self-concept** and its relationship to behavior.

People habitually observe and interpret their own behavior. Indeed, perhaps the most important things that we say to ourselves are our interpretations of our own

One by-product of the women's movement has been a reexamination of sex-role stereotypes. Many men now realize that the expression of tender emotions is an acceptable part of their self-concept and does not detract from their masculinity.

behaviors and the circumstances underlying them. This organized set of verbal self-signaling responses is called the *self-concept,* a term introduced by William James, one of the early fathers of American psychology.

As we develop an awareness of the world around us, so also do we develop an awareness of ourselves. We learn what is "I," "me," and "myself," both in a physical sense and in a psychological sense. We learn that we are tall or short, strong or weak, attractive or ugly, a success or a failure, by means of the multitude of experiences that make up our lives. We receive an enormous amount of information about ourselves, and as we develop we gradually synthesize it into the integrated and organized pattern which is the self-concept. Feedback from others about ourselves is the basic stuff from which the self-concept is formed.

One aspect of the self-concept is one's sex-role identity, the degree to which individuals regard themselves as masculine or feminine (Kagan, 1964, p. 144). Making this appraisal involves a continuing comparison by individuals of their own behavior with the sex-role standards or stereotypes of their culture. If a boy sees himself doing the things that boys typically do, he learns to regard himself as masculine. On the other hand, if he perceives a greater degree of similarity between his behavior and what girls usually do, he will come to see himself as more like a girl. Similarly, some girls may notice that the behavior they prefer does not match the traditional sex-role behavior expected of girls.

The role of sex-role self-concepts in psychological adjustment is highlighted by a study by Mussen (1962), who studied the adjustment of a group of highly masculine boys and a group of less masculine boys, both during their adolescence and again twenty years later. Although the highly masculine boys were more self-confident and felt more adequate than the less masculine boys during adolescence, the reverse was true when they were in their thirties. At that time, the men who had been more masculine as boys felt less certain of themselves and less adequate, a finding which suggests that the relationship between sex-role self-concept and psychological adjustment is a rather complex one, and that sex-role self-concepts have different meanings at different ages. Also, the concept of androgyny, as discussed in Chapter 3, may be

relevant here. It is possible that these less masculine boys may have been developing feminine psychological characteristics, which would lead to a more androgynous personality in adulthood.

Perhaps the most important aspect of our self-concept is our **self-esteem,** our personal judgment of our own worth. These two terms are sometimes used interchangeably, but most psychologists regard self-concept as the broader notion which includes self-esteem. Self-esteem is often reflected in statements to ourselves such as "I am a success" or "I am a failure," and these verbal mediational responses play an important part in determining future behaviors. These statements operate as expectations of what is to come, and they serve to set our level of aspiration for the future, much in the manner of a self-fulfilling prophecy. Thus, if we see ourselves as failures, then we will anticipate failure, and we are more likely to engage in behaviors that will lead to failure. To put it simply—nothing succeeds like the will to fail.

In an experimental test of the "will to fail" (Aronson and Carlsmith, 1962), undergraduates who expected to do poorly on an experimental task (that is, those who had an initially low self-concept) but who were told that they had performed well on the task, were found to have surreptitiously lowered their performance records. Subjects who had a high self-concept and expected to do well on the task, but were told that they had performed poorly, surreptitiously raised the record of their performance. On the other hand, subjects whose performance was reported to them as being in line with their expectations based on their self-concept made few changes in their records. Obviously, in most situations performance is heavily influenced by reality considerations such as skill and knowledge, but self-concept is also an important determinant.

It can readily be seen that high self-esteem individuals have had learning histories that have involved mostly positive rewards for their behavior, while low self-esteem individuals have had long histories of failure. We all attempt to arrange our lives to maintain and enhance our self-esteem, and involved in this process are the defense mechanisms we have been discussing in this chapter. Thus, the defense mechanisms serve not only to control our anxiety but also to maintain a positive personal judgment of our own worth.

THE DIRECT CONTROL OF ANXIETY

In this chapter we have studied the most common ways of managing anxiety, through the use of mediational or cognitive processes. There are two other ways that are much more direct: the use of drugs and the direct counterconditioning of autonomic responses. Neither of these two methods can be regarded as defense mechanisms, but since they both reduce anxiety, it is appropriate to discuss them here.

Drugs

From Chapter 4, we know that an important part of anxiety is its physiological aspects: rapid and shallow breathing, changes in heart rate, increases in stomach motility, increased perspiration, muscle tension, sleeplessness, and so on, all of which are extremely unpleasant for the person who is experiencing them.

It has been known for thousands of years that certain substances, or drugs, can have inhibiting effects upon these physiological changes. That is, some drugs counteract anxiety. Recognizing that there is also a wide variety of modern "tranquilizing" drugs that are prescribed on appropriate occasions by licensed physicians, let us review some of the drugs that are self-prescribed for anxiety reduction. The drug that is most widely used for this purpose at the present time is *alcohol,* which interferes with the functioning of the higher brain centers and thereby permits the drinker some relief from anxieties. *Barbiturates,* which are the primary ingredient of most prescription "sleeping pills," act in a similar manner. There are also *amphetamines,* the primary ingredient of most "pep pills," which produce a euphoric mood, increased alertness, and reduced fatigue. *Marijuana* appears to be somewhat like alcohol in its effects, producing in most people a mild euphoria, an increased sense of well-being, increased self-confidence, and, of course, decreased anxiety. Both alcohol and marijuana have a sedative effect, particularly when used in larger quantities. The so-called "hard drugs" such as *morphine* and *heroin* also lead to temporary anxiety reduction as one of their effects.

There are a number of other reasons for the nonmedical use of drugs; alcohol and marijuana, for example, are often integrated into complex patterns of social behavior. However, it is clear that the abuse of these substances generally stems from a desire to escape the discomfort of anxiety. The 1973 report of the National Commission on Marijuana and Drug Abuse has noted that the use of alcohol is "without question the most serious drug problem in the country today," and that the overuse of barbiturates is "America's hidden drug problem." The major drawback in using such drugs as a way of managing anxiety is that the solution is only temporary, and that the source of the anxiety remains after the effects of the drug wear off. In sum, it is important to recognize that drugs can be a potent, though temporary, way of inhibiting anxiety. We will return in Chapter 7 to an examination of the serious negative consequences of habitual drug use.

The Direct Conditioning of Autonomic Responses

Psychologists believed until recently that it was not possible to apply reinforcement conditioning procedures to responses of the autonomic nervous system, which constitute the physiological aspects of anxiety. This belief has been challenged by a number of research findings, many of them stimulated by the work of Neal E. Miller. In Miller's (1969) studies, it was suggested that laboratory animals could be trained to change their heart rate, blood pressure, and intestinal contractions by the proper application of reinforcement. In one study (Miller and Banuazzi, 1968) rats were reinforced for either increasing or decreasing their heart rate after a baseline had been established. A shaping procedure (see Chapter 2) was used, so that initially any small deviation in the desired direction led to a reinforcement; over time, larger and larger changes were required for the animal to receive the reward. Because heart rate can be decreased by slow breathing, the animals in this experiment were given curare, a drug that temporarily paralyzes the skeletal muscles that control breathing, and the animals were artificially respirated.

Although there is controversy surrounding some of Miller's original work (Miller and Dworkin, 1974), the utility of these findings for humans is now being actively explored in a number of research laboratories. Research in this area has come to be known as **biofeedback,** referring to the use of artificial feedback devices to monitor internal changes of which we ordinarily have little or no awareness. Research has shown, for example, that some persons can learn to achieve effective control of their blood pressure when they monitor it through constant feedback (Blanchard and Epstein, 1978). From these and other findings, we can conclude that it is likely that unintentional learning through the direct conditioning of our autonomic nervous system is at least one cause of problems such as high blood pressure, ulcers, impotence, and perhaps a variety of other maladies. Other possible applications of biofeedback in the treatment of human disorders are described in Chapter 7.

SUMMARY

1. This chapter has examined ways in which the individual responds to situations in which anxiety has played a major role in preventing full need satisfaction. Habitual ways of managing adjustment problems that involve anxiety are known as *defense mechanisms,* or self-protective thoughts and behaviors that usually involve some kind of self-deception. The simplest self-deception mechanism is *denial,* which can be distinguished from lying or malingering in that the individual who denies genuinely believes that his behavior involves no deception.

2. The basic concept underlying defense mechanisms is *repression,* a term used by Freud to refer to the process by which threatening needs and thoughts are "blocked" from consciousness. Repression can be better understood in terms of social-learning theory as based on the reinforcing effects of avoiding thoughts that are anxiety producing. The term *suppression* refers to the conscious and deliberate avoidance of thoughts, topics, and events that arouse anxiety. Repression, in contrast, occurs automatically, and the person is unaware or unconscious of the avoidance.

3. In the original Freudian explanation of repression, unacceptable materials were said to be somehow forced into the unconscious mind. Psychologists now speak instead of memory, and consider that repression refers to the fact that anxiety-arousing memories are brought into awareness less readily than neutral or positive memories. In the Freudian view, repression poses a problem because psychic energy is constantly required to maintain the repression; in the social-learning view, the problem is that the repressed thoughts are not available to be dealt with through conscious, logical thought processes.

4. *Displacement* refers to the mislabeling of the true source of anxiety, by selecting a stimulus that has some similarity to the true source, or one that is not the only source of anxiety. The individual thus avoids the more intense anxiety that would be aroused if the true source were acknowledged. Displacement is a special case of *generalization,* a concept discussed in Chapter 2. Although the concept of an unconscious mind is not useful today, it does make sense to talk about behavior as being unconscious or unaware. Such labels would be used when the reasons given for the behavior by the individual involved do not agree with the reasons given by expert observers, in situations where this failure of self-understanding has important negative consequences for the individual.

5. Repression can affect behavior in three ways: it can prevent the individual from adequately labeling the behavior, it can result in a disappearance of the behavior itself, and it can prevent the occurrence of thoughts that would ordinarily lead to a particular behavior. Much research has been conducted in an attempt to provide scientific demonstrations of the phenomenon called repression. Freud's original notion of repression, referring to the effect of traumatic childhood experiences on adult memory, is practically impossible to demonstrate, but repression as defined in social-learning terms can readily be shown. Thus, people automatically and unthinkingly avoid anxiety-producing thoughts just as they automatically avoid situations involving physical danger.

6. Because society expects people to offer rational and acceptable accounts of their behavior, all of us rely on defense mechanisms. Rationalization, projection, and reaction formation are three defense mechanisms in which repression plays a central part. It should be stressed that the use of these and other mechanisms is unconscious, that they are part of normal behavior, and that they are learned in the normal process of childhood socialization.

7. *Rationalization* refers to giving convenient logical reasons for our actions. People rationalize their actions in a variety of ways, such as blaming others, appealing to unfortunate circumstances, and describing their behavior as normal. *Projection* refers to an extreme form of blaming others by "seeing" one's own unacceptable thoughts, behaviors, and needs in other people, often to an exaggerated degree. In *similar* projection, other persons are perceived as having the characteristic that is threatening to the individual; in *complementary* projection, the individuals see others as trying to force them into the undesirable behavior. In *reaction formation,* the individuals defend themselves against anxiety-arousing thoughts and needs by developing thoughts and behaviors that are their direct opposite.

8. There are a number of other behavioral patterns that serve to protect one's self-esteem in frustration and conflict situations, but do not involve repression in such a direct manner as the three described above. The behaviors involved in *compensation* and *substitution* lead to satisfactions that are close to those that were frustrated, and the original needs are to some degree satisfied. In *overcompensation,* the individual

attempts to deny a weakness by excelling in that very behavior. The Freudian concept of *sublimation* refers to the behavioral expression of repressed impulses in disguised but socially acceptable form. In *compensation,* we try to get satisfaction through the successes of others, as seen in parents who push their children to excel in areas in which they themselves had always wanted to be successful.

9. Satisfaction can also be gained through *fantasy,* the imaginative representation of desired events. The use of fantasy becomes pathological when a person uses it for most need satisfactions. Related to fantasy is *withdrawal,* a way of handling conflictful situations by leaving them altogether. *Emotional isolation* is a form of withdrawal in which the individual is physically present in a situation but manages to block perception of all emotional reactions. In *intellectualization,* the person gives logical explanations for threatening events in order to avoid the emotional reaction involved. In addition to the negative aspects of defense mechanisms, it is important to recognize their positive or *coping* aspects. Also of interest is *acting-out,* or unexpected aggressive behavior that has direct negative consequences, and is usually taken to indicate a "failure" of more adaptive defenses.

10. The term *self-concept* refers to the organized set of verbal self-signaling devices by which we interpret our own behaviors and the circumstances underlying them. Feedback from others is an important source of this information. One aspect of self-concept is sex-role identity, the degree to which individuals regard themselves as masculine or feminine. Another, and perhaps the most important, is our *self-esteem,* our personal judgment of our self-worth.

11. In addition to the control of anxiety through the use of cognitive defensive processes, two other, more direct ways can be identified. First is the use of drugs—those prescribed by physicians, and usually referred to as tranquilizers; and also self-prescribed drugs such as alcohol, marijuana, amphetamines, and heroin. Anxiety management is, of course, not the only reason for the use of these latter drugs, but it is an important one. Second is the possibility of using reinforcement procedures for the direct conditioning of autonomic physiological responses, a field recently opened by research demonstrating the direct control of heart rate, blood pressure, and other such responses in laboratory animals and humans.

KEY TERMS

defense mechanisms	conversion reaction
denial	hysteria
disguise	displacement
repression	unconscious behavior
suppression	rationalization

projection

similar projection

complementary projection

reaction formation

compensation

substitution

overcompensation

sublimation

remote compensation

fantasy

withdrawal

escapism

emotional isolation

dissociation

acting-out

externalization

self-concept

self-esteem

PART THREE

PROBLEMS OF ADJUSTMENT

SEVEN

Failures of Adjustment

There is no simple definition of normal behavior.

- Different societies throughout the ages have developed their own definitions of what is normal and abnormal.

- The disease model of abnormality has had a powerful influence on our own society.

- This book emphasizes the importance of social learning in determining what is normal.

Abnormal behavior is traditionally classified into neuroses, character disorders, and psychoses.

- Neurotic behaviors, including psychosomatic disorders, usually involve attempts to avoid disabling anxiety.

- Character disorders tend to be associated with problems of insufficient anxiety. They also include addictions.

- Psychotic disorders are the most severe and disabling. They include schizophrenia and manic-depressive disorders.

IN CHAPTERS 5 AND 6 WE HAVE DISCUSSED THE PROCESS OF ADJUSTMENT, the ways in which people satisfy their psychological needs and protect themselves from stress and discomfort. Since the effectiveness of a person's adjustment tends to vary according to the time and the situation, it is difficult to find any simple way of expressing the overall quality of adjustment. In this chapter we discuss the nature of failures in the adjustment process, and we turn our attention to those persons who either fail to satisfy their needs or who achieve need satisfaction only at considerable emotional expense. In the first part of the chapter we discuss a number of important issues that must be considered in any attempt to understand failures of adjustment, and in the latter part we introduce the major kinds of adjustment failures and try to understand how they come about.

NORMALITY AND DEVIANCE

Definitions

Adjustive behavior can be conveniently approached in terms of a dimension, ranging from highly adaptive to highly unadaptive. The dimension is also sometimes viewed as referring to acceptable versus unacceptable behavior, or normal versus abnormal behavior. Because the concept of "normal behavior" is so widely used in discussing psychological adjustment, let us examine it at some length.

Statistical definitions of normality. The word *abnormal* means "away from the normal," and it implies a deviation from some clearly established norm or standard. The usual way to establish a norm is by statistical averaging procedures, which give us an accurate indication of the frequency with which a particular event occurs. Thus, a person who achieves an IQ score (intelligence quotient) of less than 70 is abnormal by this definition because IQ scores below 70 are obtained by only 2 to 3 percent of the population.

Statistical definitions of abnormality, however, raise a number of problems. First, we simply do not have adequate objective indexes for most human behavior. For instance, how could one assign a score to "happiness in marriage," or "unhappiness in childhood"? It is doubtful that these concepts could even be defined adequately. Second, many behaviors that are normal in the sense of being statistically common are also clearly undesirable, such as having head colds in the winter or being overweight. If we were to use a strict statistical definition of normality, we would be forced to conclude that having one or more colds per year is perfectly normal. Similarly, we will note in Chapter 8 that the majority of American males have had premarital sexual experiences, but the conclusion that this is therefore "normal" would be challenged by many traditional religious authorities.

A third problem in using statistical definitions of normal and abnormal behavior is that while abnormality tends to imply maladaptive behavior, it can be pointed out that IQs of 130 and above, those in the "very superior" range, are as statistically abnormal as IQs of 70 or less. In fact, the many difficulties involved in satisfying our needs in today's culture make it quite rare to find individuals who do meet all their psychological needs, so that a very well-adjusted person would be statistically abnormal—a peculiar statement, to say the least. Fourth, there is a problem of "cultural relativism," that is, the fact that there are different cultural norms in different societies and even in different segments of one society. In Chapter 8, for example, we describe major differences in sexual behavior that exist between different social classes in our own society, so that what is statistically normal for one cultural group is deviant for another. Thus, the use of a statistical definition of normality raises a number of difficult problems, suggesting that we should be very cautious about equating normality with what is most common.

"Ideal" definitions of normality. As alternatives to the statistical approach to normality, a number of different *ideal* definitions of normality have been proposed. These definitions attempt to define normality as something absolute, rather than relative. In the ideal **biological** definition, normality exists when function follows structure; that is, when the organism fully performs its biologically intended function. Thus, an organism is biologically normal when all of its organs are functioning optimally: the glands are secreting, the heart is pumping fully oxygenated blood, the digestive system is extracting the needed nutrients, and so on. The **medical** definition of normality is a special case of the biological definition, namely the absence of any disorder that might interfere with the structure's fulfilling its function. In the behavioral and psychological area, however, the biological and medical definitions are not very useful because it is difficult to say which, if any, behaviors are "natural" to our biological functioning. For example, by these ideal definitions of normality we would have to conclude that the use of birth control devices is abnormal, since they prevent the biologically natural process of conception.

Another historically important absolute definition of normality is found in *religious* prescriptions of what is normal. According to these definitions, certain behaviors are normal, correct, or moral because they are in accordance with God's will. Unfortunately, in today's society there is little agreement about the nature of God's will, so that moral absolutes provide little help in deciding what behaviors are psychologically normal.

Comment. A wide variety of professional persons, such as theologians, psychologists, psychiatrists, psychoanalysts, and social workers have been involved in the many attempts that have been made to define normality and related concepts such as "mental health," which usually implies a more positive psychological state than mere normality. Most definitions do have some usefulness in providing structured ways of viewing human behavior and goals for evaluating future behavior, provided we recognize the personal and cultural biases that influence these definitions. Bearing in mind the cautions outlined above, it is accurate to say that each society, including our own, develops fairly clear *practical* definitions of what constitutes acceptable or normal behavior and what is unacceptable or abnormal. These practical definitions tend to incorporate aspects of both the statistical and the ideal notions of abnormality. Thus, being an astronaut, while statistically rare, is not regarded as abnormal, while an adult who eats feces is unquestionably engaging in abnormal behavior. In the remainder of this chapter we will use the general term *deviant behavior* to refer to those actions which our own society regards as unacceptable, bearing in mind that deviance must be seen as relative to specific cultures and to specific times and places.

One criticism of our own society is that there is little tolerance of deviant behavior and that there is increasing pressure for conformity. In order to evaluate these criticisms, we must compare the degree to which the range of currently acceptable behavior compares with what was acceptable in earlier times. If we compare the ranges of lifestyle, dress, hairstyle, and language that were acceptable one hundred years ago with today's standards, it becomes obvious that there has been a broadening of that range. The continuing problem as to how much deviance should be permitted to members of our society is the subject matter for groups that are involved in questions of civil liberties.

Reactions to Deviant Behavior

We have concluded that, although deviance may be difficult to define in scientific terms, there is generally good agreement within each society as to what constitutes deviant behavior and how it should be handled. The response to deviance, however, varies greatly from society to society. There are certain cultures in which little or no response is made to deviant behavior, although the behavior is clearly recognized as deviant. These cultures, primarily rural or agricultural, simply accept the fact that some people behave peculiarly, and tend to overlook them. They are permitted to wander about freely, and while the village accepts some basic responsibility for their care, they are largely left to their own devices.

Another response to persons who behave deviantly is to regard their care and control as being the responsibility of the immediate family. In societies that are strongly family-oriented, each family is seen as responsible for handling its own problem members, and is expected to use whatever resources it has available to deal with them. The traditional Japanese family was expected to handle deviant behavior in this fashion, although a number of studies have shown that the greater the influence of Western culture on the Japanese family, the more likely it is to regard behavior as a problem for society in general. Similarly, as our own society has become more and more industrialized, there has been increasing pressure for the deviant individual to be handled on a formal basis. We no longer tolerate the "village idiot," and there is no place in the family dwelling for poor old "crazy Aunt

Any definition of "normal behavior" must be relative, varying from era to era and culture to culture. One ever-changing norm is the standard regulating decorum and dress. In 1921 America discovered the bathing-beauty contest, and in one show girls were required to wear hats, tunic suits, and stockings. Neither their outfits nor the restrained and formal grooming of this turn-of-the-century family would be considered normal by current American standards.

Emma." Instead, over the years we have gradually developed organized society-wide programs for dealing with deviant behavior. Persons exhibiting deviant behavior are thus seen as social problems requiring societal solutions rather than as peculiarities to be overlooked or to be handled by the family. There are some signs, however, that society is tending to rediscover the advantages of this older approach. The community mental health movement is the best example of this thrust.

Today's society is often embarrassed when publicity is given to the inadequacy of some of these societal programs. Without condoning the present state of affairs, we remind the reader that considerable improvements have been made. Thus, at one time, little distinction was made among various kinds of deviant behavior. Thieves, paupers, murderers, bankrupts, idiots, those who talked to invisible others, and all kinds of other deviants were treated in the same way. They were regarded as socially undesirable and simply excluded from the mainstream of society. In the eighteenth century such people were often placed indiscriminately in large institutions where they were chained, tortured, and beaten. Unfortunately, some of this "warehousing" of deviants still occurs, although it is rarely regarded as the preferred solution.

Explanations of Deviance

The particular way in which a society responds to its deviant members is a direct reflection of the way in which that society understands the phenomenon of deviance. Deviant behavior is as old as the recorded history of the human species, and the history of the management of deviance is highly related to the history of our understanding of its causes. The ancients tended to explain strange or incomprehensible behavior in terms of possession by evil spirits. This should come as no particular surprise, however, since they tended to explain most natural phenomena, such as floods, storms, and famine, the same way. Their methods for treating deviant behavior generally involved attempts to drive out the evil spirits, a procedure known as *exorcism*. This procedure involved the use of a variety of medications; if these failed to make the body an uncomfortable place for the evil spirits to reside, then starvation, torture, and other unpleasantries were used. There are also accounts of attempts to open the skull surgically to permit the evil spirits to depart.

The ancient Greeks took a rather different view of deviant behavior, and searched for natural rather than supernatural causes. Hippocrates (460–377 B.C.), the great Greek physician, firmly denied that spirits could cause mental disorders, believing instead that these disorders had natural causes and should be treated as physical illnesses. His specific ideas about natural causes were limited by his lack of understanding of human anatomy and physiology, and some of these ideas seem very strange to us. For example, he believed that melancholia (depression) was caused by an "adverse mixture" of the "four humors"—blood, black bile, yellow bile, and phlegm.

Reactions to deviant behavior have changed markedly through the ages. In this seventeenth-century engraving, "moonstruck" women dance through the middle of town. The moon was believed to be an evil spirit and its phases caused madness—hence the derivation of the word lunatic.

Nevertheless, Hippocrates' views are important because they represent an early attempt to explain a common kind of deviance as a natural phenomenon.

The Greeks, as well as the Romans, developed a reasonably humane system for caring for deviant individuals, placing the responsibility for their care with relatives, who were instructed to do the best they could. After the collapse of the Greek and Roman civilizations, however, there was a return to demonology as the primary explanation for deviant behavior and the use of exorcism to rid afflicted persons of the unwanted evil. Until the beginning of the humanitarian movement in the late eighteenth century, deviant individuals were treated barbarically—shackled to the walls of the so-called "asylums," exhibited for a fee to the public, and fed like animals. And because they were regarded as either active or unwitting accomplices of Satan, few voices were raised in their behalf.

During the French Revolution, Philippe Pinel (1745-1826) was placed in charge of La Bicetre, a Paris asylum, and began to release the inmates from their shackles in the belief that they would profit more from kindness and consideration. William Tuke, an English Quaker, began a similar movement in England, and by 1841 the humanitarian movement had spread to America. The changes that took place in America were accomplished primarily through the work of Dorothea Dix (1802-1887), who has been credited with the establishment of some thirty-two hospitals for the care of deviant individuals and with the complete revolution of their care both in the United States and Canada. The reformers took the view that these unfortunate persons were in fact individuals who had lost their reason because of severe social and psychological stresses. The recommended treatment was primarily "friendly association, discussion of his difficulties, and the daily pursuit of purposeful activity" (Rees, 1957, pp. 306-307), a procedure called *moral therapy*. It is interesting to note that during the first half of the nineteenth century, when moral therapy was practically the only source of treatment for these persons, at least 70 percent of them were eventually discharged from the hospitals as cured or much improved!

With the development of physical medicine in the second half of the nineteenth century, the idea was advanced that the insane were physically ill. This view was greatly enhanced by the discovery that general paresis, a disorder that often produced bizarre behavior, was caused by a gross deterioration of the central nervous system produced by syphilis. Insanity and other kinds of deviance were renamed *mental illness,* and the control of the asylums was taken away from their wardens and given to physicians, who renamed them *mental hospitals.*

The Disease Model

The prevalent view of deviant behavior in the civilized world today is the **disease model,** the view that behavioral abnormalities are simply surface signs, or symptoms, of a basic underlying "mental disease." Just as syphilis was found to be the disease underlying general paresis, and cerebral arteriosclerosis (a degenerative thickening and hardening of the arteries) was found to be the major cause of the psychological deterioration that often occurs with old age, the disease model takes the view that underlying causes, probably of an organic nature, will be found for each of the other patterns of deviant behavior. In other words, the patterns of behavior shown in schizophrenia, depression, neurosis, character disorder, and so on, are viewed as the symptoms of some underlying illness or disease, and the discovery of the underlying cause of these disorders is taken to be one of our most pressing scientific problems. Because of the wide degree of acceptance of the disease model, the notion that deviant behavior is caused by demons has been finally laid to rest, the "mentally ill" have begun to receive humane treatment, and considerable research effort has been directed toward increasing our understanding of the physiological basis of mental disorder.

The belief in underlying causes that is basic to the disease model does not necessarily have to refer to organic or physical factors, however. For example, classical psychoanalytic theory (e.g., Fenichel, 1945) regards the major forms of mental disorder as the result of serious disturbances in psychosexual development. Thus, schizophrenia is regarded by psychoanalysts as the consequence of a dramatic psychological interruption of the early part of the oral stage, so that the schizophrenic individual develops distorted relationships with both the people and the things in the world. Basic to the disease model is the strong belief that behavior pathology should be regarded as a symptom of *some* underlying condition, which can be either physical or psychological.

What are the implications of the disease model for the treatment of deviant behavior? According to this model, the treatment should be aimed at eliminating the underlying disease process, and not merely at removing the symptom. It is interesting to note that the disease model, with its roots in traditional medicine, has led many physicians to believe that whatever treatment process is involved in the management of deviant behavior should be in the hands of a physician rather than another professional person.

Arguments Against the Disease Model

There are a number of objections to the disease model, and an important one is that our search for underlying pathological processes has led us to overlook, if not ignore, the pathological behavior itself. The critics of the disease model correctly point out that most deviant behavior is not the result of a physical disorder of the brain or of anything that could be called a psychiatric disease or mental illness, but is the result of faulty or inadequate socialization. That is, most deviant behavior is learned in exactly the same way that other behaviors have been acquired.

Thomas Szasz (1961), one of the foremost critics of the disease model, though a psychiatrist himself, has taken the view that mental illness is a myth and that the so-called "sick" person simply has "problems of living." While these persons have clearly engaged in behavior that deviates from the ethical, legal, or social norms of society, to blame it on a "mental illness" is little different from blaming it on witches or demons. He notes that many persons who have been judged mentally ill are subjected to worse punishment—long imprisonment in psychiatric hospitals—than if they had been tried and convicted in court for their deviant behavior. Szasz further asserts that viewing deviant individuals as mentally ill robs them of their rights as human beings, including their right to be held responsible for their own behavior. Szasz's other objections also involve these legal and philosophical issues, and reflect his concern that people are best served if it is assumed that they are indeed responsible for their own behavior.

Ronald Laing, the British psychiatrist, goes even further. He believes that "madness" is the only reasonable solution to the mad society in which we live, and that a major mental disturbance is a positive growth experience. This is a rather extreme view, however, and one that is not shared by most mental health professionals.

Other writers (e.g., Fairweather, 1964; Braginsky, Braginsky, and Ring, 1969) have raised different objections to the disease model, based upon social and psychological factors. These critics point out that in being diagnosed as mentally ill, one is assigned to a well-defined role. It is expected by others that the mentally ill will "act crazy," will be incapable of managing their own affairs, and should be regarded as potentially dangerous to themselves and others. These expectations often serve as guidelines for the mentally ill person, who then tends to behave in accordance with them.

The role of a mentally ill person is similar in many ways to the role of a physically ill person. In both cases the patients are expected to be passive and dependent, placing themselves and their welfare in the hands of professional experts, and in neither case are they expected to enter actively into their own treatment planning or management. It is nowadays becoming clear that such an approach is not very useful in working with deviant behavior; in fact, the importance of patient attitudes and expectations is also being recognized in the management of well-known physical diseases such as tuberculosis and heart disorder. Research and clinical studies show that those patients who are actively involved in planning their own treatment—that is, who are regarded as responsible for their own welfare—improve more rapidly than those who are treated in a passive and dependent manner.

Research has also shown very clearly that persons diagnosed as mentally ill and confined in mental hospitals are *not* totally incapable of managing their own affairs, but are responsive to the role expectations that they encounter in the institution and react accordingly. For example, Braginsky, Braginsky, and Ring (1969) reported that virtually all new patients in the mental hospital which they studied learned the physical layout of the hospital, knew when and where meals were served, and were generally well aware of their surroundings. In other words, they had made a successful transition from living on the outside to living on the inside. Since, for many of them, living in a mental hospital represented an improvement in their overall living conditions, they had no particular incentive to leave the hospital quickly and face their "problems of living" once again. We do not wish to imply that there is never a need for a behaviorally deviant person to be hospitalized, but it should be recognized that hospitals often provide no more than a convenient refuge from real-life difficulties and provide little help in teaching people how to cope with their difficulties more effectively. Indeed, as Stanton and Schwartz (1954) have noted, the quiet, docile patient is preferred in most mental hospitals, and such behavior is consistently rewarded. This should not be surprising, since passivity tends to be the behavior that is preferred by most physicians from their patients.

Most of us have heard stories about the ease with which one can be admitted to a mental hospital and the difficulties encountered when one wishes to be discharged. Although these stories are by no means always true, a research study by Rosenhan (1973) has provided some support for their plausibility. Rosenhan had eight different people, including himself, present themselves for admission to mental hospitals. None of the eight was in truth suffering from any obvious psychological disturbance, and all were regularly employed prior to entering the hospital. All of these "pseudopatients" went to a hospital and reported that they had been hearing voices. These voices were unclear but seemed to be saying "empty," "hollow," or "thud." Immediately after admission, all the pseudopatients stopped pretending any deviance whatever. In other words, except for their initial statement, the pseudopatients always behaved in their usual manner. In fact, as part of the experiment, they were expected to get out of the hospital on their own, by convincing the staff that they were "sane."

In all cases the subjects in this experiment found themselves completely accepted as mental patients by the staff. Despite their previous normal history and despite the fact that their so-called "symptoms" were never directly observed by the hospital staff, not a single subject was detected as an imposter, and all but one was diagnosed as schizophrenic. Perhaps the most interesting observation reported by Rosenhan is that, although none of the staff was aware of the deception, it was quickly noted by the other patients, who accused the pseudopatients of being professors or journalists studying hospital conditions. The patients' conclusion is not surprising, since each of the researchers took copious notes. What is alarming is that the same conclusion never occurred to the hospital staff.

Rosenhan's study has generated considerable controversy, and many mental health professionals have taken the position that the behavior shown by the various hospital staffs was only to be expected. After a careful study of both sides of the controversy, Farber (1975) concluded that "one cannot establish the unreliability or uselessness of any diagnostic method by showing that pathological symptoms can be faked, and one ought not judge the effectiveness of psychiatric treatment solely by the impressions of those who know that they are normal and suspect many other patients are also

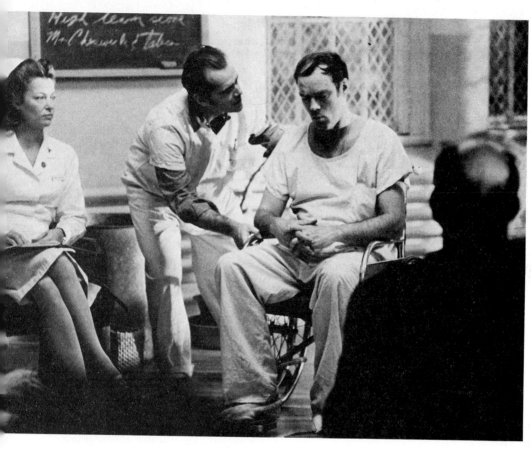

Often mental hospitals neglect to help patients cope more effectively and, instead, reinforce docile, dependent behavior. In the film *One Flew Over the Cuckoo's Nest,* the inmate McMurphy challenged authority and gave the other patients a greater sense of self-worth and dignity.

normal" (p. 619). Nevertheless, Farber also acknowledges that Rosenhan's work has sensitized us to a number of important issues: that abnormality is too often confused with guilt; that psychiatric hospitalization is often used as a way of handling persons who are seen as threatening to the community; and that difficulties created by a person's environment are often blamed on the person rather than the environment.

Alternatives to the Disease Model

What do the critics of the disease model propose as an alternative? There is no single answer to this question, but many of the critics tend to regard most behavior deviance as the simple and direct consequence of inadequate or faulty learning. In other words, they believe that the behaviorally deviant person either has learned how to "act crazy" or has not learned how to "act sane."

This view of behavior deviance is very attractive, but it tends to overlook the substantial evidence on the genetic or hereditary factors that appear to be operating in the development of certain disorders. These factors seem to be present most clearly in schizophrenia—the most dramatic and severe of the behavior disturbances—and also in the manic-depressive disorders. Although there appear to be important learned aspects to these disturbances, the present weight of the research evidence also suggests that in the serious forms of behavior pathology, the *psychoses*, something more than learning is involved.

It is clear, however, that many kinds of behavior pathology *are* directly learned, and there is little reason to invoke a disease model in order to explain these disorders. Most of the milder forms of psychological disturbance, the so-called *neuroses*, can be adequately explained in social-learning terms. Even here, however, it is possible that genetic factors might be involved in indirect ways. In our discussion of behavior genetics (Chapter 1) and of temperament (Chapter 3), we pointed out that the nature of a person's environment is indirectly related to genetic factors, and also that there probably are certain genetic differences in people's reactivity to the environment.

It should be noted that even if physical disease is involved, the way in which the disease process affects the individual will be significantly influenced by the individual's social-learning history and current environment. Consider, for example, two cardiac patients, one a successful writer and the other a poorly educated laborer, who have both suffered severe heart damage following a heart attack. The disease will be far less disabling to the writer than the laborer. While the laborer might very well be forced into retirement, there may be very little change in the writer's life except to make some alterations in diet and to begin a systematic exercise program.

THE NEUROSES

As we have discussed in Chapters 4 and 6, anxiety is highly disruptive in its effects, is difficult to extinguish, and becomes easily associated with other stimuli besides the original or primary ones. Whether or not one believes in the disease model, there is no question that anxiety and its consequences play a basic and central role in the neurotic disorders. In fact, the term **neurosis** is generally taken to refer to those behavior deviations which either involve disabling amounts of anxiety or represent attempts by the individual to avoid disabling anxiety. Thus, the different neuroses refer to different behavior patterns involving anxiety and attempts to control or limit it. Experts in mental health do not agree as to how many different neuroses there are, naming more or fewer depending on the extent to which they are willing to group different behaviors under the same label. In this chapte: we describe some of the major categories of neurosis, recognizing that additional categories have also been proposed. It is important to understand that neurotic behaviors are exaggerations of behaviors that are seen in everyday life, and that what usually leads to the use of the term "neurosis" is that either the degree of anxiety or the behaviors used to avoid anxiety interfere substantially with the routine of ordinary living.

Anxiety Neurosis

The simplest and perhaps the most easily understandable kind of neurosis is the condition called anxiety neurosis. Individuals with this difficulty experience high and disabling levels of anxiety, which may include any of the aspects previously discussed in Chapter 5, such as increased heart rate, gastrointestinal problems, and difficulty in concentrating. In addition, there is often excessive motor activity, such as pacing, sleeplessness, and exaggerated reactions to minor stresses. Anxiety neurotics are preoccupied with these disturbing symptoms and their mental and emotional functioning are usually far below their ideal levels.

The most clearcut examples of anxiety neurosis occur where the individual has been exposed to severe psychological stress of the kind experienced during war or other traumatic events. Such problems are often termed *war neuroses* or *traumatic neuroses;* they differ from other anxiety neuroses only in having a single specific cause for the condition, and in the obvious loss of effective functioning.

Grinker and Spiegel (1945) have described a number of cases of the development of anxiety neuroses in World War II, in which military personnel showed quite dramatic behavior pathology after being subjected to great physical and psychological stress. One example is seen in the case of an air crew member who had lost a number of his crewmates in different aircraft during combat, while he himself had been spared. While previously he had been a happy-go-lucky, cheerful person, he now developed a number of anxiety symptoms that interfered with his operating effectiveness. Eventually, the cues associated with flying became conditioned stimuli for anxiety, making it impossible for him to continue flying at all. Any of us who were to experience such consistent and severe psychological stress while going about our daily activities at school or work would very likely also find that these activities would serve as a cue for strong, disabling anxiety.

As we have already seen, it is not the only actual physical cues that can serve as a stimulus for anxiety; thoughts about the cues can produce strong anxiety as well. Because anxiety neurotics are therefore motivated to avoid such thoughts, they are usually unable to identify the causes of their distress, and can only talk about the

symptoms and the way in which they fluctuate in a rather vague and imprecise manner. Since these episodes of strong anxiety, often called "anxiety attacks" or **"free-
floating anxiety,"** are so upsetting and disabling, they tend to be prominent early in
the development of neurotic behavior patterns. Later, as we will see, the individual
often develops some ways of managing or "binding" the anxiety to make it more con-
trollable and less disabling. Put simply, the individual learns to avoid it. Anxiety
neuroses appear to be rather straightforward to understand and explain; once the
individual engages in efforts to reduce or manage the anxieties, explanations become
more complicated.

Psychosomatic Disorders

Anxiety often involves a substantial disruption of the physical functioning of the individual. Muscles are excessively tense, heart rate is increased, breathing is shallow and
irregular, and digestion and other physical functions are also affected. And the more
continuous the anxiety stimulus, the more continuous the physical disruption. One
clear consequence of this disruption is that the person feels mentally and physically
exhausted most of the time. Anyone who has experienced a near accident while driving or a similar psychological shock will recognize that the somatic reactions that occur
under these circumstances often bring on fatigue rather quickly. In a similar fashion,
persons suffering from chronic anxiety often report that they feel "tired," "worn out,"
and "not up to things" as a result of their chronic difficulties.

The technical name of the condition in which the individual complains of feeling tired, listless, and unable to function because of the physical changes is **neurasthenia.** Sleeplessness, general restlessness, and poor appetite are also associated with anxiety, and these problems extend the physical aspects of the condition
even further. The physical problems lead to a greater sense of inadequacy and unhappiness, and thus to even more anxiety. Neurasthenic individuals thus find themselves
in a vicious circle in which their attempts to manage the problems appear only to
increase them further.

Anxiety also results in physical difficulties when individuals concentrate their attention on a particular bodily aspect of anxiety, and focus on that one symptom as the
"real" problem. For instance, anxious persons can focus attention on heart palpitations, and come to regard themselves as suffering from heart ailments, despite their
physician's assurances to the contrary. We would conclude that in this person's view,
the problem of a "heart disease" is clearly preferable to one of "neurosis." In a similar
manner, neurotic individuals sometimes use low back pain, shortness of breath, or
diarrhea—all of which can occur as part of an anxiety reaction—as a physical focus in
order to reduce the anxiety. In all of these cases, the somatic distress is initially part of
the early "free-floating" anxiety reaction, and the individual concentrates attention on
one or more of these symptoms, treating the anxiety as a somatic disorder. Since
heart disease, breathing difficulties, and back ailments all can be used as legitimate

excuses for avoiding a vigorous interaction with life, the individual can withdraw into a more protected style of living, and thereby avoid additional anxiety, without feeling the shame of being regarded as neurotic.

There are also people who suffer from actual heart disease or other clearly identifiable illness but who respond to their illness in a maladaptive manner. For example, the patient with heart disease may resign from a job, refuse to leave home, and withdraw from social interactions, all in the name of the illness, even though such a program had never been suggested by a medical specialist. In this instance the physical disease serves as the precipitating factor in the development of a neurotic disorder, the so-called *cardiac neurosis*. Most people in our society tend to be very concerned with their physical health, and some overreact to evidence that they are not in good health, whether the disorder is psychological or physical.

Biofeedback. It is possible that certain other somatic conditions can at times be explained through the operation of psychological factors. As described in Chapter 6, Miller (1969) reported that carefully designed operant conditioning procedures, known as **biofeedback,** could be used to control directly a variety of physiological responses, such as blood volume and gastric secretions. Miller's work stimulated a surge of interest in studying stress-related disorders in humans to determine whether physiological changes could be produced by reinforcement-based learning procedures, and a substantial body of research now exists on a number of human physiological responses and disorders.

A recent book by Blanchard and Epstein (1978) provides an excellent introduction to this area, and offers the following conclusions on the findings to date. Biofeedback-based procedures have been shown to be effective in alleviating muscle-contraction headaches, and in some cases other disorders based on excessive muscle tension. The research on biofeedback-based control of blood pressure has also shown promising positive findings, and there are positive indications for the control of the circulatory disorder known as Raynaud's disease through learning to monitor skin temperature (and thus blood flow) in the extremities. Areas which show some promise but need much more research include the voluntary control of irregular heart rhythm and functions of the digestive or gastrointestinal system. The voluntary control of the electroencephalogram (EEG), or "brain waves," is another interesting area of biofeedback research, although little of practical utility has yet been discovered.

There is no doubt that further advances will be made in the understanding and treatment of psychosomatic disorders through biofeedback technology. Two cautions should be offered to the reader at the present time, however. First, in much of the existing research, it is not possible to tell whether the positive changes that occurred were indeed a result of the biofeedback technique itself or whether they were caused by accompanying behaviors such as muscle relaxation, and thus would have occurred without the use of biofeedback. The second caution is related to the first. A number of mental health professionals are now offering "biofeedback treatment" for a variety of disorders, but it is often questionable whether the use of biofeedback technology contributes anything to the positive changes that might take place. In summary, biofeedback technology should be regarded as an area of much promise for the future, but one that needs to be approached with considerable caution at the present time.

Hysteria

Another neurotic way of managing anxiety is through **hysteria,** the development of physical symptoms that interfere with the arousal of anxiety. In contrast to psychosomatic disorders, however, the physical symptoms of the hysteric involve no clear physical disorder whatever, and are often inconsistent with what is known about human physiology. For example, hysterical symptoms may involve blindness or deafness, but the individual will still show dilation of the pupils to light or an appropriate physiological response to sound. Physical symptoms that are of hysterical origin clearly serve some psychological needs of the individual. Thus, the air crew member described above might develop a "glove anesthesia" in which he would feel nothing in his right hand, with the loss of sensation resembling the area of a glove. This loss of sensation would clearly prevent him from flying, but there is no known neurological disorder that could possibly account for it.

We tend to know very little about the development of hysterical disorders. They do tend to occur more often in naive, unsophisticated people, and they seem to be less common in general nowadays than in the past. Hysterical behavior bears a close resemblance to the effects of hypnosis, and in fact hysterical symptoms can be produced in some people through hypnosis. Hysterical symptoms can sometimes also be removed by post-hypnotic suggestion. Thus, it is possible that hysteria is the result of a self-suggestion process of which the person is not fully aware. The kind of anxiety-avoidance procedure that occurs in hysterical disorders is consistent with the defense mechanism of denial.

Amnesia and fugue. Amnesia refers to the loss of personal memories, and **fugue** to the disorder of finding oneself in a strange new place with no recollection of how one arrived there, a kind of temporary amnesia. Both are regarded as a type of hysterical reaction, in that the behavior serves the psychological needs of the person, while the physical symptoms do not fit any known neurological disease. Brain disease or injury would lead to some loss of all recent memories and not just personal memories. Amnesia and fugue can both be produced by hypnotic suggestion.

How does **malingering**—the conscious, deliberate pretending of symptoms to cope with some adjustment problem—differ from hysterical disorders? The answer is theoretically easy but is difficult to apply in practice. The malingerer is pretending and is aware of it, while the symptoms of hysterical patients are not under their conscious control. Malingering usually tends to involve symptoms that are difficult to verify, such as headaches or low back pain, while hysterical symptoms tend to be more flamboyant, such as loss of memory, loss of sensation, and paralysis. Obviously, though, headaches and low back pain can be hysterical in nature, and all the above symptoms could also be physiologically based.

It is difficult to differentiate malingering from **hypochondriasis,** the exaggeration of real physical symptoms to serve psychological needs. It is a rare person who has never found it convenient to regard a headache or stomachache as too severe to be able to go to school or work, although the same malady might not be sufficient to keep us from a more pleasurable activity such as a film or a football game. It is extremely difficult to make objective assessments of pain or discomfort, to decide when people are "really sick," or to evaluate the extent to which they might be trying to fool themselves and others. But it is clear that people do often rely upon physical distress as a convenient means of dealing with anxiety. Most of us learn early in life that whenever we are ill much concern is expressed over our welfare, and we receive more affection than at other times. These learning experiences undoubtedly serve as the basis for the development of hysteria, malingering, and hypochondriasis, but it is not yet fully understood exactly how they develop, nor why one kind of behavior develops rather than another.

Obsessive-Compulsive Neurosis

As we have already noted, free-floating anxiety is extremely disabling, and the sufferer loses no time in developing ways to reduce the discomfort. **Obsessive-compulsive neurosis** represents yet another attempt to cope with anxiety and, like the other neuroses, it is only partly successful, since it usually raises new problems.

Obsessive thoughts, or persistent, irrational ideas that the individual cannot dismiss from attention, can serve to reduce high anxiety to a manageable level. Thus, instead of being anxious in response to a wide variety of cues, the obsessive thought ("something terrible is going to happen to my children," or "the house may burn down") permits individuals to limit their anxiety to these obsessive concerns and keeps the real causes of anxiety from coming to their attention. When pressed, obsessive persons readily agree that the concerns are irrational, but insist that they are quite unable to get rid of them.

All of us have an occasional obsessive thought, as when a song or a phrase "enters our head" and defies our attempts to dismiss it. For most of us the obsession is simply a catchy melody or an advertising slogan which perhaps causes some slight interference with our normal thinking and causes us to wonder why we "can't get it out of our heads." For obsessive individuals, the thoughts are often sexual or aggressive in nature—either the notion that they will engage in some immoral act, or that some terrible event will happen to them or to one of their loved ones.

In the compulsive aspect of this disorder the individual feels compelled to engage in some strange or absurd behavior. Compulsions can vary from simple acts like touching a button or washing one's hands to highly complex rituals such as cleaning one's room according to a rigid and lengthy schedule. In these complex rituals, if compulsive persons omit a single step, they feel compelled to repeat the entire ritual. A patient known to the authors, a young college student, was able to study or read only after he had counted each and every object in the room—the number of panes in the window, floor tiles, panels in the door, and rungs in the chairs. The compulsion seriously interfered with the time available for studying, and the result was reflected in grades that were well below his capability.

In sports we see a variety of compulsive or superstitious rituals—the outfielders who must touch third base before they enter the dugout, the bowlers who must wipe their hands three times before they pick up the ball, and the tennis players who must bounce the ball twice before serving. In these rather normal examples, it is not difficult to understand how the behavior develops. Whenever the individuals make a desired response—the bowler makes a strike or the outfielder hits a double—they try to note the exact characteristics that could account for the success; for example, the way in which the ball or the bat were held, or perhaps even the color of the socks worn at the time. But these are very difficult to determine, because the relevant cues are very subtle and probably beyond conscious awareness. Since the behavioral cues involved in the success are not available, they attend to the behavior they were aware of—wiping hands or bouncing the ball, and this behavior becomes reinforced by the successful events that followed it. Thus, at least some compulsive behavior is learned as a direct result of reinforcement.

On the other hand, the counting behavior of our college student seems to have been reinforced by anxiety reduction, as he apparently learned, without being aware of it, that counting interfered with the arousal of anxiety, and developed a strong compulsive counting ritual that seemed to prevent anxiety arousal. The student reported that if he did not count the objects in a room, he would become obsessed with the

thought that he would completely undress. The counting, however, interfered with those thoughts and they did not recur after he had engaged in a complete ritual of counting. This example demonstrates the commonly observed relationship between obsessions and compulsions, which are usually discussed as a single disorder. One of the most widely known illustrations of compulsive behavior is found in Shakespeare's *Macbeth*, where Lady Macbeth is preoccupied with her ritualistic attempts to wash from her hands the blood of the newly murdered King Duncan, and continues this behavior well beyond what would be physically necessary.

Phobic Disorders

The reader will recall from Chapter 1 the case of Frances, a woman with a disabling phobia of thunderstorms, and also our theoretical discussion of phobias in Chapter 4 in the context of anxiety. These strong, persistent, generalized, unrealistic fears are regarded as a neurosis, particularly when the phobia involves a set of cues that is not easily avoided, such as germs, knives, being alone, being with persons of the opposite sex, or going outside. Some phobias are undoubtedly learned directly, while some are developed in an effort to control or manage anxiety through the mechanism of displacement as discussed in Chapter 6. In the latter case, displacing or misidentifying the source of the anxiety helps the individual to reduce objective distress. It can easily be seen that most individuals would prefer to have a phobia, even one such as fear of being alone, as an alternative to free-floating anxiety with its overwhelming sense of impending doom.

We have seen that the neurotic disorders stem from strong anxiety and the attempts of the individual to reduce or manage this anxiety. A neurotic individual is one whose level of anxiety seriously interferes with everyday living or whose efforts to cope with the anxiety produce long-term negative consequences. In either case, then, the neurotic person engages in persistent unadaptive behavior.

THE CHARACTER DISORDERS

Character disorders include a wide variety of different failures of adjustment, including the psychopathic or antisocial personality, the passive-aggressive individual, the immature or socially incompetent individual, and drug addicts. Whereas neurotic persons seem to be suffering from levels of anxiety that are too high, it sometimes appears that persons with character disorders have too little anxiety. It is thought that much of their antisocial behavior stems from a failure of the socialization process, since their antisocial behavior does not arouse even ordinary amounts of anxiety. As we have previously emphasized, most of us are prevented from violating society's taboos by the anxiety that has been attached to the taboo behaviors.

Psychopaths (or **sociopaths**) are characterized by irresponsible and impulsive behavior, a disregard for what most of their peers regard as appropriate behavior, act-

ing-out of impulses, and a lack of concern for the consequences of their behavior. At the same time, the psychopath is often charming in interpersonal relationships, although these relationships tend to be rather superficial. The psychopath tends to charm others and then exploit them, and when confronted with these misdeeds, either denies involvement in the act or attaches the blame to others.

The description of the psychopath which we have just given fits many so-called confidence men, imposters, and others who tend to live by their wits. A colleague of the authors recently discovered that such an individual had impersonated him for more than a year, obtaining a professorship at a Canadian university, and had succeeded well in his deception before it was detected by accident. Ferdinand Demara, the "Great Imposter," had several different careers, including psychologist, physician, and prison warden, all based upon forged credentials (Crichton, 1959). Each time he was detected and exposed he succeeded in talking his way out of trouble and went on to a new exploit.

Our understanding of the way in which psychopathic behavior develops is rather limited. Hare (1970), in his comprehensive review of the research on this topic, has concluded that psychopaths lack sensitivity to ordinarily noxious or painful stimuli. In studies of laboratory conditioning using pain as the unconditioned stimulus, psychopaths appear to condition much more slowly than normal individuals, and their psychopathic behavior is thought to be an attempt to produce the thrills and excitement that would otherwise be missing from their lives. Whether this failure to respond to pain and to develop normal amounts of anxiety is constitutional, learned, or a combination of both biological and environmental factors has not yet been determined. The important point is that antisocial behavior is thought to occur through the failure to develop consistent anxiety, shame, or guilt. The reader will also recall from our discussion in Chapter 1 on behavior genetics that some persons with psychopathic behavior have been shown to have an abnormal genetic structure.

Some kinds of character disorders appear to involve not the absence of anxiety in situations where it would be expected, but a failure to regard it as a cue for socially appropriate behavior, so that the individual habitually "acts out," or responds in a disruptive manner that is distressing to others. Individuals with **passive-aggressive** character disorders continually express hostility, but in indirect, covert ways. They obstruct and mislead others, waste time, pout, and find reasons not to involve themselves in ongoing activities. When directly confronted with this behavior, however, they deny it. The origins of such behavior are probably found in early overdependency coupled with strong anxiety about aggression. Thus, their antagonism to authority is considered to be "counterdependent" in nature, a reaction formation to their strong dependency needs. Such individuals are rarely personally successful, and they also tend to interfere with the work and lives of others.

Another kind of problem behavior that is usually labeled a character disorder is that of the *socially incompetent person* or inadequate personality. Such people tend to be inept and ineffectual, especially in their interpersonal relationships. While neither mentally nor physically inadequate, their behavior never seems to measure up to typical expectations. They tend to hold rather menial jobs, have few, if any, long-term relationships, and generally seem to be misfits in the framework of society.

The Addictions

The behavior problems described in the two preceding paragraphs indicate that the category of character disorder tends to be a rather loose classification which includes difficulties that are neither clearly neurotic nor psychotic. Also included in this category are the problems of alcoholism and drug dependency.

As we noted in Chapter 6, there are a number of psychoactive or mind-altering drugs. The most prevalent and best understood of these drugs is alcohol. Alcohol acts as a physiological depressant rather than a stimulant, numbing the higher mental processes of thinking and problem solving. It also interferes with anxiety arousal, making the person less aware of anxiety-arousing cues. Thus, alcohol produces a reduction of behavioral controls and a sense of comfort, well-being, and expansiveness.

While most consumers of alcohol rarely cause trouble for themselves or for society, there are about 10 million Americans who are considered **alcoholics**—persons whose drinking seriously interferes with their everyday living. It is generally agreed that alcoholism is the most serious problem of drug abuse in the United States today, and it is an even more severe problem in certain countries of western Europe and the Soviet Union.

How does alcohol cause problems? Although some of the temporary psychological effects of alcohol might be desirable, its long-term physiological effects are not. Prolonged heavy drinking produces a variety of physical disorders, including damage to the central nervous system, the liver, and the heart. Alcohol, like the other mind-altering drugs, serves as a powerful reinforcer, and people become dependent on it rather easily. Alcoholics come to get most, if not all, of the reinforcement in their lives while intoxicated, and the task of obtaining and consuming liquor becomes their most important behavior. Work, family life, and even eating become less and less important in the course of alcoholism, and the individual becomes preoccupied with getting and staying drunk. Apart from the physical dangers of such a high level of alcohol consumption, constant intoxication also poses a variety of serious problems for society, such as disruption of families and a greatly increased frequency of traffic accidents.

Since alcohol is available as a potential reinforcer to everyone, we might ask why some users become alcoholics while the majority do not. Some researchers have suggested that certain individuals may be physiologically predisposed to alcoholism, especially since alcoholism tends to run in families. But the same research data can be used to support the conclusion that alcoholism is the result of specific psychological factors such as modeling based on parental behavior, since about 50 percent of all alcoholics have at least one alcoholic parent. Thus, whether alcoholism is psychologically or physically based is not known at the present. It is clear, however, that alcoholics do not cope successfully with their everyday problems, and that their use of alcohol increases their difficulties rather than decreasing them. It is for this reason that alcoholism is often classified as a psychological disorder.

Almost everything that we have said about alcohol can also be said about the other psychoactive drugs. The drugs all tend to be highly effective reinforcers: they produce a sense of euphoria or relaxation, they tend to block or reduce anxiety, and they provide a means for escaping from reality, if only temporarily. The problems that they cause stem from the facts that they can very easily be used to excess and that extensive reliance upon them leads to a withdrawal from the problems faced in daily living. Obviously, a society is in difficulty if a significant number of persons are habitually intoxicated by alcohol or other drugs.

It should be emphasized that there are important differences in the effects of various drugs, and some of these differences have been described in Chapter 6. However, there has been an unfortunate tendency on the part of our legislators and law enforcement officials to treat all psychoactive drugs, with the exception of alcohol, as having the same consequences and posing the same potential dangers to the individual and society. Most experts on psychoactive drugs now agree, for example, that both the psychological and the physiological consequences of heroin and marijuana use are quite different. While marijuana tends to produce a sense of relaxation and lassitude, somewhat similar to the effects of alcohol, heroin usually produces a kind of euphoric spasm, the so-called heroin "high," which is followed by a deep sense of lethargy and then a physiologically based craving for more heroin. It is this physiological dependence that makes heroin a far more serious danger than marijuana. Heroin also poses a serious problem of *tolerance,* in that the individual finds it necessary to take greater and greater amounts in order to produce the same effect, until an almost fatal dose is required. For marijuana, on the contrary, there is some evidence that the opposite is true, and that the same effects can be produced over time with smaller and smaller doses.

An important issue in appraising the effects of psychoactive drugs is the degree to which the substance is physiologically addictive. Some drugs, notably heroin and morphine, usually produce a physiological craving, so that signs of physical illness—running nose, nausea, perspiration—appear as the effects of the drug wear off. These signs disappear when the drug is taken once again, although, as noted above, the amount required tends to increase. The exact manner in which physiological dependency functions is not yet understood, nor do satisfactory answers exist at the present time to the questions of why some users do not develop dependency, why dependency occurs with certain drugs but not others, and how physiological dependency differs from psychological dependency. The last question is especially complex, as it is difficult to distinguish between physiological dependency and a psychological need based on a very strong reinforcer.

Despite these unanswered questions, it is clear that drug abuse, including alcoholism, represents a serious problem in Western society. There is much debate over the best way to view drug abuse—whether to regard it as criminal behavior or whether to consider addicts as medically ill or as having a psychological disorder. Even more difficult is the question of how to prevent and stop drug abuse, and here again, there are widely differing views. Until these questions are resolved, drug abuse will continue to be an ongoing problem for our society.

THE PSYCHOSES

Individuals are described as *psychotic* when their mental functioning is sufficiently impaired to interfere grossly with their capacity to meet the demands of everyday living. Psychotic individuals require assistance and supervision in order to attend to the most elementary details of life, such as eating, dressing, and otherwise caring for themselves. Their interpersonal relationships are usually so distorted that their immediate family and friends find it impossible to cope with them, and hospital care or some other form of special intervention appears to be necessary. While there is no sharp division in the degree of disability between psychotic and severe neurotic disorders, the psychotics are the more disabled. Equally important, there are certain behaviors that occur only in psychotic individuals: **delusions,** or obviously false beliefs, such as believing that one is the king of England or is being persecuted by the Kremlin, and **hallucinations,** or false perceptions, such as hearing voices that no one else hears or seeing monsters that no one else sees. The interpersonally disruptive behaviors that are shown by certain psychotic individuals, such as refusal to eat, random striking out, and constant talking to nobody in particular, and bizarre behaviors such as smearing feces, tend to make them appear threatening to others and lead to their rejection by society.

There are two major kinds of psychoses, *organic* and *functional.* The **organic psychoses** are those behavioral disturbances which stem from known injury or disease to the brain and the central nervous system. Almost any brain pathology can produce psychotic behavior, depending upon the nature and extent of the damage. Some psychologists believe that well-adjusted persons are better able to compensate for the effects of brain damage, even of a severe nature, but the research evidence on this point is not clear at the present time.

Brain malfunction and consequent behavior pathology in individuals who have had no previous adjustment problems can be caused by a wide variety of conditions. These include (1) infections, such as syphilis and encephalitis (inflammation of the brain caused by a virus); (2) brain tumors; (3) injury to the brain through accidents or surgery; (4) toxic and metabolic disturbances, including drug effects, nutritional deficiencies, and endocrine disturbances; and (5) the effects of senility, especially cerebral arteriosclerosis and cerebral degeneration. In all of these conditions there is clear evidence that the behavioral disturbance stems from the brain pathology, and in general, it can be said that any set of circumstances that causes brain malfunctioning can also lead to behavioral disturbance. This is not surprising, given the central role of the brain in the organization and integration of behavior.

The specific behavioral changes that occur with each of these brain pathologies depend more upon their extent and locus in the brain than upon the nature of the injury or disease itself. Also, there is often a relationship between the behavioral disturbance that occurs and the individual's original or premorbid level of adjustment. In general, the behavioral changes associated with the organic psychoses include (1) impairment of memory, especially for recent events; (2) impairment of orientation, so that the person is unsure of time and place; (3) impairment of judgment, comprehension, and learning; (4) emotional overreactivity; and (5) loss of a sense of reality and of control over one's own behavior. Certain specific behavioral changes are more characteristic of one kind of brain impairment than others, but these details need not concern us here. Some of these changes are reversible while others are not, depending upon whether the organic state is temporary, such as an infection, or permanent, such as an injury, and also depending upon the amount and site of the brain damage and on certain other factors. The degree of recovery that can be expected is often difficult to predict, since our knowledge in this important area is still quite limited.

The **functional psychoses** are those in which there is no known associated brain pathology. Many research workers in mental health, however, firmly believe that brain pathology also underlies the so-called functional disorders, and that it is only a matter of time before these basic causes will be uncovered. There is also an equally fervent group that believes that the functional psychoses are the result of environmental or learning factors, and that no organic pathology is involved. Many persons in the latter group, however, now believe that genetic or other biological factors also play a role in the cause of these behaviors. The two primary categories of functional psychoses are *schizophrenia* and the affective or *manic-depressive* psychoses.

Schizophrenia

Schizophrenia is a behavioral disturbance marked by an inappropriate view of reality, so that schizophrenics appear to be responding to inner thoughts as though

they were as real as the world around them. It is both the most studied and the least understood of all the behavior pathologies. Despite almost a century of research into biological, biochemical, genetic, psychological, sociological and other variables, schizophrenia remains a "riddle of the ages."

Basic to schizophrenia is a disturbance of the thought processes, so that the schizophrenic's view of reality appears to be grossly distorted. Brown (1973) has given a clear example of this distortion of reality testing. His schizophrenic patient, in an otherwise normal conversation, said, "When I get out of here I'm going to fly to Scotland where they are making a movie of *Fiddler on the Roof* because I want to try out for the lead" (p. 399). Brown notes that the following is wrong with this statement: (1) the film has already been made; (2) Scotland was not the locale of the film; and (3) the patient was far too young for the part. While there is nothing wrong with the statement from a linguistic viewpoint, it is clear that the ideas contained in it are contrary to our notion of reality. Distortions of reality are typical of schizophrenia and are regarded as the core of the disturbance.

It is important to recognize that this delusional statement by the patient is intended to be taken seriously. It is not presented as a dream or a fantasy but rather as a statement of his actual intention. However, the patient seems unable to differentiate dreams or fantasies from actual situations or events. It is also important to note that such breaks in reality testing, or delusions, only occur occasionally, even in rather severe cases of schizophrenia. The area of mental content in which delusions occur is more or less limited, and outside of that area the schizophrenic's thoughts are usually quite ordinary.

Despite the cultural and historical problems of defining reality, schizophrenic delusions seem to be present in all human cultures that are known today, and they have been reported throughout recorded history. Hallucinations are sensory events such as voices that come to the patients as though from some external source, but which are in fact purely a product of their internal thought processes.

Most of the other behaviors that occur in schizophrenia stem from the person's disturbed view of reality. If schizophrenic patients have the delusion that they are gods, and if, in their view, gods do not eat, then they will refuse all food. If the secret voices tell them not to move, then they will remain motionless. In almost all cases, the bizarre behaviors which occur in schizophrenia stem directly from the delusions or hallucinations, and it is the "break in reality" that is regarded as the paramount feature of schizophrenia.

At one time schizophrenia was known as *dementia praecox*, or insanity beginning at an early age, but it is now recognized that the disorder does not always begin in youth, and the term has fallen into disuse. The Swiss psychiatrist Bleuler introduced the term schizophrenia, or "split mind," in 1911 because he regarded the disorder as a disorganization of the thought processes plus a lack of integration between the thoughts and the emotions. Although the second aspect of Bleuler's definition is now in some dispute, his term has remained as the descriptive label for this most serious and baffling disorder.

There seem to be two rather distinct and different patterns by which schizophrenia develops. In **process schizophrenia,** the onset of the disorder is slow and insidious. The early signs, usually noted in adolescence, are gradual lack of interest in one's environment, excessive daydreaming, reduced emotional responsiveness, and inappropriate behavior. The intensity of these symptoms tends to increase gradually and the prognosis, or expectation of recovery, is rather poor. There are often periods in which the symptoms seem to have disappeared, but they usually reappear later, often in even more intense form. The life history of individuals with the disorder of process schizophrenia is usually marked by long and often continuous times spent in institutions, and they are rarely able to achieve normal patterns of living.

In the other pattern of development, **reactive schizophrenia,** the disorder has a sudden, dramatic onset, and the early life of the reactive schizophrenic does not show a long history of gradual withdrawal and loss of interest in the environment. Indeed, many reactive schizophrenics seem to have led quite normal lives until they show a sudden and dramatic breakdown. Although the course of the disorder is often stormy and can last for several years, the prognosis in reactive schizophrenia is much more favorable than in process schizophrenia. Most reactive schizophrenics seem to recover and return to reasonably normal lives.

The sharp differences in both onset and prognosis in these two types of schizophrenics have led some writers to conclude that there are really two different disorders that have some similar symptoms. Even Bleuler noted in 1911 that schizophrenics whose disorder developed rapidly were more likely to exhibit *paranoid* and *catatonic* symptoms, while the gradually developing or process schizophrenics were more likely to exhibit *hebephrenic* symptoms or *simple withdrawal*. These four patterns or syndromes of schizophrenia have also been regarded from time to time as separate disorders, and although the distinctions are nowadays not considered as important as they once were, it is worthwhile to examine each category in turn.

Paranoid schizophrenia is characterized by absurd, illogical, and often changing delusions. The cartoonist's depiction of an insane person thinking of himself as Napoleon represents a paranoid type. The delusions are usually of grandeur, such as Napoleon or Christ, or of persecution, in which the patients might be convinced that they are being spied upon or harassed. Paranoid delusions are often dramatic in nature, so such persons are the focus of public attention and concern.

Catatonic schizophrenia is marked by extremes of stereotyped behavior—either a complete lack of motion or extreme excitement. In the motionless or stuporous phase, the body of the catatonic can sometimes be moved into different poses and will remain there, a state called *waxy flexibility*. Or the patient may be extremely negativistic, refusing to move but striking out at anyone who approaches. In the excited phase the patient may pace madly about, shouting or talking constantly, and on occasion, openly and continuously masturbating. As we have noted previously, these behaviors are almost always the result of some delusion, such as the patients' believing they are possessed by devils. Some catatonics pass from one state to the other, while others show only one type of behavior.

Hebephrenic schizophrenia is characterized by emotional confusion and extreme silliness. Inappropriate laughter, childish giggling, the repetition of meaningless phrases, and bizarre speech are the most notable features of this category. The patients withdraw to a considerable extent from interpersonal activity and seem to have retreated into a childish fantasy world of their own.

Simple schizophrenia is also marked by withdrawal and seclusiveness. The patients neglect their appearance, lose interest in the external world, and show a loss of appetite, a progressive deterioration of speech, and a generalized disintegration of social behavior patterns.

As we have noted in Chapter 1 and elsewhere, schizophrenia tends to run in families. Most experts on schizophrenia agree that there is a genetic aspect to this disorder, although some consider that the experience of having a schizophrenic parent is sufficient basis for the later development of schizophrenia. Meehl (1962) has suggested an interactive theory for the development of schizophrenia, which takes the genetic evidence into account and still allows for psychological factors. In Meehl's view, the predisposition for developing schizophrenia is hereditary, but schizophrenia only develops when an individual with a genetic predisposition is exposed to "schizophrenogenic" family circumstances. The schizophrenogenic family involves a cold, dominating, overprotecting, yet rejecting mother, and a weak, passive father. The mother tends to dominate and control the children, keeping them dependent upon her, but offers them little in the way of warmth or affection. Meehl believes that when these family circumstances are coupled with a genetic predisposition, schizophrenia will develop; otherwise, only a neurotic individual will result. On the other hand, a child with a genetic predisposition who undergoes normal childhood and never experiences any unusual stress will probably not develop schizophrenia, despite the predisposition. Meehl's theory is plausible, but it is difficult to test. At the present, we still do not have a generally acceptable theory of the origins of schizophrenia. It clearly is the most complex and the least understood of the behavior disturbances.

In a recent review, Zubin and Spring (1977) have attempted to present an integrated picture of what is currently known about schizophrenia and its causes. After identifying the three major approaches to the study of schizophrenia—genetic, behavioral, and biological—Zubin and Spring propose that an important common element is the person's *vulnerability* to the disorder. Vulnerability is defined as a person's threshold for tolerating human stress coupled with the intensity of the stress itself, and is related to genetic, behavioral, and biological factors. In this view, new advances in the understanding of schizophrenia are most likely to come as researchers develop precise ways of measuring a person's vulnerability to this disorder.

The Affective Psychoses

The other major category of psychotic disorder refers to the manic-depressive or affective psychoses. While schizophrenia primarily involves a thought disturbance, the **manic-depressive psychoses** involve a serious disturbance of feelings, emotion, or mood. Most people experience some degree of shift in their moods. On some days we awake feeling happy, lively, and very much at peace with ourselves, and we look forward to the events of the day, while on other days we awake feeling sad, lonely, and misunderstood, and we find it difficult to organize our energies to get on with our daily schedule. These changes often appear to occur on a regular basis, without regard to the actual circumstances of our life. In the manic-depressive psychoses, there is a gross exaggeration of one or the other of these mood states.

In *depression,* individuals are profoundly sad and joyless. They feel that there is no reason to continue to live, and there is a sense of great emptiness and loneliness. They speak slowly and in a monotone. They may show some degree of withdrawal, and may feel unworthy and guilty of some terrible transgression. They frequently have suicidal ideas, and a substantial number of depressives (10 percent) actually attempt suicide. Some theorists consider that the depressive aspect of manic-depressive psychosis should be differentiated from the disorder known as *reactive* depression, a depressed mood state and lack of activity that sometimes follows a personal loss such as death of a loved one or failure at an important event in life. Reactive depression is often considered to be a neurotic disorder, and several explanations have been offered. Psychodynamic theorists see it as the result of expressing anger toward the self, in the context of guilt or self-punishment, rather than expressing it outward at persons or objects in the environment. Behavior theorists define depression primarily as a lack of behavior, and regard it as the result of an absence of the usual reinforcers that maintain behavior or of the usual stimuli that trigger behavior. Underlying these absences is believed to be a deficiency in the skills needed to elicit positive reinforcement for one's behaviors. The relationship between reactive depression and the depressive end of the manic-depressive cycle is not well understood at the present time.

In the *manic* state, there is an intense feeling of elation and extreme optimism. Manic individuals are highly energetic, often to such an extent that they are unable to slow down their activities sufficiently to eat or sleep. They are loud and boisterous, and easily become involved in all sorts of plans, schemes, and other activities. Their ideas often become wildly extravagant and are frequently unrealistic, and they easily become impatient with other people and the caution that they recommend.

In the affective psychoses the patient may be either depressed or manic, or may move from depression to mania in a cyclical fashion. Both the manic and the depressive phases tend to run for limited periods of time, so that virtually all persons suffering from this disorder eventually recover without treatment, although treatment by antidepressant drugs may hasten this process. However, these difficulties tend to recur at regular intervals, so that the patient will frequently experience several bouts of symptoms, sometimes separated by years. In many cases, manic-depressive disorders can be at least partly controlled by medication containing the chemical element lithium.

Like schizophrenia, manic-depressive psychosis tends to run in families, leading many theorists to conclude that there is an important genetic component to this disturbance. Once again, however, the evidence on this question is not entirely conclusive, and scientific study is made difficult by the same problems that hamper the study of schizophrenia. Thus, the most reasonable view at the present time is that genetic and environmental factors interact in some manner that is not yet understood.

SUMMARY

1. It is difficult to define what is meant by adjusted versus maladjusted or normal versus abnormal behavior, and there is no single definition that is entirely satisfactory. One possible definition is *statistical,* so that anything uncommon would be called abnormal. There are several problems with this definition; for example, it would be abnormal to have a high IQ but perfectly normal to have a cold in winter. Also, what is normal would differ from one culture to another. There are also *ideal* definitions of normality, in which any natural function is normal, and there are *religious* prescriptions for what is normal. Each society tends to develop its own *practical* notions as to what is normal; these tend to involve both statistical and ideal notions.

2. Throughout the ages, each society has reacted to abnormal or deviant individuals according to its beliefs about the causes of the deviance. In some societies, each family cares for its own deviant members, while in others, care is provided on a formal basis. In ancient times deviant behavior was thought to be caused through possession by demons, and attempts to eradicate them were known as *exorcism.* The ancient Greeks believed in more natural causes; however, there was subsequently a return to the belief in demon possession, which was replaced in the nineteenth century by the *disease model,* the belief that the insane were physically ill. Their care was taken over by physicians, and their institutions were renamed mental hospitals.

3. The disease model reflects the belief that behavioral abnormalities are simply surface signs, or symptoms, of a basic underlying "disease." This disease can be organic, as in the brain deterioration that underlies senility, or "mental," as in the psychoanalytic view that adult maladjustments are due to disordered psychosexual development in childhood. A number of objections have been raised against the disease model: much deviant behavior is known to be directly learned as the result of faulty socialization; blaming a "mental illness" is no different from blaming witches and demons; being diagnosed and treated as mentally ill robs the individual of human rights; and the individual is often encouraged to behave in a passive and helpless man-

ner. Possible alternatives to the disease model of mental illness include the social-learning model, although the role of genetic factors in psychosis should not be overlooked.

4. The *neuroses* are those behavior deviations that either involve disabling amounts of anxiety or represent attempts by the individual to avoid disabling anxiety, and they tend to involve exaggerations of behaviors that are seen in everyday life. In *anxiety neurosis*, the individual experiences very high anxiety, which may be accompanied by other physiological distress. Prolonged and severe stress, such as at the battlefront of a war, can lead to such a condition.

5. *Psychosomatic disorders* are neuroses in which there is direct bodily involvement with the anxiety. Thus, the *neurasthenic* individual feels chronically worn out and listless. Other neurotic individuals seize upon some physiological difficulty as a reason for avoiding a more vigorous role in life; thus, patients with *cardiac neurosis* protect themselves to a far greater extent than their actual heart disorders would warrant. The extent to which certain forms of headache, high blood pressure, and other disorders can be directly learned and unlearned through operant conditioning procedures is the subject of much current research interest. Treatment methods involving these procedures are known as *biofeedback*.

6. Another neurotic way of managing anxiety is through *hysteria*, the development of physical symptoms that interfere with anxiety arousal. *Amnesia* refers to the anxiety-motivated loss of personal memories, and *fugue* to the disorder of finding oneself in a strange place with no memory of getting there. It is often difficult to distinguish these disorders from *malingering,* the conscious and deliberate faking of symptoms in order to cope with adjustment difficulties. Somewhat similar to malingering is *hypochondriasis,* the exaggeration of real though minor physical symptoms in order to serve psychological needs. *Obsessive-compulsive* neurosis represents yet another way of coping with anxiety. Obsessive thoughts are persistent irrational ideas that serve to keep the real causes of anxiety from coming to the individual's attention, while compulsions are motor activities that the individual feels compelled to perform, once again interfering with anxiety-producing behaviors. *Phobias,* discussed in Chapter 6, are strong, persistent, unrealistic fears of specific objects or events, such as sharp knives or going out of doors.

7. The category of *character disorder* includes a wide variety of adjustment problems, in which, in contrast to the neurotic's problem of too much anxiety, the individual often seems to have too little anxiety. The *psychopath* engages in irresponsible and impulsive behavior, with a lack of concern for its consequences. Individuals with a *passive-aggressive* character disorder continually express hostility, but in indirect ways that are overtly denied. *Addictions* are also classified as character disorders, and the most prevalent is alcoholism. Alcohol serves to reduce anxiety, but when taken to excess it can seriously interfere with everyday living, and it can eventually cause a vari-

ety of physiological disorders, including damage to the central nervous system, the liver, and the heart. There are important differences in the degree to which different mind-altering drugs are psychologically and physiologically addictive, and it is a mistake to treat them all as highly dangerous. Much more research is needed in this area.

8. The *psychoses* are the most serious of all behavioral disturbances, and psychotic individuals often require assistance in coping with the simplest demands of ordinary living. In the *organic* psychoses, the difficulty is linked to a known injury to the brain, such as a tumor, accident, senility, or disease. In the *functional* psychoses, there is no apparent physiological disorder. Psychotic individuals usually show gross distortions in their perception of reality and in their interpersonal relationships. Also common are *delusions,* or obviously false beliefs, and *hallucinations,* or obviously false perceptions.

9. The most common psychosis is *schizophrenia,* the least understood of all the behavior disorders, which has been noted in all known cultures, both present and past. Some researchers distinguish two different patterns in the development of schizophrenia: *process* schizophrenia, with a gradual onset which includes withdrawal, reduced emotional responsiveness, and a poor prognosis; and *reactive* schizophrenia, with a sudden, dramatic onset and favorable prognosis. Distinctions have also been made between four patterns of schizophrenia according to their symptoms or behaviors. The *paranoid* schizophrenic experiences delusions, usually of persecution and of grandeur, the *catatonic* schizophrenic shows either a marked lack of physical motion or else extreme excitement, the *hebephrenic* schizophrenic shows silly, childish behavior, withdrawal, and emotional confusion, and the *simple* schizophrenic shows withdrawal, seclusiveness, and a gradual deterioration of behavior. Theories of schizophrenia must take into account both genetic and environmental factors.

10. The *affective* psychoses refer to manic and depressive disorders. In psychotic *depression,* the individual is profoundly sad and lonely, feels worthless and guilty, and may attempt suicide. In the *manic* state, there is intense elation, a speeding up of activity, and often wild and extravagant ideas. Manic and depressive problems may appear in cyclical fashion in the same person. In understanding the affective disorders, both hereditary and environmental factors must be considered.

KEY TERMS

biological	biofeedback
medical	hysteria
disease model	amnesia
neurosis	fugue
"free-floating" anxiety	malingering
neurasthenia	hypochondriasis

obsessive-compulsive
  neurosis

character disorders

psychopaths

sociopaths

passive-aggressive

alcoholics

delusions

hallucinations

organic psychoses

functional psychoses

schizophrenia

process schizophrenia

reactive schizophrenia

paranoid schizophrenia

catatonic schizophrenia

hebephrenic schizophrenia

simple schizophrenia

manic-depressive
  psychoses

EIGHT

Human Sexuality

Scientific knowledge about sexuality has been greatly advanced by the work of Alfred Kinsey and Masters and Johnson.

Masters and Johnson studied the anatomy and physiology of the human sexual response through direct laboratory observation.

- Sexual arousal in both sexes brings about myotonia and vasocongestion.
- The sexual response cycle can be divided into four phases: excitement, plateau, orgasm, and resolution.
- Societies differ in their patterns of sexual behavior.
- Despite popular belief, sexual attitudes and behaviors have not changed much in recent years.

Sexual behavior is mostly learned.

- Biological factors can affect sexual functioning.
- Sexual identity is predominantly learned, through the child's early assignment to a specific sex role.
- Homosexuality is a complex concept, and covers a wide range of behaviors and attitudes.
- The disorders of impotence in males and orgasmic dysfunction in females are found to be mostly learned.

SEXUALITY IS ONE OF THE MOST IMPORTANT ASPECTS OF HUMAN BEHAVIOR. We have previously discussed the central role given to sexuality or libido in psychoanalytic theory by Sigmund Freud and his followers. We have also seen that sex training constitutes one of the universal aspects of the socialization process, and that there is a great deal of anxiety and guilt attached to sexual behavior in our society despite the many changes in sexual customs and attitudes that have occurred in the past fifty years. In this chapter we will attempt to provide a systematic though brief overview of human sexuality and adjustment, discussing in detail some of the issues raised earlier and introducing some new ones.

Scientific knowledge about human sexuality has been greatly advanced in the recent past by the work of two research groups: Alfred C. Kinsey and his coworkers (1948, 1953) at Indiana University, and William H. Masters and Virginia E. Johnson and their staff (1966, 1970) at the Reproductive Biology Research Foundation in St. Louis, Missouri. Kinsey's monumental studies involved individual interviews with more than 18,000 people, in which questions were asked concerning the intimate details of their sexual experiences. The two resulting volumes, reporting on the sexual behavior of men and women, provide the most comprehensive and intensive survey of human sexual behavior yet available. In contrast to the interview procedures used by Kinsey, Masters and Johnson (1966) developed techniques that permitted the direct observation and recording of sexual responses in laboratory settings. Their research was focused primarily on the anatomy and physiology of the human sexual response, in an attempt to answer the question: "What do men and women do in response to effective sexual stimulation?" The subjects for their research were 382 female and 312 male volunteers, all of whom were screened for obvious physical and psychological abnormalities.

Although Kinsey's work was carried out earlier than that of Masters and Johnson, it is more appropriate to begin our discussion with the later work, which has provided us with the most comprehensive understanding to date of the anatomy and physiology of sex. Once having understood the unlearned, biological aspects of the subject, we will be in a better position to study the effects of learning and social factors. It is assumed that most readers will have been exposed in the past to sex education, but most of these programs tend to focus on reproduction rather than purely sexual matters. Also, many of them were developed before the work of Masters and Johnson was generally available, and some that have been developed subsequently have not paid much attention to this work.

THE ANATOMY AND PHYSIOLOGY OF SEX

The Work of Masters and Johnson

As we have said, Masters and Johnson addressed themselves to the study of the effects of sexual stimulation, using the method of direct laboratory observation. The first step in the procedure was always to establish an atmosphere of mutual trust and to gather biographical and personal data about the subjects. Following these procedures, they observed each of their subjects while engaged in a sexual act. These acts included: (1) automanipulation (masturbation) and other kinds of self-stimulation; (2) artificial intercourse or coitus (for women, using a plastic penis-like object containing sensitive recording instruments); and (3) natural intercourse, typically with one's husband or wife. Their data included: (1) gross behavior observation; (2) direct physiological recordings; and (3) direct questions before, during, and after the sexual act. Masters and Johnson (1966) estimated that they were able to observe at least 10,000 complete cycles of sexual response, and it is upon these observations that their conclusions are based.

Although these observations were made under conditions that were obviously unusual and involved subjects that probably were not closely representative of people in general, the results are clearly the most definitive that are available about human sexual responses on the direct physiological level. Also, the consistency of many of their findings suggests that the basic physiological processes studied are largely unaffected by psychological and social factors. Let us examine the findings in summary form, first for males, then for females, and then for what they have termed the cycle of sexual arousal.

William H. Masters
and Virginia E. Johnson

Male Anatomy and Physiology

The external genital organs of the male consist of the penis and the scrotum, the sac in which the testes or testicles are located. Figure 8-1 presents a cross-sectional view of the male pelvis, showing the external genitalia. The adult penis is composed of three cylindrical bodies of erectile tissue. As shown in Figure 8-2, two of these spongy bodies, the corpora cavernosa, lie parallel to each other and just above the third cylinder, the corpus spongiosum, which contains the urethra. It is these structures that permit the penis to enlarge upon sexual stimulation and become erect, a process involving **myotonia,** an increase in the muscle tension in the genital area, and **vasocongestion,** an increase in the blood supply in the penis. These cavernous bodies are responsible for giving the erect penis its inverted triangular shape. The erection is lost when the blood supply to the penis is reduced, primarily through the constriction of the arteries that lead to it.

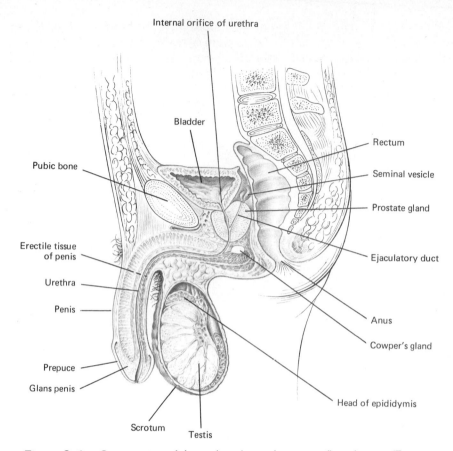

Figure 8-1.   Cross section of the male pelvis with penis in flaccid state. (From Eric T. Pengelley, *Sex and Human Life,* Reading, Mass.: Addison-Wesley, 1974.)

In the adult male, the length of the average penis when flaccid or limp is from 8 to 10.5 cm, its diameter is somewhat over 2 cm, and its circumference about 8 cm. When tumescent or erect, the average penis extends from 12 to 17 cm in length and is about 4 cm in diameter. There are, of course, wide individual differences in the size of both the erect and flaccid penis. However, there is little or no relationship between the size of the penis when flaccid and when erect, since the increase in size for a large penis is in general less marked than for a small one. There is also little or no relationship between penile size and general body size. Males are commonly concerned about their penis size, which has traditionally been presumed to reflect sexual prowess. Masters and Johnson discovered, however, that size of penis had little relationship to a marital partner's satisfaction in sexual intercourse, since the vagina accommodates itself to the size of the male organ.

The penis, and especially the *glans,* its smooth, conelike head, is markedly sensitive to sexual stimulation, as are the scrotum and the rectum. As we previously noted, sexual stimulation results in vasocongestion and myotonia; also, as arousal increases, color changes may occur in the penis, especially in the corona. The corona, and sometimes the entire glans, may become mottled reddish-purple in

Figure 8-2. Longitudinal and cross-sectional views of the male penis. (From Eric T. Pengelley, *Sex and Human Life,* Reading, Mass.: Addison-Wesley, 1974.)

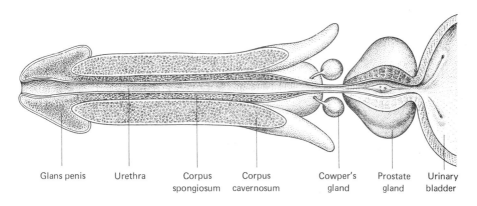

| Glans penis | Urethra | Corpus spongiosum | Corpus cavernosum | Cowper's gland | Prostate gland | Urinary bladder |

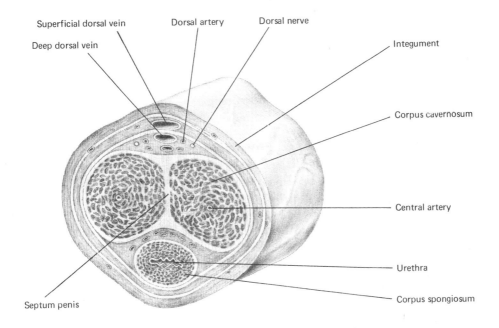

color, changes which usually signal the approach of orgasm, although these changes are highly variable and are not found in all males. Also, as arousal continues, the testicles are enlarged and elevated in the scrotum and the scrotum thickens and darkens in color.

As sexual tension mounts, a preorgasmic secretion can usually be observed as it escapes involuntarily from the penis. It is important to note that this secretion usually contains active sperm cells, so that impregnation is thus possible prior to ejaculation. The source of this emission and the reasons for it are as yet unknown, although it is frequently attributed to Cowper's glands, the two small structures at each side of the base of the penis.

Female Anatomy and Physiology

The external genitalia of the human female, or vulva, are shown in Figure 8-3, and include the labia majora (major or outer lips), the labia minora (small inner lips), and the clitoris. The labia majora, when sexually unstimulated, normally meet in the midline and protect the underlying structures—the minor labia, the vaginal outlet or vestibule, and the urinary meatus. In sexual arousal the major labia thin out and usually flatten in order to expose the minor labia and the vaginal outlet.

The minor labia undergo a variety of changes during sexual arousal. They increase in size, often two to three times in diameter, and the enlarged minor labia then protrude through the thinned major labia. The minor labia also become slightly elevated in an upward and outward direction away from the vaginal outlet, and they undergo a marked change in color, usually from pink to bright red in women who have not borne children. Masters and Johnson believe that the more brilliant and definitive the color change, or *sex skin*, the more intense has been the woman's response to sexual stimulation. The expansion in size and the color changes are brought about by vasocongestion, as in the case of the male penis.

The **clitoris** is a small cylindrical node of tissue, rich in nerve endings and containing two sponge-like cavernous bodies, which fill with blood upon sexual excitation much in the manner of the penis. When engorged with blood, the clitoris is substantially enlarged, especially in its diameter, frequently becoming twice its normal size. The function of the clitoris is entirely one of sexual excitation; the penis, on the other hand, is also involved in the transportation of semen and in the nonsexual function of urination.

The *vagina* is a muscular tube which receives the erect penis during coitus. As is true of the external genitalia, the vaginal opening has many nerve endings and blood vessels that respond to sexual stimulation. According to Masters and Johnson, the first physiological evidence of the human female's response to any form of effective sexual stimulation is vaginal lubrication. Within 10 to 30 seconds after effective sexual stimulation, either physical or psychological, a "sweating" response can be observed on the walls of the vaginal barrel, much like perspiration

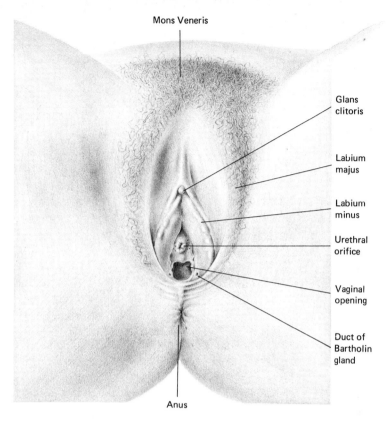

Figure 8-3. The external female genitalia. (From Eric T. Pengelley, *Sex and Human Life*, Reading, Mass.: Addison-Wesley, 1974.)

on the forehead. This sweating provides the necessary lubrication for coitus and occurs rather early in sexual arousal.

As sexual tension further increases, the vaginal barrel expands in both length and diameter. Since the walls of the unstimulated vagina actually touch, this expansion of the barrel is necessary in order for the vagina to accept the erect penis. During orgasm, there are strong contractions of the lower or outer third of the vagina, a section that Masters and Johnson have termed the orgasmic platform. These contractions are the only vaginal responses that were noted during orgasm, and their duration and intensity were found to vary from woman to woman and also within the same individual from experience to experience. Figure 8-4 shows the changes that occur in the female as a function of sexual stimulation.

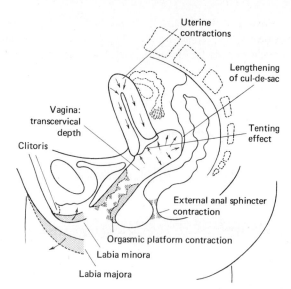

Figure 8-4. Cross section of the female pelvis showing the physiological changes which typically occur in orgasm. (From Eric T. Pengelley, *Sex and Human Life,* Reading, Mass.: Addison-Wesley, 1974.)

The *uterus,* or womb, is a hollow, pear-shaped muscular organ that opens into the vagina. Early in sexual arousal, the position of the uterus becomes more elevated on the pelvis and considerable vasocongestion occurs. This increase in the blood supply of the uterus can be up to two or three times the unstimulated supply. Masters and Johnson have reported that prolonged sexual stimulation without orgasm can result in fairly generalized engorgement with blood of both the internal and external female genitalia, causing cramping, genital pain, low back pain, irritability, and sleeplessness. Both the pelvic vasocongestion and the subjective discomfort completely disappear within ten minutes following orgasm.

What conclusions can be drawn from these data about female sexuality? It should be obvious that the pattern of physiological responses in the human female is roughly parallel to that of the human male, and involves vasocongestion of the internal and external genitalia, changes in the size, shape, position, and lubrication of the genitalia, and heightened muscle tension. The work of Masters and Johnson has also made clear something that has not been so apparent, namely, that the physiological responses of the human female are probably more complex than those of the human male.

The Human Sexual Response Cycle

We now turn our attention to what occurs during the sexual cycle, recognizing that we have already noted some of the specific changes that occur in the genitalia.

Masters and Johnson have arbitrarily divided the **sexual response cycle** into four phases: (1) excitement; (2) plateau; (3) orgasm; and (4) resolution. The same cycle occurs for both men and women, although women do not show the refractory period that is experienced by men in the resolution phase immediately following orgasm. Figure 8-5 gives a schematic representation of the cycles for men and women separately.

All four phases involve both specific genital changes and general bodily reactions. For both males and females, the excitement phase develops in response to any form of effective sexual stimulation, either physical or psychological. In the male, the excitement phase is marked by penile erection and some elevation of the testicles, as well as thickening and elevation of the scrotum. In the female, there is vaginal lubrication, flattening and elevation of the major labia, and some thickening and expansion of the vaginal barrel. For both males and females there is nipple erection, a superficial flush over the face and body—the "sex flush"—and increased muscle tension throughout the body.

If sexual stimulation is effectively maintained, the second or plateau phase is entered. Here the degree of sexual tension is more intense, and there is more vasocongestion, not only in the pelvis but throughout the entire body. There is a marked reduction in the degree to which the individual responds to stimuli other than sexual ones, and both hyperventilation (excessively rapid and deep breathing) and tachycardia (excessively rapid heart action) can be observed. The changes in the genitalia outlined above become more marked, and the individual is now at a level from which it is fairly easy to move to orgasmic release of the accumulated physiological and psychological tensions that have been built up.

For human males the orgasmic phase is entered when there is a sensation of "feeling the ejaculation coming." This sensation appears to arise from a series of contractions of the accessory sexual organs of reproduction—the vas deferens, seminal vesicles, ejaculatory duct, and prostate. From the onset of this sensation until the moment of actual ejaculation there is a period of two to three seconds during which the male can no longer constrain, delay, or in any way control the process. Masters and Johnson have termed this the period of "ejaculatory inevitability." The seminal fluid is compressed and ejected along the penile urethra, and the contractions, which now include the muscles in the penile shaft, continue until all of the seminal fluid has been discharged from the urethra.

For human females, orgasm is a suffusive, short-term reaction which usually includes contractions of the internal genitalia. As noted above, orgasmic patterns vary markedly among women and also from experience to experience. These variations are illustrated in part by the three different patterns, A, B, and C, in Figure 8-5. Pattern A shows two rather intense orgasmic reactions separated by a brief return to the plateau phase. Pattern B shows a series of low intensity orgasms, perhaps of such low intensity that they might not even have been regarded as orgasms. Pattern C shows a single orgasm without much time in the plateau phase,

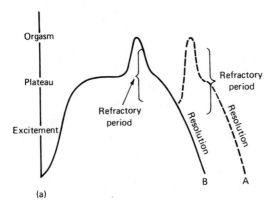

(a)

Figure 8-5. The human sexual response cycle: (a) male; (b) female. (Adapted from Masters and Johnson, 1966.)

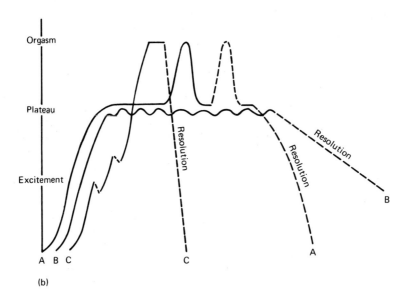

(b)

followed by a rapid resolution. While each of these patterns tends to be characteristic of some women, there are other women who show all three patterns in the course of their sexual experience. Despite these differences in pattern, Masters and Johnson state that female orgasm has its onset in contractions of the muscles of the uterus, and that these contractions quickly move downward to the orgasmic platform of the vagina. It is the contractions of both areas that the human female identifies as orgasm. Masters and Johnson found no sharply discernible changes in the clitoris during orgasm.

One question that is commonly asked in this context is whether there are differences between vaginal and clitoral orgasm. Masters and Johnson answer this question with an unequivocal no. From their physiological and anatomical records they state that, regardless of the genital area stimulated or the nature or quality of the stimulation, there is a single physiological pattern of orgasmic response, involving the vagina and clitoris in exactly the same fashion. They conclude their discussion of this question by noting that "clitoral and vaginal orgasms are not separate biologic entities" (1966, p. 67).

A somewhat different answer to this question, however, is offered by Fisher (1973), who has reported the results of interviews on the sexual responses of 300 middle class married women. Fisher found that his subjects were able to differentiate clitoral from vaginal orgasm on the basis of their own sensations. Although there were no differences in the reported ease with which the subjects could reach clitoral or vaginal orgasm, two-thirds chose the clitoral orgasm when asked to make a permanent choice between the two.

Additional research is obviously necessary to resolve these apparently discrepant findings, but it is worth noting that Fisher relied upon self-reports, while Masters and Johnson drew their conclusions from physiological data. One can compare and contrast these studies according to their methodological differences, but a more important question would seem to be whether one's stated personal preferences (i.e., self-report data) are more significant in the management of one's life than physiological data. In any event, both sets of investigators point out that most women preferred and needed both kinds of stimulation in order to reach orgasm.

A somewhat different position is presented by Hite (1976), who insists that the current preoccupation with orgasm as the central focus of the sexual response, especially for women, is not in the best interests of overall human adjustment. She argues instead that her research findings strongly suggest that arousal is as important as orgasm, and that the focus of sexuality should be the pleasure of intimate physical contact rather than orgasm.

To return to our general discussion of the orgasmic phase of sexual response as reported by Masters and Johnson, males and females show a number of similar general body reactions to orgasm, including more intense hyperventilation and tachycardia than was evidenced in the plateau phase, specific skeletal muscle contractions, and contractions of the external rectal sphincter. There are also some

interesting differences. The female's orgasm can be terminated at any point by the unexpected introduction of some external distraction, such as a loud noise. Once a male's ejaculatory process has been initiated, however, the orgasmic response will continue regardless of interruption.

Also, there is an acute refractory phase for the male which is not found for the woman. The post-orgasmic woman usually can return to the orgasmic level (pattern A in Figure 8-5, females) but this is not possible in the human male. During the male's refractory phase, the level of sexual tension usually falls below that of the plateau phase, and any form of sexual stimulation will bring about only a partial erection at best. Only after this refractory phase has run its course can the male be restimulated to higher levels of sexual tension and successive orgasms (pattern A in Figure 8-5, males). The human female, however, is capable of multiple orgasms if restimulated, without the level of sexual tension ever falling below the plateau phase.

Because of the work of Masters and Johnson, we now have a great deal more knowledge about the specific physiology of the human sexual response than was previously available, especially in regard to the nature of the arousal and dissipation of sexual tension. Masters and Johnson were able to show that many assumptions which had traditionally been made about the nature of the human sexual response were in fact incorrect, and they also demonstrated that it is possible to conduct careful scientific biological work in the area of sexuality. Their work shows that there is little difference between men and women in the basic physiological aspects of the sexual response; for both, the basic response is vasocongestion with myotonia, with other physiological changes of secondary importance. It is also clear that there is considerable variation in sexual responsiveness from individual to individual and also within the same individual from time to time.

BIRTH CONTROL

Of basic importance in human sexuality is the question of birth control. There are at present four major types of birth control measures in addition to abstinence: (1) rhythm, (2) mechanical, (3) chemical, and (4) surgical. There are male and female versions of each major type of **contraception,** and they vary widely in their certainty of success. These methods and their degree of effectiveness are summarized in Table 8-1. We have *not* included in our list one widespread effort at birth control, **coitus interruptus,** or withdrawal of the penis immediately before ejaculation. The reason is simple—it is a very uncertain and ineffective procedure. Not only is it often difficult for the male to withdraw prior to ejaculation, but active sperm cells are almost always contained in the pre-ejaculatory fluid.

Couples who use the **rhythm method** engage in intercourse only during that time of the menstrual cycle when pregnancy is thought to be unlikely to occur. In a normal cycle of 28 days, pregnancy can be avoided by refraining from intercourse during ovulation, a period of approximately 24 hours occurring 12-16 days after the beginning of the previous menstrual period. The efficacy of this method depends upon how accurately ovulation can be determined. Since many women do not have completely regular cycles, it is often difficult to determine when the "safe period" begins and ends, and this method has very low reliability.

The primary mechanical means of contraception is the **condom,** a rubber sheath that is worn by the male during intercourse. The condom mechanically pre-

Table 8-1
The Various Modes of Contraception and Their Effectiveness

Type	Male	Female	Effectiveness
	Gender of user		
(1) Rhythm	Abstinence	Abstinence	Low
(2) Mechanical	Condom	Diaphragm	Moderate
		Intrauterine device	Good
(3) Chemical	None available	The pill	Excellent
(4) Surgical	Vasectomy	Tubal ligation	Excellent

vents the sperm from entering the vaginal opening; instead, the sperm are collected inside the condom. Care must be taken to prevent rupturing the condom
and also to avoid spillage into the vagina after ejaculation. Used with care, the condom is a fairly effective means of contraception, although some men report that it
reduces their sensation and their satisfaction.

The female counterpart of the condom is the **diaphragm,** a dishlike, soft rubber
device which is placed in the vagina at the mouth of the uterus before intercourse.
The diaphragm blocks the sperm from entering the uterus, thus preventing conception. In order to be effective the diaphragm must be properly fitted, usually by a
physician, and it must be left in place after use until the sperm are no longer alive.

Another mechanical device which prevents conception is the **intrauterine
device** or IUD. The IUD, a small, irregularly shaped piece of sterile plastic, is
placed by a physician in the woman's uterus, where it remains until pregnancy is
desired. The IUD prevents pregnancy for reasons that are still not clear, perhaps
because of chemical or other changes in the uterus produced by this foreign body.
It can, however, cause severe cramping and discomfort in some women, and more
rarely, it can perforate the wall of the uterus and produce dangerous infection. It is
also possible for it to be dislodged without the woman's knowledge, and pregnancies have occurred with the IUD in place.

The use of a **douche,** the rinsing of the vagina with a water spray into which
some spermicidal chemicals may have been added, is a popular contraceptive practice, but it is not an effective procedure. By the time a douche can be used the
sperm will have already entered the uterus, where no rinsing can reach. The widespread use of this technique, despite its lack of effectiveness, shows that many
people are limited in their knowledge of effective birth control measures.

The most recent and the most successful way of controlling conception is **the
birth control pill,** a chemical which inhibits ovulation. Taken by the woman on a
regular basis, the pill has proven its effectiveness in both laboratory and field
studies. Although it is constantly being improved by research, the pill still produces
undesirable side effects in some users—weight gain, nausea, and enlargement and
tenderness of the breasts. Research has also shown a possible increase in disorders
such as circulatory diseases and diabetes in women who are predisposed to these
disorders. Probably the most dangerous side effect is an increased risk of blood
clots for some women. It is interesting to note that most side effects appear within
the first six months of use, and that follow-up studies of women who have used
the pill constantly over a number of years show no clear long-term adverse effects.
A recent report on the seventeen-year history of oral contraceptives (Beral and
Kay, 1977) has found that this method is still the most effective available, and
highly recommends that users should minimize the dangers through ongoing medical consultation.

Efforts have been made to develop a "morning after" pill for use by women, and
also a pill for males which would affect either sperm vitality or production. While
progress has been made on the "morning after" pill despite its unpleasant side

effects, the extent of the side effects of the pills for males has as yet prevented their introduction to the general public.

Spermicidal creams, jellies, and foams have also been developed. A measured dose must be inserted into the vagina before intercourse; each dose is supposed to be adequate to kill the sperm deposited during that sexual act. Although laboratory tests indicate that these measures should be highly effective, especially for spermicidal foam, human forgetfulness and error make the foams and creams less effective in actual practice. Also, many couples find their use unaesthetic and unpleasant.

It is possible to curtail fertility by surgical means for both males and females. In a **vasectomy,** the male's vas deferens are clipped and tied by a physician so that the sperm are not part of the ejaculate fluid; instead, they are absorbed by the body without any physical effects. In a **tubal ligation,** the woman's fallopian tubes are clipped and tied so that the ova can no longer enter the uterus. In both cases these are relatively permanent surgical procedures and are usually recommended only for persons who have already had children. Because the changes are permanent, most birth control centers insist upon careful psychological assessment and counseling before these surgical procedures are used.

The final surgical technique of birth control is **abortion,** the destruction of the fetus. Although this can be done quite easily, especially early in pregnancy, there are clear ethical and financial problems involved. Discussion of these issues is beyond the scope of this book; rather, let us ask why abortion is necessary at all. Since most of the birth control techniques that we have discussed are easily available, why should an abortion ever be desired, except in the case of rape or occasional contraceptive failure?

The answer lies in our attitudes to sexuality, especially our difficulties in accepting our own sexuality. Although the prevention of unwanted pregnancy must be seen as a joint responsibility of both partners, a quick review of the above discussion of contraception will show that the most effective techniques are those that are used by the female and require forethought and planning. Thus, the woman must be able to recognize fully her own sexual impulses and desires, and plan for the necessary steps to prevent pregnancy. For many women, including many married women, this is impossible to do. In studies conducted in abortion clinics, many of the patients insisted that their pregnancy was an "accident" and that there was no reason to consider using contraceptives regularly since "it can never happen again." Because of the importance of these attitudes and the rather distressing number of multiple abortions, most abortion clinics have begun to include birth control counseling and planning as part of the total abortion program.

PATTERNS OF SEXUAL BEHAVIOR

The work of Masters and Johnson has told us much about the physiology of the sexual response in humans, but it is important to remember that sexual behavior is less dependent upon physiology for humans than for any other species. The pattern of physiological arousal described by Masters and Johnson is, of course, basic and probably unlearned, but social-learning factors determine such things as the circumstances under which these patterns are permitted to occur, their frequency, and in many cases, the effectiveness of the sexual stimulation.

In mature humans the sexual drive is relatively stable for both sexes. In contrast with other mammals, for example, in which female sexual drive is dependent upon hormonal factors associated with the female ovulation cycle, the human female experiences sexual desire throughout her monthly ovulation cycle. For example, female chimpanzees are attracted to males and are sexually responsive only during the six days in the midportion of their menstrual cycle (Jensen, 1973; Michael and Herbert, 1963). Thus, it would appear that female primates solicit sex when ovulation is imminent and impregnation is thus more likely. On the other hand, most human females express more sexual desire at those times when ovulation is least likely and the probability of impregnation is therfore lower (Ford and Beach, 1951). Thus, sexual behavior in humans appears to be more closely related to sexual satisfaction than to propagation. No longer dependent upon the limitations of the woman's fertility cycle, human sexuality has become more closely tied to experience or social learning, and the brain rather than the glands has become the dominant organ in determining sexual behavior.

Anthropologists have collected a considerable amount of information on differences in sexual behavior among various human societies (Ford and Beach, 1951). Let us illustrate some of these differences. In our own society kissing is probably the most universal behavior linked with sexual arousal, but there are some societies where kissing is unknown. For instance, although the Siriono have no prohibition against kissing, it is simply not part of their pattern of love making. The first time members of the Thonga society saw Westerners kissing, they laughed and were surprised that such otherwise civilized people could "eat each other's saliva and dirt." Kissing was also found to be unknown to the Balinese, but they had substituted for it a facial caress that involved sufficient closeness that each could smell the perfume of the other and feel the warmth of the other's skin with slight movements of the head. It is this behavior that Westerners have wrongly termed "rubbing noses."

Stimulation of the female's genitalia by the male, especially the clitoris, is commonly practiced in other societies than our own, including the Crow, the Dahomeans, and the Marianas. In some cultures, fingering the woman's genitalia often serves as an initial erotic advance. For example, among the Crow Indians the male crawls up to the woman's lodge, attempts to locate her bed, puts his arm in her bed roll, and stimulates her clitoris, while remaining outside the lodge himself. If he is successful in this behavior, the woman frequently responds by having intercourse with him. And among the Trobriand Islanders it is believed that if a man subjects his finger to a magical charm and inserts it into a woman's vagina, she will find him sexually irresistible. Such differences in sexual behavior among human societies, of which these are only a small selection, provide clear evidence for the strong influence of social learning in the determination of sexual behavior.

The Kinsey Studies

The most definitive evidence to support the role of social learning in determining sexual behavior in our society comes from the two research reports of Alfred C. Kinsey and his coworkers (Kinsey *et al.*, 1948, 1953), the first on males and the second on females. Over a period of 30 years, the Kinsey team interviewed over 18,000 people about their sexual experiences. These individual interviews were indeed all-inclusive, covering a total of 521 items (Kinsey *et al.*, 1948, pp. 63–70), and it should be noted that it was Kinsey and his professional colleagues themselves, rather than assistants, who did the actual interviewing.

In both of Kinsey's research reports, the interview responses were analyzed according to six major forms of sexual outlet: (1) masturbation; (2) spontaneous nocturnal orgasms; (3) heterosexual petting; (4) heterosexual coitus; (5) homosexual relationships; and (6) animal contacts. Information was also collected on the socioeconomic status of the respondents, their religious affiliation, the degree of their religious devoutness, and their educational level. In our brief overview of Kinsey's findings, we shall emphasize the results based upon differences in educational level, since these were the most striking. Kinsey used three categories of educational background: (1) those with thirteen or more years of education (the college group); (2) those with nine to twelve years of education (the high school group); and (3) those respondents with eight or fewer years of education (the grade school group).

In regard to masturbation, 95 percent of Kinsey's males reported having masturbated to orgasm, while approximately 60 percent of the females reported this behavior. There were slight differences in the males as a function of education: 96 percent of the college group, 95 percent of the high school group, and 89 percent of the grade school group. The differences in educational level were more striking for the women, for whom the respective percentages were 63, 59, and 34. One interesting difference between the sexes is that the reported frequency of masturbation declined sharply in males after the teens, while it increased in females until middle age and then became fairly constant.

Spontaneous nocturnal orgasms were reported by a very high percentage of the men in Kinsey's sample; what may be more surprising is that 37 percent of the women also reported this experience. Indeed, 70 percent of the women interviewed reported dreams of specific sexual content, and over half of them reported that the dreams led to orgasm. Since, however, female nocturnal orgasm leaves no physical traces, it is difficult to judge the accuracy of this estimate. For both men and women, greater educational attainment was associated with higher reported frequency of nocturnal orgasm.

Kinsey defined heterosexual petting to mean any deliberate sexual arousal between persons of the opposite sex that did not lead to coitus. His data for males, especially on petting to orgasm, show striking differences as a function of education, with 61 percent of the college group, 32 percent of the high school group, and 16 percent of the grade school group reporting this behavior—a 100 percent increase for each level of education. For women, on the other hand, only 39 percent reported orgasm as a result of petting, and there were no differences as a function of educational background. For both males and females there was a strong "generational" effect, with those born later in the century, especially after 1920, reporting more experiences.

The findings on heterosexual intercourse were categorized into premarital, marital, and extramarital relationships. With respect to premarital intercourse, there were again striking differences among the males as a function of education, with 67 percent of the college group, 84 percent of the high school group, and 98 percent of the grade school group reporting this behavior. There were also striking educational differences among the women, but in the opposite direction to those of the men; for women, 62 percent of the college group, 47 percent of the high school group, and 30 percent of the grade school group reported premarital intercourse. In discussing these findings, Kinsey pointed out that the lower percentage of premarital coitus in the female grade school group was primarily due to the extremely early age at which marriage occurred in that group, giving them much less opportunity for such activity. Examination of the data for single women aged 20 and above showed no educational differences in premarital intercourse.

Some interesting differences as a function of educational level emerged from an analysis of marital coitus among males. The grade school group reported, for example, that early in their marriages, 80 percent of their total sexual outlet was in marital intercourse, and this percentage increased to 90 percent after a few years and remained constant. For the college group, however, marital intercourse comprised 85 percent of the total male outlet early in marriage but dropped later to 62 percent. For the grade school group, 47 percent reported extramarital coital relationships early in their marriage, dropping steadily to 19 percent at age 50. In contrast, the college group showed a steady increase in the percentage reporting extramarital intercourse during the same time span (15 to 27 percent). Interestingly, the grade school males tended to have their extramarital relationships primarily with prostitutes, while the college males tended to have them with women married to their friends and neighbors. As one would expect from the previous statement, the reported frequency of extramarital intercourse by women was also related to educational level, with 31 percent of the college educated women but only 24 percent of the other two groups reporting this behavior.

In regard to homosexual activity, Kinsey found that by age 45, 37 percent of the males and 13 percent of the females had had homosexual experience leading to orgasm. For males, 34 percent of the college group, 29 percent of the high school group and 27 percent of the grade school group reported at least one homosexual experience by age 30. For women, a similar trend in regard to educational level was found, with 10 percent of the college group, 6 percent of the high school group, and 5 percent of the grade school group reporting at least a single homosexual experience by age 30. We return to the topic of homosexuality later in this chapter.

Sexual contacts with animals were found to constitute a negligible sexual outlet for both males and females, producing considerably less than one percent of the total outlets for either group. Most sexual contacts with animals occurred in preadolescent boys living in rural settings.

In addition to Kinsey's differences in reported sexual behavior as a function of educational level, the results showed one important general finding with regard to religious differences. The sample included the three major American religious faiths—Catholic, Protestant, and Jewish—and each respondent was further classified as either devout or inactive on the basis of participation in regularly organized religious activities. In general, there were no differences in the reported sexual behavior among the three religions, but there were large differences between the devout and inactive groups, regardless of the specific faith involved. The religiously

Has there been a sexual revolution, or were the sexual activities of past generations shrouded in secrecy and hypocrisy? This 1886 illustration from the *National Police* *Gazette* depicts "the orgies indulged in by Yale students and their female friends in a subterranean cave at New Haven, Connecticut."

inactive were more sexually active than the devout in all respects, including frequency of marital intercourse. Since the teachings of the three faiths with respect to sexual behavior are highly similar, the similarities in their reported sexual behaviors are not surprising. Also, the findings in regard to devout versus inactive practitioners are consistent with the fact that all three religions counsel sexual restraint. They are also consistent with the fact that human sexual behavior is heavily dependent upon social-learning experiences, including the effects of formal religion.

Taken as a whole, the findings reported by Kinsey strongly suggest that there are as many differences in sexual patterns among the various segments of American society as there are among different societies, again indicating the importance of social learning in sexual behavior. It is particularly interesting that each of these social groupings tends to regard its own pattern of sexual behavior as the "natural" or "normal" one, and the patterns of other segments as peculiar or perverse. For example, premarital virginity for males is most likely to be found in the college-educated group; yet at the same time, collegiate life is popularly viewed as "wild" or "licentious." Kinsey felt that the reason for this view of college life lay in the fact that it was the college male who was most likely to engage in petting to climax, a behavior which is regarded as unacceptable and even perverse by persons in lower education groups. Knowledge of such differences in sexual mores makes an important contribution to our understanding of the conflicts that are often observed between the different social levels in our society.

Besides reporting differences in the frequency with which given sexual outlets are used in the various segments of American society, the Kinsey volumes report many other differences in sexual behavior and attitudes among the three educational groups. For example, there are notable differences as to the sources of erotic stimulation, the frequency with which intercourse is performed in the nude as compared to partial dress, whether in the dark or the light, and whether or not petting precedes coitus. In general, each educational level tends to have its own clear-cut pattern of both sexual behaviors and sexual attitudes; and, of course, educational level is highly related to socioeconomic level in American society. The consistency of these patterns, and the fact that they are regarded as standards of appropriate behavior for most group members, offer further important support for the conclusion that sexual behavior is learned.

There is yet another important general finding that supports the conclusion that sexual behavior is learned. This is the fact that the pattern of sexual behavior developed in early adolescence continues to be rather stable for at least the next 35 to 40 years, especially for males. Males who reach puberty early not only begin their sexual activity earlier than those who mature late, but they also maintain a higher frequency of sexual activity throughout their lives and have a broader sexual repertoire. It is possible to ascribe sexual activity to hormonal or other physical differences, but the differences in broadness of sexual behavior cannot be accounted for in this manner. Further, Kinsey pointed out that there are long-term consistencies not only in sexual behavior but in sexual attitudes as well, with those males who lead very active sexual lives reporting greater interest in sexual matters very early in life, often as early as 7 or 8 years of age.

Kinsey's data and his conclusions have been severely criticized because of a number of possible shortcomings in his research methods, but his results are very much in line with those of other investigators who have done less extensive work. The Kinsey research also withstood the examination of a special committee of the American Statistical Association that was appointed to review its scientific merits. The committee concluded that, in comparison with other studies in this area, Kinsey's work was markedly superior, and that although certain specific aspects of his findings were open to question, the conclusions were substantially correct (Cochran, Mosteller, and Tukey, 1953).

Is There a Sexual Revolution?

One problem that arises in applying the information of the Kinsey reports to today's world is that the data are now more than 30 years old. Since the time of Kinsey's work there has not been a single follow-up study of sexual behavior that comes close to the scope and thoroughness of the original work. The past ten years have seen the publication of the Hunt study (1974) and the *Redbook* study (Levin and Levin, 1975), but neither of these two more recent studies is as comprehensive or thorough as the original Kinsey work. The Hunt study involves 2,026 questionnaire responses, which represent only a 20-percent return on the total number of questionnaires mailed out. While the *Redbook* study reports data from more than 100,000 respondents, the sample is biased in a number of ways, making it difficult to know how representative these findings are. Thus, since up-to-date information of the type presented in the Kinsey reports is not available, it is difficult to know whether or not major changes are now occurring in society with regard to sexual behavior.

In the absence of hard facts, the answer that each one of us gives to this question will depend on what we believe about the sexual behavior of earlier times. If one assumes that the members of the generation immediately preceding us (that is, our own parents) were virginal before marriage, completely faithful to their spouses, and sexually inhibited in general, one would be likely to conclude that society is now engaged in a sexual revolution. If, on the other hand, we assume that the preceding generation was rather sexually active prior to marriage, and that there was considerable extramarital activity and other forms of forbidden sexuality, but in the context of much more secrecy and hypocrisy, then we would conclude that the revolution is not in sexual behavior but in truthfulness.

Kinsey's results tend to be consistent with the latter of these two assumptions, namely, that earlier generations are about as sexually active as succeeding generations. Kinsey also pointed out that while the changes in sexual behavior and sexual

attitudes from generation to generation tend to be rather small, each older generation believes that the world is becoming more licentious and perverted. Thus, it is most likely that any current sexual revolution is in attitudes rather than in behavior, so that people of today are more likely to be open about matters that our parents' generation would have kept secret. The very inclusion of this chapter in a psychology text can be taken as some indication of changes in sexual attitudes. Even as recently as 20 years ago, it would not have been possible to include such a frank discussion of human sexuality in an undergraduate textbook.

Still, it is possible to find substantial evidence that the revolution in sexual attitudes is not widespread, or at least not as widespread as many college students would like to believe. At least one relatively recent, large-scale popular survey of social attitudes showed that American youth still holds moderate or conservative views about a number of issues, including sex. In January 1970, *Life* magazine reported the results of a Harris poll involving 26 million Americans between the ages of 15 and 21. Among the findings were the following: 26 percent agreed that sexual experience before marriage would contribute to later happiness, but 50 percent disagreed; 96 percent agreed that it was important for a married man to be faithful, while 97 percent agreed that it was important for a married woman to be faithful; and 52 percent agreed that young men still consider virginity until marriage important in a woman. As in the case of Kinsey's earlier findings, there were differences between those respondents who were college educated and those who were not. For instance, 52 percent of the college group agreed that sexual relations were permissible between a couple planning to marry, but the majority of the noncollege group disagreed.

The findings of the Hunt study, despite their limitations, are somewhat similar. This study reports that by the end of their senior year in college, 40 percent of the females and 60 percent of the males have engaged in sexual intercourse, compared with Kinsey's figures of 25 percent and 50 percent respectively. Given the great increase in the number of persons attending college and the difference in the nature of their socioeconomic background, these figures can hardly be regarded as indicating any major change. If a revolution involves a radical break with the past, the two sets of findings suggest that there is little evidence to support the claim of a revolution in sexual behavior in America today.

THE LEARNING OF SEXUAL BEHAVIOR

Throughout this chapter we have emphasized that, except for the basic response of vasocongestion, sexual behavior is learned. We also noted in our earlier discussion of socialization that Western society is quite restrictive about sexuality, and that early childhood socialization in sexuality mainly involves the teaching of "shall nots." Most middle class parents, in fact, teach their children very little about the specifics of sexual behavior, and tend to discourage any interest that is displayed in these matters. However, there are some societies in which children's early interest in sex is encouraged, where children are free to observe and imitate adult sexual behavior. Ford and Beach (1951) identified a number of societies where children observe adults in sexual acts, although the child's own mother is sometimes excluded from observation; and they cite still other cultures where the children are given fairly careful formal instruction in sex, often as early as age 5. With such opportunities for learning, together with a generally permissive atmosphere about sex, these youngsters should experience no difficulties in achieving competence in the sexual area.

How are sexual responses learned in our own culture? This is a very interesting question, since there are few opportunities for observational learning, especially in the preadolescent years, and our society is generally "closed" about sexual matters. Kinsey's findings showed that in our society, the teaching of sexual behavior is done almost exclusively by peers, and that this teaching begins rather early in child-

Much sexual knowledge is acquired informally through self-exploration or interaction with peers. Rather early in childhood, children become interested in their genitals and in the appearance of the opposite sex.

hood. Children, or at the latest, preadolescents, teach each other that it is to be done "this way" and not "that way." Even before the current relaxation of censorship and the ready availability of explicit sexual material, there were very few youngsters, especially males, who had not seen and shared with each other published materials of a very explicit sexual nature. These materials, either verbal or pictorial, further enhance the peer group teaching.

As a specific example of the learning of sexual behavior, we can cite Kinsey's report that nearly all of his male subjects recalled having heard of masturbation from their peers before they attempted it themselves, and that a high proportion of them had actually observed their companions in masturbation (1948, p. 501). Romantic literature contains many stories of fathers arranging for their son's sexual "education"—of some older woman initiating an inexperienced young man into the "pleasures of the flesh"—but as we have stated, Kinsey's research data has shown that the teaching of sex is traditionally done by one's peers. This fact undoubtedly helps to explain why such teaching is often so poorly done, and why there is so much misinformation about sexuality in our society.

What would be the result if people were never taught how to perform the sexual act? In order to answer this question, we would need to rear a number of humans in complete isolation both from each other and from all human society. Then we would need to place a mature male and a mature female together for some time and discover what transpired. For obvious reasons, it is extremely unlikely that such an experiment will ever be performed, and thus we can give no definite answer to this question. Some information on this issue, however, is provided by the research of Harry Harlow and his associates at the University of Wisconsin, who have studied the consequences of social isolation for the behavior of monkeys (Harlow and Harlow, 1965). When monkeys reared in complete social isolation were paired for breeding purposes, the experiment ended in complete failure. Not a single female was ever mounted, even after the couples were given numerous opportunities at appropriate times in the females' ovulation cycle. Nor did any of these animals demonstrate a normal pattern of sexual behavior when they were later paired with monkeys who had been reared normally. None of the males ever appropriately mounted the cooperative and experienced females, even with their help; all of them showed inappropriate and disorganized behavior which continued over many successive opportunities. When an experienced and normally reared male approached an isolation-reared female and attempted to position her for coitus, she usually collapsed on the floor. This happened even at the height of her ovulation cycle, when normally reared females are extremely receptive to sexual overtures. Four of the eleven females reared in isolation were finally impregnated, but "only through the patience, persistence, knowledgeability, and motor skill of the breeding male" (p. 167).

If we are willing to extend these findings to apply to humans, we can conclude that sexual behavior must be specifically taught, and at some time before the person is completely mature. At the least, it can be stated that humans reared in isolation would probably have considerable difficulty in determining what behavior was necessary for mating and in carrying it out successfully.

LEARNING TO BE AROUSED

Earlier in this chapter we described the human sexual response cycle that follows effective sexual stimulation, but deliberately avoided any discussion of what constitutes effective stimulation. It should come as no surprise that the process of effective sexual stimulation involves the principles of learning that we have seen to underlie the overwhelming majority of human behaviors. From a physical point of view, it is clear that certain kinds of physical contact, such as kissing, genital fondling, oral-genital stimulation, and other types of fondling and caressing, are natural and automatic precipitators of the human sexual response cycle as described above.

A variety of other stimuli can acquire the capacity to become effective sexual stimulators. Some of these are, for example, other persons engaged in sexual stimulation, either in real life, in visual form (both still and motion pictures), in verbal description, or in imagination. While males tend to report greater arousal to such stimuli than females, it is clear that they constitute an important source of stimulation for both sexes. In this connection, it is interesting to note that when a sexual scene has an affectionate or romantic component, such as kissing, females and males are equally responsive (Katchadourian and Lunde, 1975). Although the specific processes by which cognitive stimuli acquire the capacity to trigger the cycle are not well understood, the influence of learning, particularly in late childhood and early adolescence, should be readily apparent.

Fetishism. The role of learning becomes much clearer in sexual disorders such as fetishism. **Fetishism** refers to sexual arousal by an object or a part of the body that is not ordinarily considered to be erotic, such as the foot, the elbow, or women's undergarments. Interestingly enough, reports of fetishism are almost entirely confined to males, a fact that again underscores the differences in sexual psychology between men and women, and perhaps also a lack of research attention to female sexual attitudes and behavior.

Considering the enormous array of objects that are associated with sexual arousal in everyday life, the development of a fetish is not difficult to understand. Any neutral object which has been associated with a pleasant sexual experience can take on sexually arousing properties by a process of simple classical conditioning. That a man can be aroused by the perfume of his mistress or his wife would surprise nobody. Rachman (1966) created a mild boot fetish in the laboratory by pairing a photograph of a pair of woman's boots with pictures of sexually arousing nude females. His male subjects continued to show sexual arousal later in the experiment when the picture of the boots alone was shown to them.

When does fetishism become a kind of sexual dysfunction? Probably when the behavior involved in the fetish leads to negative consequences; for example, fetishists frequently steal the objects that are involved, such as panties and bras. Also, the fetish is often used not only for sexual arousal but as a stimulus for masturbation, and the husband who would prefer to masturbate over a pair of his wife's panties rather than engaging in intercourse with her must be considered to have a sexual problem. On the other hand, an adolescent masturbating over a sexually provocative photo should not be a cause for concern.

Hormonal Influences on Human Sexuality

While experience or learning factors play a central role in the initiation, development, and maintenance of sexual behavior of humans, biological factors also exert an influence. Let us now examine this area.

The successful development of secondary sex characteristics depends on the hormones secreted by the gonads or sex glands. The gonads have two functions: the production of reproductive cells, and the secretion of the hormones that produce the physical changes occurring in adolescence—the rapid spurt of growth, the development of pubic hair, the enlargement of the female breasts, and the development of facial hair and changes in the pitch of the voice in males. The male sex hormones, or **androgens,** of which testosterone is the best known and understood, are produced by the testes. If the testes are removed (castration) or are damaged before puberty, the male secondary characteristics do not develop. The body shape remains typically childish or becomes obese; the voice remains high pitched, and the beard is either nonexistent or very light.

The female sex hormones, or **estrogens,** are secreted by the ovaries, and function in the same way as the androgens in producing and maintaining the secondary sex characteristics of females. If the ovaries are removed or destroyed before puberty through illness or injury, the woman does not develop the usual secondary sex characteristics.

Recent research (Money and Ehrhardt, 1972) has shown that males and females secrete both androgens and estrogens, so that in discussing hormone secretion, it is appropriate to consider the androgen-estrogen *ratio*. They have also concluded that it is androgen that is responsible for the partial regulation of the intensity and frequency of sexual arousal for *both* men and women. The higher androgen-estrogen ratio in males may account for some of the differences that were found by Kinsey in the frequency and range of sexual behavior between men and women.

What happens to human sexuality if the hormonal influences are eliminated? We have already noted that the secondary sex characteristics do not appear if this loss occurs prior to puberty, but the situation is rather different if the loss occurs after puberty. Although there might be a slight reduction in the frequency of sexual activity, sexual behavior will continue even after the elimination of the sex hormone. This effect has also been noted in other animals, such as cats and dogs; sexual behavior does not disappear after castration in animals who have had previous sexual experience. Thus, the effects of hormonal loss may be minimized through experience, in both humans and animals.

We are certainly not suggesting that human sexual behavior is free of hormonal influence, only that the effects of some of these biological factors can be reduced by experience. *Severe* disruption in hormonal supply does produce changes in sexual functioning that are not compensated by the individual's previous experience. For example, surgical removal of the pituitary gland, which monitors and controls the operation of the other glands, including the gonads, clearly disrupts sexual functioning. When surgery is necessary, as in the case of advanced carcinoma, there is a marked decrease in sexual desire and responsiveness. In less severe changes in hormonal balance, however, social factors continue to play the dominant role in determining sexual responsiveness.

The Learning of Sexual Identity

We have been concentrating our attention on the way in which learning experiences are involved in the development of human sexual responsiveness. Let us now ask to what extent learning is involved in the development of a sexual identity, that is, the creation of a gender role as either a man or a woman. It is now time to return to this topic, which was touched upon in Chapter 3, and to examine more carefully the process by which we develop a sexual identity.

Most people assume that the process of differentiating between the sexes—the first step in the learning of sexual identity—is perfectly straightforward. As explained in Chapter 1, when the human body produces germ cells for reproduction, a process of reduction division occurs so that the sperm and egg cells each carry 23 chromosomes, or half the total number to be found in the new organism. One pair of the 23 complete pairs of chromosomes is called the sex chromosomes, and is responsible for determining the sex of the child. The female egg always carries an "X" sex chromosome while the male sperm cell carries either an "X" or a "Y" chromosome. If the sperm cell that fertilizes the egg is carrying an "X" chromosome, the resulting fetus will have two "X" chromosomes and will be a female. If the egg is fertilized by a sperm carrying a "Y" chromosome, the "XY" chromosome combination will result in a male fetus. Thus, the gender of the new person produced by this process is a biological matter and is immediately obvious by inspection of the external genitalia at birth.

There is abundant evidence at both the primate and the human levels that mothers have rather different patterns of behavior toward male and female infants. Jensen's (1973) studies of mother-infant relationships in monkeys showed that mothers were more punitive toward infant males and carried, cradled, and retained them less than infant females. He concluded that the consequence of this differential handling is the greater independence which is typical of the male monkey in later life. On the human level Kagan (1969) concluded that "human mothers unconsciously or instinctively have one 'program' for female infants and another for male infants and that they put one of these into effect as soon as their child is born" (Jensen, 1973, p. 24).

As Money and Ehrhardt (1972) have pointed out, however, this "ideal" picture of sex differentiation is very much simplified. A more complete sex typing would have to include the following indices of sexual differences: (1) *genetic* sex, as revealed by a chromosomal count; (2) *hormonal* sex, or the androgen-estrogen ratio; (3) *gonadal* sex, or whether the internal glands are testes, ovaries, or mixed; (4) the nature of the internal reproductive organs; and (5) the nature of the external genitalia. When all of these indices agree, as they nearly always do, sex differentiation is straightforward, and the learning of a sex role can begin. When contradictions exist, the label **hermaphrodite** is used, and a study of these persons reveals much about the process by which gender roles are learned.

Without exception, these studies of hermaphrodites demonstrate that gender is *not* determined by the preponderant genetic or hormonal constitution but by early assignment to a sex role. Females with the disorder known as Turner's syndrome have external female genitalia but no functioning ovaries. If untreated, they never develop secondary sexual characteristics or have menstrual periods. Nevertheless, they have the same aspirations as hormonally normal females, and appear to be psychologically similar (Hampson, 1965).

Research findings of this nature suggest that it might be possible to take a biologically normal person and deliberately misassign him or her to the improper gender role. If this deception could be maintained until adolescence, when secondary sexual characteristics would create some obvious problems, we would have created a person whose psychological sexual characteristics would be opposite to all of the physical indices of gender. The clinical literature, of course, contains many examples of this

state of affairs with both hermaphrodites and normal individuals, and the situation is extremely confusing for the person involved.

It is very tempting to believe that the above process of gender misassignment plays an important role in the development of homosexuality. Hooker (1965), after studying extensively a group of exclusively homosexual males, has reported little support for this hypothesis, however. While homosexuals obviously fail to fulfill the male gender role in one sense, namely, their choice of sexual partner, there is much variability in the degree to which other aspects of the male gender role are fulfilled. Some of the homosexuals in Hooker's study rejected most of the male gender role and could be characterized as effeminate in their appearance, manner, dress, occupation, and interests, but there were others whose only deviation from the traditional male role was in their sexual behavior. Apart from that, their appearance, dress, manner, occupation, and pattern of interests were reported to be typically masculine. It is the former group of homosexuals who are likely to be recognized as sexually deviant by the rest of society because of their distinctive overt characteristics, though it is popularly believed that total rejection of the male role is typical of all homosexuals. Hooker concluded that male homosexuals do *not* in general show the expected close correspondence between gender identity and pattern of sexual behavior.

It should be recognized that the term homosexuality covers a considerable range of behaviors and attitudes. As Kinsey (1948, p. 638) was careful to point out, homosexuality is not an all-or-none category; rather, homosexuality–heterosexuality is best regarded as a continuum, as shown in Figure 8-6. In Kinsey's scheme, a person's rating along the continuum depends upon two factors: active engagement in homosexual behavior; and "psychologic reaction," that is, the degree to which a person can be sexually aroused by someone of the same sex. Since most research, including Kinsey's, indicates that the majority of people have had strong feelings toward another person of the same sex at some time in their lives, there would be few of us who would have a stable rating of "0."

The position of any individual on this continuum might well change from time to time, especially before sexual behavior tends to stabilize, which occurs in early adulthood. For instance, most of Hooker's homosexual subjects were classified as "6" at the time of her study, but since most of them had engaged in some heterosexual behavior earlier in their lives, they would have received a lower rating at those times. The important points to remember are that homosexuality represents a range of behaviors, and that these behaviors are not entirely stable over time, especially during adolescence.

It is unlikely that any single explanation will account for the divergence in sexual identity that exists among us, and a variety of theories have been put forward. Most theorists on homosexuality tend to look to the family relationships of homosexuals to account for their behavior. For example, Bieber et al. (1962) interpreted their research findings to indicate that male homosexuality is generally caused by a dominant, seductive mother and a weak or absent father. Other writers have concluded that the critical

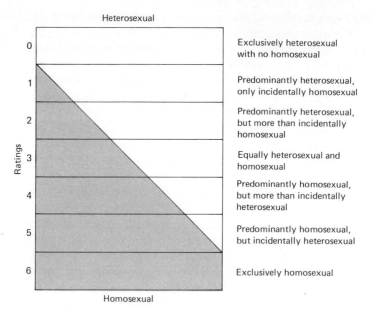

Figure 8-6. A rating scheme for evaluating the degree of homo-sexuality-heterosexuality of an individual. Ratings are based both on psychological reactions and on overt experience. (From Kinsey, 1948.)

combination is a strong, controlling mother and a detached, rejecting father. In regard to female homosexuality, a number of studies have concluded that the cause is found in disturbed family relationships, overemphasis on the evils of sex, and the lack of strong affectional ties between the girl and her family. The difficulty with these explanations is their vagueness. Not only is it possible to find many nonhomosexuals whose backgrounds fit these patterns, but there are many homosexuals whose personal histories do not fit such descriptions.

Is the cause of homosexuality to be found in genetic or hormonal factors rather than in the social-learning experiences of the individual? Although occasional studies have reported some genetic or hormonal differences between homosexuals and nonhomo-sexuals, these findings have not been clearcut and have not been substantiated by further research. Perhaps the best evidence against a purely biological explanation of homosexuality is the finding that imprisoned male homosexuals who were given large doses of the male hormone testosterone were observed to increase the vigor and fre-quency of their *homosexual* responses. Thus, it is likely that hormones influence the degree of sexual drive, but that the direction or object of the drive is learned.

One consistent finding in research on the causes of homosexuality is the existence of strongly pleasurable homosexual experiences before adolescence, and before the development of a well-differentiated heterosexual pattern of behavior. Such early and successful homosexual experience may be regarded as an instance of the *canalization* of the sexual drive (a concept introduced in Chapter 3), in much the same way that our early eating experiences canalize, or set the pattern for, the way we satisfy our hunger drive. It can perhaps be said, then, that homosexuality is in many instances an acquired behavior that is shaped fairly early in life, although we do not clearly understand the specific circumstances under which this behavior is developed.

We conclude our discussion of homosexuality by drawing attention to the statement made by Ford and Beach (1951), who suggest that homosexuality should not require any special explanation. According to the cross-cultural and cross-species comparisons made by these authors, there is a basic biological tendency for sexual inversion that is inherent in most if not all mammals, including humans. This tendency is said to be obscured in contemporary Western society, which forbids such behavior and classifies it as unnatural. If one takes the viewpoint of Ford and Beach, the task is not to explain homosexuality in our society, but to explain its absence.

The Content of Gender Role

In Chapter 3 we identified four elements that were involved in the learning of gender role. To repeat, these elements are: (1) the early and continual labeling of differences in the gender roles, so that the child becomes highly aware of the differences in the way males and females behave; (2) observational learning, especially of the same-sex parent, and self-reinforcement of this learning; (3) direct reinforcement of appropriate gender-role behaviors; and (4) observational learning of the negative consequences of performing inappropriate gender behavior. By these processes, which are sometimes referred to as *identification*, the child learns his or her appropriate gender role.

But are there no natural or unlearned sex roles? Probably not, apart from childbearing. Obviously, males and females have different overt primary sex characteristics, and these differences are directly associated with the process of producing children. In addition, there are secondary sex differences: men in general are taller, heavier, hairier, and have a higher muscle-to-fat ratio which usually gives them greater physical strength. Let us examine the findings of a now classic study by Murdock (1937), who studied the division of labor by sex in 224 primitive societies. A summary of these findings is presented in Figure 8-7.

Murdock's results show that the men of these societies were usually the ones to engage in activities that were strenuous, required long periods of difficult travel, and involved cooperation with others. Woman, on the other hand, were more likely to be engaged in activities that were physically less demanding, required less mobility, and involved less cooperation from others. These differences among primitive societies can be readily attributed to the physical requirements of hunting for food, a task assigned to males, while the females cared for their dependent children. In other words, this distribution of labor can be seen as a plan that led to the most effective and convenient pattern of living.

Activity	Number of societies in which activity is performed by				
	Men always	Men usually	Either sex	Women usually	Women always
Pursuit of sea mammals	34	1	0	0	0
Hunting	166	13	0	0	0
Trapping small animals	128	13	4	1	2
Herding	38	8	4	0	5
Fishing	98	34	19	3	4
Clearing land for agriculture	73	22	17	5	13
Dairy operations	17	4	3	1	13
Preparing and planting soil	31	23	33	20	37
Erecting and dismantling shelter	14	2	5	6	22
Tending fowl and small animals	21	4	8	1	39
Tending and harvesting crops	10	15	35	39	44
Gathering shellfish	9	48	7	25	
Making and tending fires	18	6	25	22	62
Bearing burdens	12	6	35	20	57
Preparing drinks and narcotics	20	1	13	8	57
Gathering fruits, berries, nuts	12	3	15	13	63
Gathering fuel	22	1	10	19	89
Preservation of meat and fish	8	2	10	14	74
Gathering herbs, roots, seeds	8	1	11	7	74
Cooking	5	1	9	28	158
Carrying water	7	0	5	7	119
Grinding grain	2	4	5	13	114

Figure 8-7. The division of labor by sex in 224 primitive societies. (From Murdock, 1937.)

Social evolution has changed the nature of these gender roles and has opened up other alternatives, but it is still traditional to regard the male's role as that of the provider and the female's role as that of the child rearer. There is no adequate evidence to suggest that these gender roles were "natural" in primitive societies. Rather, it should be remembered that all of us have been subjected to a long process of socialization in which we have learned the traditional gender roles of Western society, and it is this long experience that makes some gender roles seem natural and right while others seem unnatural and wrong.

SEXUAL DYSFUNCTION

So far in this chapter we have avoided the question of what constitutes sexual deviance. Let us now approach this topic, by considering two possible ways of defining deviance. In the conservative, traditional view, sexual behavior is considered to be deviant when it varies from the stated sexual standards or mores of a society. For people inclined to accept this definition of sexual deviance, note should be made of Kinsey's (1948) conclusion that more than 95 percent of the total male population had probably transgressed the legal sexual code of the state in which they were resident at some time in their lives. Even if this percentage were found to be somewhat exaggerated, no competent observer of American sexual behavior could question the fact that there is a marked discrepancy between our formal sex code—our social and legal sanctions concerning sexual behavior—and our actual sexual behavior. It makes little sense to regard virtually everyone as "deviant," but this seems to be a peculiarity of the sexual aspect of American life.

The more contemporary view is to regard as deviant or dysfunctional only those sexual behaviors that result in dissatisfaction or unhappiness for the person engaging in the behavior, such as impotence or frigidity, or for the person who is the target of the behavior, as in the case of rape. Thus, for example, homosexuality would be regarded as a problem only if it causes the individual greater negative consequences than he or she is willing to accept. In this view, sexual responses, like any other behaviors, are evaluated in terms of their consequences, both short-term and long-term. Thus there would be some persons for whom homosexuality would not be regarded as sexual dysfunction.

Many people would disagree with this conclusion about homosexuality. For example, many mental health professionals, especially psychoanalysts (Bieber *et al.*, 1962) argue that homosexuality is pathological because it is not consistent with what is regarded as the normal pattern of psychosexual development. Others point out that because of society's negative reaction in general to homosexuals, and the disdain in which they are usually held, it is practically impossible for them to achieve an adequate level of psychological adjustment. It is interesting to note, however, that the American Psychiatric Association has now removed homosexuality from its *Diagnostic and Statistical Manual,* the "official" list of psychiatric disorders.

The same points and arguments can be raised in regard to each of the sexual behaviors studied by Kinsey, and the same disagreements would appear. Let us therefore simply acknowledge the existence of these disagreements, and move on to a study of behaviors that *are* generally regarded as problematic or dysfunctional.

Sexual Inadequacy

The inability to function sexually in a normal manner is usually called **impotence** in the male and **frigidity** in the female. As Masters and Johnson point out in their more recent book, *Human Sexual Inadequacy* (1970), there are occasional circumstances under which all of us might be sexually inadequate; for example, when we are over-tired, emotionally upset, or intoxicated. Therefore, it is necessary to establish criteria for deciding when sexual inadequacy should be regarded as a problem.

Masters and Johnson define male impotence as the failure of the individual to achieve and maintain an erection that is adequate for coitus in at least 25 percent of his attempts. They also distinguish between two kinds of impotence: primary and secondary. In primary impotence, the male has *never* been able to achieve or maintain an adequate erection for coitus, while in secondary impotence, there must have been at least one successful coital experience. Masters and Johnson report that the major factors involved in impotence are "untoward maternal influences, . . . religious orthodoxy, involvement in homosexual function, and personal devaluation from prostitute experience" (1970, p. 137). It is interesting that in spite of the obvious disruption that impotence would cause to a marital relationship, Masters and Johnson report having encountered marriages of up to 18 years duration without intercourse.

Although the number of cases of impotence studied by Masters and Johnson in their research sample was rather small, the consistency of their findings is quite striking. In general, impotent males were sexually naive as well as inexperienced, and so too were their wives. The typical courtship had involved only hand-holding, and there were many inaccurate beliefs, misconceptions, and unresolved feelings in regard to sexual taboos. Further, all the impotent males reported high anxiety about sexual performance—the concern about "doing it right" that is typical of males in our society and is prominent in almost all kinds of male sexual inadequacy. In view of these factors, there should be little surprise that the initial attempts at intercourse made by these men should lead to failure, and that their subsequent shame and anxiety should actively interfere with the development of competent sexual responses. The reader is reminded of the behavior of Harlow's monkeys who, after having been reared in isolation, were never able to figure out what to do sexually.

Impotence involves more than fear and anxiety, or a lack of knowledge, however. There is a disturbance of the basic physiological response involved in sexual arousal, namely, vasocongestion. As we noted in Chapter 6, there is now clear evidence that a variety of psychophysiological responses can be conditioned, and it is possible that erectile failure can be explained by the principles of conditioning. Despite the problems that it raises, erectile failure can be reinforcing if it removes the possibility of further sexual performance and the anxiety associated with it. It is also worth noting that primary impotence is the condition that Masters and Johnson found to be the most resistant to treatment, with only half of these cases responding successfully to their treatment program. It appears that even a single positive experience of erectile competence is enough to improve the chances of success in treatment.

For women, **orgasmic dysfunction** (the term Masters and Johnson prefer over frigidity, which implies more than simply a failure to reach orgasm) is more complex than impotence in males. Since both erection and ejaculation are much more easily observed than female orgasm, it has been far more difficult to study the problems of the female. Also, society has not taught women to accept and value their sexual feelings in the same way as men, so that women have often tended to develop "romantic" notions of marriage rather than realistic sexual expectations. Further, since female orgasm is not necessary for either the male's sexual release or for conception, its importance has tended to be overlooked both scientifically and clinically, and it has not received much attention until fairly recently. Yet, as we indicated earlier in this chapter, women's physiological capacity for sexual response and orgasm is greater than that of men.

Masters and Johnson have not differentiated between different kinds of orgasmic failure in women but have been primarily concerned with those women who have never experienced orgasm under any kind of sexual stimulation, a condition they call primary orgasmic dysfunction. In view of society's restrictiveness in providing sex information for women, it is not surprising that there are many women who are unsure as to whether or not they have actually experienced orgasm.

The primary factor in the development of orgasmic dysfunction in the cases studied by Masters and Johnson appeared to be a background of religious orthodoxy. Almost all of their cases came from strict and traditional religious homes, where sex was never openly discussed, any sensual pleasure was frowned upon, and there were constant admonitions to be a "good girl." Given a lifetime of learning that sex is evil and that good girls "don't," it is not in the least surprising to find that changes cannot be made simply by a wedding ceremony. Further, in many of these cases the women were involved in rather unsatisfactory marriages, where the husband was seen as inadequate either sexually or for other reasons. Thus, the marriage relationship itself often further augmented and complicated the orgasmic failure. It should be apparent from these findings that, as in the case of male sexual inadequacy, orgasmic dysfunction is based in large degree on psychological or learning factors.

We have not identified as a problem the opposite end of the continuum of sexual behavior, that of excessive sexual needs or demands, called *satyriasis* in males and *nymphomania* in females. Given Kinsey's data (1948, 1953) showing the wide range in frequency of sexual behavior, it would be difficult to know where to set the basis for making a judgment of satyriasis or nymphomania. At least one man, a successful lawyer, reported an average of 30 ejaculations per week throughout his adult life without suffering any obvious negative consequences for either his health or his career. On the basis of what is known today about the diversity of sexual behavior, it is

Research indicates that there is little evidence linking pornography to the commitment of sexual crimes.

difficult to regard satyriasis or nymphomania as worthy of serious attention. Perhaps the most useful definition of excess in this context would be when one's frequency of sexual behavior interferes with other aspects of adjustment.

INFLUENCE OF PORNOGRAPHY

To what extent does pornography contribute to sexual dysfunction? Despite the concerns that are frequently voiced about the negative effects of reading pornography, research has shown that the major consequence of reading pornography is simply the reading of more pornography. There is no evidence whatever that reading pornography leads to sexual crimes such as rape or child molesting. To understand these disorders, we should take note once again of the fact that any neutral object can take on sexually arousing characteristics through conditioning. Sexually disturbed individuals, those most likely to injure or frighten others by their sexual behavior, more often than not become sexually aroused in unusual ways; one recently arrested rapist, for example, became sexually aroused when reading the Bible, and the elimination of pornography would obviously do little to curb his behavior! Pornography can often be legitimately regarded as lacking in good taste, and one might even argue that reading it is a waste of time, and likely to become an even greater waste of time, but there is no evidence that pornography leads to serious negative consequences.

There are many other kinds of sexual behaviors and pathologies that could be discussed, but the central point has been made: in all but a very few instances, it is psychological and social factors that determine sexual behavior. Not only do learning experiences determine the nature and quality of one's sexual life, but they also account for the deviations from what is ordinarily considered an adequate sexual adjustment.

SUMMARY

1. Scientific knowledge about sexuality, one of the most important aspects of human behavior, has been greatly advanced by the work of Alfred Kinsey and of Masters and Johnson. Kinsey's work involved detailed interviews with more than 18,000 people on their sexual experiences. Masters and Johnson studied the anatomy and physiology of the human sexual response through direct laboratory observation of volunteers engaging in a variety of sexual behaviors, including masturbation and intercourse.

2. The male external genital organs consist of the penis and scrotum. Penile erection involves increases in muscle tension (*myotonia*) and blood supply (*vasocongestion*). The size of the penis tends to be unrelated to body size or to the partner's satisfaction, despite popular beliefs to the contrary. The female external genitalia consist of the labia majora, the labia minora, and the clitoris. As with the male,

female sexual arousal brings about vasocongestion, causing color changes and size increases. The vagina also undergoes changes, expanding and providing a secretion that serves as a lubricant. The position and the blood supply of the uterus also undergo changes.

3. The human sexual response cycle can be divided into four phases. *Excitement* develops in response to any form of effective sexual stimulation; in the *plateau* phase, there is a further increase in sexual tension and other physiological changes; the *orgasm* involves intense sensations and muscular contractions; and in the *resolution*, these changes gradually dissipate. The work of Masters and Johnson has shown that there is little difference between men and women in the basic physiological aspects of the sexual response.

4. There are four major types of *birth control:* rhythm, mechanical, chemical, and surgical. In the rhythm method, intercourse is engaged in only during that part of the female fertility cycle when pregnancy is unlikely to occur. The primary mechanical means of contraception are the condom, worn by the male, and diaphragm and IUD, worn by the female. The use of a douche involving spermicidal chemicals is popular but not very effective, and the same is true of spermicidal creams and jellies. Most successful is the birth control "pill," which at times has some serious side effects. Surgical procedures include vasectomy for the male and tubal ligation for the female. Abortion, a fairly simple surgical procedure if done early in pregnancy, is now legal and relatively easy to obtain.

5. Human patterns of sexual behavior differ from those of the lower animals, and there are also considerable differences among societies. The importance of social learning is shown by the research of Kinsey and his co-workers, who interviewed a wide range of people in great detail. Their results were analyzed according to form of sexual outlet; socioeconomic status, religious behavior, and educational level. Different social groupings were found to have their own stable patterns of sexual behavior, and each grouping tended to regard its particular pattern as the "normal" one. Kinsey also found that sexual patterns learned early in life often tend to be stable for many years.

6. Except for the basic response of vasocongestion, sexual behavior is mostly learned. In our culture, the learning comes almost exclusively from peers, and in a rather piecemeal fashion. Research with monkeys has shown that animals reared in social isolation were rarely able to engage in sexual activity, even when considerable help was provided. Certain biological factors, such as hormonal changes, can affect sexual functioning, but the effects of these changes can often be minimized by prior learning. Severe disruption in hormonal supply can have more permanent effects.

7. It is commonly believed that sexual identity is purely an anatomical matter, but the study of hermaphrodites shows that gender is predominantly learned through the child's early assignment to a specific sex role. It is tempting to believe that *homo-*

sexuality is caused by assignment to the wrong gender role, but this is too simplified a view of the concept, which covers a wide range of behaviors and attitudes. Some theorists believe that the causes are to be found in the homosexual's early family relationships; for example, the presence of a dominant, seductive mother and a weak or absent father. One consistent pattern is the existence of strongly pleasurable homosexual experiences before adolescence. It seems that there are no "natural" gender roles; rather, through socialization, certain behaviors seem "right" for each sex while others seem unnatural.

8. Although people tend to disagree as to what behaviors should be regarded as sexually deviant, there is agreement that certain behaviors do constitute problems. *Impotence* in males, the inability to maintain adequate penile erection, is related to inexperience, anxieties, and faulty beliefs in regard to sex. The basic failure is in the response of vasocongestion. *Orgasmic dysfunction* in women, a more complicated problem, has been shown to have somewhat similar bases, particularly a background of religious orthodoxy. Both of these disorders are largely learned. There is no evidence that pornography contributes to sexual disorders.

KEY TERMS

myotonia

vasocongestion

clitoris

sexual response cycle

contraception

coitus interruptus

rhythm method

condom

diaphragm

intrauterine device

douche

the birth control pill

spermicidal creams, jellies,
   and foams

vasectomy

tubal ligation

abortion

fetishism

androgens

estrogens

hermaphrodite

impotence

frigidity

orgasmic dysfunction

NINE

Adult Adjustment

The process of human development continues throughout life.

- Four phases of adult development are adolescence, the novice phase, settling down, and middle adulthood.

A major area of adjustment challenge to adults is love and marriage.

- Adolescence is a time of change and conflict.
- Dating choices are usually based on physical and social attractiveness.
- Expectations and fantasies, particularly "romantic love," play a large part in the decision to marry.
- The needs served by marriage have changed markedly in the twentieth century.
- Childbearing and child rearing have been traditional functions of marriage, but women are now taking other roles in the community.

Another major area of adjustment for adults is in work and career.

- Few career choices are made on an entirely rational basis.
- Career choice can be seen as an extension of personality development.
- Intrinsic rewards are extremely important in vocational satisfaction.

Retirement has become a topic of major concern to society.

- To be satisfactory, retirement should be planned and structured.
- New patterns of satisfactions must be developed.

ALTHOUGH THE STUDY OF HUMAN DEVELOPMENT IS ALMOST 100 YEARS OLD, until quite recently it was assumed that the developmental process was largely completed at adolescence. It has been only recently that the notion of **adult development** has emerged, the notion that there are changes in values, attitudes, skills, aspirations, and similar attributes throughout the life cycle. As we noted in Chapter 3, much of the impetus for an interest in adult development stems from the work of Erik Erikson (1963), who extended the psychoanalytic notion of stages of psychosocial development into the adult years.

In this chapter we explore some of the recent research and theorizing about the developmental process during adult life. We then turn our attention to a more detailed analysis of two broad developmental areas in which adults face adjustment challenges: (1) love and marriage; and (2) work. It is interesting to note that when Freud himself was asked what one must do to be genuinely mature, his reply was brief and pointed: *"Lieben und arbeiten."* To be truly mature, one must be able to *love* and *work*. The challenges encountered in these two areas are universal ones, and the decisions that we make here—choosing a mate and a career—have such obvious long-term consequences that these two decisions are among the most important that we will ever make. Thus, our personal understanding of these areas should have some positive effect on our efforts to cope with everyday problems.

ADULT DEVELOPMENT

We have seen the powerful effects of socialization and formal education in providing the developing child with the skills and competencies necessary for coping with the demands of the world. As we move from the world of the child to the world of the adult, the necessary skills and competencies change dramatically. Further adult life experiences require different skills and competencies at various times. There appears to be an identifiable set of stages or life crises that occur in the adult life cycle, "passages" (Sheehy, 1976) from one phase of adult life to another. This section of the chapter identifies and describes each stage in turn.

Adolescence

Adolescence is the period of transition from childhood to adulthood, and may be regarded as the first of the stages of adult development. Adolescence, typically the period from age 12 through the late teens, is marked by a series of obvious and important physical changes. There is the adolescent *growth spurt* where, after a period of rather slow, steady growth during the later years of childhood, the average boy gains almost 15 inches in height in four years and the average girl almost 10 inches in the same period. There is also a gradual development of the sexual organs and of the *secondary sexual characteristics,* such as breast development in females, facial hair in males, and pubic hair in both. It takes about two years for these sexual changes to occur, and **puberty,** or biological sexual maturity, is the culmination of these changes. Puberty is marked by menstruation in the female and the production of sperm cells by the male.

Variations in onset of puberty. There are a number of interesting and important variations in the onset of adolescence. Females generally begin the process about two years earlier than males, usually around the age of 11 for girls and 13 for boys. While the boys eventually catch up and surpass the girls in size and weight, the typical seventh and eighth grade classroom is filled with rather mature, tall young women and rather immature, smaller young boys. These are often times of awkward and difficult social interactions between the sexes of the same age.

Even more important are the large differences among individuals in the age at which these physical changes begin. What are the implications of being the last girl in the class to begin to develop breasts or have menses, or the first? Does it matter if you are the last boy in the class to grow to full height or develop a beard? The research findings suggest that the effects of early and late maturing are rather different for males and females. At the time when these changes are occurring, earlier maturing males are more popular with their peers and appear to be making a better social adjustment. This is not surprising given the importance placed on physical size and strength during these years, especially in such sports as football and basketball.

The findings for females are less clear and less striking. Early maturing girls are often seen as less attractive than their later maturing peers. Since many of these girls are larger than most of the other girls and virtually all of the boys, this finding is not unexpected. However, early maturing girls are more attractive to older boys, particularly if they are physically appealing. Thus the relationship between maturity and peer group acceptance appears more complex for girls than boys. The most general finding is that those youngsters who mature very late are disadvantaged, having less positive self-concepts and poorer social relationships (Weatherly, 1964).

Are these differences between early and late maturing adolescents long-lived? Do they have any lasting effect? Clausen (1975), after reviewing all the available evidence, concluded that there are indeed significant long-term effects of early maturing, at least through senior high school. The early maturers of both sexes are more self-assured and assertive and less dependent than the late maturers. He pointed out, however, that these effects are tempered by both social class and general physique. Among middle class boys, more of whom are college bound and thus interested in careers in which physical size and strength are less important, the late maturers do not devalue themselves as much as do the late maturing lower class boys who are not college bound.

The data for the girls are less clear, and no simple conclusions can be drawn from them. In regard to physique, Clausen concluded that the available research strongly suggests that general body build, which does not change during adolescence, is a more important determinant of personality characteristics and adjustment than the more transitory phenomena of early or late maturity. For example, *mesomorphs*— those who are muscular and large-boned with relatively little fat (see Chapter 1)—are consistently seen as more active, more likely to be in leadership roles, more likely to engage in fights, and happier, regardless of social class or the age at which maturity occurs. While there are some differences in the effects of physique as a function of both class and age of onset of maturity, the general body build characteristics are the more important determinants of other people's reactions to these boys.

The data on the *very* long-term effects of early or late maturity are inconsistent. Clausen (1975) noted that one major study reported early maturers to be more dominant and better adjusted than late maturers, while another major study reported no differences between these groups. Both studies involved long-term longitudinal research carried out within several years of each other in California, and there is no ready explanation for the discrepant findings. It would thus appear best at the present time not to draw any firm conclusions about the very long-term effects of the age of maturity.

Socialization. Not so long ago, there was no period of adolescence as we know it today. Many children and almost all teenagers worked at jobs, much as adults. The early days of the Industrial Revolution saw the need for large amounts of cheap unskilled labor, and children and teenagers provided much of it. While children and adolescents fulfilled adult work roles, their social roles were less than adult. They were not permitted to vote, drink intoxicants, enter into contracts, or marry without parental permission. During the early days of the Industrial Revolution, employers were given parental authority over these youngsters who did not attain full legal maturity until age 18 or 21.

As the Industrial Revolution proceeded, there was less and less need for large numbers of unskilled workers and more and more need for trained technicians. As the labor of children and adolescents has become less necessary for society, the period of schooling has been extended, either by legal sanctions or by custom and tradition or both. Over the past century, every decade has seen an extension of the length of schooling, and it is clear that formal education now plays the major role of socializing the developing youngster into the adult world.

This contemporary dependency on formal education for socialization is in marked contrast to much earlier times when the future roles of children were exemplified by the roles of their parents. Thus, before the Industrial Revolution, children learned about the adult world by observing their parents as both generations went about the business of life in the context of the family home. Today, neither parents nor adolescents spend so much time in the family home. Work is done in factories and offices, and socialization occurs in schools formally and in peer groups informally. One of the clearest consequences of the Industrial Revolution has been the change in the family and its impact on the socialization of the developing person.

Our current approach as a society is to view adolescence as a transition period—a time-out—during which the young person develops the skills and attitudes that are necessary for future success. But there are many strong and conflicting pressures upon the adolescent which directly contradict this view. There are the marked physical changes noted earlier, and the development of strong sexual impulses in the face of traditional prohibitions about satisfying these impulses. Parents are usually less than helpful about such issues. For example, Sorensen (1973) found that approximately 70 percent of adolescents of both sexes reported that they never openly discussed sexual matters with their parents. Whatever discussion did occur was couched in fairly general terms and was not directed toward helping the individual adolescent deal with his or her own personal sexual problems or concerns. The typical adolescent view of parental hypocrisy may stem in part from this evasiveness in dealing with sexual issues, especially during our current era of general societal openness about sex.

Of equal importance is the contradiction that while adolescence is seen as a time of preparation for the world of work, there is little direct exposure to this world, except for occasional part-time and summer jobs. The Report of the Panel on Youth of the President's Science Advisory Committee (Coleman, 1974) raises serious questions about the adequacy of our schooling for the development of the necessary skills, attitudes, and involvements that are necessary for seeking, holding, and progressing in meaningful jobs and for managing one's own affairs. They argue cogently for experimenting with other strategies—cycles of school and work, work leaves, public service job opportunities especially for adolescents, youth communities, and so on—for the development of a more effective citizenry.

It is interesting to note that while we have been postponing the entry of the developing person into the adult world of work, we have been granting adult rights and responsibilities at an earlier age by reducing the age for voting, entering into legal contracts, and other matters. Such contradictions about the nature of adolescence can hardly help the developing person clarify his or her own role in society.

Identity. In Chapter 3 we noted that, stemming from Erikson's revision of the psychoanalytic stages of development, adolescence was the time for developing a separate sense of **identity,** for incorporating new physical and sexual attributes into a comprehensive sense of self, an integrated self-concept. While there is clear recognition by society that adolescence is a time of change which should facilitate the development of a more adult self-concept, we have seen that there are a number of contradictions and inconsistencies that pose difficulties. Also, our complex and pluralistic society offers adolescents a bewildering variety of options, choices with which, as we have seen, they are ill-prepared to deal. Thus, more likely than not, contemporary adolescents experience an "identity crisis," a period of time during which there is considerable uncertainty about who one is, one's capabilities, one's social role, and one's future directions.

An identity or an integrated self-concept involves the development of values and moral standards, concepts that provide standards of conduct for the person and for those whom the person encounters. Such values are initially learned in the process of socialization and, in the child, these values are largely those of the child's parents. As the child grows older and moves away from the primary influence of the parents, these values are modified by other agents of socialization, such as the school and the church. During adolescence, the peer group, which had been important to a greater or lesser degree in childhood, assumes paramount importance. The adolescent peer group often advocates values and standards that differ from those initially held, placing the individual in strong conflict.

For the first time, the developing person may experience a "values dilemma," having to make certain specific behavioral choices but not knowing what to do. Should the adolescent boy join his friends in driving a "borrowed" car and risk parental wrath, or should he refuse and experience peer group ridicule and rejection? Will the adolescent girl accept her parents' moral views or her peer group's more casual view of sexuality? These double approach-avoidance conflicts are frequently painful for the adolescent involved in them, yet they are necessary for the development of an independent identity. How can one develop an integrated and functional set of values if they have never been tested under conditions of real temptation? Certainly adolescence is the time when difficult behavioral choices are regularly posed for the developing person, and it is the way in which these continuing choices are made that determines the ultimate nature and quality of one's belief system.

The Novice Phase

As we have noted earlier, there has recently been an increasing awareness of and interest in adult development. Some of the most important theory and research in this area has been developed by Daniel Levinson and his colleagues (Levinson, Darrow, Klein, Levinson, and McKee, 1977; Levinson, 1978), who have intensively studied

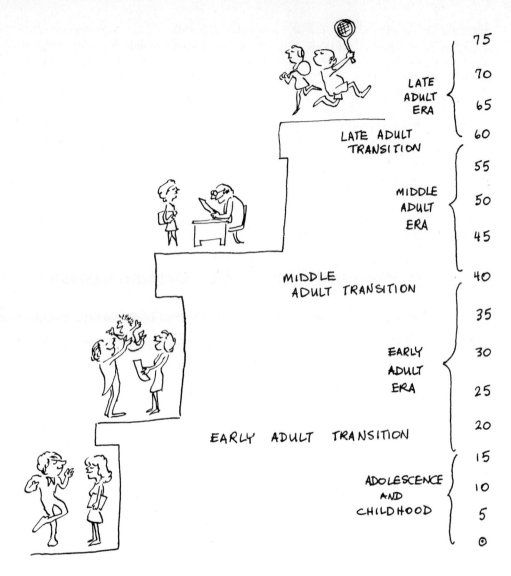

40 men, aged 35-45 at the time of the last report. These studies have involved ten men in four occupational groups: industrial workers, business executives, college teachers of biology, and novelists. Each participant was initially seen in 1969 and 1970 for a total of 10 to 20 hours of interviewing and psychological testing over a period of three months, and was then followed up at later times. While unfortunately no women were included in this study, the results are rather instructive about the nature of personal development for males in the post-adolescent years. Naturally, we must

await the findings of such studies with women in order to construct a more complete theory of adult development. Also, Levinson has tended to state his findings with somewhat more authority than his data allow, so that the reader should regard the categories and phases simply as tentative guides.

Levinson's data led him to conclude that the process of achieving full maturity is more complex and lengthy than was previously believed. He has estimated that it takes about 15 years (from about 17 to 33 years of age) for a young man to move from adolescence to a stable, adult life. The achievement of this stable adult life occurs with the movement through a series of phases or stages, the first of which he terms the *Novice phase.*

The **Novice phase** involves the exploration of the adult world, developing one's own adult interests and values, and making critical choices about work and love. The length and importance of the Novice phase caused Levinson to subdivide it into three distinct periods: Early-Adult Transition (age 17-22); Entering the Adult World (age 22-28); and the Age-30 Transition. Although these periods are called by various names in Levinson's different writings, the central themes are consistent within his work.

One of the basic tasks of the *Early-Adult Transition* is separating oneself from the family, an event which occurs on several levels. Overtly, it involves moving away from home, becoming financially independent, and establishing new roles. Psychologically, it means further differentiating oneself from one's family and creating some psychological distance from family members. It is interesting to note that men who enter college or the military have an institutional structure to ease the transition—a structure that provides specific expectations and controls, as well as continued reinforcements. Also, privacy and autonomy coexist with support and control in this situation. On the other hand, those men who go directly from high school to work often do not have

such structural support for the transition, and it may therefore take longer. They often continue to live at home, in a kind of "semi-boarder" status, leading their own life but marginally attached to the family. Men in the Early-Adult Transition are still at the boundary between the family and the adult world—those in college or the military because they have no independent home of their own and those who are working because they are still living in the family home.

During the *Entering the Adult World* period, the young man's central focus shifts from his family of origin to a new home base, and much of his energy is involved in establishing an adult life of his own. He endeavors to establish himself in his occupation, or at least to establish some clear occupational direction or career path, one that is congruent with his own experienced interests, values, and self-concept. His relationships begin to take on a more adult quality, involving greater intimacy in Erikson's sense. This period is very much a time of exploration and initial choice in which there is exploratory searching, the making of provisional choices, and searching for tentative confirmation of these choices.

The last period of the Novice phase is the *Age-30 Transition,* which is marked by the development of a sharper focus on work, family, and one's own interests. It is a time of tentative confirmation and the enactment of the initial stages of one's life plan. As with all transitions, this is a period of change—of shifting from youth to maturity and of developing a firm sense of oneself as an adult engaged in adult pursuits.

Four tasks. According to Levinson, there are, generally speaking, four central tasks to be accomplished during the Novice phase: forming a Dream and giving it a place in one's life structure; forming mentor relationships; establishing an occupation; and establishing love relationships, including marriage and family. Perhaps the most crucial of these is the formation of the Dream, a vision or plan for one's own future. Most often the Dream is found within the context of a job—becoming president of a company or of a union, winning the Pulitzer Prize, or receiving some great honor for personal achievement. At the beginning of the Novice phase, during the Early-Adult Transition period, the Dream is poorly formed and usually has only a tenuous relationship to reality. The ways in which the Dream is connected to the rest of the man's life are critical in determining what role the Dream plays in steering the man's development. A Dream may be blocked by one's parents, the lack of opportunity, an unplanned pregnancy, or other factors. The Dream provides a central organizing focus, offering a sense of aliveness and purpose for those men who are, in some sense or another, living out their Dream. While the man whose Dream is blocked may be successful by external criteria, he will feel unfulfilled and that his life lacks purpose.

The **mentor relationship** is one that received little attention prior to Levinson's work. The mentor, typically a man a dozen or so years older than the person, is sufficiently older to provide experience, wisdom, and authority, but close enough in age and attitude so as not to be the "wise old man" or patriarch. The mentor may be a teacher, supervisor, or more experienced coworker who takes the younger man "under his wing," shows him around, and helps him learn the ropes. The most important function that the mentor plays is to bestow his blessing on the younger man's Dream. While the mentor may serve as a role model for the younger man, one that he can admire and emulate, what is more important is fostering the younger man's development from a child-with-adults relationship to an adult-with-peers relationship. The mentor provides counsel and moral support to the younger man, especially in times of stress, but most importantly, he both explicitly and implicitly assures the younger man that his Dream can come true.

The end of the mentor relationship provides some of Levinson's most interesting data. This relationship lasts anywhere from two to ten years, with shorter rather than longer relationships the more typical. The relationship occasionally ends when circumstances such as a move to a new city or a new job make its continuation difficult. More often, however, there is an emotional end to the relationship with residual ill will between the pair. Levinson calls the mentor relationship a "love relationship" and, like all such intense relationships, it rarely ends simply or pleasantly. Most often, the younger man experiences feelings of loss, abandonment, and anger, coupled with a sense of relief and freedom, while the mentor feels a lack of gratitude, a sense of having been used, and a sense of relief from the burden of having to "carry" the younger man.

In a similar longitudinal study of adult development, Vaillant (1977) also found that his subjects required equivalent supportive relationships with benign individuals in order to achieve personal maturity. Vaillant's subjects were 94 men initially selected on the basis of professional judgments of high achievement potential between 1939 and 1944 at an exclusive men's college in New England—young men the college officials were "glad we admitted." These men have been followed for over 30 years with clinical investigative techniques much like those used by Levinson. Although Vaillant has been less concerned than Levinson with constructing an overall theory of adult development, the two studies yield strikingly similar findings.

The central point of this discussion is the importance of a mentor relationship in the development of the younger man, particularly in providing a new, different, and more approachable model for further personal growth. It is worthwhile to note that, while neither Levinson nor Vaillant studied female subjects, Epstein (1970) concluded that a lack of available mentors has been a major obstacle in the professional development of women. One must wonder who will serve as mentors for the younger women now entering the work force, for clearly there are few older professional women available to serve in the mentor role. While some men can perhaps serve portions of the mentor role with a younger woman, they certainly cannot provide a completely suitable role model. In addition, sexual and other issues are likely to interfere with the mentor relationship between men and women. Given the demonstrated importance of mentors in male adult relationships, this would appear to be a problem worthy of serious consideration by our society.

The last two tasks to be accomplished in the Novice phase are those of establishing an occupation and establishing a marriage and family. Again, we encounter the two major themes of adult life—work and love. These two basic themes are so important that we have devoted the final portion of this chapter to a detailed examination of each of them. In the meantime, we continue with our overview of adult development.

Settling Down

The Novice phase ends with the Age-30 Transition and its preoccupation with a shifting focus. The next major phase, according to Levinson, is **Settling Down.**

Beginning in the early thirties, this is a period of deeper commitment—to one's work, family, and valued interests. Within the framework of this life structure, the man conceptualizes and begins to pursue his longer-term plans and goals.

Two principal themes share the man's energies and attention during this phase: *establishing oneself* and *"making it."* On the one hand, he is concerned with establishing his niche in society, building his own family and its home, and pursuing his career interests within a sharply defined pattern. The need for order, stability, security, and control characterize this theme. On the other hand, he is equally concerned with "making it," by which Levinson means the attainment of certain major goals according to an inner timetable that the man attempts to follow. Such goals might involve completing the family by age 35, achieving tenure or a vice-presidency by age 40, or similar matters. Mobility and ambition characterize these themes.

Both of the central themes of the Settling Down phase, establishing oneself and "making it," run counter to being open to new experiences or moving outside of one's already existing life structure. Thus the man in this phase is often seen as single-minded, preoccupied, and unwilling to consider alternatives to what he is presently pursuing. He comes to believe that he is fully adult and that there are no developmental changes ahead for him.

But the man's occupational goals, his interpersonal relationships, and his beliefs about what is really important in life tend to be based upon an illusion. The illusion is that one's life structure is now complete. This is not the case, however, for there are many aspects of the individual that must still be considered in order to develop further, aspects that were overlooked or temporarily set aside in order to Settle Down. For instance, Levinson notes that the man typically believes that he is autonomous during this period. While he may be relatively free of the influence of his parents, he is not free of what Levinson and others call the "tribal" influence, the belief system of our society, where, for example, we believe that we can "make it" given hard work and dedication. One set of guidelines has merely been exchanged for another.

The Settling Down phase reaches its peak with the period of *Becoming One's Own Man,* which occurs near the end of the Settling Down phase, usually the late thirties. This period is the high point of early adulthood and is marked by the awareness that, no matter what he has accomplished to date, he is still not really autonomous. He may feel that he has not freed himself from his mentor's influence, or that he is too dependent upon peer influence, or that he has not adequately stood up to his boss. During the Becoming One's Own Man period there is a conscious and deliberate attempt to free oneself of such constraining influences, both in the job and elsewhere. Not only is the relationship with the mentor finally ended, but the man may also terminate his marriage or other relationships that are experienced as constricting or binding. Thus, the man may end a marriage of ten or more years at the very time when he is almost at the peak of his development. Such behavior cannot help but cause much anguish to the other persons who are involved, and more often than not, nobody has much understanding of how such a rupture fits into the individual's own needs.

During this period, the man vitally needs some external affirmation of himself. He needs indications such as a promotion, a new job, or an award to serve as signals that he has indeed "made it." The event of external affirmation, regardless of what it is, has a crucial symbolic significance. If it is forthcoming, he believes he has "made it." Otherwise he may conclude that he is without value and that his life has been without purpose. While he is waiting for the event, the next transition, the Mid-Life Transition, begins.

The *Mid-Life Transition* occurs between two fairly stable periods of adult development—Settling Down and Middle Adulthood. The transition itself, however, is typically a turbulent and troublesome one. The central issue involves facing up to the discrepancy between the man's accomplishments and his goals, between the Dream and reality. Implicit in this period also is a comparison between the Dream and one's life structure. One can achieve a Dream that is not consistent with one's own interests, values, and sense of self and thus experience only a hollow victory. In order to weather this phase successfully, the Dream must be realized in some sense. Equally important, the Dream itself must stand examination by the Mid-Life man and be found to be worthy.

There are a number of other issues which ordinarily are raised for the first time during the Mid-Life Transition and are continued into Middle Adulthood. First is the sense of bodily decline and a sharp awareness of one's own mortality. Second is the development of a sense of aging, where the man sees himself as old rather than young. Finally, there is a significant change in the man's sense of his own masculinity with the acceptance of more feminine aspects of the self. There is often a development of greater nurturance and less preoccupation with the sexual aspects of relationships with women. These changes sometimes follow the achievement of greater self-acceptance and the growing awareness of having "made it" as a person.

Middle Adulthood

By the middle forties the Mid-Life Transition is largely completed, and there is a period of restabilization as the man enters **Middle Adulthood.** Middle Adulthood is seen by Levinson as divided into three major subphases: Entering Middle Adulthood, Age-50 Transition, and the Culmination of Middle Adulthood. These phases are followed by another transition, now into Late Adulthood.

We will not elaborate further on these later stages, for two reasons. First, Levinson's theorizing is incomplete because his subjects are still in the period of Middle Adulthood. Second, we have now adequately demonstrated the ongoing nature of adult development, its roots in the earlier socialization process, and its complexity. While there is much yet to be done, Levinson's work is a reasonable start toward meeting Erikson's hope that his brief description of the adult life cycles would be expanded into more detailed descriptions based on longitudinal data.

We previously noted another ongoing longitudinal study of adult development, reported by Vaillant (1977). Although Vaillant has not been concerned with providing an overall description of the pattern of adult development, we have said a little about his work. One major finding from Vaillant's study is relevant here. Although all of Vaillant's subjects were chosen because they were persons who were doing well in life, none of them escaped major pain, emotional upset, or anxiety in the course of their lives. Vaillant found that those men who used their adversity to develop mature coping mechanisms—altruism, humor, suppression, anticipation, and sublimation— were far more successful in life than those who were not able to do so. Such findings support the belief that psychological strength develops as much through adversity as it does through prosperity. A similar conclusion was drawn by Elder (1974) in his study of children who went through adolescence during the Great Depression. It would thus appear that many persons learn to cope by being forced to cope.

Vaillant's study also provides some interesting information about the antecedents of coping. Those men who made the best adaptations as adults tended to have happier childhoods than those who made poorer adaptations. However, it is noteworthy that the ratings of such behaviors as "shy," "introspective," or "inhibited" obtained during adolescence were not related to adjustment ratings in mid-life in this investigation. Also noteworthy is Vaillant's consistent reliance upon the two behaviors of love and work as the twin themes of adult maturity. It is to these themes that we now turn our attention.

LOVE AND MARRIAGE

In contrast with more traditional societies, the choice of a mate in our society rests with the two individuals involved. The interaction between the sexes that is permitted and encouraged during adolescence and early adulthood is intended both to train the individual in heterosexual relationships and to provide the basis for mate selection.

Dating provides us with opportunities to experiment with relationships with a variety of persons of the opposite sex, and hopefully, to test and refine our judgments about the kind of person with whom we are most likely to establish a mutually satisfying, long-term relationship. There are a number of challenges involved in this process that must be successfully met in order for young people to develop adequate self-awareness and a healthy basis for mate selection. In this section we examine some of these challenges and the nature of marriage itself.

The Dating Game

As we have stated above, dating is supposed to provide the individual with opportunities to discover and test various kinds of interpersonal relationships, but this does

In the dating-rating game, each individual is evaluated according to the standards of his or her peer group. Compatible couples are expected to have similar status ratings in the areas of looks, popularity, and family background.

not always occur. Even among early teenagers there may be pressures to "go steady"—to choose one partner and maintain just one relationship. Stable relationships of this kind can often provide valuable training in learning how to solve the problems that emerge in long-term relationships, but going steady can prevent a person from experiencing the variety that is necessary for making wise judgments about mate selection. Also, it often becomes extremely difficult, if not impossible, for one of the partners to break the relationship when it is no longer mutually satisfying. They may lack the skills necessary to end it without causing pain or prolonged feelings of guilt or anger, they may be unwilling to risk hurting each other, and there may be strong pressures by the peer group or by parents to maintain the relationship. Also, there may be great reluctance to give up the comfort and security, as well as the sexual gratification, that have been part of the relationship. Of course, these factors are all involved in maintaining a marriage, but they should also be recognized as important in premarital relationships. Obviously the dating process should aim for a balance between the individual's need for diversity of experience and the need for an intense and sustained experience.

Although there are definite advantages in basing the choice of dating partners on psychological factors such as the compatibility of needs and interests, this does not always happen. Indeed, as Margaret Mead (1949) has pointed out, dating choices in our society have traditionally been made on the basis of "ratings" of the two people involved. These ratings involve a kind of average of the implicit evaluations made of each individual by his or her peer group, and they tend to be based upon such factors as the visibility of the person in the group, physical attractiveness, and social status of the family. In this traditional "dating-rating game," the handsome, rich, popular captain of the football team is expected to date the pretty, popular captain of the cheerleaders whose family is of equal status. Similarly, the slightly built, acned son of a janitor is expected to date someone with an equally low rating. When the dating-rating rules are broken, there are strong negative peer sanctions against the relationship; for example, "I just can't see what Peggy sees in *him!*"

These informal peer ratings provide a crude index of the social status compatibility of the couple, but they fail to take psychological characteristics into account. The captain of the cheerleading squad might find that the slightly built, bespectacled boy from the "wrong side of town" is less competitive, more willing to deal with her needs in an open, direct fashion, and more entertaining than the boys that her friends might choose for her. It would appear that reliance upon the dating-rating game tends to diminish with age and is less a factor in college than high school dating. However, since many marriages are contracted during high school, especially by couples who do not go on to college, it is important to understand these factors, and they perhaps offer some bases for understanding why so many marriages fail.

During the teenage years the dating game can provide an opportunity for developing self-awareness and interpersonal competence, but it can also be the focus of much concern and anxiety. For example, the heavily competitive flavor of much teenage dating may cause the person with a low "rating" to develop a sense of being unattractive or unwanted. Such people may be led to withdraw from the game or to enter early marriages as a way of protecting themselves from having to face the anxieties involved. Also, the dating-rating game may lead the successful players into developing an exploitive and shallow view of interpersonal relationships—an interest only in persons who enhance one's own image. Obviously, dating ought to provide the opportunity for youth to learn how to develop meaningful relationships with members of the opposite sex, but our current system is probably not the best way of doing it.

Sexual factors. The natural needs for sexual exploration and expression add further complications in dating. Even if one does believe that there has been a "sexual revolution," there are few revolutionaries to be found among the parents of teenage girls, and not many more to be found among the parents of teenage boys. Most parents hold quite traditional attitudes toward premarital chastity and use all the means at their command to prevent sexual experimentation. Jessor and Jessor (1975) reported that high school students who had engaged in sexual intercourse were more independent of their families than those who had not, suggesting the importance of peer values in determining such behavior.

While there seems to be some shift in sexual attitudes among teenagers themselves, Packard (1968) reported that more than two thirds of his college male sample would be "troubled" if they knew that their wives had had premarital relationships with someone else. More recently, Pietropinto and Simenauer (1977) found that one-third of their sample of 4,000 males still would have preferred to marry a virgin. Perhaps even more important, only 2 percent would want to marry a woman had had relations with many men. Thus, there are still strong inhibitory forces, both external and internal, against much sexual experimentation at the same time that sexual appetites are very strong. These sexual pressures often lead to early marriage—either to permit full sexual activity or to cope with the guilt from premarital sexual activity. In other words, when a society discourages sexual experimentation as a natural part of premarital relations, sexual pressures often lead to premature marriages, marriages that cannot stand the test of time.

This problem is intensified when an accidental pregnancy occurs during premarital sex. While abortions are now legal in this country, and have become easier to arrange, most of us are acquainted with marriages that were "arranged" because the girl had become pregnant. Of course, adequate information on birth control procedures is more easily available nowadays, but adult society is reluctant to appear to be condoning adolescent sex by publicizing availability of such information to teenagers. And the fact that many adults are uneasy with their own sexuality makes it all the more difficult for their maturing children to develop attitudes with which they can be comfortable.

Mate Selection

We have discussed some aspects of the context of mate selection, and we are now ready to explore further the bases on which selection is made. Two contradictory claims are often made for the development of human relationships: "birds of a feather flock together," and "opposites attract." Both of these appear to be true in mate selection, depending on which characteristics of the relationship one examines.

By and large, people tend to choose a marriage partner from a background that is rather similar to their own. Thus, college graduates marry college graduates, Catholics marry Catholics, and whites marry whites. This tendency for people to choose mates of a similar background, especially from similar social and economic backgrounds, is called **homogamy.** The fact of homogamy is not surprising when we consider that we tend to spend more of both our work and our leisure time associating with people whose background is similar to our own, and thus have greater opportunity to meet an eligible partner with similar characteristics. Also, homogamy tends to produce couples that share similar values and interests, without which it would be unlikely that stable marriages would ever occur. Although there are some obvious exceptions, a stable marriage requires some sharing of religious beliefs, some agreement on the ways in which the family income is spent, some sharing of the importance placed upon one's vocational success, and agreement on a variety of other factors. Without shared beliefs, values, and interests, marriage would be a continuous struggle between opposing forces. Selecting a mate with a background similar to one's own tends to increase the chances of having a high degree of similarity in values and interests.

Personality characteristics, however, are pretty much independent of social background factors, and it is in this area that opposites have been said to attract each other. Thus, various writers (Winch, 1958, 1963) believe that, within the limits of homogamy, we select a mate whose psychological or personality needs are complementary to ours. Thus, a dominant person would choose a submissive other, and a person with strong protective or nurturant needs would choose a mate who needs to be protected or nurtured. In other words, the complementary need hypothesis suggests that most people marry somebody whose personality characteristics are the mirror images of their own, so that the partnership provides each individual with a direct means for satisfying his or her own needs.

Although the complementary need hypothesis sounds sensible, it is not strongly supported by the available research evidence (Udry, 1966; Winch, 1963). First, not all needs have opposites, and a similarity of needs often appears to produce a more harmonious relationship. For example, it is likely that a relationship in which both partners had similar achievement goals would produce less friction than one in which there were strong differences. Second, even when one partner can meet the needs of the other in a complementary fashion, this may not lead to mutual respect or even liking. For example, a submissive man might select a dominant woman, but might also strongly resent her domination. Third, role expectations are also important, so that the pairing of a submissive male with a dominant female—a situation generally regarded as incompatible with normal sex-role expectations—might lead to difficulties in relating to other couples, conflict regarding role models for the children, and other problems. It is probably safest to conclude that the complementarity of psychological needs plays a yet-to-be determined role in mate selection, and future research will probably find that only a few needs are actually involved in a complementary manner.

Of much more importance are the expectations and fantasies about marriage that the two people bring to the relationship. Romantic love, an intense emotional relationship between two people, is typically regarded as the most important element in the decision to marry. Unfortunately, romantic love has been regarded as a more appropriate subject for poets to write about than for psychologists to study. As a consequence, we know very little about the nature of this kind of love and how it operates in mate selection. It is clear, however, that this intense emotional reaction tends to diminish over time, and those relationships that survive the waning of romantic love are known to involve other, more stable elements.

A substantial amount of research has been done to determine the characteristics that young people look for in selecting a mate. One study that was conducted over a period of 25 years revealed that the four most important qualities sought in a mate by college males have been found to be dependability of character, emotional stability, mutual attraction, and a pleasing disposition (Coleman, 1969). The characteristics sought by college women are quite similar and were also stable over the 25-year period. We tend to know much less about the way in which these characteristics are assessed during dating and courtship, the way in which one's expectations vary according to the availability of prospective mates, and the degree to which romantic love interferes with accuracy of perception.

Recently, Murstein (1976) has attempted to develop a theoretical framework within which these findings on choosing a marriage partner might be explained. Called Stimulus-Role-Value Theory, its essence is that "attraction and interaction depend on the *exchange value* of the assets and liabilities each of the partners brings to the situation" (p. 107). Murstein's own research findings have provided a moderate amount of support for his theory. His most important findings are that two aspects were matched among the mates: physical attractiveness, and an accurate understanding of the other person's self-concept. A number of Murstein's hypotheses were not supported by his empirical findings, however, reinforcing the conclusion that mate selection is a very complex process that is not adequately understood at this time.

Courtship

Once two people agree that they are suitable as marriage partners, a period of more-or-less formalized relationship begins—the engagement. In our society, this includes a considerable amount of ritualized behavior, such as the giving of a ring, parties and showers, and formal announcements. The engagement is a period in which the relationship is supposed to be examined and tested, but there are many obstacles to the use of the engagement period for this purpose. For example, although the engaged couple are expected to see a good deal of each other, the taboos against complete sexual intimacy still exist. Even when these taboos are minimized it is often difficult for the couple to arrange to spend time alone with each other in circumstances which permit mutually satisfying intimacy.

Perhaps the major problem with the engagement tradition is that, while it is regarded as a testing period, there are strong pressures against coming to a negative judgment about the planned marriage. Long engagements are regarded as better than short ones—the couple can get to "know each other better"—but there is little or no expectation that their increased knowledge might lead to dissolving the relationship. Rather than being a period of mutual interpersonal exploration, American engagements seem to include all the psychological pressures of marriage but with less opportunity to work them out.

It is interesting to note that prolonged engagements, especially those involving postponements of the wedding, often reflect strong ambivalence in the couple's feelings about each other. In this special case of an approach-avoidance conflict, as the wedding day approaches the negative valence increases and the conflict is temporarily resolved by postponing the date. But the longer the engagement, the more difficult it is to break, so that the couple are trapped in a more and more insoluble conflict.

A case seen by one of the authors nicely illustrates how an approach-avoidance conflict operates in a lengthy engagement. A young woman sought help from a psychologist, complaining that every time the wedding plans were being finalized, her fiancé developed a variety of symptoms, including nausea, heart palpitations, dizziness, and an occasional blackout. In joint counseling sessions with the woman and her fiancé, it quickly became apparent that the young man had grave doubts about the wisdom of the marriage, doubts that he could not share readily with the young woman who was convinced that this was an arrangement "made in Heaven." As he was able to fully express his ambivalence to her (and as she began to experience some slight doubts herself), they were able to reach a rational decision to move ahead with the wedding, sharing their concerns openly.

Marriage

There has been a quiet revolution in marriage during the past century, a revolution whose effects are still unclear. This revolution stems from a number of social and economic changes that directly affect the marital relationship. Consider the following: In the past 100 years the life span for persons in the Western world has more than doubled, with the current life expectancy rising to 76 years for females and 69 years for males. There is increased mobility, with almost half the population living outside the state of their birth. There has been a large increase in the number of women who work, with a third of the current work force in the United States being female. The development of convenient and reasonably safe contraceptives has given both men and women more options about their sexual conduct. Divorce is more socially acceptable, with over one-third of all American marriages terminating in divorce. Each of these changes has had some impact on the institution of marriage, and these changes are continuing.

The needs that are served by marriage have changed markedly in this century as we have gradually moved from a rural to an industrial society. The roles of the husband and wife on the small family farm were clear-cut, and both partners had their specialized functions to perform. The husband tilled the fields, took care of the livestock, and did the butchering and other heavy manual chores, while the wife did the cooking, baking, sewing, and childbearing. Even the members of families who lived in town and were engaged in one of the skilled trades had similar specialized roles to fulfill. In that era, the needs to be met by the marriage were survival needs, and the partners were interdependent because of their specialized roles. If both of the partners were able to fill their roles, that is, if both had the competencies to meet the family's survival needs, the marriage was regarded as successful.

Today, it is the psychological needs served by the marriage that are of central importance. Although child rearing and economic support are still important functions of marriage, they are not the principal ones, especially among college-educated persons. Rather, marriage has increasingly come to be regarded as a vehicle for meeting one's personal, psychological needs and for achieving self-fulfillment. The degree to which a marriage provides an intimate, intense, and mutually rewarding emotional relationship is nowadays the most important criterion of its success. Clearly, such a relationship requires much interpersonal competence on the part of both partners, including self-awareness and sensitivity, a desire for and a capacity to give emotional support, communication skills, and skill in the use of a variety of techniques of interpersonal conflict resolution.

It is not at all clear how these skills are acquired in our culture, particularly at a high enough level to provide the satisfactions that marriage is supposed to yield. Certainly very few people regard their parents' marriage as having provided an adequate model to use in their own behavior. And the idealized marriages that are typically portrayed in films and television are also unlikely to provide much in the way of adequate models. Thus, at the same time that our cultural expectations about the role of marriage have been on the rise, little or nothing has been done by society to provide the experiences that would make these expectations a reality.

Further, since we are living twice as long and the age at which we get married has significantly decreased (by almost three years), the period "until death do us part" has more than doubled in the past century. Thus, we have both rising expectations for marriage and a much longer time during which these expectations may or may not be met. Also, our earlier discussion of the developmental changes during the adult years clearly suggests that a marriage which may have fulfilled mutual psychological needs at one time may fail when the needs of the two people involved change in different

Over the past century, the institution of marriage has been changing. Nowadays, the criterion of success depends upon the degree
to which marriage provides a mutually
rewarding emotional relationship. Closed
marriages are giving way to relationships that
permit flexibility of roles, personal freedom,
and growth.

ways or on a different time schedule. Given these circumstances, the high rate of divorce and the current discussions about the future of marriage as an institution are not surprising.

One attempt to deal with this dilemma has been termed the **open marriage** (O'Neill and O'Neill, 1972). In the traditional, or "closed," marriage, the roles of each partner are fixed, both by social tradition and by the particular history of that couple. For instance, the woman cooks the dinner because that is "woman's work," and disagreements between the partners are usually settled in a particular manner, such as emotional outbursts followed by tearful apologies. Also, the closed marriage encourages a possessiveness of each partner by the other, and an exclusiveness in which it is pretended that the partners can fulfill all of their psychological needs within the confines of the relationship.

In contrast, the O'Neills suggest an open marriage in which the relationship is seen as an interpersonal contract between the partners that should be frequently renegotiated. The concept of an open marriage recognizes that people's values, expectations, and needs change over time, and that a workable marriage must take these changes into account. A marriage that acknowledges that changes will and must occur permits flexibility of roles, renegotiation, and growth. Specifically, the open marriage involves the following: living for the present, based upon realistic expectations; privacy; open and honest communication, including self-disclosure and feedback; flexibility in roles, including sex-role reversal; open companionship; equality; identity; and trust.

Two of these points deserve special mention: privacy, and open companionship. The first simply recognizes the need of most people for moments or places where they can be left alone. All too often such a need is regarded as neurotic, and is taken by the other partner as rejection. The second, open companionship, involves a freedom for each partner to have significant independent relationships with other people, a pro-

WE DECIDED IT WOULD SAVE A LOT OF TROUBLE IN THE END TO HAVE LAWYERS DRAW UP THE MARRIAGE CONTRACT IN THE FIRST PLACE.

posal that does not fit with the American ideal of marital "togetherness." The O'Neills use the term "couple-front" to refer to society's expectations that married people should always appear together as a couple, and their ideas are instructive in seeing how marriage can sometimes limit many of the individual's options and lead to a feeling of personal constriction.

Carl Rogers (1977) makes a very similar point in discussing what he terms **satellite relationships,** that is, close emotional relationships that either partner may form outside of the marriage. He notes that such secondary relationships, which are not necessarily sexual, cause both pain and growth. Pain occurs because these relationships violate the general expectation that the marriage should provide all the emotional support and affection either person requires, thus giving rise to jealousy, suspicion, and feelings of inadequacy. Growth occurs because satellite relationships prevent the primary relationship from becoming "overloaded," and because the openness required to work through the feelings about these relationships enhances the communication between the marriage partners and can be important in the development of mutual trust.

The work of both the O'Neills and Rogers provides interesting ideas that are being used to reconceptualize marriage as an institution. It is difficult, unfortunately, for many people to make use of these ideas because of the strength of their traditional beliefs and the nature of their interpersonal needs. Nevertheless, these statements do provide a new and potentially useful way of making marriage provide the satisfactions we expect of it. They also form one of the several foundations for a variety of "marriage enrichment" experiences and workshops that are regularly attempted by churches and other organizations.

Children

As we indicated earlier, child rearing is one of the traditional functions of marriage which continues to occupy a central position in that institution. However, certain critics of the nuclear family, especially those in the various women's liberation movements, have suggested that more child rearing responsibilities be assumed by the fathers and by other institutions, such as day nurseries and preschools. Mothers would then be freed to take other roles in the community, and especially to enter the labor market. This suggestion might be seen as an extension of two already existing trends in our society—the shift in the focus of education from the home to the school and other formal institutions, and a continuing increase in the number of women in the labor force. At the present time it is not possible to predict the extent to which this suggested change would alter the role of the family as an institution. It is important to remember that marriage and the family are everchanging institutions, although the changes for the most part are slow.

Today, most married couples continue to want and have children. It is clear that there are many pressures on married couples to produce children, especially after several years of marriage. The parents of the couple begin to inquire insistently about potential grandchildren, many of the couple's peers have already begun a family, and it begins to seem "the natural thing to do." Also, the role of "being a mother" is a central part of the traditional sex-role stereotype to which all females in our society are exposed. There is no recognized biological need for a woman to become a mother, but this fact is certainly not obvious from the way motherhood is publicized. For example, virtually throughout their socialization, women are told in popular magazines and through the advertising media that bearing and rearing children will provide them with a sense of fulfillment, and that only through motherhood can they achieve their personal destiny. It is small wonder that women come to fertility clinics with a deep sense of guilt, and that psychological counseling is an important aspect of the work of these clinics.

Most commonly, however, the decision to have children is made without a great deal of discussion, and in a rather casual manner. We know very little about the way in which these decisions are made, but it would appear that the couple have usually decided much earlier about the general advisability of having a family. Still, it seems likely that adequate consideration is usually not given to the consequences of this decision, especially in view of the extent of the changes that children produce in a marriage.

Most new parents are surprised to find how time consuming and demanding a baby is. As we pointed out in Chapter 3, the infant operates on the pleasure principle and demands immediate gratification of its needs. When these demands occur at 4 a.m., an already exhausted parent may find it difficult to respond cheerfully. The new infant, with its demands for care and feeding, is very frequently more time consuming than had been anticipated and the couple find themselves in some conflict about reorienting their lives around the infant.

Female sex-role training does appear to prepare the new mother for meeting these demands, however. Although they often feel tired and harassed, many new mothers do adjust to and find satisfaction in their new role. Men may sometimes experience conflicts in adjusting to the new demands. The training that society provides in the male sex role gives little attention to fathering other than as the "breadwinner," so that the new father may feel incompetent about participating in child care, and may believe that such behaviors are not masculine. The findings of a study by Feldman and Rogodd (1969) are interesting in this regard. It was found that when the couple were especially close and interdependent prior to the birth of the child, the new baby led to a decrease in marital satisfaction. On the other hand, when the couple were rather distant and independent prior to having a child, the new baby led to an increase in marital satisfaction. This study clearly indicates that the effects of a new baby on a marriage depend upon the nature of the marriage before the baby is born. Nevertheless, it is clear that the birth of a baby requires a good deal of readjustment, and must be regarded as one of the critical periods in the marriage.

WORK AND CAREER

Now that we have examined the first of the two major themes of adult life—love and marriage—let us turn our attention to the world of work. This is the second major area in which we all must make a basic life adjustment. The discussion is organized around three major issues: (1) career choice, (2) vocational satisfaction, and (3) retirement.

Career Choice

Since most adults spend between one-third and one-half of their daily lives at work or in work-related activities, it is not surprising that the choice of a vocation is a central issue in the lives of most young people. Indeed, probably the most frequent question asked of young people is "What are you going to be when you grow up?" There is much pressure upon our youth to make an early and definite career decision, and one of the popular middle class myths is that for each of us there is a single, best vocation. If, for whatever reasons, we fail to discover our "true destiny," we are presumably doomed to a life of vocational dissatisfaction. We will return later to this myth; first, let us examine the notion of a career, usually defined as one's chosen pursuit or life's work.

The concept of a career refers largely to middle class, white-collar, professional occupations. Studies of the lower socioeconomic classes and blue-collar workers, especially those individuals in unskilled or semiskilled jobs such as truck driver or laborer, clearly show that they have no concept of a career but rather tend to see themselves "working for a living." Their initial job choice seems to be largely a matter of chance, and they are willing and able to shift jobs on the basis of economic and other factors.

For middle class professional persons, however, a career or work role is a major part of their identity as a person. Kuhn (1960) has shown that the most frequent responses of middle class people to the "Who am I?" questionnaire, in which the respondent is required to list 20 self-characteristics, are standard career roles. Thus, the authors of this book would respond to the questionnaire with "psychologist," "professor," or "textbook writer." These kinds of responses show the centrality of career in the life of middle class professional persons in forming an important part of their identity, and one can recognize how difficult it is to change careers without disrupting this sense of identity. We can now understand why unemployment is so disruptive to the lives of professional persons, and why there are so many pressures against midlife career shifts.

Recognizing that we are talking about only a portion of the work force, let us examine how people go about choosing an occupation. Ginzberg *et al.* (1951) have identified three developmental stages in the process of career choice. Up to age eleven, children are in the *fantasy stage* in which they more or less assume that they can become anything they want to become in their adult life. The choices at this stage are most often either those with which the child is most directly familiar, including the occupations of parents, teachers, and the family physician, or those that are glamorous and familiar through film and television, such as astronaut, soldier, or explorer. The choice does not depend upon any attempt by the children to match their own abilities and interests with those required by the career, and it is for this reason that the period has been labeled the fantasy stage.

In the period from age eleven to seventeen, children gradually become aware of their own differential abilities and interests, and recognize that these factors ought to be considered in making a vocational choice. In this *tentative stage,* they may know, for example, that they like to write and are rather successful in literature and English courses. Thus, they may begin to consider journalism as a career choice, as such a choice would permit them to simultaneously express their interests and maximize their abilities. In this stage teenagers are generally more able to come to negative decisions than positive ones, so that they find it easier to reject careers that they would not choose than to actually select a career. All too often, however, parents and teachers fail to see these negative judgments as part of an emerging career choice, and they prematurely insist upon a definite positive choice. In the tentative stage, individuals begin to come to grips with the need to integrate their interests and abilities in a realistic fashion, allowing for such factors as the length and cost of the necessary education.

The final stage identified by Ginzberg and his colleagues is the *realistic stage,* which is usually reached around age seventeen. In this stage, individuals have worked out the integration of their interests, abilities, and values into a realistic vocational plan. They have compromised their desires with the realities of their life. They have explored their choice by reading and perhaps by actual work experience, they have used their exploration to narrow the choice of alternatives, and they have developed a commitment to a specific occupational goal.

While this description of the vocational choice process adequately emphasizes its developmental nature, there would seem to be very few persons who are so systematic or rational. Certainly many college or university students have no clear idea at all of their vocational future; for example, the case of Ed, described in Chapter 1. At the other extreme, some persons make their vocational choices in early childhood, choices that persist into adult life. For instance, Paul, a 29-year-old physician, is now completing his formal training in surgery and is seeking a post in academic medicine. From all accounts, he "decided" at age 5 to be a physician, like his maternal grandfather who lived in the same small town in which he was growing up. Although neither of his parents was involved in medicine, they supported his choice, which seemed to stem from his early experiences with his grandfather. An intelligent and industrious student, Paul graduated from high school with outstanding grades, entered the university as a "pre-med" major, did exceptionally well academically, worked in a research laboratory during his summer vacations, and applied for and was accepted into medical school without ever openly questioning his decision. While Paul is clearly unusual in his clarity of vocational choice at an early age, such cases do raise questions about the universality of the scheme advanced by Ginzberg and his colleagues.

A different approach to vocational choice has been taken by Holland (1973) and other writers, who see vocational choice as an extension of one's personality development. Holland characterizes people by their resemblance to each of six personality types, which are more or less self-explanatory: social, realistic, investigative, artistic, enterprising, and conventional. These types are said to be the end products of one's socialization. Based on our socialization experiences, we learn to prefer some activities to others, and these preferences become strong interests as they are reinforced by our social environment. These interests, in turn, lead to the development of patterns of competencies and skills. The combined interests and competencies that each individual develops constitute that person's type in Holland's scheme.

For example, a person who resembles the social type is likely to seek out social occupations such as teaching, counseling, or the ministry. Such people are seen by both themselves and others as social and friendly. They place greater value on social interactions, such as helping others with their personal problems, than on "realistic" behaviors, such as using tools or understanding machines, and they also have greater competencies in social areas.

Holland also believes that there are six environments: social, realistic, investigative, artistic, enterprising, and conventional. Each of these environments is dominated by persons with the corresponding personality type, since the tasks to be performed in each of the environments are best handled by people with that particular combination of skills, competencies, and interests. For example, laboratories engaged in pure research would be dominated by persons of the investigative type. The fact that all

work environments are dominated by one of these types leads each to have a special social environment that is determined by that particular type.

Vocational choice, according to Holland's theory, involves a person's development into one of these personality types (or combination of types) and the continual seeking out of a supportive environment. Thus, as a person develops more and more into an artistic type, he or she will more and more seek out artistic environments which, in turn, will further this type of development. Holland acknowledges that people are hardly ever "pure types," but rather are best understood in terms of how much they resemble a type; and also that there are mixed types, although for both people and environments some types are more closely related than others. It should be clear, for example, that an enterprising-conventional combination would be more likely to occur than a conventional-artistic one.

In Holland's theory, vocational satisfaction, stability, and achievement are determined by the similarity or congruence of the individual's personality and the environment (which is largely composed of other people). In contrast with Ginzberg's notion of a single specific career choice, Holland's approach suggests that there are a number of occupations in which an individual can find a reasonable match between personality type and environment. Thus the enterprising personality type can find success and happiness in business, sales, politics, broadcasting, and any other occupation that requires acquisitive, ambitious, dominant, and self-confident persons.

It should be noted that most occupational titles mask a variety of different functions. Therefore, in many occupations, particularly those that require a college degree, one can find a variety of different types doing rather different work, although they have the same title. For instance, an "engineer" may be involved in investigative work, in sales, in quality control, or in helping customers solve their problems, each of which involves a rather different combination of personal skills and competencies. Most experts on vocational behavior point out that there is often considerable opportunity for people to shape their own work, especially over time, even though the basic dimensions of the job are spelled out in the job description.

Holland's theory has received a considerable amount of research support. His approach to career choice is a developmental one, and it suggests that career development is a continuous process involving changes throughout one's life. However, as we noted above, there is a strong cultural belief that each of us is entitled to only one career. Sarason (1977) calls this the one life–one career imperative. As we have just indicated, people can, over time, reshape the nature of their jobs, but this is typically done without any dramatic shift in their career path. What about the individual who has achieved some success in a career, at least by external standards, and now decides that "enough is enough"? While this decision may be explained as the consequence of a poor match between personality and environment types according to Holland's theory or as a Mid-Life Transition according to Levinson's scheme, it is not likely to be accepted or understood by one's family or friends. Indeed, most students of mid-life career shifts note that it is easier to change a mate than a career.

Yet all of us know of someone, either directly or indirectly, who left a successful career to try something else. One of the authors is acquainted with a man who, at age 44, quit a successful insurance brokerage to become a baker in a health-food shop. Clopton (1973) has studied a small sample of mid-career "shifters" by comparing them with a matched group of "persisters." Clopton himself was a shifter, leaving his job as a daily columnist for a major American newspaper to enter graduate school in psychology. Somewhat surprisingly, he found no major psychological differences between the two groups. Not only were the shifters as successful in their careers as the persisters, but they also seemed as stable in their adjustment to life, and perhaps a little better adjusted than the persisters.

Clopton notes that there are three distinct patterns of shifting: (1) shifts as a consequence of some major event, such as involvement in psychotherapy, religious conversion, or a serious illness or accident, that causes a reformulation of one's life goals; (2) shifts that result from a growing awareness of the inappropriateness of one's life goals, consistent with Holland's notion of an incongruence between personality and environment types; and (3) shifts that involve a mounting boredom with one's initial career, where the second career is initially an avocation but gradually develops into a full-time commitment. Interestingly, all of Clopton's shifters but only a quarter of the persisters had the necessary financial resources to facilitate the shift. One might wonder if the one life–one career imperative is simply a justification for most of us to do what we cannot avoid doing.

While the developmental nature of vocational choice and research data such as Clopton's are important considerations, we must not overlook the fact that important specific decisions are made in the process of career choice and that each of these decisions reduces other alternatives. For example, studying engineering makes it highly unlikely that a person would ever study law, and majoring in art would probably prevent a person from entering medical school. Each of us has only one life to lead, and each life decision both closes certain options and opens others. It is usually rather difficult to make these kinds of decisions, especially for people who have multiple potentials, and a variety of approach–avoidance conflicts can be involved. The emphasis upon making a final "best" decision and closing out attractive options are both important factors in these conflicts. To resolve the problem successfully, one must recognize and accept that the vocational-educational decision must be made, and that we can no longer become Renaissance men or women. The mature individual can look back upon all the major decisions or points of choice and recognize, without regret, that very different lives would have emerged had one or more alternative decisions been made. And nowhere is this more apparent than in the area of vocational planning and development.

Vocational Satisfaction

In American society, work is seen as one of the primary means of achieving personal satisfaction. One's vocation is expected to provide not only the means for satisfying

Job satisfaction may be more than monetary success. Richard Pearson is a skilled English sheep shearer who wanders around the world seeking the "Four T's" (no Taxes, Tools of the trade provided, plenty of Tucker, and plenty of Touhey, Australian terms for food and beer.) He works nine months a year and spends the other three months traveling and enjoying rest and recreation. He says it's a jolly good life.

basic economic needs but also psychological needs for achievement, self-esteem, and self-fulfillment. While these needs were rather easily satisfied in the "craftsman" era of history, prior to the Industrial Revolution, the development of modern technology has made many occupations very much less satisfying.

Mass production, especially the assembly line, has made it difficult for most workers to find any sense of achievement or pride in their vocational accomplishments. Due largely to the influence of the American management expert Frederick Taylor (1923), work in the industrial sector has for many years been broken down into its simplest components, such as turning a screw or tightening a bolt, so that there would be little room for errors of judgment. Initially, assembly line factories operated with reasonable success, especially when most of the labor force was composed of uneducated immigrants, but this is no longer the case. For example, one British worker was convicted of destroying an industrial machine costing over $500,000 by throwing a chunk of metal into it. After drilling holes in flywheels, 74 an hour for eight hours a day over ten years, his defense was: "Try to imagine doing that job, day in, day out, for ten years. I began to find the working conditions terrible. Most of all it was the boredom." His gesture of protest made him something of a hero, and provides an appropriate social comment on the nature of much industrial work.

Many recent strikes, especially in the automotive industry, reflect the worker discontent that has been increasing as the work force has become younger, better educated, American-born, and more articulate. In addition to strikes, there are absenteeism, sabotage, and high turnover in personnel, all of which are indices of the discontent and dissatisfaction of industrial workers. Originally, the objectives of workers and their labor unions were adequate wages and protection from extreme physical hazards and stress. While there certainly are still occupations where such risks are still present, such as mining, the major concern now seems to be the boredom and monotony that are involved in most industrial jobs.

It should be emphasized that this boredom often affects many white-collar and professional workers as well as those on the production line. For instance, in one study of job satisfaction among computer programmers, Herzberg (1968) found that, despite their high salaries and excellent fringe benefits, most of his respondents were simply bored with their jobs and quite dissatisfied. He found that, after an initial period of challenge, most of these highly competent and technically trained specialists found their jobs to be routine drudgery.

Additional insights about job satisfaction and dissatisfaction can be gained from research that has asked employed persons whether they would choose the same work again. Summarized in Table 9-1, these data represent more that 3,000 workers in sixteen industries in the Detroit metropolitan area, plus a sample of professional and other personnel (Kahn, 1973). The results clearly suggest that the higher the status of the occupation, the more satisfied are the persons engaged in it, but another possible conclusion is that those persons whose jobs permit the greatest autonomy—that is, those who have the greatest independence and freedom of choice in their daily activities—have the highest degree of job satisfaction, and that these are the jobs with the highest status. They are also the jobs that provide the greatest degree of self-actualization, the highest on Maslow's (1954) hierarchy of needs as discussed in Chapter 3.

Although the data in Table 9-1 strongly suggest that persons in high status occupations would choose them again, we should not conclude that they are completely satisfied. Since World War II there has been an enormous increase in the number of persons exposed to higher education in the United States. Most of these people were attracted by the promise of the good life following their education—by the expectation of a life of work rather than a life of labor. As Sarason (1977) notes, however, this goal is much less attainable today than it was 30 years ago. It is often impossible for people, even highly educated people, to perceive any relationship between what they do at work and any useful outcome for society. Also, the increasing bureaucratic control over work, especially over the professions, has tended to reduce the potential

Table 9-1
Percentages of Different Occupational Groups
That Would Choose the Same Occupation Again

Occupation	Percent	Occupation	Percent
University professor	93	White collar workers (nonprofessional)	43
Mathematician	91		
Physicist	89	Paper mill workers	42
Biologist	89	Skilled auto workers	41
Chemist	86	Skilled steel workers	41
Lawyer (working in law firm)	85	Textile workers	31
		Blue collar workers	24
School superintendents	85	Unskilled steel workers	21
Washington correspondents	82	Unskilled auto workers	16
Skilled printers	52		

fulfillment that the work once offered. Finally, the highly specialized nature of much work also tends to reduce personal fulfillment. Thus, Sarason believes that those persons who should be the most fulfilled at their work are often unfulfilled because they also have the highest expectations concerning the personal rewards that their work should provide.

Sarason goes on to note that highly educated and successful persons can express their dissatisfactions with work only indirectly, because candor tends to bring forth disbelief and even direct disagreement. While laborers or truck drivers might complain about their jobs, how can eminent surgeons or successful stockbrokers complain about theirs? Yet, according to Sarason, their families are quite sensitive to these poorly hidden dissatisfactions, and much of the disenchantment of the children of apparently successful middle class families stems directly from their awareness of the failure of their parents, particularly their fathers, to find fulfillment in work.

Psychologists who study work and job satisfaction are becoming more aware of the complex nature of work motivation and work satisfaction. Herzberg's research, mentioned above, suggests what he terms a two-factor theory of work motivation. *Hygiene* factors, such as the attractiveness of physical facilities, salaries, and fringe benefits, create dissatisfaction if they do not exist. Their mere presence, however, does not provide positive motivation. A second set of factors, *motivators*—the challenge of the task, responsibility, the opportunity to utilize one's skills and talents—are necessary to produce positive motivation. In other words, Herzberg believes that beyond a certain level, improvement in hygiene factors has little effect upon workers, and that the only way to increase both work satisfaction and productivity is to increase the motivating factors.

The traditional view of management has emphasized the importance of the hygiene factors, virtually to the exclusion of the motivators. This approach to management, characterized by McGregor (1960) as the **Theory X** approach, views the typical worker as lazy, disinterested, unambitious, and motivated only by extrinsic rewards. The alternative, or **Theory Y** approach, takes a rather different view of human behavior in the work environment, more consistent with Herzberg's beliefs. In this view, it is assumed that workers want to be challenged, want satisfaction and achievement from their work, and respond to intrinsic rewards. And there is a growing body of evidence to support this view.

The best known study in this area was originally reported in 1948 (Coch and French, 1948) and reconfirmed by a 20-year follow-up study (Seashore and Bowers, 1969). Briefly, three different groups of operators in a clothing factory were paid on a modified piece-rate basis. The three groups were matched with respect to efficiency, age, and degree of group cohesiveness. In each of the three groups a work change was introduced by one of three methods. (1) In the control condition, the change was introduced in the traditional manner. The staff told the operators what was necessary and why the change was required. (2) In the participation-by-representation condition, the group elected a representative to meet with management to work out the manner in which the change was to be brought about. (3) In the total-participation condition, the entire group of operators met with management and worked out the method for producing the desired change.

The results are strikingly clear-cut. The workers in the first, traditional condition group reacted as usual. Once the change was introduced there was a decrease in production with a very slow upward return and a high degree of worker resistance, as evidenced by direct hostility to the supervisors, lack of cooperation, and other factors. In the second, representative-participation group there was a considerable difference. While there was the same dramatic initial decrease in productivity, it picked up again more quickly and the relearning time was cut approximately in half. Also, there were

fewer instances of resistance on the part of the workers. The third, total-participation groups, however, were clearly superior to those in the second condition. There was much less of a decrease, much more rapid relearning, and final production was distinctly greater than in either of the other two conditions. The follow-up data, after 20 years, showed that those segments of the organization that practiced "management by participation" were still more productive and more satisfied with their work. These data strongly support the argument that those work situations that take the psychological needs of workers into account, in this case their need for an increased sense of control over their own destiny, will enhance job satisfaction.

A recognition of this "Theory Y" position has led many employers to reexamine their basic assumptions about their reward systems, and a number of alternative proposals have evolved for providing more intrinsic satisfactions in the work setting. Such alternatives are variously termed **work enrichment,** "the humanization of work," and "the democratization of work." Let us examine several of these proposals.

One proposal involves the concept of work modules or time-task units (Kahn, 1973). Such modules represent the smallest allocation of time that is both psychologically and economically meaningful that can be devoted to a job. Kahn suggests that a two-hour module can fit most industrial jobs: two hours of typing, two hours of operating a drill press, or two hours of inspecting units on an assembly line. Conventional jobs usually do consist of four two-hour modules—an eight-hour shift broken into four segments by coffee and lunch breaks—but all the modules involve exactly the same activity. Consider, on the other hand, how the typical farmer, physician, or professor organizes these modules. Although these workers may spend more or less time in each module, may have more than four modules per day, and may work more than an eight-hour day, their modules are varied and they are free to organize the sequence of the modules to suit themselves.

In Kahn's notion of work modules, the workers would be allowed both to choose and to organize the modules in which they would spend their days, with the recognition that there are a variety of different tasks that must be done. His simplest example involves a supermarket, where a single worker could choose modules such as unpacking and price-marking merchandise, operating the cash register, and sacking the customers' purchases. In the usual supermarket, each of these tasks is done by a single worker and there is no work diversification. Kahn recognizes the complexity of his suggestion and points out that it would require a set of fair and objective rules, a flexible management, and in certain settings, some computer time.

Another approach to work enrichment has been described as an "open system," "total system," or "sociotechnical system" (Katz and Kahn, 1978). In this instance the workers—even the unskilled assembly line workers—are actively encouraged to influence their working environment, and attempts are made to integrate the technological systems with social systems, so that the work serves human needs as well as corporate needs. This approach is an interesting application of "Theory Y" to management. In one application of this approach, the management of a food-processing plant attempted to analyze the plant's operations in terms of the workers' psychological needs—their desire for accomplishment, autonomy, increased skill and knowledge, and higher self-esteem—and then restructured the operations of the plant in order to meet these needs. For example, the plant was organized into teams which were given real responsibility for planning and scheduling their own work. This arrangement permitted more worker autonomy than would be possible in the typical factory. Also, management minimized the size of the work force in order to make each job more challenging, in contrast to the usual tendency of management to overstaff and over-manage.

As the plan eventually evolved, there were two teams, a processing team and a packing-warehousing team, operating on three shifts. Each team member learned and performed every job required of the team. There were no machine operators, no fork truck drivers, no boiler operators, only team members. This unique arrangement provided challenge and the opportunity for developing new skills, both of which are important in developing increased self-confidence. It is interesting to note that this arrangement actually resulted in lower production costs than those of a conventional plant. Also, the reactions of all persons involved were uniformly positive, especially in regard to their increased job satisfaction. A similar program has been adopted on a company-wide basis by a large European automobile manufacturer, with highly positive consequences for both morale and rate of absenteeism.

In a recent research report Alber (1978) surveyed 58 American business organizations that had utilized a work enrichment program. He found that absenteeism was reduced by an average of 15 percent, a highly important factor since the average cost of absenteeism was estimated at $57 per person-day. Even more important was the reduction in employee turnover which decreased by an average of 18 percent, since the average replacement cost for an employee who quits was estimated at $2,330. Although there were no layoffs as a result of these programs, reductions in the work force as a result of natural attrition enabled the organizations to save over $4,000 per month in labor costs. Finally, and most important from our point of view, 54 of the 58 organizations that were involved reported measurable improvement in job satisfaction as a function of job enrichment. While these programs are still far from widespread, they reflect the growing awareness of management about the nature of the workers and the importance of the psychological aspects of the work environment.

Women and Work

Work has traditionally had a rather different meaning for women than for men. Despite the fact that approximately one-third of our labor force is female, the socialization of women has emphasized their roles as potential wives and mothers rather than as persons engaged in gainful employment outside the home. Consequently, the employment histories of men and women have traditionally differed widely, as have the satisfactions that each obtained from work.

YES, MARTHA HAS HAD A LOT OF TROUBLE FINDING HIGH QUALITY AND REASONABLY PRICED CHILD CARE WHEN SHE WENT BACK TO WORK.

Women often work from the time they conclude their formal education until their first child is born. Working may then be resumed after the youngest child reaches an age where the mother feels that she can absent herself from the home on a regular basis. The major problem confronting mothers who work outside the home, however, is the unavailability of high quality and reasonably priced child care. While mothers who work are becoming more common, reflecting the increase in availability of child care, most mothers still experience some anxiety and guilt about leaving their children. Some studies of working women (e.g., Rossman and Campbell, 1965) have reported that economic necessity is the major reason why women work. Studies of male workers, on the other hand, indicate that most men would continue to work even if there were no economic necessity (e.g., Morse and Weiss, 1962). Our traditional patterns of sex-role socialization are such that the basic sense of identity and the intrinsic satisfactions that men are expected to obtain from work have not been part of the sex role for most women.

Women's sex-role training has led them to find much of their identity in their roles and skills as wives and mothers. And their status in the community has traditionally been a reflection of their husbands' occupations. It is only very recently that career development and advancement are beginning to be considered legitimate aspects of a woman's role in American society.

Sex-role considerations have also been important with respect to the kinds of employment that women were typically expected to enter. There have been the traditionally "feminine" careers, such as nursing, teaching, and secretarial work, and the traditionally "masculine" careers, such as architecture, dentistry, engineering, and motion picture projection. These "masculine" careers have not involved any clear masculine attributes such as physical strength; rather they have been largely closed to women through historical accident followed by prejudice, discrimination, and an unwillingness of institutions to change. As a result, there have traditionally been only a few women in these careers, and such women have shown certain differences from women in general. For example, Rossi (1964) showed that more women in traditionally feminine careers have been married, and they married earlier, than women in traditionally masculine careers. In another study, Bancke (1972) found that women in traditionally masculine careers handled their aggressive impulses more directly than women in traditionally feminine careers, whose defense mechanisms were primarily "intellectualization" and "turning against the self."

All these considerations led Bloustein (1968) to state that a "marriage-career" hoax has been perpetrated on American women. This hoax prevents those women who desire it from looking forward to a career as a homemaker that could be fulfilling and rich, especially in our affluent, leisure-oriented society, and instead forces them into poorly paid, unsatisfying work. Bloustein proposes that we should follow one of two alternatives. The first would be to modify the socialization of women in order to prepare them for a full entry into the world of paid work, a procedure that would necessitate changing work itself to make it more compatible with the simultaneous roles of wife and mother. The second alternative would be simply to allow women to be comfortable in their more traditional roles as wives and mothers.

Retirement

One of the consequences of our advancing techology is that the human life span has undergone quite a remarkable increase. Along with the fact that many people now live to an advanced age, there is much disagreement as to how longevity should affect a

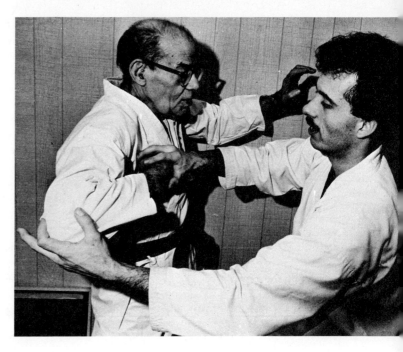

Jim Elliot, 68, is a retired photo finisher who didn't want to become inactive after his retirement. He has achieved the level of brown belt at a local karate academy and works part time as a bundler in a neighborhood market.

person's work life. The usual age of retirement in the United States has been 65, an arbitrary limit which was originally set in the late nineteenth century in Bismarck's Germany. For many years there has been strong pressure in the United States to reduce the age of retirement to 60 or even 55. More recently, there has also been a reverse trend—to extend the work life to 70 or even later. These contradictory movements seem to reflect our cultural ambivalence about retirement.

Although work may indeed be harsh and unfulfilling for many persons, it does provide most men and some women with a sense of identity, and it also takes up a great deal of time. The demands of work and the time involved give the lives of most adults a structure that otherwise would be lacking. Getting ready to go to work, traveling to the job, and the job itself provide a basic schedule not only for the worker but for the entire family. The loss of this structure, particularly on an arbitrary basis, often has important negative consequences and is now being resisted by more and more persons.

While retirement seems very attractive to most workers as an abstract idea, many find the reality harsh and unpleasant. They find it difficult to organize their lives in this new-found vacuum after spending most of their adult years engaged in work, and the adjustment to leisure is not easy to make. The idyllic picture of the happily retired couple now free to pursue their hobbies on a full time basis is rarely true in fact. Most of us have not developed either the interests or the competencies that would allow us to spend the bulk of our time in such pursuits. Also, retirement prevents us from obtaining whatever satisfactions have been involved in work, which we have already identified as an important source of need fulfillment for many adults.

Work represents a means of earning a living, a source of status and prestige, a way of achieving personal independence, a way of providing social contacts, and a way of taking up time. Let us see to what extent these need satisfactions are met in retirement.

In regard to economic needs, it is well agreed that the retirement incomes of most presently retired individuals are not sufficient to fully meet their requirements. Although the economic aspect of retirement has received far more attention than other aspects, and although economic planning for retirement is often the only kind of planning that is done, most workers still approach cessation of work without adequate economic resources. These potential difficulties cause obvious concerns, since they threaten the ability to satisfy basic physiological needs. The economic aspect of retirement is, however, receiving attention, and labor unions and management have both placed increasing importance on adequate pension plans as a major area of concern.

We have noted that many workers view their work as a source of status and prestige. What is the status and prestige conferred by retirement? This is a far more difficult question to answer, as the general cultural attitude toward retired workers has as yet not been adequately assessed through careful research. On the one hand, retirement is seen as a reward for a lifetime of productive effort and successful achievement; on the other, retired workers are frequently seen as people without a role or purpose in life, and their status and prestige are probably to a large extent a function of their former occupational status. The problem of assessing attitudes toward retired workers and developing methods for modifying these attitudes in a positive direction deserves careful attention.

A question frequently raised is whether retirement is good or bad. The answer is straightforward: retirement is both good and bad, just as work is both good and bad. All stages of life have both their pleasures and their problems, and retirement is no exception. All too frequently, an unrealistically rosy picture of retirement has been painted, which ignores its limitations and problems. Retirement is pictured as the golden age of life, a stage of life when all dreams come true. Most workers find it difficult, if not impossible, to see these dreams as realistic to any degree. Workers approaching retirement need help in facing their own ambivalence about retirement, help in exploring both their positive and negative feelings about becoming retired members of the community. Any approach that emphasizes only one side cannot be regarded as really useful in helping people to adjust to this stage of life.

To what extent does retirement permit personal independence? Potentially, retired persons can be the most independent members of society: freed from the daily obligations of work and having earned their economic security they could find that retirement can mean real independence. But this independence is rarely achieved. As noted above, most retired workers do not have economic independence, and they are frequently placed in the position of having to rely on either their families or the state. The question of failing health in old age poses the additional crucial problem of physical dependence.

Work provides an important source of social interaction that does not seem to be met in most retirement situations at the present time. Studies of workers indicate that the friendships of the work group are among the most important satisfactions yielded by work for all groups of workers; retirement simply does not provide for these needs. Thus, the social needs of the retired worker should be permitted to play a very important part in retirement planning, both by society and on a personal level. The success of retirement communities and retirement housing is in no small measure due to the fact that they satisfy the individual's social needs that are otherwise unmet.

While work takes up time and provides a day-to-day schedule for living, retirement provides a complete absence of structure and activity. Many workers welcome retirement as a time in which to do things that they have never had time for in the past, but others see it as unwelcome inactivity. Work, even burdensome and dangerous work, seems to be particularly important as a *routine*. It is something familiar, around which the pattern of life is organized, and some workers seem to fear that if work stopped so would life itself. This problem is complicated by what has been called the "honeymoon attitude" toward retirement. This refers to the plans made by some retiring workers to move their place of residence—to Florida, from the country to town, or from town to the country—without any real understanding of what these changes entail, especially in one's daily existence. Planning for such moves is an important step, but retired individuals must also have specific plans for spending their time. Perhaps these needs for structure can be summarized by saying that every retired individual needs something to do, but nothing that has to be done *today*.

Retirement is a time of intense personal change. Habits that have been relatively stable over the past 40 or 50 years must be completely modified. Roles that have become comfortable and customary must be given up. Retirement is a new way of life. Yet little is currently done to help the worker make the important change of accepting this new way of life, with its problems and promises. This is especially noteworthy in view of the help that is provided, through professional counseling programs, during other important life changes such as entry and exit from school, entry into marriage, and choosing a career. The need for extensive, well-conceived retirement counseling programs seems obvious. These counseling programs should be available early enough to provide for long-range planning, and thorough enough to help solve the problems of the transitional period into retirement itself.

SUMMARY

1. Chapter 9 examines the various adjustment challenges that are faced by all of us as we progress through adult life, from adolescence through retirement. Two areas appear basic to adult adjustment: *love and marriage,* and *work*.

2. Adult development begins with *adolescence,* involving obvious physical changes which begin around age 11 for girls and age 13 for boys. There is considerable individual variation in the age at which these changes begin, and this variability results in distinct psychological differences between early and late maturers. The very long-term effects of the differences are unclear, however.

3. The nature of adolescence has changed markedly in Western society over the past 200 years and currently is seen as a transition or time-out period involving preparation for the world of work. Adolescence is also a time of conflict over moral and personal values, when all of us must establish our own identities and belief systems separate from those of our parents.

4. Recent research by Daniel Levinson has identified three further phases of adult development for the male population. In the *Novice* phase, extending to age 30-35, the young man first separates himself from his childhood home and family. He endeavors to establish himself in an adult life of his own, in a clear occupational direction and in other aspects of an independent adult life. Other aspects of the Novice phase involve the Dream and the mentor relationship.

5. In the next phase, *Settling Down,* the two principal themes are establishing oneself and "making it." The man may terminate relationships that are too constricting, and he seeks affirmation of his success. The remainder of Levinson's stages, the next of which is *Middle Adulthood,* have yet to be fully elaborated.

6. It is through the process of *dating* that adolescents are presumed to develop the interpersonal knowledge that enables them to select an appropriate marriage partner. It would seem most sensible for dating choices to be based on similarity of needs and interests, but in practice the major factors are usually physical and social attractiveness. Individuals who are low in these characteristics may develop inferiority feelings. Sexual matters provide further complications in dating, and can create problems such as strong guilt feelings, accidental pregnancies, and unsuitable marriages.

7. The widespread tendency to choose a marriage partner from a background similar to one's own is called *homogamy,* and this practice enhances the probability that the couple will have similar values and interests. In regard to personality characteristics, it is popularly believed that "opposites attract." This is not supported by the research evidence, however, which shows that the decision to marry tends to be based on expectations and fantasies, particularly the existence of "romantic love."

8. The *engagement* has traditionally been a time after the formal commitment to marriage in which the partners are expected to examine and test the relationship, but few such opportunities exist, since there are still taboos against sexuality and against breaking the engagement. The needs that are served by marriage have changed markedly in this century; in a rural society survival needs were primary, while today psychological needs come first. Many persons have not had the interpersonal learning experiences that are necessary to enable them to utilize marriage in this manner, and alternative marriage styles have recently been proposed. In the *open marriage,* the interpersonal commitment would be frequently renegotiated, and there would be greater flexibility of roles and opportunity for personal growth.

9. The topic of *work and career* is discussed under four headings: career choice, vocational satisfaction, women and work, and retirement. *Career choice* is a topic of concern for most young people in the middle and upper socioeconomic classes, while those in the lower classes tend to see themselves simply as "working for a living." In Holland's view, vocational choice is an extension of personality development, within the framework of six types: social, realistic, investigative, artistic, enterprising, and conventional. There are six corresponding types of work environments. It is a strong cultural belief that each of us should have only one career, and there are substantial problems involved in attempting to shift careers in mid-life.

10. *Satisfaction* in one's vocation was perhaps easier to attain during the "craftsman" era of history, whereas modern technology has made many jobs quite dissatisfying. These feelings of dissatisfaction, particularly boredom, are reflected in high rates of turnover and absenteeism in many industries, while satisfaction is greatest in jobs with a high degree of status and personal autonomy. Work motivation appears to be best viewed in terms of two factors: hygiene factors, such as salary and attractiveness of the physical facilities; and motivators, such as the challenge of the task and the opportunity to use one's talents. Management's traditional view has emphasized the importance of the hygiene factors; more recently, "work enrichment" programs based

on motivators have been developed with substantial success. These programs have included the development of work modules or time-task units, in which workers choose and organize their own tasks, and the "open system" approach, in which the work system is integrated with the social system.

11. With the modern increase in life span, retirement has become a major topic of concern to society. Society's current indecision as to whether the retirement age should be raised or lowered reflects our cultural ambivalence about this area of our lives. Retirement is often an unpleasant experience, as it forces an end to the sources of satisfactions formerly provided through work. Retirement incomes are often not sufficient to meet economic needs, and it is difficult to find new sources of prestige and status. New patterns of social interaction must be developed. For retirement to be a satisfactory experience, it must be preceded by careful structuring and planning.

KEY TERMS

adult development

puberty

identity

Novice phase

mentor relationship

Settling Down

Middle Adulthood

homogamy

open marriage

satellite relationships

Theory X

Theory Y

work enrichment

PART FOUR

ASSESSING AND IMPROVING ADJUSTMENT

TEN

Assessing Psychological Adjustment

The most common methods for alleviating adjustment problems are dynamic psychotherapy, behavior therapy, and modern "tranquilizing" drugs.

Dynamic psychotherapy attempts to increase a person's self-understanding.

- Basic tools of psychotherapy are transference and interpretation.
- Thought and language play important roles in therapeutic change.
- Two specialized kinds of psychotherapy are psychoanalysis and nondirective therapy.

The behavior therapist is an expert in applied learning theory and designs learning-based procedures for behavior change.

- Behavior therapy begins with systematic observation of the problem behaviors.
- Behavioral techniques include simple positive reinforcement, systematic desensitization, and extinction.
- "Token economies" can be developed for behavior change in institutional settings.
- The ethics of behavior therapy have been the subject of recent debate.

The community mental health movement is shifting the location of public mental health care from the state hospital to the community.

THERE ARE FEW AREAS IN PSYCHOLOGY THAT HOLD AS MUCH FASCINATION as the assessment of the psychological state of another person, the "reading" of personality. This is also an area which has had far more than its share of popular but invalid theories and methods, together with a plentiful supply of quacks, charlatans, and hustlers who have practiced them. Below we identify some of these *ascientific* methods and try to view them objectively.

Legitimate approaches to assessing psychological adjustment can be divided into two categories: the everyday or "naive" approaches which we all use to try to understand our friends and acquaintances, and the more technical or professional methods used by psychologists in their work. Both are discussed below, and as we shall see, they overlap to some degree.

ASCIENTIFIC ASSESSMENT METHODS

We use the term **ascientific** to refer to those methods of assessing others that predate the development of psychology as a science. Even though it is now clear that they are uniformly of no use, some of them remain in vogue today and new ones are regularly being proposed. Let us take a brief look at three of the best known ascientific assessment procedures: astrology, palmistry, and phrenology. More detailed accounts may be found elsewhere (Lanyon and Goodstein, 1971).

Astrology, the attempt to forecast events on earth through observation of the fixed stars and other heavenly bodies, is thought to have originated about 25 centuries ago. The belief that the stars were powerful gods led the ancients to conclude that human affairs could be foretold by study of the heavens. The personalities of individual persons and the course of the events in their lives were determined by the person's horoscope (the configuration of the stars at the time of birth). Assessment was accomplished by noting the exact moment of the person's birth and then getting the appropriate predictive information from one of a number of elaborate manuals or almanacs, not unlike the daily horoscopes that are still to be found in many newspapers.

Palmistry refers to the attempt to describe personality and predict future behavior by interpreting the various irregularities and folds of the skin of the person's hand. Palmistry is known to have existed as a standardized system in China as early as 3000 B.C., although its early beginnings and theoretical roots are lost in antiquity. In palmistry, importance is given to the lines of the hand, as well as to the swellings or monticuli between these lines. Each of these "signs" is interpreted in a specific manner. Thus a large Mound of Saturn, that portion of the palm directly below the third joint of the middle finger, indicates wisdom, good fortune, and prudence. Palmistry provides for a complete personality assessment of individuals by the reading of these signs.

Phrenology, the art of personality assessment through the measurement of the external shape of the human skull, was given its major impetus by Franz Joseph

Gall, a German physician and anatomist, late in the eighteenth century. Gall's basic assumption was that the human brain is the locus of control over human behavior, a view which is now uniformly accepted by psychologists. At the turn of the nine-teenth century, however, the operation of the cerebral cortex was poorly under-stood and the current scientific view favored a strict localization of cortical action, with each function or faculty centered in a definite and specific region of the brain surface. The size of these regions created corresponding and observable alterations in the size of the skull, which could be used by the phrenologist to assess the many characteristics of the individual, including personality. For example, a protrusion of the skull in the area of honesty would indicate an honest individual. As was the case with astrology and palmistry, phrenology enabled its practitioners to give a complete personality assessment, based in this case upon the protrusions and con-tours of the skull.

It is interesting to note that Gall was essentially empirical in his approach to the development of phrenology, attempting to relate behavior to brain functioning and skull shape through personal observation. To gather information about the brain, he examined the skulls of living persons and then attempted to study their brains through autopsy after death. He also examined the skulls of persons in mental hos-pitals, prisons, colleges, and other places where individuals of exceptional deficien-

cies or endowments could be found, hoping to be able to relate skull shape with the characteristics which had brought these persons together. Unfortunately, Gall must have permitted a great deal of observational error to enter his work, since the more recent scientific study of phrenology has confirmed none of the relationships which he claimed to have found.

It is nowadays clear to psychologists interested in personality assessment and prediction that none of the methods described above, nor similar methods such as tea-leaf reading or crystal ball gazing, has any validity. Carefully controlled studies clearly show that the predictions made from such data simply do not come true. A man thought to be honest on the basis of the shape of his head, or the configuration of his palm, or of the stars at the time of their birth, turns out to be neither more nor less honest than anyone else. Why, then, have these methods persisted despite the massive evidence against them? There are several reasons. First, they are part of the folklore of our culture, so many persons have grown up believing that they are valid and reliable. Cultural "truths" of this nature are extremely difficult to dispel. Second, many practitioners of these methods rely on other information about the person being assessed, such as appearance, manner, and conversational cues, to make their assessments and predictions. Thus, much of what they say to others seems quite sensible and may indeed be accurate.

The third reason for the persistence of these methods is that many of the statements that are made could be true about practically anybody, and provided they are positive, people are generally eager to believe them. For instance, to tell a typical college student "There are times when you and your parents do not see things the same way" does not require any special psychological understanding, but can nevertheless convince the student that the speaker has a high level of "insight." Finally, some ascientific methods of personality assessment form a lucrative branch of the entertainment industry, and are promoted with advertising and with exaggerated but plausible claims. Thus, they are appropriately regarded as part of the culture but not a part of our established knowledge, and as such they rank with cards telling "your weight and your future" and with fortune-cookie slogans.

Let us briefly examine another assessment procedure that has recently become extremely popular and is being promoted by commercial methods: the evaluation of a person's **biorhythms.** According to the theory of biorhythms, as promoted by George Thommen (1973), our day-to-day effectiveness is governed by our position on three "cycles"—physical, emotional, and mental—which are fixed according to the moment of our birth. Since each cycle has a different period, they can periodically combine to produce an occasional "triple-low" day and corresponding "triple-high" days. The more the cycles stacked against us on any particular day, the more likely things are to go wrong, and vice versa.

Once again, there is no apparent reason why this rather silly scheme should give useful information, and a number of scientific studies (e.g., Shaffer, Schmidt,

Zlotowitz, and Fisher, 1978) have shown conclusively that it does not. It is certainly true that there are changes in one's energy level and motivation over time. What is inconceivable is that the pattern of these changes should be fixed absolutely by the moment of one's birth. Nevertheless, the notion of biorhythms is attracting a growing cult of "true believers" and is being commercially promoted as a viable approach to the prediction of human behavior.

EVERYDAY METHODS OF EVALUATING PEOPLE

All of us are constantly evaluating ourselves and others in a variety of ways. When we are introduced to a stranger, we often try to judge what he or she is "really like." If we are interested in dating, we try to assess the probability that the person in whom we are interested will accept a date, and whether our interests and personalities will be compatible. Obviously, we need to make the best judgments we can about such matters before we act. If a friend, an acquaintance, or a TV character does something for which there is no ready explanation, we become more comfortable once we have considered the possible reasons for the behavior and selected one that fits best for us. The process of arriving at these judgments is technically known as *making attributions,* and the study of the attribution process is a lively field within social and personality psychology. A related field of study is the communication of information through *nonverbal behavior,* and this is also an essential component in our everyday judgments and predictions about others.

Making Attributions

Attribution theory is concerned with how people make inferences about the causes of behavior. It primarily focuses on the methods used by the average person in attaining an understanding of the behavior of the self and others. Although this area was referred to in 1958 by psychologist Fritz Heider as "naive psychology," Heider also indicated that people often do have an adequate understanding of others and make accurate predictions about them. Apart from a need to explain the behavior of another person and to predict it in the future, people make attributions in order to have some control over future events. Thus, if we decide that an acquaintance is a violent person, we can prevent being injured by him if we avoid him in the future. In fact, social psychologist Harold Kelley (1972) believes that the basic purpose of attempting to determine the cause of another person's behavior is to achieve effective control of our own environment. Ironically, it is when people have strong needs to control their environment that their attributions, or judgments about causality, are least likely to be accurate. Let us now look in more detail at some of the research findings in the area of attribution—how people go about assessing the behavior and adjustment of others, and how they go about assessing their own behavior (Jones and Nisbett, 1972; Kelley, 1972; Shaver, 1975; Vernon, 1964).

Self versus others. One interesting and important fact is the "pervasive tendency for actors to attribute their actions to situational requirements, whereas observers tend to attribute the same actions to stable personal dispositions" (Jones and Nisbett, 1972, p. 80). In other words, we tend to perceive that our own actions are controlled by our environment and not by our internal needs and personal dispositions, while we see other people's behavior as due to their personal dispositions and not to the influences of their environment. For example, you may believe that an angry remark which you made to another person was the culmination of a long series of provocations by that person, and that you rarely make angry remarks to others. However, a person observing the interaction would be more likely to conclude that the angry remark was a typical sample of your behavior and that you generally are a very angry person.

One possible reason for this difference is that each of us has a great deal more information about our past reactions than do observers. The observer has only the information immediately at hand to use as a basis for understanding. In addition, each of us has information about our inner states and intentions at the time, information that is not available to our observer. Another possible reason for the difference is that the aspects of other people to which we attend most closely are differ-

The process of arriving at judgments about what others are "really like" is known as making attributions. What evaluation of the various people in this photo would you make by observing such characteristics as sex, age, and mode of dress?

ent from the aspects of ourselves to which we pay most attention. In particular, we tend to view others as a package of personality traits and ourselves as a package of underlying values and strategies brought into being by particular cues in our environments (Jones and Nisbett, 1972). Some psychologists believe that the approach we take to viewing ourselves is a more scientifically accurate way of perceiving a person than the approach we take to viewing others (Mischel, 1968).

Two further points are worthy of our attention. The first point is that in judging others, we tend to overattribute the causes of their behavior to personal dispositions at the expense of considering environmental influences. In looking at others, we tend to see a stable constellation of traits, and we tend to overemphasize these traits in explaining the other person's behavior. Second, it appears that our own motivations can lead to some of the differences between the way in which we perceive our behavior and others perceive it (Jones and Nisbett, 1972). For example, the maintenance of our self-esteem may be involved. Thus, if we fail a test we may explain the failure as the result of the unfairness of the exam, or the fact that we had a headache, or the prejudice of the instructor against us. But when we do well on an exam, it is because we are intelligent and studious. This strategy of explaining our failures in situational terms and our successes in dispositional ones maintains and enhances our self-esteem. This can be regarded as an example of the defense mechanism of *rationalization,* as described in Chapter 6.

Some of the above points have been made on an intuitive basis by popular author Robert J. Ringer (1977) in his book *Looking Out for Number One*. Carrying some of the arguments to their extreme, Ringer emphasizes the importance of recognizing that people in general tend to view situations in accordance with their own needs, and that in matters of judgment most of us will tend to draw the dividing line in such a manner as to benefit ourselves rather than other people, particularly when the matter involves our own emotions. He also believes that some persons do this deliberately, while retaining clear awareness of the realities of the situation, while others remain unaware, acting in the belief that their behavior and attitudes are a completely objective response to the situation. While Ringer's motive is to warn us that other people's distortions can easily have negative consequences for us, we can go still further in pointing out that each of us also engages in these distortions in our own attributions. This can prevent us from making adequate coping responses in our own lives, a point to which we will return in Chapter 12.

The ability to judge others. Psychologists are nowadays not as interested as they used to be in identifying the types of people who are the best judges of other

people's characteristics. However, some interesting facts were discovered on this topic some years ago. Vernon (1964) has summarized this research, which tends to show that the ability to judge others is perhaps very slightly better in women, is slightly related to intelligence, and increases with age in children. As would be expected, people are more accurate in judging others who come from a comparable socioeconomic and cultural background. Persons with artistic and literary interests appear to do slightly better in judging others, while persons with dogmatic, authoritarian attitudes do significantly more poorly. There is some evidence that academic training in the sciences serves to enhance the ability to judge others accurately. Finally, several studies showed that the better judges tended to possess better psychological adjustment than the poorer judges.

Improving the accuracy of judgments. What can people do to increase their skills in judging the characteristics of others and predicting their future behavior? Perhaps the most obvious thing is for the judge to improve his or her ability to empathize with other persons (Jones and Nisbett, 1972). Essentially, to empathize means to become aware of a situation in the same way as the other person becomes aware of it, by experiencing similar perceptions, thoughts, and feelings. The importance of **empathy** as a skill for enabling psychotherapists to better understand their clients has been emphasized by many writers, most notably Carl Rogers (1957).

Can people be trained to become more empathic? Although psychologists know relatively little about this area, we do have some knowledge about it in the context of counseling or psychotherapy skills. For example, Truax and Carkhuff (1967) demonstrated that structured learning techniques could be used to train beginning psychotherapists to increase their therapeutic skills, of which empathy was perhaps the most basic.

As already stated, another factor affecting our accuracy in perceiving the characteristics of others is motivation, and a special case of motivational influences involves the situation where the judge has an emotional connection with the person being judged. This source of distortions in judgment was recognized by Sigmund Freud many years ago, and Freud went so far as to insist that all fully trained psychoanalysts must be free of emotional difficulties themselves and must thoroughly understand all their minor emotional biases and weak spots. Most professional mental health workers recognize this point in varying degrees, and at the least, decline to work with a person as a client if they have any other kind of relationship with the person.

A third factor which can be brought to bear in increasing the accuracy of our perceptions of others involves attending to the relevant cues. Clearly, not every aspect of people is relevant in assessing or predicting things about them. To make accurate judgments, the judge must attend carefully to those aspects of a person and those behaviors that contain the needed information. Little research in this area has yet been done, although some was included in the training procedures of Truax and Carkhuff (1967) described above.

TECHNICAL AND PROFESSIONAL METHODS

We have discussed some of the popular but invalid methods that people have used over the years to explain and predict the behavior of others. We have also reviewed what is known about the informal ways in which people assess, or make attributions about, the causes of their own behavior or that of others. We now turn to the study of the ways in which professional psychologists assess the quality of a person's adjustment. One of the major aspects of training in professional psychology is in the nature and use of psychological *tests*. It is through the use of tests that psychologists are able to make more accurate assessments than are possible on the basis of informal methods alone. Information obtained from skillful interviews and from the person's past history is also important to mental health professionals in doing formal assessments, although a discussion of these areas is beyond the scope of this book. We first discuss tests of *skills* and *abilities,* then *personality* tests, and finally we touch more briefly on tests that assess *vocational* and *occupational* interest areas.

Abilities and Skills

In the understanding and assessment of psychological adjustment, the need frequently arises for the assessment of abilities, aptitudes, or achievements. Consider the case of a child who is causing concern because of poor performance in school. There are a variety of possible reasons for the behavior, the most obvious being a lack of the necessary intellectual or problem-solving ability. Thus, one of the first steps to be taken by the counselor would involve an assessment of this ability. Should the child be found to be more able than is reflected in school performance, then the counselor is likely to focus attention on motivational, personality, and other possible variables in an attempt to account for the problem.

Another widespread use of ability tests in relation to human adjustment comes in the area of vocational and educational guidance. Does Jack have the necessary ability to succeed in a career as a lawyer? Should Margaret major in mathematics, which is the area of her greatest interest? In Jack's case, he will in all probability have to sit for the Law Aptitude Test in order to apply to most major law schools. In Margaret's case, she would be ill advised to enter an area for which she did not have adequate ability (as would be true for anybody), and the counselor might well refer to the mathematics section of Margaret's college board examinations to provide a standardized basis for evaluating her ability relative to other students.

There are basically two kinds of ability tests: **achievement tests** and **aptitude tests.** Intelligence can be regarded as a general kind of aptitude—the aptitude for

Are aptitudes such as musical ability inborn or taught? How important are training and reinforcement in developing competence?

learning in general. Using this distinction, achievements can be defined as what individuals can demonstrate that they have learned—their present level of competence; and aptitudes, how well a person is likely to be able to do something if given the right training—a prediction of future competence.

By inquiring whether Jack has the ability to succeed in law school, we are asking about his *aptitude*. If, several years after completing law school, we ask whether Jack is in fact an able lawyer, then we are inquiring about his *achievements*. The distinction between aptitude and achievement is a time-oriented one. Achievements refer to current level of competence, while aptitudes refer to potential future level of competence, usually after additional training. Measuring achievement is a fairly straightforward task: obtain a behavior sample; that is, give a test that samples what the person can do. Aptitude assessment is an appraisal of current competence in areas that are regarded as predictive of the skills to be learned. In general, the people who have the greatest aptitude in a particular area should eventually show the greatest achievement, provided that all have been given equal learning opportunities.

Why do people appear to have widely differing aptitudes, in such areas as music, art, or athletics? To what extent are these inborn qualities, and to what extent are they simply the outcome of training and practice? There appears to be little question that some are inborn. For instance, musical aptitude requires a high degree of pitch discrimination skill and tonal memory, while athletic aptitude involves gross muscle coordination and visual-motor timing. These individual differences in basic skills are to some extent genetic; it is equally clear, however, that such skills require an enormous amount of training and reinforcement if the individual is to develop any degree of useful competence.

While we often talk of the "natural athlete," it should be apparent that most professional athletes spend years of preparation and hours of daily practice to maintain this so-called natural ability. Or, let us consider the development of musical talent. Suppose that a child with good pitch discrimination and the other basic qualities that are necessary for developing a good musical talent is born into a nonmusical family, where little music is heard, and where little reinforcement is offered for any expression of interest in music. Such a child would be at a marked disadvantage when compared to one born into a musical family, who has a vast array of opportunities and models for developing musical skills, and who receives enthusiastic rewards for any interest displayed in this area. Tests of musical aptitude, when administered to children or adolescents, do not just measure innate qualities but also evaluate the current level of achievement, to which innate predispositions and training, both incidental and formal, have contributed.

Perhaps the issue is clearer in examining mechanical aptitude. Figure 10-1 is a sample item similar to those found on commonly used tests of mechanical aptitude. Clearly, knowing the correct answer requires the application of a simple physical principle—the lever. Knowledge of such principles could have been acquired

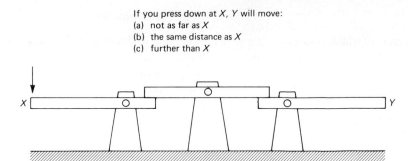

If you press down at *X, Y* will move:
(a) not as far as *X*
(b) the same distance as *X*
(c) further than *X*

Figure 10-1. Item similar to those used in tests of mechanical aptitude.

formally, through a knowledge of high school physics, or incidentally, through tinkering with motors or other mechanical devices. In any event, a good understanding of basic principles will permit the individual to acquire a knowledge of advanced physical priniciples more quickly. Thus, in a certain sense, this aptitude test is a simple achievement test. It can also be noted that the amount of incidental learning in a field is an index of a person's interest in the field.

An individual's current achievements would thus be expected to be consistent with innate predispositions, learning opportunities, and the extent of the reinforcements available. A substantial discrepancy between a person's actual achievement and that predicted by aptitude test scores is often an early sign of psychological maladjustment.

Intelligence testing. As long as we consider more or less neutral behaviors such as athletics and mechanical aptitude, our division of ability testing into aptitudes and achievements causes little controversy. What about intelligence? Do intelligence tests measure aptitudes or achievements? As previously noted in Chapter 1, practically all formal measures of intelligence reflect the individual's earlier experience in problem solving. Indeed, test questions asking about the meaning of different words (*vocabulary* items) are usually among those which correlate best with overall performance. Thus, achievement appears to be an important aspect of intelligence tests.

Because most formal learning situations tend to be somewhat similar, what we already have learned is a good predictor of what we will learn in the future. Thus, people who can correctly define many abstract words will clearly do better in most advanced educational programs than people who cannot. It must therefore be agreed that intelligence tests are a kind of aptitude test as well. Perhaps we can summarize by saying that if we consider intelligence to be one's aptitude for learning, then this aptitude is determined in part by one's early learning experiences and in part by genetic and other factors.

Personality and Clinical Diagnosis

A person's abilities and skills play an important role in determining the career avenues which will lead to better or poorer personal adjustment, and specific personality attributes are also important in this regard. A persuasive, happy-go-lucky extrovert might make a highly successful salesman but a terrible accountant, while the opposite could well be true of a persistent, shy, conscientious person. Likewise, anybody who reacts badly to personal rejection would be well advised to steer clear of politics, a potential scholar must enjoy reading, and a creative thinker would never be comfortable as an army sergeant. In planning the maximum use of capabilities, therefore, and to achieve the best possible adjustment, it is wise for individuals to spend their time in activities which are compatible with their general personality.

The other area where assessment plays an important function in adjustment is, of course, the understanding of psychological problem areas, their probable causes, and possible ways of alleviating them. Consider the case of John who, as he enters his senior college year in engineering, finds that his interest in keeping his work up to date is rapidly dwindling, and that he is scarcely motivated enough even to attend the minimum number of classes. He spends increasing amounts of time playing the guitar, for which he has developed a sudden enthusiasm, and even enrolls in an evening course in music theory. He also volunteers for political campaigning work, even though there is no imminent election. He accepts his declining grades with a fatalistic attitude, and finds himself engaging in lengthy discussions with his peers about the

meaning of life. His girlfriend, viewing the dramatic behavior change with some alarm, persuades him to make an appointment with the college counseling service.

What are the causes of John's difficulties? Perhaps there is essentially no problem at all, and he has finally faced up to the reality that a career in engineering is of no interest to him whatever. Perhaps he is showing the early signs of a serious psychological disorder such as schizophrenia. Alternatively, John's behavior may represent attempts to avoid situations which arouse strong anxiety, in which case he would be classified as neurotic. Or maybe John is simply "doing his thing" before taking on the responsibility of beginning a career.

These possible explanations range from benign to extremely serious, and the amount of effort which John would need to put forth in order to surmount his difficulties would also vary widely according to their basic causes. Psychological tests, while not always useful, can often be of considerable help in pinpointing possible sources of difficulty and excluding others. Let us examine some different kinds of personality and psychodiagnostic tests that might be used.

Personality and Adjustment Inventories

Adjustment questionnaires had their origin during the First World War, when it became apparent that there were not enough psychiatrists to examine adequately all the potential recruits. The need at that time was to identify in advance persons who might suffer some kind of psychological breakdown when under the stress of battle, and a committee of psychologists went to work on the problem. The result was the Woodworth Personal Data Sheet, a standardized psychiatric interview in printed form. More than 200 questions were initially considered for use, and the number was reduced to 116 on the basis of preliminary testing with both college men and draftees. Typical questions dealt with physical symptoms ("Do you ever feel an awful pressure in or about your head?"), fears and worries ("Are you troubled with the idea that people are watching you on the street?"), and adjustment to the environment ("Do you make friends easily?").

Woodworth's questionnaire was an immediate success, and led to the development of a number of similar inventories. Critics of this method of assessing psychological adjustment, however, were quick to point to the ease with which such a test could be faked in both "look-good" and "look-bad" directions, and to the fact that many sources of maladjustment were rather more complex than a simple test could show.

The MMPI. An important step forward came in 1940, with the development of what is now the best known and most widely used of psychological questionnaires, the **Minnesota Multiphasic Personality Inventory,** or **MMPI** (Hathaway and McKinley, 1951). Like the Woodworth test, the MMPI was developed to meet a practical need, that of rapid and standardized psychiatric diagnosis. Rather than assessing overall psychological adjustment, the MMPI was designed to predict which of nine common diagnostic categories a patient was most likely to fit, such as depression, hysteria, paranoia, schizophrenia, and so on. Thus, the MMPI is to be used primarily with persons suspected of having a definite psychological disorder.

One way to build a questionnaire for making psychiatric diagnoses would be to ask the same questions that the diagnostician would ask in the interview, in the same manner as the Woodworth test. The authors of the MMPI, however, wanted to avoid the easy susceptibility to faking and other criticisms of such an approach. To do this, they made use of many **subtle items;** that is, questions whose relevance to a particular disorder is not easily apparent but can be shown by experiment. For example, patients diagnosed as depressive actually answer "True" to the item "I sometimes tease animals" much more often than normal persons do. Therefore, this item can be used, in conjunction with a number of others, to assess the likelihood of a person being diagnosed as depressed, and the fact that the item does not obviously relate to depression makes it difficult to fake.

Selection of test items according to the way they are actually answered by the criterion group in question is called the **empirical** approach to test development, and it was considered to represent a definite advance over Woodworth's *rational* or **face-validity** approach. The best inventories today utilize both empirical and rational aspects in their development, plus additional refinements through factor analysis and other complex statistical procedures.

The manner in which the MMPI is commonly used can be illustrated by reference to Figure 10-2, which shows the *profile* of scale scores obtained by a college student seeking help at a mental health center. The numbers on the sides of the chart represent a standard score system with a mean of 50 and standard deviation of 10. The four scales at the right are validity scales, designed to show whether the respondent is being deliberately evasive, or defensive in a more subtle manner, or may be responding in some other invalid way. The clinical scales (numbered one through nine) show the degree of similarity between the patient's responses and those of nine different well-defined psychiatric groups. In addition, research conducted in the past twenty years has shown it is possible to identify profile *patterns* which are associated with various psychological characteristics and disorders.

The relatively low scores on the validity scales *L, F,* and *K* show that our student has responded to the questions honestly and conscientiously. The high peak on scale two (*D,* or depression) indicates similarities to depressive patients, while the peak on scale seven (*Pt,* or psychasthenia) shows some similarity to patients with obsessive-compulsive disorder, and a high degree of anxiety, guilt, and ruminative worrying. From the profile pattern as a whole it can be suggested with a fair degree of confidence that if a psychiatric label were given to the patient, it would involve some category of neurosis. Detailed information about such profiles is summarized in Lachar's (1974) reference manual, which reports the results of empirical studies of the characteristics of persons with different MMPI profile patterns. The most common (and discriminating) complaints of patients represented by the profile in Figure 10-2 include insomnia,

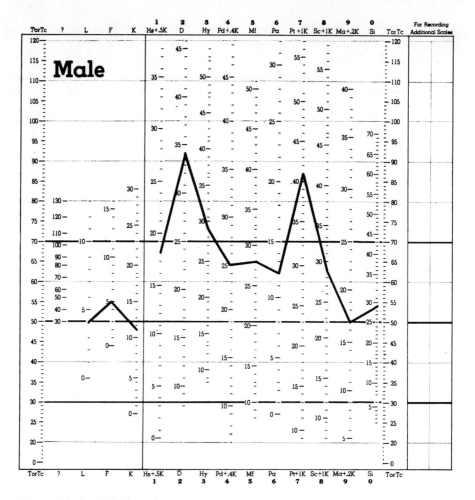

Figure 10-2. MMPI profile suggesting anxiety and depression. [Profile forms copyright © 1948 by The Psychological Corporation]

obsessions, anxiety, depression, nervousness, tension, worry, tiredness, and gastrointestinal problems. They typically have high standards of performance, are capable of developing good emotional ties, and tend to become overwhelmed and dependent under accumulated stress.

The CPI. The **California Psychological Inventory** or **CPI** (Gough, 1957) was specifically designed for the multidimensional description of normal personality. The test consists of 468 personal statements, of which 200 also appear in the MMPI, to be answered "true" or "false" in the same manner as the MMPI. The CPI yields scores on 15 personality scales, most of which were developed using the empirical approach. Thus, the Socialization scale was derived by comparing the responses of juvenile offenders and high school disciplinary cases with those of normal high school students (Gough and Peterson, 1952). The Dominance scale was developed by asking fraternity and sorority members to nominate the five most dominant and five least dominant members of their group (Gough, McClosky and Meehl, 1951). Several other scales were constructed through internal consistency analyses, combining a rational selection of initial items with statistical refinement of the item pool. In addition, there are three validity scales, which are similar in nature to the validity scales of the MMPI.

To facilitate the clinical interpretation of the CPI, the 18 scales are organized into four groups or clusters: (1) measures of poise, ascendancy, and self-assurance; (2) measures of socialization, maturity, and responsibility; (3) measures of achievement potential and intellectual efficiency; and (4) measures of intellectual and interest modes. In interpreting a test profile, the test *Manual* suggests initially observing the overall elevation of the profile as an index of the respondent's social and intellectual functioning, and then comparing the relative levels of the four scale clusters. Further information is gained by observing the highest and lowest scale scores and by studying combinations of scales. The *Manual* also provides lists of adjectives that are descriptive of high and low scorers on each scale, plus a considerable amount of additional information about the scales, to serve as a basis for further interpretative hypotheses and research.

To illustrate the use of the CPI, Figure 10-3 presents the CPI profile of a 41-year-old male research scientist who was tested as part of an industrial management development program. As was the case with the MMPI, the numbers on the sides of the chart represent a standard score system with a mean of 50 and a standard deviation of 10. The 18 CPI scales are presented in abbreviated form along the horizontal axis.

This man would be viewed as a self-assured, poised, rather forceful person with little self-doubt or uncertainty about himself. At the same time his sense of responsibility, his willingness to accept rules and proper authority, and his self-control seem less well developed; and his achievements, both those gained through conformity and those gained through independence, are probably modest. Quite aware of and sensitive to others, he is quite open to change and may even be impulsive at times. However, he appears rather satisfied with himself, and can be rather closed-minded and intolerant of others, especially when he feels that his principles are being violated. One might conclude that this man is an ambitious and socially skillful individual who lacks the impulse control and conscientiousness necessary to realize his ambition. His sensitivity to others coupled with his unwillingness or inability to respond completely to this awareness might lead others to view him as manipulative and controlling.

This characterization was very much in keeping with the man's supervisory evaluations, which noted that he "has never realized his potential as a scientist." These evaluations further noted his very high needs for autonomy, making it very difficult for

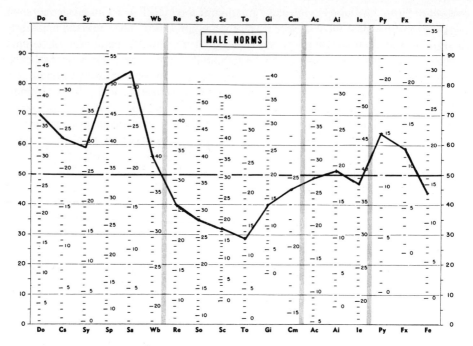

Figure 10-3. CPI profile suggesting mild personality problems. [Profile forms from *California Psychological Inventory*, by Harrison G. Gough, copyright © 1957 by Consulting Psychologists Press Inc.]

him to hear or accept supervisory feedback. His impulsiveness and his impaired interpersonal relationships led to a variety of morale problems in his laboratory and he was generally regarded as having limited potential for higher managerial positions or promotions.

Screening tests. Another use of objective inventories is in routine screening procedures that attempt to identify individuals with adjustment or other problems that need professional attention. The Psychological Screening Inventory (PSI) was developed for such a purpose, and is used in community clinics, probation courts, medical facilities, and other places where a brief evaluation could be helpful in the ultimate prevention of more serious problems (Lanyon, 1973). Screening procedures differ from comprehensive individual assessments in that they do not attempt to make the most accurate possible assessment of each individual, but rather to make an improvement in the overall quality of the service provided, through identifying, at minimal costs, some of the individuals who could benefit from further attention.

There are many other adjustment inventories besides the MMPI and the CPI. These two, however, are among the best known and most satisfactory from the viewpoint of validation through research evidence. The question of which test to use in a particular instance, and the broader question of whether to use tests at all in the understanding of any particular adjustment problem is, of course, an important and interesting one. In most cases, the tools used by the psychologist or counselor and the particular method followed in approaching the problem will be a matter of individual preference, and satisfactory results can be achieved in a number of different ways. The case materials presented at the end of this chapter show examples of the manner in which adjustment problems might commonly be approached by the psychologist.

Lie-detector tests. Let us also look briefly at an assessment procedure which is becoming increasingly popular as a tool in legal work, the **lie-detector test.** This is one example of a *behavioral* test, in which actual samples of the respondent's behavior are taken in a structured manner and are compared with norms for that behavior over the population at large. Lie-detection test procedures record an individual's physiological emotional responses while answering a series of questions, and are based on the premise that the pattern of such responses while lying will be different from the pattern while telling the truth. The subject's psycho-physiological behavior, such as heart rate, blood pressure, skin resistance response (sweating), and muscle tension, is closely monitored while he or she is asked a series of questions, and it is presumed that the patterns of responses can be inspected to determine the topics, if any, on which the subject was probably untruthful.

How effective is lie detection? Despite its rapidly growing popularity, research psychologists who have studied the matter carefully agree that the majority of the

claims for accuracy made by the lie-detection industry are invalid. Thus, Lykken (1974, 1978) has pointed out that in two recent studies, approximately half of the innocent subjects were erroneously classified as having lied! However, out of the many complex procedures employed in lie-detection work, there do appear to be several that have the potential for much higher accuracy in cases to which they are applicable. Unfortunately, most professional polygraphers are ignorant of these matters, and the field continues to flourish on the basis of its popular appeal and its economic success.

Projective Techniques

Of all the various activities that psychologists engage in, one of their most traditional and best known roles has been psychological assessment using projective tests. The development of projective tests began in the 1930s, when it was popular to regard "mental" problems of the mind as analogous to physical problems of the body. In this view, it was considered that the causes of mental problems lay beneath the "surface" of the mind in "unconscious" areas, just as the causes of most physiological problems lay beneath the skin and thus hidden from direct observation. A rather extreme form of this analogy was to liken projective tests to "mental X-rays," with which the structure of a person's mind could be laid bare without disturbing the surface aspects, in much the same manner as an actual X-ray indicates the structure beneath the physical surface of the body.

We have seen in earlier chapters that psychological or behavioral adjustment problems cannot be fitted neatly into the analogy of physical illness, and thus the use of projective techniques is in a strict sense somewhat obsolete. Experienced clinical psychologists, however, are often able to gain a wealth of helpful practical information about a person's psychological problems from projective tests, which have become a more-or-less permanent part of the clinical psychologist's procedures. We now discuss several of the best known projective tests, and give illustrations of their use.

The Rorschach test. In administering the **Rorschach test,** perhaps the best known of all projective techniques, the respondent is shown a series of ten symmetrical inkblots, and is asked to describe "what you can see in them," or "what they remind you of." The order of presentation is always the same, and the examiner records everything the individual says and does during the testing procedure. Following this free-association period, there is an inquiry or post-test interview in which the examiner repeats the individual's responses back and asks exactly what it was about each blot that led to each specific response.

This test was initially developed in the early part of the twentieth century by a Swiss psychiatrist named Hermann Rorschach (1942), whose original interest was in the experimental study of fantasy. When he began to use his patients as subjects for these perceptual experiments, Rorschach was surprised to note that there were stable relationships between certain inkblot perceptions and psychiatric symptoms. Encouraged by these findings, he began a more systematic investigation of the responses of different patient groups, and started to speculate about the reasons for these relationships. Since Rorschach was primarily interested in perception, he paid particular attention to the formal aspects of the individual's responses rather than to the content. He noted the number of responses, the reaction time, whether the response was determined solely by the form of the inkblot or whether color or perceived movement were also involved, and many other characteristics. These relationships form the basis for the manner in which the test is traditionally interpreted. However, it is also common for psychologists to analyze the content of the responses for symbolic meaning in much the same manner as the psychoanalytic patient's free associations.

Figure 10-4 shows a reproduction of Card IV from the ten Rorschach inkblots. Klopfer and Davidson (1962, p. 10) have described the stimulus characteristics of this card as follows:

The blot material of Card IV appears massive, compact, yet indistinct in shape. This card is black-gray all over and highly shaded. Because of its massive structure and dense shading, it appears ominous to some people. Thus monsters, giants, gorillas, or peculiar-looking people are seen sitting or approaching, or the blot looks like a dense forest with mountains and lakes. The frequency of the giant,

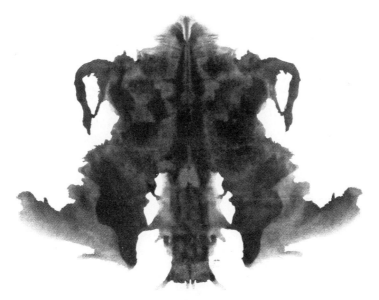

Figure 10-4. A reproduction, approximately half-size, of Card IV from the ten Rorschach inkblots. [From H. Rorschach, *Psychodiagnostics*, Bern: Hans Huber, copyright 1921, 1948; reproduced by permission of Grune & Stratton, Inc.]

ape, or monster type of response has prompted some clinicians to refer to this card as the "father card." They believe that attitudes toward paternal authority are revealed because of the combination of masculine aggression and dependent needs related to shading.

Subjects who are prone to select details for their responses may perceive the large side areas as "boots," or the top side areas as "snakes" or a "female figure diving." Two other areas that are easily delineated are the lower center portion and the small top center area, frequently associated with sexual responses.

The shading of the card, if not disturbing to a subject, may suggest furriness; in that case the blot is frequently seen as a fur rug.

Paula, a 23-year-old woman who had consulted a psychologist because of her personal problems, gave the following responses to this card. The question marks in the inquiry phase indicate places where the examiner asked clarifying questions about the *location* of the percept (What parts of the blot are you referring to?) and its *determinants* (for example, What about the blot suggested a monster?).

Free Association Phase	Inquiry Phase
IV 1. Sort of looks like a monster with big feet.	A cute little thing. Really a dashing little monster. Such a friendly little guy. Got a big tail, though. (?) The whole blot. (?) Really looks like a monster, but a friendly one.
2. When I turn it round, it just looks like—when you mount an insect it has wings and legs—looks like a mounted insect. Sort of cute insect. Maybe a little moth.	You lay him out flat. Only partially mounted. Person hasn't finished yet. You can tell by the lighter color that its wings are turned over. (?) The lighter gray. (?) Again, the whole blot.

In a formal analysis of the first response, it would be noted that the location of the percept was the whole blot, that the determinant was form, or shape, that the form perceived was appropriate or realistic, and that the content of the percept was humanlike. The second response is also a whole response, and has realistic form integrated with the perception of achromatic color and animal content. In interpreting the responses, at least three kinds of material are considered to be significant: the formal scoring categories, namely, the distribution of percepts over the various location and determinant categories; the nature of the perceived content; and the general language with which percepts are described. Only the most tentative hypotheses would be made from each individual percept, and heavy reliance is placed upon the response pattern as a whole.

Predominance of "whole" locations, when combined with a high level of form appropriateness, is traditionally interpreted as reflecting the ability to organize material, to relate details, and to be concerned with the abstract and the theoretical. A high degree of form appropriateness is also considered to indicate a concern with the reality situation. The presence of achromatic color responses in any quantity is interpreted as indicating either hesitation in responsiveness to external stimuli or an unhappy mood. With regard to content and language, the client's recognition of a "monster" and the manner in which she divests it of its threatening nature ("cute," "little," "friendly") might be seen as illustrating one method of adjustment to perceived threat, by denying and even "reversing" the threatening elements. This is a possible example of reaction formation, a concept discussed in Chapter 6. The fact that a satisfactory compromise is reached at the end of the inquiry ("a monster, but a friendly one") might be taken as a tentative indication that this particular defense mechanism operates satisfactorily for the client. This hypothesis might be tempered slightly after examining the next response, in which the percept has been reduced not only to an insect, but a dead one, and the client again calls it "cute," perhaps suggesting that she is still finding it necessary to reassure herself that no threat exists. Pinning it out on a board might be seen as yet a further attempt to remove the threat. The use of "him" rather than "it" in the inquiry might be taken as a tentative cue that the threat has its basis in human interactions, particularly involving males. Obviously, such statements as these would only be regarded as tentative hypotheses, to be confirmed or negated by the client's responses to the other nine cards.

Thematic Apperception Test. Commonly known as the **TAT,** the **Thematic Apperception Test** (Murray, 1943) is another traditional projective device. The stimulus materials consist of 31 cards, 30 depicting various scenes and one blank card. In the standard presentation, the respondent is shown 20 cards chosen according to sex and age, although in the typical clinical presentation fewer than 20 cards are generally used. The TAT is introduced as a "test of imagination," and the respondent is asked to tell as dramatic a story as possible about each card. The respondent is instructed that each story should include what has led up to the event depicted in the card, what is happening at that moment, what the people in the story are feeling and thinking, and finally the outcome of the story. The examiner records the stories exactly as they are given. Murray also recommended that the examiner attempt, in a post-test interview, to determine the source of the story—whether personal experience, from friends, or from books or movies. It is generally assumed that the respondent "identifies" with a major figure in each story, so that a close examination of the stories will reveal much about the respondent.

Figure 10-5 shows one of the stimulus cards of the TAT. Ways in which respondents tend to react to this card are as follows (adapted from Henry, 1956, pp. 254-256).

Murray's description. *The portrait of a young woman. A weird old woman with a shawl over her head is grimacing in the background.*

Manifest stimulus demand. *An adequate accounting will include only the two figures plus some explanation of their being together in this position. Generally, the interpretation of subjects is about as Murray gives it. However, recently we have*

Figure 10-5. A reproduction of one of the TAT stimulus cards. [Reprinted by permission of the publishers from Henry A. Murray, *Thematic Apperception Test,* Cambridge, Mass.: Harvard University Press, copyright © 1943 by the President and Fellows of Harvard College.]

seen in female subjects over seventy interpretations in which the "weird old woman" becomes a gently smiling and helpful person. Close examination of the face of the older figure suggests that "weird" and "grimacing" are not necessary connotations.

Form demand. *The two figures are the only major details, though the facial features of the older woman can be differentially perceived.*

Latent stimulus demand. *In subjects in the middle-age range, this appears to be a stimulus relating older to younger. Thus, for the mature woman, threats of old age appear prominent. In the younger adult, apprehension over control by an older woman appears more prominent. A basic stimulus selected by many subjects, especially women, is one which portrays the old woman as some symbolic representation of a part of the younger; her evil self, her self when aged, and so on.*

Frequent plots. *Most generally, the younger woman bears a family relationship to the older woman who is influencing or advising in some way. In about one-third of the stories, the older woman is seen as adversely influencing. In about one-third of the stories, a second plot will appear in which the older woman is a symbolic representation of the younger woman.*

Significant variations. *Of importance here is the issue of whether the subject sees the two figures in the same reality plane (mother-daughter) or whether one is a symbolic representation (my bad self, me when old). In addition, if treated in this fashion, the particular ideas toward the good and evil or other parts of the self should be specially viewed. In the light of the possibility of some, especially older, subjects seeing the background woman as kindly, responses to her should probably be watched more carefully and attention paid to the extent to which projection rather than reality observation is involved in attributing adverse influences.*

The following story was given by the same 23-year-old female who contributed the Rorschach material discussed earlier in this chapter.

Well, there's a young woman in the foreground and an older woman in the background, and the older woman looks as though she has planned something that will be harmful to the younger woman, who looks very naive. And in fact the older woman has planned to keep the younger woman captive, and to make her serve her, for the rest of the older woman's life. But although the girl is naive, she's also rebellious; and by asserting herself with other people and getting a group of friends she's able to move out of the—not exactly spell, but she's able to break the bond that the older woman has around her. Right now she's just beginning to realize that she is being put in a position like this, but she's still very much under the control of the older woman, because these two have lived together for a long time. In fact, the younger woman was raised by the older woman. She's still very much under her control as I said, and she has strong feelings of guilt and fear of facing the world on her own. But fortunately she is able to make friends. At this point, though, she hasn't broken the bonds and she feels very confused, like she's being drawn between two poles. Ultimately, she's able to go out and make friends, and getting to know people and the different ways they have from the ways the old woman had taught her, she's able successfully to face the older woman, and defy her control, and go out and live a life of her own.

This story follows the stimulus demands of the card to a considerable extent; that is, the client reacted to the card much like most people her age. Thus, we would not be justified in coming to an immediate conclusion that she has any special problem in her relationships with older women. Also, a typical TAT interpretation would draw material from ten or more cards, and would regard whatever hypotheses are gleaned from an individual story as quite tentative, to be strengthened or contradicted by the remainder of the stories. From the present story, the following details might be considered of greatest interest.

The older woman's control over the younger is perceived as longstanding and as having caused some rather central personality problems. However, the younger woman is seen as taking the initiative in developing other friendships in order to provide emotional support for the break which she plans with the older woman. Her ambivalence over these plans is seen in the use of the words "rebellion," "guilt," and "confused." The younger woman is perceived as displaying perhaps a somewhat lesser degree of anger and resentment toward the older than one would expect after having been trained as a lifelong captive and servant; and the severity of the confinement, together with the younger woman's expression of guilt rather than anger, suggest a situation where anger is perhaps repressed. There is also the younger woman's determination and ultimate success, though this comes about through defiance of the older woman rather than a resolution of conflict, again suggesting more anger than is overtly acknowledged.

Although themes of apprehension over control by an older woman are relatively common in stories given by younger persons to this picture, the strength of the conflict as represented by the guilt, the severity of the control exercised, and the absence of appropriate expressions of anger by the younger woman suggest the tentative hypothesis that such a conflict does exist for this client. The client's inability to resolve the fantasy conflict successfully lends further support to this hypothesis. A TAT analyst might also suggest that the client's ability to put forward a rational plan for the younger woman while still acknowledging her confusion and naivete suggests good potential for improvement in psychotherapy. Naturally, experienced clinicians would seek additional support for these tentative hypotheses elsewhere in the client's TAT responses.

Vocational Interest Tests

It is well understood that people differ in their suitability for different careers. Much of the difference is due to variations in skills and abilities, as we have discussed earlier in this chapter. A significant part, however, depends on personality characteristics, attitudes, areas of nonintellectual competence, aspirations, motivations, and a variety of other influences. These factors, as related to vocational satisfaction, we call *vocational interests*. Although some persons may make a decision fairly early in life as to the kind of career they would like to follow, many do not have the opportunity to make such a decision with any degree of maturity. In some cases an occupational field may be completely unknown to young persons, and it is an important part of the vocational counselor's job to make them aware of the possibilities. In some cases there is a fine line between personality characteristics and vocational interests, since both involve interpersonal behavior and competencies. Vocational interest tests, however, involve concepts which are directly related to the world of work, such as "scientific," "outdoors," and "computational" interests. We now discuss two of the best known tests in the vocational interest area.

The Strong-Campbell Interest Inventory. An outgrowth of the original Strong Vocational Interest Blank, which was first developed in 1927, the **Strong-Campbell Interest Inventory** assesses the similarity between a person's interests and those of successful persons in a large variety of occupations (Campbell, 1974). Respondents are asked to indicate their likes and dislikes among a list of 325 occupations, school subjects, kinds of people, hobbies, and so on, regardless of whether they possess any special training that might be required. Using objective scoring keys developed by the empirical method and based on the responses of persons who are known to be following successful careers, each respondent receives a score indicating degree of interest in 67 different occupations for males, and 57 for females. These occupational scales are shown in Table 10-1.

The Strong-Campbell also yields scores on two other types of scales: Basic Interest Scales and General Occupational Themes. The 23 Basic Interest Scales represent occupational areas such as agriculture, social service, and sales. The six General Occupational Themes are the styles or types developed by Holland (1973) and discussed in Chapter 9: realistic, investigative, artistic, social, enterprising, and conventional. As the reader will recall, Holland's theory of vocational choice suggests that each of us is predisposed to enter a vocational field that is congruent with our particular occupational style.

Careful longitudinal research with the Strong VIB has indicated that most people's vocational interests tend to remain remarkably stable from the years of career decision through middle age. For example, Strong (1951) reported that the average correlation between the interest scores of individuals in their senior year of college and a retest 22 years later was as high as .75.

The Strong-Campbell is very tedious to score by hand, and answer sheets are generally sent out by the counselor for professional scoring by computer. The output is a profile sheet on which one receives a set of standard scores indicating one's degree of similarity to the interests of each of the occupational groups listed in Table 10-1, and additional scores indicating degree of interest in the Basic Interest areas and in the General Occupational Themes.

Table 10-1
Scales Available for the Strong-Campbell Interest Inventory

Men

Accountant	Merchant Marine Officer
Advertising Executive	Minister
Agribusiness Manager	Musician
Air Force Officer	Navy Officer
Architect	Nurse, Licensed Practical
Army Officer	Nurse, Registered
Artist	Optometrist
Banker	Personnel Director
Biologist	Pharmacist
Business Education Teacher	Photographer
Buyer	Physical Scientist
Cartographer	Physical Therapist
Chamber of Commerce Executive	Physician
Chiropractor	Police Officer
College Professor	Priest
Computer Programmer	Psychologist
Computer Sales	Public Administrator
Credit Manager	Purchasing Agent
Dentist	Realtor
Department Store Manager	Recreation Leader
Dietitian	Reporter
Elementary Teacher	Sales Manager
Engineer	School Superintendent
English Teacher	Skilled Crafts
Farmer	Social Science Teacher
Forester	Social Scientist
Funeral Director	Social Worker
Guidance Counselor	Speech Pathologist
Highway Patrol Officer	Veterinarian
Interior Decorator	Vocational Agriculture Teacher
Investment Fund Manager	
Lawyer	
Librarian	
Life Insurance Agent	
Mathematician	
Math-Science Teacher	
Medical Technologist	

SOME ACTUAL ASSESSMENT CASES

The case of Ed. Let us now become reacquainted with two of the persons we first met in Chapter 1. Ed, the 23-year-old college graduate who has been living on a commune, has spent several sessions with a psychological counselor, who has persuaded

Women

Accountant
Advertising Executive
Army Officer
Art Teacher
Artist
Banker
Beautician
Business Education Teacher
Buyer
Chemist
College Professor
Computer Programmer
Credit Manager
Dental Assistant
Dental Hygienist
Dentist
Department Store Sales
Dietitian
Director, Christian Education
Elementary Teacher
Engineer
English Teacher
Entertainer
Executive Housekeeper
Flight Attendant
Guidance Counselor
Home Economics Teacher
Instrument Assembler
Interior Decorator
Language Interpreter
Language Teacher
Lawyer
Librarian
Life Insurance Agent
Mathematician
Math-Science Teacher
Medical Technologist

Musician
Nurse, Licensed Practical
Nurse, Registered
Occupational Therapist
Optometrist
Pharmacist
Physical Education Teacher
Physical Therapist
Physician
Physicist
Psychologist
Radiologic Technician
Recreation Leader
Reporter
Secretary
Social Science Teacher
Social Worker
Speech Pathologist
Veterinarian
YWCA Staff

him to undergo a full evaluation of his potential. Though he is very distrustful of the establishment, Ed's fears are allayed to some extent when he discovers that the psychologist-in-training who is to do the evaluation at a local university clinic is a young man who appears to share many of his values. Because the psychologist suspects that one reason for Ed's "dropping out" may have been undue pressure to settle into a middle class achievement-oriented existence, questions of vocational interests and academic achievement are left until last. He does learn, however, that Ed majored in business administration and was expected to join his father and older brother in the family business, a small but profitable concern.

It does not seem important to make a careful evaluation of Ed's intelligence; careful questioning reveals that he did very well in high school, had above-average college board scores, and managed to pass all his college subjects although many were extremely distasteful to him. His best grades were in his electives: philosophy, graphic arts, and creative writing.

In order to assess the possibility of formal psychological disorder, Ed was given the MMPI and Rorschach tests. The TAT was also given in an attempt to understand some of the motivations underlying his actions and feelings. The psychologist trainee, aided by his faculty supervisor and by his books and notes on test interpretation, determined several things. First, the probability of Ed's being psychologically disturbed, or potentially so, was small but not out of the question. Second, the tests indicated a surprising amount of anger, the nature of which Ed appeared to be unaware. Third, an artistic sensitivity and flair for creative work was suggested. Fourth, it became fairly clear that Ed's typical response to anxiety or interpersonal pressure was simply to withdraw to a safe psychological distance from the situation.

The results of the Strong-Campbell Interest Inventory, with high scores in the occupational areas of social service, art, and writing, confirmed that Ed's choice of a college major had been quite inappropriate. The one main inconsistency, how Ed had managed to make himself stay in college through the entire four years, was clarified later in counseling when he realized that he had never intended to join the family business, and had viewed college as a way to escape from it. With his graphic arts skills, creative talents, and knowledge of business, Ed was able to qualify easily for a part-time, no-obligation post with a newly developing magazine, and he continues in therapy to resolve his guilt at having let the family down and his anger at their failure to understand his needs.

The case of Donna. The parents of Donna, the nine-year-old girl who was unable to function in a regular classroom, were seen by a clinical psychologist who specialized in problems of learning and development in children. After the initial interview, a complete history of the problem was obtained from the parents by one of the social workers at the clinic, with emphasis on Donna's intellectual and social development prior to her illness, her current difficulties both at home and at school, and the parents' own feelings about this highly emotional aspect of their lives. The psychologist spent several sessions with Donna herself, during which she administered the Stanford-Binet Scale of Intelligence (Form L-M), and used the Thematic Apperception Test and a structured play situation to assess the degree to which Donna was able to relate interpersonally. Also obtained was information from the two school teachers in whose classrooms Donna had been. These sources of psychological information were supplemented by hearing and vision tests, and by neuropsychological tests in an attempt to assess the extent of disability due to physiological brain damage.

The assessment data yielded the following important points of information. Donna's intellectual functioning was discovered to be in the Dull Normal range, and not mentally retarded as her parents and teachers had thought. Although Donna's initial behavior at the clinic was quiet and passive, her main behavioral problem for the past two years had been hyperactivity and bursts of uncontrollable rage, during which she would shout at the top of her voice and throw objects around the room. It was this behavior that had led her to be excluded from school classrooms, and her parents had readily accepted the school's explanation that Donna's severe illness had permanently damaged her intellectual and emotional development. The extreme guilt that was felt by her parents had so far prevented them from making a realistic assessment of the situation, and their response of giving in to her tantrums had strengthened this behavior to the point where it dominated their lives. During the assessment procedure, however, the clinical psychologist had set firm limits for Donna's behavior and had calmly and systematically withheld the attractive rewards which were available to Donna until her tantrums ceased. With supporting evidence from the TAT, it was thus apparent that Donna was quite capable of appropriate interpersonal behavior, and the psychologist worked with the parents for several months in order to improve their skills in managing their child. The neuropsychological tests indicated some possibility of brain damage and problems in learning ability, presumably due to her earlier illness, but it was clear from the overall assessment that Donna could look forward to a much more satisfactory level of adjustment than was apparent when she first appeared at the clinic. Currently, Donna is enrolled in school in a class for exceptional children, and there is a fair probability that she will eventually be able to function as a more or less independent member of society.

SUMMARY

1. Ascientific assessment methods are those which predate the development of psychology as a science. Three well-known ascientific methods are *astrology*, *palmistry*, and *phrenology*. The use of *biorhythms* for human assessment, while new, is essentially prescientific in nature.

2. People are constantly evaluating each other informally. The process of making these everyday judgments is technically known as *making attributions*. People tend to attribute their own actions to situational requirements but those of others to stable personal predispositions. The accuracy of one's informal judgments about others can be improved by specific training, which could involve increases in empathy, in motivation, and in the ability to attend to relevant cues.

3. Technical and professional methods of assessing the adjustment of others involve information from a variety of sources, particularly psychological tests. Tests

can be grouped into three categories: (1) skills and abilities; (2) personality; and (3) vocational and occupational interests.

4. Ability, or what a person can do, can refer either to *achievements,* what a person has learned; or *aptitudes,* what a person could do with appropriate training. It is difficult to measure aptitudes separately from achievements, and children who have not had the usual learning opportunities are sometimes erroneously regarded as lacking aptitude.

5. Personality and adjustment *inventories* are widely used by psychologists and counselors as an aid in understanding personal problems. The Minnesota Multiphasic Personality Inventory (MMPI), the most widely used of these tests, was originally developed to make rapid and standardized psychiatric diagnoses. In constructing the MMPI, use was made of the empirical approach, which is nowadays used in combination with the rational approach. Interpreting MMPI profiles is a complex skill, but research-based interpretive manuals can sometimes simplify the psychologist's task.

6. The California Psychological Inventory (CPI) yields scores on 15 dimensions in the range of normal personality, such as Dominance and Socialization. Procedures for interpreting the scores are given in a manual that accompanies the test, and both the CPI and the MMPI include several "validity" scales that give the psychologist information as to whether the respondent understood the instructions and answered honestly. Screening tests are designed to provide basic information at minimal cost, and not to achieve the accuracy of more comprehensive tests.

7. *Projective tests* occupy a traditional place in the assessment of psychological adjustment, and were developed in an era when problems of the mind were seen as directly analogous to problems of the body. The most famous of the projective techniques, the Rorschach inkblot test, was developed by a Swiss psychiatrist who accidentally discovered relationships between his patients' perceptions of inkblot patterns and their particular disorders. In interpreting responses to the Rorschach test, three kinds of material are considered: formal or structural categories, the content of the patients' percepts, and other aspects of their language and behavior.

8. Another well-known projective technique is the Thematic Apperception Test (TAT), in which the respondent is shown a series of pictures depicting people in various activities, and is asked to make up a story to go with each picture. The content of the stories is analyzed for information about the respondent, who is assumed to have identified with a major figure in the story.

9. *Vocational interest tests* are designed to assess interests, attitudes, motivations, personality characteristics, and other influences as they relate to vocational satisfaction. Some vocational interest tests, such as the Strong-Campbell Interest Inventory, use objective scoring methods to determine the similarity between each respondent's interests and those of persons who have followed successful careers in a large variety of different fields. For many persons, vocational interests have been shown to be surprisingly stable from the years of career decision through middle age.

KEY TERMS

ascientific

biorhythms

attribution theory

empathy

achievement tests

aptitude tests

Minnesota Multiphasic Personality
Inventory (MMPI)

subtle items

empirical approach

face validity

California Psychological
Inventory (CPI)

lie-detector tests

Rorschach test

Thematic Apperception
Test (TAT)

Strong-Campbell Interest
Inventory

ELEVEN

Alleviating Adjustment Problems

The most common methods for alleviating adjustment problems are dynamic psychotherapy, behavior therapy, and modern "tranquilizing" drugs.

Dynamic psychotherapy attempts to increase a person's self-understanding.

- Basic tools of psychotherapy are transference and interpretation.
- Thought and language play important roles in therapeutic change.
- Two specialized kinds of psychotherapy are psychoanalysis and nondirective therapy.

The behavior therapist is an expert in applied learning theory and designs learning-based procedures for behavior change.

- Behavior therapy begins with systematic observation of the problem behaviors.
- Behavioral techniques include simple positive reinforcement, systematic desensitization, and extinction.
- "Token economies" can be developed for behavior change in institutional settings.
- The ethics of behavior therapy have been the subject of recent debate.

The community mental health movement is shifting the location of public mental health care from the state hospital to the community.

IN THIS CHAPTER WE DISCUSS WAYS OF ALLEVIATING PROBLEMS OF PSY-chological adjustment. The history of the modern treatment of psychological problems essentially began in the late nineteenth century with the work of Freud and his early colleagues; before that time, there was little or no formal knowledge in this area. Such "treatments" as did exist included hot and cold baths, the use of magnets, and attempts to drive out demons through exorcism. It is likely that effective methods of coping with some of the less serious adjustment problems were known to particular cultures at certain times, but no formalized body of knowledge was developed.

Freud's work, which was radical and highly innovative for its time, offered the first treatment that was associated with a serious intellectual attempt to formulate a theory of human behavior. Though Freud's methods were very complex and extremely time-consuming, they attracted widespread interest. One of the difficulties associated with them, in fact, is that they have often been pressed into service for problems for which they are unsuitable. Since their origin they have been updated and modified in many ways, but most contemporary psychotherapy is still based on the procedures orig-inated by Freud. This kind of therapy, with a heavy emphasis on the psychody-namics of the patient and on the relationship between patient and therapist, is the subject of the first part of this chapter. Our presentation emphasizes the special con-tribution of Dollard and Miller (1950) in reformulating Freudian theory and practice in more scientific terms. Two other traditional methods of psychotherapy, classical Freudian psychoanalysis and nondirective psychotherapy, are also discussed.

The latter part of this chapter is devoted to another group of therapeutic pro-cedures, the **behavioral therapies.** These are based on the more recent research findings of behaviorally oriented psychologists, and are in some instances radically dif-ferent from the methods originated by Freud. The field of behavior therapy has grown at a rapid rate in the recent past, both in research and in practice, and while it is much too early to assess the full impact of these procedures on the mental health industry in general, it is clear that they are here to stay.

Mention should be made of three additional procedures that have been employed to alleviate psychological problems: electroshock therapy, psychosurgery, and the use of drugs. The first two, used exclusively for problems of a very serious nature, have now been almost completely replaced by the rapid recent development of modern tranquilizing drugs. The effects of most drugs are usually temporary, and their use is generally accompanied by psychotherapy or behavior therapy to bring about more lasting changes.

Electroshock therapy originated in the late 1930s, and was based on the erroneous observation that patients who had epileptic convulsions never suffered from schizophrenia. Therefore, it was reasoned that if epileptic-like convulsions could be somehow induced in schizophrenic patients, their condition would be gradually alleviated. For a number of years, considerable effort was expended in exploring the ways in which such convulsions could best be produced—through electrical stimula-tion of the brain, through very high doses of insulin, and through the inhalation of carbon dioxide. Since the electrical method was the safest and most easily controlled of these procedures, it became a standard therapeutic technique for the treatment of patients in mental hospitals. Most of the research on the usefulness of electroshock therapy suggests that its major utility is with the problem of depression, but even here it has been largely replaced by other psychotherapeutic procedures.

Psychosurgery also began in the 1930s, and was based on the assumption that if a temporary disruption of the frontal lobes of the brain produced temporary relief from psychotic behavior, then a permanent alteration in that area of the brain should produce permanent relief. A variety of surgical techniques were developed for destroying selected portions of the frontal lobe, and these procedures are known under the general term of prefrontal lobotomy. Follow-up research on patients subjected to lobotomy has shown rather limited positive therapeutic effect, except perhaps for some decrease in assaultive behavior in certain patients.

The development of **psychoactive drugs,** broadly referred to as tranquilizers, intensified during the 1950s. The success of these drugs in treating patients, especially in mental hospitals, has been so great that their use has been regarded as a revolution in patient care. The average length of stay in psychiatric hospitals has been greatly reduced, and psychoactive drugs now form the major therapeutic program in most institutions. Unfortunately, not a great deal is known about the specific ways in which these drugs affect the operation of the brain. However, a variety of drugs have been developed, primarily by trial and error, to produce a number of different psychological effects, such as mood elevation, alleviation of anxiety, suppression of bizarre and dangerous behavior, and reduction of psychotic thought processes. Since many of these drugs also produce undesirable side effects, and can be used only over limited periods of time, they are far from a complete answer. Also, as one of our patients remarked, "I want to be tranquil, not tranquilized." Drugs are most useful as an adjunct to psychotherapy or behavior therapy, and it is to these therapies that we now turn our attention.

DYNAMIC PSYCHOTHERAPY

Patient, Therapist, and Setting

We begin our discussion of dynamic psychotherapy by defining its nature and goals, and by examining the usual characteristics of patient and therapist. Most textbooks on psychotherapy emphasize that this form of treatment for psychological problems is not suitable for everybody, and it should not be expected that the result will be an "ideal" person. Rather, for those persons for whom psychotherapy is appropriate, the goals are specified in terms of particular problems and changes. **Psychotherapy** focuses on increasing the patient's self-awareness and self-understanding, and many patients come to the psychotherapist with life dilemmas that they want to explore. In our current society, with its loss of the extended family and its superficial interpersonal relationships, little opportunity is provided for obtaining informal, nonprofessional help for personal problems. As Schofield (1964) has noted in his book *Psychotherapy: The purchase of friendship,* the professional therapist can sometimes fill this need. Clearly, the person who comes to the therapist with vaguely defined problems of self-under-standing and self-direction is unlikely to be a candidate for either drug therapy or behavior therapy. In the intimate and confidential relationship that develops in dynamic psychotherapy, however, the therapist attempts to serve as an interested listener who is also professionally skilled in helping the patient to develop self-aware-ness and self-understanding. It should be clear that the therapist does not set moral values for patients nor provide them with formulas for producing happiness.

While people have long been interested in ways of influencing the actions of others, the concept of psychotherapy (and also behavior therapy), involving a clear agree-ment between two people that their joint goal is to improve the thoughts, actions, and feelings of one of them, is a very modern one. This is the first essential characteristic of psychotherapy: a specific agreement between two people as to the nature and pur-pose of their relationship. Another essential characteristic is the possession of certain skills by the therapist, and certain motivations by the patient. Both of these are dis-cussed below. Third, there must develop between the two a positive regard for each other, so that they respect each other and are comfortable in working together. The therapist must develop and display genuine liking for the patient, and a real empathy for the patient's problems. Obviously a patient and therapist will sometimes be incompatible.

These three conditions, originally identified by the well-known psychologist Carl Rogers (1951), are the essential ingredients for psychotherapy. Proponents of differ-ent therapeutic systems suggest others, but virutally all agree on the above. Let us briefly distinguish psychotherapy from psychological **counseling,** a term that refers to a situation in which clients' problems do not involve general psychological disturbance so much as specific difficulties in adjusting to certain factors in their current environ-ment. Examples might be a college student trying to grapple with vocational decisions, a couple with a handicapped child, or a single girl trying to decide whether to terminate a pregnancy. A significant part of the process of counseling usually includes the provision of new information—scores on aptitude and interest tests, the availability of special child treatment facilities, abortion information—that would be central in making the decision in question. Also, it is assumed that the problem can be resolved within a rather short period of time, whereas psychotherapy frequently extends over one or several years.

The patient. Individuals come to psychotherapy for a variety of reasons. Some are referred by the courts or other public agencies, and there is an implied threat of punishment as an alternative. Some may come in an attempt to appease a family member or on the very strong advice of a physician or other professional person. Some have a physical ailment for which no organic basis can be found, and they are reluctantly considering the possibility that it may be psychological in nature. And some are simply curious. For all of these persons, the probability of receiving benefit from psychotherapy is rather low. The person whose chances of improvement in dynamic psychotherapy are highest is the one who is willing to put forth real effort in the hope of achieving it.

There are a variety of additional characteristics that improve patients' chances of success. First, since the treatment process relies on verbal expression of the difficulties being experienced, it is desirable for the patient to be at least average in verbal ability. A second and related point is that since the patient's ability to think clearly is an important tool in bringing about improvement, psychotherapy is much less likely to be effective if the problem involves a disorder of thinking, such as schizophrenia. Third, because psychotherapy is lengthy, cumbersome, expensive, and sometimes painful, the patient must be highly motivated. For most patients, this means that a considerable amount of anxiety or other subjective distress must be present, and it also virtually rules out the use of psychotherapy for patients who are experiencing little discomfort, as in many cases of character disorder. Fourth, the expense involved in psychotherapy would tend to limit its availability to persons in the middle or upper socioeconomic classes. It is also known that improvement in psychotherapy seems to involve a shift in the patient's system of personal values toward those of the therapist.

A summary of these factors indicates that the ideal patient for psychotherapy is intelligent, neurotic, in considerable distress, willing to invest time and money, and usually relatively young. Within this group of persons, psychotherapy is often quite effective. In our following discussion, the reader should keep these qualifications in mind.

The fact that psychotherapy has always been restricted in its application and that not everybody has benefited from it has led some psychologists to write it off as worthless. In a now famous paper, British psychologist Hans Eysenck (1952) argued that the chances of patients improving as a result of psychotherapy were about two out of three, which was about the same as their chances of showing spontaneous improvement without psychotherapy. However, if the evaluation is limited to well-trained therapists and to patients who are suitable candidates for psychotherapy, the improvement rate is much higher. Indeed, if one regards psychotherapy as an attempt by one person to influence the behavior of another person, then it is simply foolish to take the position that psychotherapy does not work. However, we do not wish to minimize the difficulties of making scientific evaluations of the success of these complex interpersonal encounters.

The therapist. Becoming a **psychotherapist** requires extensive training. Persons undertaking it are usually in the professions of psychology, medicine, social work, education, or the ministry. It requires a substantial formal knowledge of human behavior and of the various theories of personality and psychological disorder, plus an extensive period of supervised technical experience or apprenticeship in the actual practice of psychotherapy. Since a key tool in the process is the interpersonal relationship, it is also necessary for therapists to be well aware of their own psychological makeup and problems. Psychotherapists were once required to undergo extensive personal therapy of their own; nowadays, this is not considered necessary but is highly desirable if the potential therapist does not have a high degree of self-awareness, emotional stability, and flexibility. Since most people have difficulties being objective and sensitive about another persons's problem area if it is very similar to their own, the psychotherapist usually refers a potential patient elsewhere if their problem areas overlap too much.

The Therapeutic Relationship

Why has so much emphasis been put on the therapist's adjustment and interpersonal competence? It is because a basic tool of psychotherapy is the *relationship* between patient and therapist. Furthermore, it is the therapist who structures the relationship, sets its limits for the patient, and uses it to bring about the desired changes for the patient. Therapists have to contend with their own interpersonal needs—being liked and approved of, sexual feelings, aggression, the need to earn a living, and so on, and it is important for them to be able to distinguish between those aspects of the relationship that stem from their own needs and those that come from the patient's. Thus, they must be able to identify their own needs and put them aside in order to concentrate on the patient's, and must be able to relate to the patient in a natural and spontaneous manner, despite the wide variety of patient personalities.

Transference. It is usual for therapists to provide little or no information about themselves, and to deliberately remain as personally ambiguous as possible. Such behavior

facilitates the development of **transference,** which refers to the fact that patients come to feel and behave toward the therapist in the same way as they did toward significant persons in their childhood, usually authority figures such as parents. Thus, some of a patient's feelings and behaviors toward the therapist are determined by the reality of the situation, and some by the patient's own "projections." Behaviors, feelings, and thoughts that are unusually friendly and positive are referred to as positive transference, while inappropriately hostile or other negative feelings are called negative transference. Therapists must be alert to the development of counter-transference, or instances where they feel and act toward the patient as they did toward an important figure in their own past.

It can be noted that transference is a special case of generalization, in which the response the patient makes to the stimulus complex presented by the therapist is determined by previous learning experiences in interpersonal relationships. This generalization of response is heightened by the fact that so little of the therapist's personal background is revealed.

The development of transference is considered necessary for progress to be made in therapy, for it is through an examination of the transference that the therapist gets important information about the way patients feel and act toward significant people in their lives, including their maladaptive or neurotic interactions. In a sense, the therapist permits and encourages the therapeutic relationship to develop into a situation that clearly mirrors the ways in which the patient tends to react to people in general. Colby (1951) has listed five common roles in which patients might cast their therapists. First, they may perceive therapists primarily as givers of affection, and may attempt in various ways to gain affection from them. Second, they may set up the therapist as a powerful authority, whose protection can be assured by being exceedingly polite and careful not to offend. A third perception of the therapist is as an ideal model for dress, posture, and whatever else the patient can learn about the therapist. Fourth, patients may come to perceive their therapists as competitive rivals, and may attempt to compare themselves in economic status or to compete in matters of general knowledge or in those pertaining to the therapy situation. A fifth role, particularly when the patient is older than the therapist, is that of favorite child, who has the potential for growing to embody the ideal that was never achieved by the patient-parent.

Interpretation. Through transference the therapist is able to observe patients reliving situations and conflicts that they may not be able to put into words. It also affords the therapist many opportunities to point out, or *interpret,* the patients' behavior to them. The purpose of **interpretations** is to make the patients aware of aspects of themselves of which they were formerly unaware. The therapist must be cautious and skillful in presenting interpretations to avoid a negative reaction or a direct denial from a patient, since the patient's lack of awareness is often serving the function of protection against anxiety. A mistake sometimes made by inexperienced therapists is to give too many interpretations, confusing their patients and making them defensive about their problems.

THE PROCESS OF PSYCHOTHERAPY

To understand the process of psychotherapy from a more theoretical point of view, it is helpful to discuss three psychological areas and their role in the process. These areas are language and thinking, fear and anxiety, and the concept of unconscious or unaware behaviors. All have been introduced in earlier chapters; here, we focus on their importance in psychotherapy.

The Role of Language and Thinking

In our initial discussion of learning in Chapter 2 it was seen that thoughts tend to obey some of the same learning principles as observable behaviors. Thus it can be useful to regard thinking as "covert" behavior, since it cannot be observed directly.

Labeling. Giving verbal labels to one's events and experiences is an aspect of language and thinking that has particular importance for psychotherapy. If people give the same label, "dangerous," to two aspects of the environment, such as crossing the street and playing with a ferocious dog, they will be more likely to respond to both in the same way (with caution, timidity, and avoidance), even though the two are quite dissimilar in many respects. Conversely, giving different labels to two similar aspects of the environment such as "angry father" and "happy father" increases the likelihood of making different responses to them. These examples illustrate the role of language or labeling in enhancing or *mediating* the processes of generalization and discrimination in behavior. Therapists often point out that the labels the client has been using are inappropropriate. For example, the therapist could help the client make a more appropriate discrimination by saying: "You really do seem to be reacting to your boss as though he were your father, and that seems to be getting you into trouble."

Language rewards. Another important use of language in psychotherapy is its capacity to serve as reinforcement, both when given by others and when given by oneself. Thus, verbal praise and approval such as "I approve" and "that's good" serve to increase the frequency of the behavior that they follow, whether made by others or the behaving person. Clearly, one of the several functions of the therapist is to verbally reward the client's efforts to explore his or her behaviors in the therapy hour and to attempt more adjustive behavior outside the hour. Thus a therapist might say: "Mark, I'm delighted that you called that girl to ask for a date."

Vicarious problem solving. Thinking or reasoning might be seen as the substitution of symbolic or covert responses for overt behavior. By using our thinking skills in the solution of problems, we can "rehearse" possible responses symbolically rather than overtly, and anticipate some of the consequences of doing different things. Not only can we thus plan our future behavior, anticipating some of the difficulties that various responses will pose and also the rewards that such responses can perhaps yield, but we can also analyze our past behavior, recognizing what has been effective in producing rewards and what has been ineffective. The application of efficient thinking processes can do much to eliminate responses that raise more problems than they solve and also responses that may be temporarily satisfying but lead ultimately to undesirable consequences. According to Dollard and Miller (1950), the inability of the individual to "think straight" by the efficient use of higher mental processes in this way is one of the main characteristics of the maladjusted person in our culture. These failures of rational thinking can often be explained in terms of the inhibiting effects of fear or anxiety on the higher mental processes, a topic which is discussed below.

Anxiety

The importance of anxiety in learning and maintaining maladjustive behavior has been discussed earlier in this book, and here we repeat the most important points about anxiety as it relates to psychotherapy. In this context anxiety is best seen as a complex group of aversive responses (emotional arousal) which automatically accompany pain, and which become easily associated with, or conditioned to, *any* stimuli or events that happen to be present at the same time.

Generalization of anxiety. Through classical conditioning, stimuli that have been previously associated with painful events now come to elicit the same emotional reactions as the events themselves. The power to elicit anxiety can be generalized to still other cues, and this generalization can be either enhanced or inhibited by labeling, in the fashion discussed previously. For example, in a child who has been badly frightened by (or in the presence of) a particular dog, the degree of generalization of this fear depends on the verbal label attached to the stimulus. The fear could thus generalize to large, black, growling dogs, or further to all dogs, or even to all animals.

Generalized anxiety is characteristic of most maladjusted individuals, and considerable effort in psychotherapy is often devoted to developing an understanding of the manner in which the anxiety was acquired—information that is considered crucial to an adequate understanding of neurotic behavior. The "inexplicable" or "silly" fears of the neurotic, fears of success, of people, of making decisions, and so on, can usually be explained in terms of learned anxiety reactions to particular cues. What makes much neurotic and maladjusted behavior so difficult to comprehend is that we do not know what circumstances of learning were involved in the acquisition of these anxieties; moreover, maladjusted persons themselves are also usually unable to recall these events.

Learned avoidances. Any behavior that results in anxiety reduction will be learned by the individual. There are many potential anxiety-reducing responses available in any situation, and there will be considerable variability among individuals as to which response is acquired. Some individuals simply leave an anxiety-arousing situation and avoid it in the future, some deny the presence of the anxiety cues, and some engage in the other defense mechanisms discussed in Chapter 6. Those responses which serve the individual best as anxiety reducers become acquired as an important part of that person's behavior. Many anxiety-reducing behaviors have later undesirable consequences, although they do serve as immediate anxiety reducers, and it is these later behaviors that are sometimes termed symptoms, the distressing problems that are often the main reasons for seeking psychotherapy in the first place.

Unconscious Processes

As we have discussed above, the higher mental processes of language and thinking play an extremely important role in adaptive behavior, since they enable the individual to engage in foresight and planning. Behaviors for which the individual has no thoughts or language, or where the thoughts are inappropriate ones, are important in understanding and dealing with maladjustment. As discussed in Chapter 6, behaviors of which the individual is unaware are traditionally referred to as *unconscious*.

Dollard and Miller (1950) have distinguished two different types of unconscious behavior. The first refers to responses that were acquired very early in life, and prior to the development of the individual's higher mental processes. Thus, one reason why it is impossible to recall the very early aspects of one's life is that the memories were never tagged with verbal labels because language skills had not yet been developed.

Repression. The second type of unconscious process, which is far more important for understanding maladjustive behavior, involves those responses for which anxiety has inhibited the thoughts. As described more fully in Chapter 6, thought or language responses can come to elicit anxiety in exactly the same way that any previously neutral cue can come to elicit anxiety, and this process has been called *repression*. The repression of the reasons for one's actions is one of the factors that makes maladjustive behavior appear silly or stupid. Individuals may engage in behavior that is clearly maladaptive, frequently even to themselves, but cannot explain why they are behaving in that fashion. This state of affairs often leads to the development of rationalizations—socially acceptable but incomplete or inaccurate explanations of the behavior—a process that inhibits adequate self-understanding even further.

Examples of repression. The avoidance by individuals of thoughts about certain responses often causes a failure to see the connections between different aspects of their behavior. Let us examine, for example, the repression involved in the case of an underachieving high school student and his father, who had high expectations of achievement for his son. The son was not able to see that his scholastic failure served as a way of expressing his hostility toward his father. In this boy's life, practically all direct expressions of hostility as well as the thoughts underlying such expressions had been severely punished. Using his scholastic failure, the boy could recognize that his father was upset and angry, but could deny any direct responsibility in causing these feelings and could blame his academic difficulties on a variety of other circumstances. Since the son was unable to correctly label his own failure as a subtle form of hostility because such an admission would be too anxiety arousing, he continued to fail, much to his own dismay as well as that of his teachers. The father, even though he was indeed very angry, could not punish the son for his hostility, but only for his underachievement. These unconsciously determined responses were obviously maladaptive for the son because of their long-term consequences, although they had certain short-term reinforcing aspects.

In another example of the way in which repression interferes with thinking and adjustment, a vocationally undecided college junior was unable to choose among major fields for which her aptitudes and interests qualified her, although she had avail-

able considerable information about the fields and the opportunities that they presented. The psychologist to whom she turned for assistance recognized that she was unable to take responsibility for making any important decisions which affected her life, and further discovered that a similar pattern of avoiding responsibility ran through the student's history. However, the student was quite unaware of this pattern and was thus unable to plan remedial courses of action. In this case, psychotherapy proceeded by examining the student's dependency problems and the manner in which her anxiety about dependency interfered with an adequate understanding of her behavior.

In these examples we can observe that repression, the avoidance of anxiety-producing thoughts, led to the patients' failure to adequately label their own maladaptive behavior and to see certain connections among their responses or between the environment and their responses. In general, the anxiety-motivated failure to "think straight" can lead to inappropriate behavior, to the lack of any behavior, to faulty generalizations of discriminations, to an inadequate or unrealistic self-concept, and to an entire range of maladaptive and neurotic problems.

The Course of Psychotherapy

Let us now see how the process of psychotherapy operates to untangle the kinds of problems described above, to relieve patients' subjective distress, and to enable them to be more positively adaptive in their behavior. For a variety of more detailed accounts of the therapeutic process in behavioral and other terms, the reader should consult the writings of Dollard and Miller (1950), Patterson (1973), and Pietrofesa and others (1978).

First, it should be emphasized that therapists serve in a number of ways as good *models* for their patients. They are prestigeful and hold many of the values that patients also hold. Thus, the therapist's sheer attention is reinforcing, and therapists give their patients their complete and undivided attention. They are also accepting, uncritical, nonpunitive listeners, creating a situation for their patients that is usually very different from the patients' previous interactions with prestigeful authority figures.

Second, therapists instruct and encourage their patients to *free-associate;* that is, to say anything and everything that happens to come into their thoughts, no matter how fragmented, trivial, or unacceptable. The fact that this material is accepted uncritically frees patients from the burden of having to be precise and logical, and enables them to express fragmented thoughts and ideas that may be important in regard to their problems but partly repressed because of anxiety. The uncritical acceptance of this material and also of material which the patients know to be anxiety arousing, such as sexual matters or anger toward a loved one, gives them freedom and encouragement to explore further these areas which they have formerly considered taboo. In the absence of punishment, the high anxiety associated with these topics gradually diminishes.

Third, therapists help their patients to *discriminate* and *label.* Patients must learn to discriminate between the past and present, since behavior that was once punished might now bring a variety of rewards. Also, they must learn that having thoughts about certain behaviors is not the same as actually performing the behaviors themselves. In these and other ways, patients' attention is drawn to the disproportionate nature of their fears, given the realities of the present. They are helped to recognize the inappropriate verbal labels that they have used for certain thoughts and actions— "wicked," "ungrateful," "wrong," and so on—and to substitute new and more adaptive labels, such as "fun," "reasonable," and "necessary." Patients are also assisted to label groups of feelings and thoughts which in the past were too fragmented or too anxiety arousing for them to have integrated and labeled.

Fourth, once these feelings are recognized, defined, and labeled, they are available to be thought about and dealt with consciously and rationally. In other words, "repressions" have been removed, and patients are enabled to intensify their thinking in critical problem areas by bringing to bear the full weight of their intellectual skills—reasoning, judgment, adaptive planning, and further fear-reducing discriminations and labels.

Fifth, with reduced anxiety and an improved understanding in critical problem areas, patients' motivations for change are strong enough that they now try out new and more adaptive behaviors in real-life situations. The reinforcement provided by the environment for these new behaviors motivates them to continue and to enter more challenging situations, so that their therapeutic changes become generalized into real life. Throughout the entire process, therapists play an important role in "dosing" their patients' anxiety; that is, in seeing to it that the stimuli with which patients are currently dealing, whether thoughts or behaviors, are not too anxiety-arousing for them to handle. In other words, therapists see to it that their patients engage in a graded series of learning situations in which each new step represents just a small increase in anxiety over the last.

Formal Psychoanalysis

Traditional or dynamic psychotherapy, as we have described it, is a later development from the early work of Sigmund Freud. Freud's original procedure, psychoanalysis, is still practiced to some extent today, although the development of effective but briefer methods of treatment has caused it to become somewhat outmoded.

In **formal psychoanalysis** the patient is seen four or five times a week, for as long as five years. (This may be compared to psychotherapy, as described above, in which the patient may be seen once or twice a week for one to three years.) To ensure that the patient receives little information about the therapist, so that the development of transference will be as full and as rapid as possible, the patient lies on a couch with the therapist sitting behind. Relying heavily on the patient's free-associations and also on dreams, the psychoanalyst tries to reconstruct with the patient the emotional aspects of the early childhood years. The Freudian theory of personality development is used as a framework for pinpointing childhood stresses and difficulties that could be the origins of the patient's current problems. A major goal of psychoanalysis is to have the

patient understand the nature of these origins, and not much attention is paid, except at the very end of treatment, to the patient's current adjustment problems. Rather, the view is taken that the current problems, or symptoms, will disappear once the "original causes" are treated.

The viewpoint that "insight," or a full awareness of the nature and causes of one's difficulties, is sufficient by itself to bring about improvement does not seem to be supported by research and clinical findings. Rather, it appears that anxiety reduction is most likely to occur after the patient has discussed and explored anxiety-producing material with anxiety actually occurring in the therapeutic situation. In has often been noted (Hobbs, 1962) that unless "insight" is accompanied by the expression of emotionality, it is not likely to lead to changes in the patient's adjustive behavior.

Nondirective Psychotherapy

More than 30 years ago, psychologist Carl Rogers (1942, 1951) developed a variation of psychotherapy which he called client-centered or **nondirective therapy.** Rogers put special emphasis on six factors that are present to some extent in most kinds of verbal psychotherapy, but which Rogers considered to be sufficient (and necessary) for bringing about constructive personality change. The first is simply psychological contact between patient and therapist; second, patients must be in a state of "incongruence," referring to a discrepancy between the way they perceive themselves and the way they would ideally like to be. The next three conditions refer to therapists: they must "be themselves" in the relationship and must be continually aware of their true feelings; they must genuinely and unconditionally like their patients, and they must communicate that liking. Finally, patients must actually perceive these qualities in their therapists.

In nondirective therapy the task is to provide patients with the kind of interpersonal environment in which their natural tendencies toward positive change and personality growth can flourish most effectively. Therapists consistently direct their patients' attention to the feelings accompanying the difficulties, rather than to the content of the problems. In other words, nondirective therapists selectively attend to their patients' statements about their feelings, and try to make the patients aware of them also. As a somewhat oversimplified example, a particular therapist, in response to a patient's statement that he didn't feel very good about his visit the previous evening with his mother-in-law, might perhaps respond with "You didn't feel very good?" rather than emphasizing the content of the statement ("Your mother-in-law?").

According to Rogers' formulation, as patients find themselves talking more and more about their feelings to a kind, warm, empathic therapist who really seems to consider them worthwhile persons, the therapist is able to clarify the difficulties, to formulate self-concepts that are more positive, and to set goals that are more realistic in terms of each patient's personality and abilities. No special academic qualifications are considered necessary to be a successful nondirective therapist, so that it is possible for persons such as ministers, social workers, and school counselors to learn the skills, provided they possess the appropriate personality characteristics. Because nondirective therapy does rely rather heavily on patients' ability to formulate their own difficulties, it tends to be most successful with persons who would be good risks for any kind of verbal therapy—that is, patients who are young, intelligent, neurotic, highly motivated, and whose problems are not too serious.

THE BEHAVIORAL THERAPIES

Traditional psychotherapy, or relationship or dynamic therapy, as it is also called, has many limitations as a tool in treating psychological maladjustment. Its effectiveness is confined for the most part to the neurotic or anxiety-based disorders, it is extremely time-consuming, it generally requires rather elaborate training on the part of the therapist, and it requires at least average verbal intelligence on the part of the patient. Thus, psychologists, psychiatrists, and other mental health workers have been trying for many years to develop methods of treatment which are more efficient and more widely applicable. In all these efforts, there have been two significant developments, both receiving their initial impetus in the 1950s. The first, as discussed above, is the development of a wide variety of psychiatric drugs, which can bring about dramatic changes in feelings and behaviors while the patient is taking the drug. The second is the development of the *behavioral therapies,* or behavior modification, based on the principles and research knowledge of behavioral psychology.

In order to understand and apply the basic elements of the direct behavioral approach, it is necessary to understand that many patients seek therapeutic help for rather specific problems, such as phobias, specific unadaptive habits, and distressing sexual behaviors. Such specific behaviors can be formulated in concrete and specific terms using a behavior therapy approach. This simplicity and rigor has led some traditional mental health workers to conclude that the procedures are simply too artificial, mechanistic, and cold to have any real and lasting effects on human problems. However, there can be no question that the behavioral therapies have been successful in alleviating a rather wide variety of problems to date, and without any significant negative effects.

Patient, Therapist, and Setting

The fully trained behavior therapist possesses three major characteristics: (1) a sound fundamental knowledge of behavioral learning theory and a mastery of specific ways of applying it; (2) good general clinical skills; and (3) specific ways of thinking and acting. Let us discuss these characteristics in turn.

In order to approach a problem within a behavioral framework and conceptualize it for behavior therapy, it is necessary to make a behavioral assessment, also termed a functional analysis of behavior. In other words, the problem must be restated and viewed using the language and framework of behavioral learning theory, and of all the activities involved in behavior therapy, it is this one that requires the greatest amount of knowledge and skill. Once the problem has been formulated for treatment, however, it is often possible to utilize in the treatment program the services of mental health personnel whose knowledge and training are much more limited.

Behavior therapists require the same basic training in clinical and professional skills that psychodynamic therapists have. This point is often overlooked in the emphasis on technical knowledge; however, it is still necessary for the behavior therapist to relate to the patient and to communicate sensitively about disturbing personal problems. Also, patients in behavior therapy become angry, anxious, or manipulative, just as in relationship psychotherapy. Behavior therapists must have the skills to deal with these relationship issues, and learn to perform more as instructors.

There is another important reason why it is essential for behavior therapists to be thoroughly trained in basic clinical skills. They make it their responsibility to determine the nature of the problem (in behavioral terms), to select the treatment procedures, to actively tutor patients in the systems of behavior change that have been designed for them, and all this in a relatively short span of time. Thus, they take the welfare of the patients actively into their own hands, and could possibly cause their patients some harm if they did not have an adequate understanding of their patients as whole persons. There are, of course, a number of behavior therapy procedures that can be conducted by individuals who do not have such a complete training. For example, it is possible for almost anyone to conduct a simple program for cutting down smoking or increasing study time, and research has shown that a considerable amount of useful behavior modification can often be done by persons with limited training under adequate supervision.

Behavior therapists should be able to think and act in certain ways. For example, they should feel comfortable in the role of exerting direct influence over patients, a stance that is very different from that of nondirective therapists, who believe that in order for proper growth to take place, patients must make all their own decisions in their own time. In addition, behavior therapists must enjoy structuring and planning the activities of other people; or at least, they must learn to do it. Essentially, behavior therapists accept the patients' problems more or less as stated, try to fit them into the language of behavioral psychology, plan new learning experiences for the patients, and then have the patients engage in these new experiences. Thus, any therapist who is not able to take an active, structured, planning role would probably not be successful in this area.

Behavior therapists regard themselves as directly responsible for bringing about the patients' behavior change. If a patient does not improve, it is the therapist's fault, and not the patient's. On the basis of the initial assessment, the therapist decides what new learning experiences and situations will be necessary for the patient, and also assesses whether or not it is possible for the therapist to arrange them. If the therapist is able to perceive sufficient cooperation from the patient—that is, if the patient permits the therapist sufficient access to the patient's environment (both internal and external)—then it is the therapist's responsibility to produce the desired behavior change. Behavior therapists may decline to work with patients who do not permit sufficient entry into their lives and environments.

The behavior therapist is less directly concerned than the dynamic therapist with the therapeutic relationship. Naturally a positive relationship will usually develop, but the therapist does not analyze it or discuss it with the patient unless aspects of it are interfering with treatment. Behavior therapists are appropriately viewed as instructors, who teach their patients how to eliminate old behaviors and engage in new ones. They set homework assignments for the patients, and make it clear that the amount of progress the patients make will depend directly on how carefully they do their homework, just as in any instructor-student situation. Thus, behavior therapists use the relationship to monitor and reinforce the patients' behavior.

Approaching Problems Behaviorally

As we have said above, not all adjustment problems can be helped by behavioral methods. It must first be possible to view a given problem as a problem in behavior.

Most simply, it is necessary to regard the patient as possessing either (a) behaviors whose frequency is excessive and should be reduced (smoking, tantrums, high anxiety, tics); or (b) behaviors whose frequency is insufficient and should be increased. There are two kinds of behaviors whose frequency is insufficient: those that the patient knows how to perform but does not currently perform, and those that the patient does not know how to perform, and which must first be taught before their frequency can be increased. Examples of the first kind of insufficient behaviors would include sleeping for patients with insomnia, cooperation from a stubborn child, and any kind of behavior at all in depressed patients. Behaviors for which some initial instruction might be necessary include social skills in a shy adolescent, study behavior in an underachiever, and the appropriate expression of anger toward feared authority figures.

There are two further points to mention about defining problems behaviorally. First, some of the behaviors mentioned are voluntary or under conscious control (smoking, social interaction), while some are involuntary or under autonomic control (sleeping). There are also many problem behaviors that are intermediate between these two extremes (tics, vomiting), and the degree to which they are voluntary may vary from patient to patient. It is important to understand that the same behavioral learning principles can be applied to all these behaviors, although the practical manner in which the principles are approached will vary. Second, as we have indicated a number of times throughout this text, our definition of behavior does include "covert" or internal processes such as thoughts and feelings. It is usually necessary to rely on the patients' self-reports to observe internal behaviors, although the recent development of sophisticated electronic psychophysiological recording devices now enables some covert behaviors to be observed directly.

Assessment and Planning

Let us see how a psychological adjustment problem might be assessed within a behavioral framework, and how a treatment program might be designed. As we have said above, it is assumed that the problem is one that can be approached as either a deficit or an excess of specific behaviors.

Observation and recording. The first step in behavioral assessment is the gathering of careful information about the problem behavior. First, it is necessary to define the behavior in such a way that it can be reliably observed. A patient of one of the authors had sought help in overcoming her habit of fingernail biting, but was at first unable to keep careful records of the extent of this behavior because she did not know exactly what should be called biting and what should not. Sometimes she would sit and stare at a nail, wondering if she should bite it. Or she would put a finger up to her mouth, but not inside. Sometimes she closed her teeth over a nail but did not actually tear any off. It was arbitrarily decided to define "biting" to include the last of these, and she was instructed to count an instance of the problem behavior every time she closed her teeth on a nail, which gave her an objective measure.

FIRST WE WANT TO WORK ON YOUR BEHAVIOR WHEN YOU ARE AFRAID.

People are often unaware of important aspects of their problem behaviors. As we have discussed in Chapter 6, it is common to remain unaware of, or to repress awareness of, events that would arouse anxiety if acknowledged. Thus, another patient would physically abuse his wife, but was not able to recognize the events that would consistently lead up to these attacks. In this case, a detailed description of a number of these events provided by the wife (who, incidentally, also failed to recognize some of *her* problem behaviors at these times) helped the patient to become a more reliable observer of his own behavior.

Many behavior therapists stress the importance of keeping actual physical records of the frequency of problem behavior. These records can be kept in a number of ways. Some problems, such as smoking and obesity, permit natural built-in record keeping, by counting the number of cigarettes consumed (or the number remaining in the package), and by weighing oneself. Other behaviors, such as an inability to put in sufficient time studying, or frequent periods of depression and crying, can be recorded as the actual amount of time spent in the activity, a record that can be kept on an index card and brought up to date several times during each day. Sometimes it is necessary, especially for a person with severe adjustment problems, to rely on another observer to keep the records. In a hospital setting this function is often performed by nurses and attendants; also, as we have stated above, increasing use is now being found for sensitive electronic instruments that can monitor certain bodily responses that might be closely associated with a problem behavior. It is frequently found that the very act of making close self-observations often results in an immediate reduction in the frequency of the undesired behavior, perhaps because the increased self-attention makes the individual more aware of the aversive consequences of the behavior.

The context of problem behavior. It should be clear from previous chapters that behavior therapists consider problem behavior to be maintained by specific events, either in the patients' external environments or in their internal environments. These events must always include a *consequence* (reinforcement or punishment), although it may be extremely difficult to locate, and they may also include stimuli that consistently trigger the problem behavior. When we ask *why* a person engages in unadaptive behavior, the answer comes in terms of specifying the triggering (or discriminative) stimuli and the consequences. Traditional psychological assessment procedures, as described in Chapter 10, can sometimes be helpful in suggesting directions to explore in getting this information.

It can be seen that there is much more observing and recording to be done than simply counting the frequency or duration of the problem behavior. Discovering the "why" of the behavior requires careful observation of the environmental setting, including the patient's thoughts and feelings, and of the results of the behavior. Sometimes these factors can be extremely difficult to discover; fortunately, however, behavior therapists do not always have to know them to bring about change. They do not have to know enough of them to be able to design new learning environments that encourage adaptive behavior and contain as few as possible of the factors maintaining the unadaptive behavior.

A good example of behavioral analysis and treatment planning is seen in the case of a college student who found herself gagging uncontrollably several times a week, leading her to dread certain situations for fear of embarrassment, and to drastically restrict her social activities. Careful observation failed to isolate any specific environmental stimuli, but did point to one associated behavior and one consistent *consequence* — she would experience high anxiety in the gagging situation and she would immediately leave it. Treatment proceeded by preparing a list of actual situations in which she had gagged in the past or felt likely to gag in the future, and using systematic desensitization (see below) to reduce her anxiety in these situations. Soon she found herself gagging less, and eventually came to recognize the gagging as an excuse for escaping from certain interpersonal situations that involved anxiety and embarrassment for reasons other than gagging.

The behavior therapist's ability to deal effectively with a psychological problem depends on a number of things in addition to an adequate behavioral formulation. The most important of these factors is that it must be possible, from a practical point of view, to rearrange the patient's environment in whatever ways are seen as necessary. With cooperative patients and favorable circumstances, this might be accomplished simply by telling them what changes they should arrange. At the other end of the continuum is the closed hospital ward, where the patients' external environment is structured and controlled for them. Obviously, it is desirable from both an ethical and an economic viewpoint for patients to retain as much control over their own behavior as possible.

Procedures for Behavior Change

There are a variety of ways in which basic psychological principles can be employed to bring about behavior change. Let us examine several of the major ones, bearing in mind that it is common to use a combination of procedures, and also that theorists sometimes disagree as to the precise way in which a given procedure has its effect.

Simple positive reinforcement. The basic principles of reinforcement learning have been discussed in Chapter 2. To increase a behavior by using reinforcement, something that is desired by the individual is arranged to occur every time the individual performs the behavior. For example, the small boy who receives a cookie when he comes home from school *if* he hangs up his coat will come to perform this behavior with increased frequency, and will also be in a position to be taught more easily other "neat" behaviors. There are a number of conditions that are known to make the use of positive reinforcement more effective. For example, the boy's mother should make it clear in words that a cookie will follow coat-hanging, she should use the smallest possible cookie that will be effective, and she should deliver it immediately after the desired behavior.

As another example, let us consider a college student who had a study problem. In this case, the desired terminal behavior of three hours' study every evening was not initially within his capability. A shaping procedure of successive approximations was therefore used, in which reinforcement was initially available for a first step in the direction of the goal. Thus, his goal in the first week was 15 minutes of study every evening. The student also arranged to call his girlfriend every evening after performing his study assignment, which provided an immediate reward. She was to inquire if he had done the assignment and to hang up on him if he had not. Obviously, a prior agreement about honesty was necessary. As an additional reinforcer, she agreed to cook dinner for him once a week, but only if he had done the study assignment six out of seven evenings. After every such reward, the necessary period of study was to increase by 15 minutes, until the goal of three hours was reached.

Desensitization of anxiety. Mental health professionals have long been interested in finding methods for relieving the subjectively distressing experience of anxiety. A brief review of Chapter 4 will remind the reader that the concept of anxiety is a complicated one, and that we should be cautious about approaching it in any simplified manner. On the other hand, it is also clear that the learning and maintenance of a vast amount of neurotic behavior, thoughts, and feelings is based on the avoidance of this aversive experience. No matter whether one takes a strict Freudian view or a strict behavioral one, anxiety is a key problem in psychological disorders, both as a distressing difficulty by itself and in the creation and maintenance of other difficulties.

Behavioral procedures for alleviating anxiety were explored as early as the 1920s (Jones, 1924), but it was not until the 1950s that serious efforts were made to develop practical techniques that would be applicable on a large scale. The major credit for this work must go to the psychologist and psychiatrist Joseph Wolpe (1958), who, while working in South Africa, experimented with a variety of possible conditioning procedures. Basing his studies initially on work with laboratory cats, Wolpe found that a phobia, or fear specific to a particular stimulus, could be alleviated if the fearful organism (animal or human) was exposed very gradually, in small steps, to progressively stronger fear stimuli, while at the same time engaging in some alternate behavior that would produce an internal state that was incompatible with anxiety. Wolpe called this procedure **systematic desensitization,** and it is widely used to day for the treatment of specific anxieties.

The case of Frances. While there are several variants of systematic desensitization, and some controversy among applied behavior theorists as to exactly how it works, it is clear that this procedure is often effective. Usually the alternate response that is employed is deep muscle relaxation, and the fear stimuli are presented to the patient in the form of vivid fantasies or mental images. We illustrate it by describing the treatment of Frances, the housewife introduced in Chapter 1, who had been terrified of thunderstorms for some 25 years. During the summer months, when thunderstorms were more frequent, she would begin the day by listening to the early weather forecast on at least two television channels. Next she would call the local weather service, and then she would begin her day-long series of inspections of the sky. On days when there was no possibility of rain, she would be happy and relieved, while the slightest possibility of a thundershower could cause her to revise her plans for the entire day to avoid being alone or caught in the rain. An extended assessment did not turn up any "secondary gain" that might be maintaining the patient's behavior through positive reinforcement.

Several half-hour periods were devoted to teaching Frances how to achieve quickly a complete state of physical relaxation, using instructions adapted from the original work of Jacobson (1938), and including daily homework practice. Next, several half-hour periods were spent teaching her how to engage in vivid fantasies. The third preliminary step was the construction of a **fear hierarchy,** a carefully graded list of situations involving progressively greater and greater anxiety. Three different hierarchies were developed for this patient, each devoted to a slightly different aspect of the fear, and some of the items from each are listed in Table 11-1.

The actual desensitization procedure was begun by teaching the patient to become completely relaxed in a reclining chair, and then having her imagine vividly the lowest item on the first fear hierarchy. If she experienced the slightest anxiety, she was instructed to raise a finger, whereupon the therapist would tell her to dismiss the fantasy and devote her attention to improving her state of relaxation. After two successive presentations of the item for fifteen or twenty seconds during which no anxiety was experienced, the next item in the hierarchy was presented. The entire procedure took twelve one-hour sessions, and at the last session the patient was able to experience the vivid fantasy of driving through a violent thunderstorm without the slightest feeling of discomfort. At session six she reported feeling less concerned after hearing a weather forecast that predicted rain, and at that time she was instructed to start keeping a written record of her feelings after each daily forecast, and to say to herself during the forecast "it doesn't really matter whether it rains or not." By the last session she was deliberately going outside during threatening weather, had entirely ceased

Table 11-1

Selected Items from Three Fear Hierarchies
Used in the Desensitization of Anxiety about Thunderstorms

Subject	Selected items
Morning television weather forecasts	1. Hearing that the weather will be perfect, with no chance of rain. 5. Hearing that there will be cloudy skies, with some possibility of rain. 10. Hearing that there will be a major thunderstorm during the afternoon.
Looking out of the window at home	1. Seeing a perfect, blue sky. 4. Seeing half blue sky, half white clouds. 7. Seeing a gray, overcast sky. 9. Seeing a very dark patch of clouds that seem to be getting darker.
Miscellaneous, away from home	3. Seeing a slight drizzle while driving home from the supermarket. 7. Feeling a slight drizzle when getting out of the car to go into the supermarket. 10. Seeing heavy rain out of the office window while at work. 15. Driving on a strange highway during a thunderstorm.

listening to weather forecasts, and was looking forward to the next major thunder-storm so that she could adequately test her newly acquired freedom from fear.

Decreasing undesired behavior. The elimination of problem behaviors, such as tantrums in children, drug use, excessive drinking, marital discord, and insomnia are all of concern to the psychologist. It is well known to learning theorists that punishing undesired behavior is usually not a good way to get rid of it. The punished individual will first look for some way to escape the punishment, and will often start performing a behavior that is even less desirable. Therefore it is extremely important that the individual should be first taught, or made aware of, an adaptive behavior that will lead to positive reinforcement. Once the adaptive behavior is being performed at the desired frequency, punishment might then be used, either in the form of aversive imagery, mild electric shock, or some other aversive event agreed to by the patient, to make the undesired behavior less attractive. A good example can be seen in the treatment of homosexual patients who seek help in achieving a heterosexual adjustment. These problems can be regarded as double approach–avoidance conflicts, in which there are simultaneously strong anxiety and strong positive feelings over both heterosexual behaviors and homosexual behaviors. The first step in treatment usually involves procedures to strengthen approach behavior toward normal sexual activity and to reduce the anxiety associated with it. Once this is accomplished the patient's interest in homosexual affairs will sometimes diminish, due to the social aversion that is connected with them, and aided by the new availability of heterosexual satisfactions. If homosexual impulses continue and are not desired, an aversive procedure might then be employed. Other instances in which aversive procedures might be used include circumstances where it is a matter of saving the patient's life, such as in continual vomiting (Lang, Melamed, and Hart, 1970), or where a patient with a distressing disorder volunteers in the expectation of fairly rapid improvement (Lovibond and Caddy, 1970). In general, problems that involve an excess of a behavior can often be reformulated in a way that involves a behavioral deficit, treatable by positive reinforcement. For example, a disruptive child in a school classroom can readily be seen to be engaging in a variety of behavioral excesses, but a moment's thought will also indicate the possibility of defining the problem as a deficit in sitting-at-the-desk behavior. This desired behavior, which is incompatible with the undesired behavior, can then be clearly specified to the child and reinforced whenever it occurs.

Wider Applications

There are many additional ways to apply the principles of behavioral psychology in treating problems of personal adjustment. Three of them are discussed briefly: problems involving parents and children, marital conflict, and what have been called "token economies."

Parents and children. Because the major part of a child's interpersonal environment consists of his or her parents, the psychological problems of children can frequently be viewed in the context of interaction with their parents. It is often true, for example, that the quickest way for a child to get a parent's attention is to hit another child or to be disruptive in some other way. Parents, for their part, often provide their children with models for unadaptive behavior by engaging in aggressive behavior themselves when frustrated. Another example can be seen in the case of children who have an apparent phobia about going to school. On closer examination it often becomes evident that the mother is maintaining the child's behavior of staying at home by making statements about her own ill-health, and that she is excessively dependent on the child for company and emotional support. In such cases, the child's staying-home behavior is being negatively reinforced by the anxiety reduction available through being constantly in the presence of the mother and thus receiving reassurance that no harm was befalling her.

In working with children it is often fairly easy to identify the causes of the problem behavior, since they are likely to be present in the child's current environment. In many instances, the child behavior therapist will choose to work entirely with the parents, despite the fact that the parents may have identified the problem as the child's. For some problems, it is possible to train the parents to act as direct therapists in modifying the child's behavior. An example reported by one of the authors (Goldstein and Lanyon, 1971) involved a ten-year-old boy with a serious psychological disturbance known as autism. Among his many problems, the boy was grossly retarded in his development of speech skills, and was able to utter only a few words, which could be understood only by his parents. Using small portions of the child's evening meal as reinforcers over the course of 125 days, the parents were able to increase his language skills to the point where he could carry on limited conversations with others. Their most important achievement was to enable the boy to speak well enough for other persons to begin responding to him, so that the further development of his speech would be reinforced by his success in interacting with the environment.

Marital problems. It is at times possible to approach marital difficulties in a behavioral manner. In this view, the husband and wife can be seen as reinforcing each other's unadaptive behavior while failing to provide sufficient reinforcement for adaptive behavior. The decision as to whether a couple *should* try to work out their difficulties is not a behavioral question; once the decision has been made, however, both partners are asked to specify what behaviors they would most like to see increased or decreased by their partners. A bargain is then made, in which each agrees to reinforce some specific change in the other by making a change of his or her own. In one case known to the authors, the husband's most distressing habit was to make fun of his wife's fears (of elevators, crowds, and so on) in front of the children. The wife in turn made fun of her husband's neurotic attachment to his mother, laughing when he compulsively called her every night after supper to receive his daily scolding. After some careful assessment and prolonged bargaining the details of mutual changes were agreed on, and the couple were able to eliminate both of these behaviors. They eventually succeeded in reducing their bickering to the point where one of the children prepared an elaborate document for them saying how pleasant it was to be a member of their family. It should be pointed out that certain other problems, for example, the husband's frequent overspending and the couple's disagreement on how to manage their oldest boy, were not changed by this particular program, but required further programs of their own.

The "token economy." About fifteen years ago, several psychologists made an attempt to improve the lives of severely regressed psychiatric hospital patients by structuring their environment in such a manner that practically everything but the air they breathed was to be "earned" as reinforcement for performing minimal but socially desired behaviors (Ayllon and Azrin, 1968). Following the initial success of this program, a great many psychiatric hospital wards have been set up to run on similar lines, and a number of institutions for the mentally retarded have also adopted these procedures. Basically, artificial or token money is used to reinforce the patients for all desirable behaviors, such as getting out of bed before a specified hour, washing, dressing and becoming tidy, eating meals appropriately, socializing, performing assigned chores satisfactorily, and volunteering for tasks requiring personal responsibility. The token currency can be used by the patients to purchase meals (beyond the minimum ones provided), sleeping quarters (beyond the bare essentials), and a whole variety of options such as freedom to move within the hospital, passes to leave the grounds, preferred clothing, work assignments, and recreational activities. Some of the **token economy** systems that are now in operation have become quite complex, and their goal is to approximate as closely as possible the reward systems that operate in the "real world," to retrain the patients for life outside the hospital. Further information on token economies can be found in recent reviews by Kazdin (1977) and Krasner (1976).

Ethical Questions

People often ask whether it is morally right to manipulate the lives of others, as behavior therapists appear to be doing. When a patient voluntarily comes to a therapist and asks for help in changing behavior, and where nobody will be harmed by the change, there would appear to be no ethical problem. When behavior modification procedures are administered, however, in involuntary settings such as to inmates in mental hospitals and prisoners in correctional institutions, a moral dilemma is posed. Some psychologists feel that in these settings, each inmate should be given the opportunity to participate voluntarily in a behavioral program. In this sense, behavior therapy becomes simply one of the optional treatments, similar to group therapy or occupational therapy. An extreme viewpoint is that behavior therapy should be applied whenever it is appropriate, regardless of the inmate's willingness to participate. Persons holding this view offer several arguments in support: that inmates are not capable of making the choice themselves, that the treatment will be to their benefit in the long run, and that the behavior in question often poses a danger to society. Consider the case of a man who is arrested and convicted of child molesting, and who is confined to a hospital for the criminally insane. Should behavior therapy be used to try to eliminate this behavior that is so distressing to society? Or does the person have the right to refuse the treatment? The danger is, of course, that the principle of involuntary treatment, once accepted, could easily be generalized inappropriately to the case of an individual who engages in a homosexual act with a consenting adult, or a person engaged in unpopular political dissent. The recent criticisms of Soviet psychiatrists for participating in "thought control" have been based on precisely this issue.

This discussion raises the broader question of behavior control through behavior modification on a society-wide basis. Now that the extent of the possibilities of behavior control based on behavioral technology is beginning to be appreciated, many groups in our society are expressing some degree of alarm at the potential loss of freedom that might be involved. Some of these issues have been discussed and debated at length (Kazdin, 1977; Krasner, 1976), and the basic question appears to be one of ensuring adequate controls and ethical responsibility on the part of the controllers.

At present, the fact that the channels through which control could be exercised — radio, television, and the press—are not in the hands of a single agency prevents a single point of view from becoming absolute. Behavior control would be more likely to become a reality if this diversity of influences did not exist, as in some countries which have a monolithic pattern of government control. Some of the techniques used by these governments to achieve their ends can in fact be regarded as consistent with behavioral psychology. On the other hand, socially accepted forms of persuasion, such as advertising, organized religion, and political campaigning, also make use of these principles.

Some persons speculate that behavioral change procedures could in the future become the subject of formal social controls, limiting their use to qualified and ethically responsible persons who would be held legally accountable for their actions. An opposite view is that behavioral change procedures are largely ineffective, and that the current attention now being paid to behavior therapy will soon diminish and all but disappear. It can at least be said that there will continue to be controversy and argument, and that both are necessary and healthy in the ultimate development of formal ethical principles to guide the use of behavioral procedures for therapeutic purposes.

THE COMMUNITY MENTAL HEALTH MOVEMENT

No discussion of the treatment of psychological adjustment problems would be complete without an account of the widespread changes that have come about since the early 1960s in the nature of publicly financed mental health services. Prior to that time

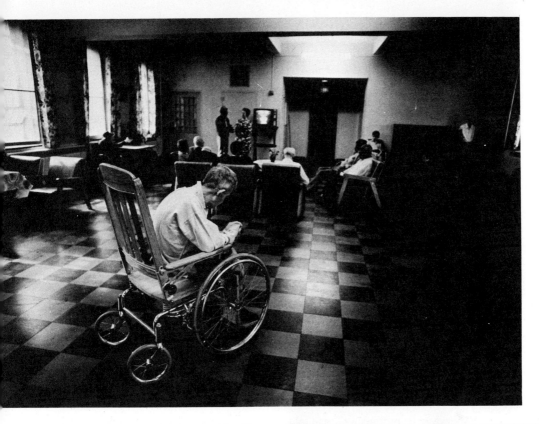

Many of the old, isolated mental health
institutions are giving way to new programs
which emphasize teaching patients the
basic self-help skills they need in order to
lead more independent lives.

the major, and for many people the only, provider of mental health services was the state mental hospital, typically an old and uninviting institution located in a rural area at a "safe" distance from the city, and often surrounded by a farm. In the 1950s a number of influences, both social and scientific, led to the federal government's appointment of a Joint Commission on Mental Illness and Health, and the publication in 1961 of a set of recommendations, *Action for Mental Health*. Based on these recommendations, the Congress in 1963 enacted the Community Mental Health Act, calling for the development of a national network of community mental health centers. This law provided the basis for a new view of mental health, as a challenge to be dealt with by local communities, with extensive involvement by relevant social systems such as schools, churches, the police, community service organizations, and individual families. The plan calls for the limited use of certain state hospital facilities for chronic or severely disturbed persons, while short-term hospital care is provided in the patient's own community. For a detailed account of the development of the community mental health movement, the reader is referred to the introductory text by Bloom (1975).

These major changes have many advantages. They promise a much more effective approach to treatment than the state hospital system was able to provide, they set the stage for removing the stigma from mental illness, and they utilize the services of those persons in the community who are able and eager to help. Scientific bases for the changes include the fact that antipsychotic drugs can now control many of the more obvious and distressing aspects of major mental disorder, that the mental hospital environment has tended to make some patients needlessly worse, and that mental illness is becoming increasingly understood as a social or behavioral problem, to be treated in a social context rather than in isolation.

The changeover from the state hospital system to community mental health service facilities brings new emphases: on early recognition of adjustment problems, and prevention rather than treatment; on the development of new kinds of treatment facilities, such as day hospitals, halfway houses, sheltered workshops, and crisis centers; on an increased use of volunteers and paraprofessional workers with specialized and limited training; on a view of patients' difficulties as "problems in living" rather than as illness; and on patients' positive strengths and resources rather than their weaknesses. The movement has not been without its difficulties. Some state hospitals have discharged patients "to the community" before community resources have been adequate to receive them. Some traditional mental health bureaucracies and bureaucrats have found it difficult to adapt to the changes, and have resisted wherever possible, either consciously or unconsciously. And some communities have found the whole idea threatening and difficult to understand. Nevertheless, there is no question that the benefits of the community mental health movement are immense, and that improvements will continue to be made in the system as new scientific and social understandings are developed.

SUMMARY

1. This chapter discusses methods for alleviating adjustment problems. Freud's were the first to be based on serious scholarship; nowadays, the three major methods are: dynamic psychotherapy (an outgrowth of Freudian procedures), behavior therapy, and the use of modern tranquilizing drugs (which produce a marked though temporary effect). Much less common are electroshock therapy, still used at times for depressive disorders, and psychosurgery, or lobotomy.

2. The best known treatment for psychological disorders is dynamic or relationship psychotherapy, which attempts to increase an individual's self-understanding. Chances of improvement are greatest for those patients who are willing to work hard, are at least average in verbal ability, are able to think clearly, are young, and whose problems are neurotic in nature. The therapist must have substantial formal training and supervised experience, and must be self-aware and reasonably free from personal problems.

3. A basic tool of psychotherapy is the relationship between patient and therapist. The therapist deliberately remains as ambiguous as possible to facilitate the development of *transference,* referring to the fact that patients come to feel and act toward the therapist as they did toward significant figures in their childhood. Transference can be regarded as a special case of generalization, and it is by examining the transference that the therapist gets important information about the patient's ways of reacting to people in general. Patients may perceive their therapist in any one of a number of ways: as a giver of affection, a powerful authority figure, an ideal model, a rival, or perhaps as a favorite child. The therapist attempts to increase the patient's insight by making cautious *interpretations,* pointing out connections between different aspects of thoughts, feelings, and behaviors.

4. The process of psychotherapy relies heavily on the use of *thought and language*. Thinking and reasoning are basic components of problem-solving activity. The verbal *labeling* of the patients' events and experiences helps to clarify similarities and differences among them. Language can also be used as reinforcement (through praise), and also to convey information. *Anxiety* plays a prominent role in maintaining much problem behavior, through the reinforcement generated by anxiety-avoidance, and its generalization to new stimuli often creates the impression that the patients' fears are silly. Processes for which an individual has no thoughts or language are referred to as *unconscious;* these include responses which the individual acquired prior to language development, and those which are *repressed* due to their association with anxiety.

5. The course of psychotherapy may be summarized as follows: therapists serve as good models for their patients, and are nonpunitive listeners. They encourage their patients to free-associate, and they accept all material without making value judg-

ments. They help patients to discriminate and label different thoughts, feelings, and behaviors, in order that they can be dealt with consciously, and they encourage the application of this new learning to real-life situations. In *formal psychoanalysis,* of which psychotherapy is an outgrowth, the patient is seen intensively for a long period of time, and the analyst attempts to reconstruct all the major emotional aspects of the patient's childhood years. In nondirective or *client-centered therapy,* therapists simply attempt to provide a warm, empathic, and understanding interpersonal environment in which patients can "be themselves," on the premise that the patients' natural tendencies toward positive personality change will take over and flourish.

6. The *behavioral therapies,* which have developed recently and are growing rapidly, are rather different from dynamic psychotherapy. The behavior therapist must have a sound basic clinical training and must also be an expert in applied learning theory. If the patient's problems can be stated as specific problems in behavior (including thoughts and feelings), learning-based procedures for behavior change can usually be designed. A high degree of structure and planning is required, and the therapist's role is somewhat like that of an instructor.

7. Behavioral assessment and planning begin with the gathering of careful observations about the problem behavior, and actual written records are often kept. It is also necessary to determine whether the behavior is being maintained by any particular reinforcers, either positive or negative, and whether it is under the control of any particular stimuli. In order to be effective, the therapist must be able to change the patient's responses and/or the environment to enable new learning to occur.

8. Learning principles can be employed to bring about behavior changes in a variety of ways. To increase a behavior through *simple positive reinforcement,* a reinforcer must be arranged to follow the desired behavior. *Systematic desensitization* is a procedure for reducing anxiety, and may be carried out in conjunction either with real stimuli or with vividly imagined stimuli, which are presented in a series of carefully graded steps. The exact way in which desensitization works is not well understood. *Undesired behavior* can be decreased using punishment or extinction, but it is usually preferable to concentrate instead on increasing alternative desirable behaviors.

9. Behavior therapy has a wide range of applications. Adjustment *problems of children,* when analyzed behaviorally, sometimes are found to be maintained by parental behavior; in other cases, parents can sometimes be trained as behavior change agents for their children. *Marital difficulties* may sometimes be approached behaviorally, by determining the ways in which each partner is maintaining the unadaptive behavior of the other, or is failing to provide adequate positive reinforcement for desired behaviors. Another application is in the *"token economy,"* in which groups of individuals in a restricted environment, such as chronic patients on a state hospital ward, are positively reinforced with tokens for performing the expected routine behaviors of daily living, and can use the tokens to purchase desired goods and privileges.

10. The use of powerful and direct procedures for behavior change raises difficult questions about the ethics of controlling the behavior of others, particularly the question of whether society ever has the right to insist on the behavioral treatment of persons who are dangerous to themselves or to others. Questions of the dangers of government control through behavioral procedures are also raised.

KEY TERMS

behavioral therapies	transference
electroshock therapy	interpretations
psychosurgery	formal psychoanalysis
psychoactive drugs	nondirective therapy
psychotherapy	systematic desensitization
counseling	fear hierarchy
psychotherapist	token economy

TWELVE

Enhancing Human Adjustment

Procedures for self-directed behavior change are becoming increasingly common.

- Some of these procedures can be used in escaping from "social traps."
- They include changing existing patterns of reinforcement and learning new responses.
- Overeating is a social trap that is amenable to self-directed behavior change.
- Self-awareness plays an important part in self-directed behavior change.

Altered states of consciousness have been suggested as a method for enhancing human adjustment.

- These states can be produced either chemically or behaviorally.

Group training and encounter experiences originated in the 1940s.

- Some group experiences are based on transactional analysis, some are based on gestalt therapy, and some are based on psychoanalytic techniques.
- Group sensitivity experiences have been shown to be beneficial in some ways, but can also have harmful effects.

Organizational development refers to the group training of intact organizational units.

IN CHAPTER 11 WE EXPLORED SOME OF THE MAJOR APPROACHES TO THE alleviation of human adjustment problems. Many psychologists have recently become interested in developing ways of extending or enhancing the adjustment of persons who are more or less problem-free. These psychologists believe that a major task for their profession should be the enhancement of human potential rather than just the treatment of human maladjustment. This movement regards the facilitation of psychological growth of adequately functioning persons as the primary and neglected issue confronting professional psychologists and other mental health workers.

In this chapter we discuss many of the approaches and techniques that have been developed recently in an effort to enhance human adjustment. While much of the writing about human potential has taken an existential viewpoint, our approach will be primarily a social-learning one. This approach has been adopted not only to maintain consistency with the remainder of the book, but also because we believe that the issues

Self-help groups, such as this Parents Without Partners meeting, help members cope
with a common problem and attempt to set
a climate for increased personal growth and
effectiveness.

and techniques that are involved in the human growth movement can and should be
included in a social-learning approach to human adjustment. In general, two directions can be taken in the enhancement of human potential—the *individual* or *self-
directed* approach, and the *group* or *encounter* experience. Let us turn first to the individual approach.

SELF-DIRECTED BEHAVIOR CHANGE

In Chapter 9 we pointed out that human personality develops and changes throughout the life cycle. Adults change their life interests, change careers, and sometimes
change spouses. However, there are few cultural resources to facilitate these changes.
Until recently, our formal educational system operated as though the only need for
such opportunities was for persons aged 25 or younger. This chapter describes some
of the opportunities that have recently become available for adult learning, especially
in the area of interpersonal skills and emotional growth.

Consider the case of a young man who had been very anxious in the presence of
women and had been successfully treated for this anxiety. He might still lack the interpersonal skills and competencies necessary to interact successfully with women. How

might our patient begin learning these skills? In most communities the resources for improving one's interpersonal competence are quite limited, if they are present at all. For persons who had been successfully treated for anxiety about driving automobiles, it would be a simple matter to arrange for them to learn to drive. In the case of interpersonal behavior, however, most of us acquire these skills informally during adolescence and early adulthood, through modeling and shaping by our peers. Once someone reaches adulthood, the opportunities for this kind of learning are extremely limited. Rather, socially inept individuals are simply avoided by their peers, and their inadequacies are left unchanged. Even when people recognize their inadequacies and try to work on them, it is usually quite difficult to arrange for suitable help.

Some agencies for providing help do exist. Commercial enterprises such as the Dale Carnegie Institutes and the Arthur Murray Dance Studios provide people with opportunities for overcoming interpersonal inadequacies. Similar programs are also offered through a variety of civic and community organizations such as YMCA's and YWCA's. Many of these programs, however, are poorly designed, quite expensive, and provide only limited assistance to the person in need.

Another source of help and support for people in need is **self-help groups,** such as Alcoholics Anonymous, Parents Without Partners, and Divorce Recovery. Levy (1976) has suggested that self-help groups tend to have five defining characteristics: (1) the express purpose of the organization is to help its members with their problem and to improve their psychological effectiveness; (2) the origins of the group and its sanction for existence come from the members themselves and not from some external agency; (3) the group relies upon the skills, efforts, knowledge, and commitments of its own members, not upon those of professionals; (4) the members share a common problem or concern; and (5) the structure and modes of operation of the organization are determined by the members with only minor external direction from a national or regional organization. These characteristics set a climate for the kind of personal growth and increased effectiveness that until quite recently has been largely overlooked by mental health professionals.

Social Traps

Let us now consider some of the problems involved in changing our own behavior. Consider an individual who wishes to quit smoking, or somebody who wants to diet in order to lose weight. Although these people have recognized that the short-term advantages of their current behavior (pleasurable feelings) are outweighed by its long-term disadvantages (increased possibility of lung cancer or obesity), they will probably find it difficult to know where to begin.

Platt (1973) has used the term **social traps** to describe these situations in which an individual or a group gets started in some behavior that later proves to be unpleasant or even lethal. Platt's notion of a social trap is derived from his understanding of a fish trap, where the fish is drawn in by the bait and, once the initial movement is made, cannot reverse its course and extricate itself from the trap. So, too, does the smoker or the overeater embark on a course from which it is difficult to escape. The concept of social traps is applicable to groups and individuals, although we are concerned here primarily with individual social traps.

One of the primary explanatory concepts that we have used throughout this book is *reinforcement*. We have emphasized that behavior is shaped to a greater extent by the immediate reinforcers, those available in seconds or minutes after a response is made, than by more remote reinforcers, that may be hours, days, or months away. Thus, in regard to smoking, the immediate biochemical and social positive reinforcers are more potent than the delayed punishment of lung cancer. In the case of overeating, there is the pleasure of tasting the food and perhaps parental approval, versus the long-term social disapproval of obesity and the increased risk of a heart attack. In these simple social traps, immediate positive reinforcement is more effective than delayed punishment.

In another kind of one-person trap, the problem is not one of simple delay but rather *ignorance* of the delayed aversive consequences. The fish that enters the fish trap does not know that it has just arranged for its own demise. Obviously, ignorance of the consequences of one's behavior can be as lethal as actions based on full awareness. "I didn't know the gun was loaded" offers no solace once the gun has been fired.

Yet another type of one-person trap occurs because of the changing quality of the reinforcer. *Sliding reinforcers*, to use Platt's term, change or deteriorate as one repeats the behavior, gradually losing their reinforcing properties. However, once having learned the behavior, the individual continues it in the hope that the original positive consequences, or "kick," will return. Perhaps the clearest example of sliding reinforcers is found in drug addiction, where the original effect is soon gone, and larger and larger amounts of the drug are used in the search for the same experience. To make matters worse, the individual becomes physiologically dependent upon the narcotic.

The major characteristic of these traps is that immediate reinforcement leads to self-maintained or stereotyped behavior that is difficult to modify. It should be emphasized that much stereotyped, or locked-in, behavior is functional. We must be able to brush our teeth, comb our hair, dress, and walk without much active concern or attention. Problems arise, however, when we find that a particular locked-in behavior is no longer useful and we try to change it.

Not only are social traps difficult for the individual to modify because of the reinforcement schedule that has been involved in learning the behavior, but the behavior frequently becomes embedded in a transactional relationship among two or more people. These transactional relationships further strengthen the behavior in very damaging and complex ways. In his volume *Games People Play*, Eric Berne (1964) presented a variety of locked-in transactions. The alcoholic, for example, begins drinking because of the immediate reinforcing properties of alcohol, and without concern for the various negative physical and social consequences. This behavior, however, is further locked-in by a variety of interpersonal transactions—with a long-suffering spouse, friends, the neighborhood bartender—and patterns of mutual reinforcement develop and become stable. It is clear from Berne's work that individual traps quickly become interpersonal traps, making escape even more difficult.

How can one escape from a social trap? Platt describes five different methods. First and most obvious, one can change the delay of reinforcement, converting long-term consequences into more immediate ones. This procedure is involved when alcoholics take medication that creates nausea whenever they drink alcohol, or when warning labels are put on each pack of cigarettes stating that cigarette smoking is a health hazard. One limitation in this approach is that it is often difficult or impossible to change the schedule of reinforcements, and further complications are brought about by the various interpersonal transactions in which the behavior may be involved. Israel Goldiamond (1973), a well-known psychologist who has been paralyzed by an automobile accident, vividly describes realizing that many of the other people in his life were unintentionally conspiring to keep him crippled and dependent upon them.

A second way of eliminating social traps is to add immediate counterreinforcers to encourage desired behavior or discourage undesired behavior. For instance, we can use social incentives or punishment, such as immediate praise or reproof, in connection with behaviors such as smoking, drinking, or eating. If we were praised every time we took out a cigarette but then did *not* smoke it, this strategy would modify our pattern of cigarette smoking. The major difficulties of this procedure concern the task of arranging for counterreinforcement to be consistently present, and the fact that such social reinforcement may not be as potent as the positive reinforcement that is produced by actually smoking the cigarette. To circumvent the first problem, Kanfer and Phillips (1970) have suggested that people should develop techniques of self-reinforcement which would enable them to monitor and self-control the behavior of concern.

Platt's third technique is to change the nature of the long-term consequences of the behavior. This would in many cases involve new inventions, such as the development of noncarcinogenic tobacco, or alcohol that does not produce liver damage or brain disorders, or food without calories. If we could succeed in changing or eliminating the long-term negative consequences of a behavior, we need no longer be reluctant to enjoy its short-term positive rewards.

A fourth method of eliminating social traps is to provide reinforcement for competing responses that do not have negative long-term consequences, so that the competing response is made instead of the original one. For example, in order to break the habit of avoiding studying, a student might arrange a program of reinforcement for successively greater amounts of studying behaviors. Thus, she might plan to call a friend only after she has finished reading twenty pages of an assignment, or to go downstairs for a coke only when she has mastered the tough calculus problem. More systematically, she could keep a record of the number of hours she has studied and, when she has met the target, reward herself with dinner at her favorite restaurant.

The fifth procedure for changing the reinforcement patterns of locked-in traps involves the use of external resources. You might contract with your spouse or a friend not to allow you to turn on the television until you have reached a certain behavioral objective, or else have them reward you by taking a stroll or preparing a special meal. Similarly, a young man could contract with his girlfriend that she *not* talk to him when he calls until he can report that he has completed his assignment. One can always cheat under the terms of a behavioral contract, but very few people do in fact cheat once they have gone to the trouble of making the arrangements. An important aspect of using external control of the reinforcement schedule is that it forces us to set clear behavioral objectives and to negotiate a contract for meeting the objectives. It breaks the habit of procrastinating and promising to get started "soon" by requiring a public commitment and providing a pleasurable consequence for fulfilling the commitment.

Burchard and Harig (1976) have summarized the research on the use of external reinforcement controls to change the locked-in behavior of delinquent children. Delinquents are usually reinforced by the attention that their behavior evokes, through the admiration of their peers and the excitement of being chased by the police. The delinquent, the police, parents and teachers, friends, and others are all locked into self-maintaining transactions that reinforce the delinquent behaviors. In their studies, Tharp and Wetzel (1969) would identify an outsider to these transactions, such as an adult friend or a teacher, who would observe the child and give immediate reinforcement for more appropriate and functional behavior. For instance, the outside resource person would make marks on a record sheet for paying attention in class or reading a book, and a specific number of marks would entitle the child to extra television viewing, or horseback riding, or some other highly pleasurable reinforcement. As the behavior became more adaptive over time, the other persons in the child's life—parents, teachers, and friends—would begin to admire the child for these new behaviors and thus begin to lock in a new and more adaptive transactional pattern. At this point the outside resources would no longer be necessary and could be withdrawn.

The clear purpose of the outside resources in these situations is to reinforce the emerging, new responses until they are clearly part of the individual's repertoire and readily receive "natural" reinforcement from others.

An example. Platt's analysis of social traps provides useful illustrations of the way in which an analysis of various patterns of reinforcement can help us understand our own behavior and successfully program our own behavior change. In order to make these ideas clearer, let us take a specific problem of behavioral self-control, and examine in detail ways of programming our own behavior more effectively. We choose the problem of regulating food intake for the purpose of weight control.

In dieting, the critical point to remember is that one must control the amount of food intake. In order to lose weight we must consume fewer calories than are required by the energy balance in our body. There is little or no evidence that "fad diets" are of any help in weight control. Nutritionists agree that "permanent" weight loss can only result from a well-designed diet, based upon the learned appetites of the individual, and sustained over a long period of time. The need for studying and programming weight control is widespread: heart disease, strokes, and high blood pressure are closely related to overweight. Also, studies of the social impact of obesity show that obese individuals are less socially acceptable than those with physical handicaps.

It is clear that weight control depends basically on changing one's eating behavior and maintaining those changes in a permanent manner. Most people are intellectually aware that calories are important in weight control and that we need to count our calories; unfortunately, most of us also love high-calorie, high-fat foods, such as ice cream, soft drinks, french fried potatoes, and desserts. Further, eating is often a social occasion, and our patterns of feeding are locked in by many of our interpersonal transactions. Also, since eating is a pleasurable activity it can serve other functions besides hunger reduction, such as reducing anxiety. Indeed, there are probably as many or more Americans who use eating to reduce their anxiety than there are using alcohol and drugs combined.

Recognizing the difficulties that most of us encounter in diet control, how can we use the behaviorally based techniques of self-control to help us in the management of our food intake? First we must accept that it is necessary to bring about a permanent change in our eating behavior, and that weight control represents a change in lifestyle. Unless we can accept this basic premise, the suggested procedures are not likely to work. Second, we must design our weight loss program in a realistic and sensible fashion. We must decide how many pounds we wish to lose and how many weeks it will take, figuring at the rate of a pound or two a week. The general plan of weight reduction and one's general state of health should ordinarily be checked by a physician, but we should be aware that the techniques suggested here really aim at learning new patterns of eating—a psychological process.

Once the program is set we need to arrange a chart which can be posted in an obvious place near the scale. The chart (see Figure 12-1) shows present weight and

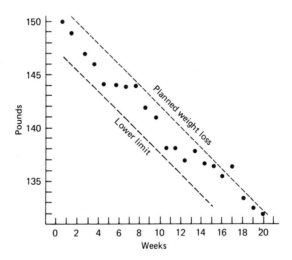

Figure 12-1. A sample weight control chart showing the planned weight loss and the actual weight loss over a 21-week period.

planned weight, and establishes a series of subgoals against which success can be checked. The chart makes it clear that only gradual reductions are expected; also, a lower limit is set (typically three to five pounds below the basic weight loss line) and the goal is to maintain one's weight between the two lines. If one's weight rises above the planned line, then a further reduction in food intake is required; if it falls below the lower limit, then an increase in intake is required. Most people show a more rapid weight loss early in such a program; however, after this initial loss many persons find it difficult to continue on the diet because the losses are less dramatic and more tedious to maintain. The major point, however, is inescapable: if one cuts down on food intake, one must lose weight over time. The charting procedure provides an obvious and ready means of checking how well the weight loss is being sustained. Most authorities recommend charting one's weight daily, taking the measure at the same time and place each day. Mahoney and Mahoney (1976) have suggested, however, that daily weighings tend to move the person's focus away from eating behavior and on to the scale. Since home-scale readings are quite variable from day to day, there is the danger that daily weighings can provide some unintended negative feedback.

Reinforcement procedures can be worked into the charting process. Crossing the line is to be regarded as a punishment (week 17) and keeping between the lines as a reward. One can use the chart for further reinforcement by planning to see a movie after keeping between the lines for a two- or three-week period, for example. Alternatively, the visual image of the chart, depicting failure to reach the goal for the previous week, might serve as a punishment. Thus, as we reach for a second helping of pasta, the image of the chart should inhibit the reaching, especially after some progress has been made and it becomes a matter of pride to maintain the same rate of improvement.

Once we have set our behavioral objectives, we must decide upon a specific method for monitoring and limiting food intake. There are three direct techniques to control food intake—counting calories, restricting or eliminating certain foods, such as cakes or pastries, and following a menu plan. All of these strategies work well, but one must be chosen and used consistently. Calories must be counted every day, and a record kept of exact caloric intake. If one is to restrict or eliminate certain foods, these foods must be specified in writing in order to make clear the self-arranged behavioral contract. The written list should be shown to as many relevant people as possible in order to make a public commitment and to get help in reinforcing the prohibitions. If menus are to be used, a considerable amount of advance planning is necessary.

After a technique for monitoring food intake has been chosen, the next major issue involves responses to food cues. Most eating behavior tends to be somewhat automatic, so that people are more likely to eat when in the presence of food. Food, rather than hunger, serves as the cue for eating, and this is particularly true for obese persons (Schachter, 1971). Also, we are more likely to experience hunger if the food is appetizing. Other cues include a television commercial break, seeing food on the television screen, and the recognition that it is "time to eat." Thus, a variety of external cues (rather than internal hunger cues) can serve to elicit eating, and the task of reduc-

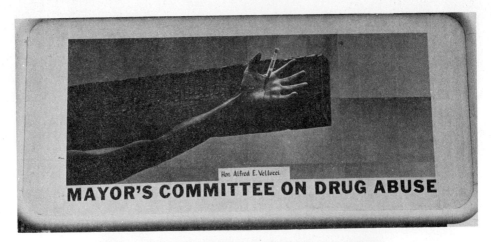

Posters such as those shown here capitalize on the use
of visual imagery to associate undesired behaviors with
aversive thoughts and feelings. The object is to make the
behaviors themselves less pleasant.

ing one's food intake requires us to change or inhibit our usual responses to these cues.

Let us examine Platt's strategies to help plan for changing our eating behavior. His first strategy is to make the long-term negative consequences of behavior more immediate. One way to do this is through the use of visual imagery. For example, if, as you reach for a large piece of chocolate cake, you can visualize yourself as a fat corpse, lying on the examining table dead at forty years of age from a heart attack, with the bereaved family standing about, the reinforcement value of that piece of cake is sharply reduced. Similarly, you might imagine that someone you love now begins to be repelled by your obesity. Most people can easily fantasize a detailed scene in which rejection takes place. You should have the loved one—a spouse, a lover, a child, a parent—recoil from you in disgust, withdrawing from any physical contact with you, horror-stricken by your appearance. Imaginative persons might be able to visualize themselves as enormously obese, tearing off rolls of fat from themselves like sticky tar, only to have it grow back instantly, while crowds of people guffaw at their discomfort. Such imagery can serve to make eating less reinforcing by making the negative consequences of eating immediate, rather than long-term.

With some systematic practice, these images will come to mind spontaneously and strongly affect the way a person behaves in the presence of food cues. It is well known that associations of this nature are formed naturally; this is the way most of us learn food aversions, or aversions of any kind. What is different in the present context is that we use the development of images and their aversive consequences deliberately to produce planned change in our own behavior. Since imagery is very much a personal matter, individuals should develop their own specific aversive scenes for use as immediate punishers for undesired behaviors.

Platt's second strategy, which overlaps to some extent with the first, is to use additional reinforcers to encourage or discourage the behavior. In the case of the self-control of eating, we can again use visual imagery. This time, however, we would use pleasant imagery to reinforce the response of not eating. As we push away the second helping, as we turn from the sandwiches to the salads, we can conjure up images that reinforce our self-control. For instance, we can see ourselves walking down a beautiful, sunny beach clad in a bathing suit, attracting the eyes of persons of the opposite sex because we are so physically attractive. Or we may be asked to attend a party by someone whom we have long admired, as they comment on our fit and healthy appearance. Again, the most effective imagery for each person is an individual matter, and the essential ingredient is that it should have strong positive reinforcing properties to be used for rewarding self-control. The self-directed behavior change system can also be designed to include a more major reward, such as a trip to Europe or a new stereo, when one achieves a major weight loss goal.

Changing the nature of the long-term consequences of our behavior is Platt's third strategy. Unfortunately, there is no such thing as noncaloric food, at least not at the present time. However, there are many foods that are very low in calories, such as many raw vegetables, and these can therefore be eaten with considerable freedom.

Thus, while we have not been able to change the long-term consequences of eating, it is possible to capitalize on those alternatives that do not have serious long-term negative consequences.

The fourth strategy suggested by Platt is to provide reinforcement for competing responses that can be substituted for the behavior to be changed. For instance, you can keep a bag of carrot sticks and celery in your room and reinforce yourself for eating them (with visual imagery or with points toward a desired reward) when everybody else sends out for a pizza. Or take a walk instead of eating and use imagery to reinforce the walking. Reinforcement could also be used for *not* buying high-calorie snack foods at the supermarket, or for buying diet soda. Instead of responding to examination anxiety by eating a candy bar, you could telephone a friend. The important aspect in all of these examples is that the alternative responses are made more attractive than might otherwise be the case by adding additional reinforcement.

Platt's final strategy involves the use of external help in changing the reinforcement patterns that sustain the behavior. We have already suggested a number of ways in which this can be done, such as by having friends praise us when we reject fattening foods, or raise an eyebrow when we do not. Also, we can ask for assistance in making certain that fattening snack foods are not kept in the house, and we can share in planning the menu.

All five of Platt's strategies could be used together in extricating oneself from the trap of overeating. We have used overeating as an example for the purpose of outlining a series of behavioral steps for modifying behaviors that we wish to change. Each success in using these strategies makes the next time easier. These procedures can be readily adapted for a variety of self-initiated programs of behavior change, provided one necessary factor is present—a genuine willingness on our part to work consistently on the program.

Health specialists have recently become acutely aware of the need for personal change strategies in order to preserve the health of all of us. Sound evidence now exists that most of the major diseases of adult life, such as heart disease, lung disorders, and premature aging, can be largely prevented by changes in lifestyle, involving better diet, continued exercise, and thoughtful management of life stresses. Indeed, many experts believe that we now know enough about the physiological aspects of these diseases that future efforts should be concentrated on behavioral programs, focused on the development of overall or holistic health.

Self-Awareness

In the example that we have just discussed, involving the self-control of eating, there is little problem of self-awareness. The condition of being overweight and needing to diet is usually perfectly obvious. However, this is not always the case.

Let us consider an example of a social trap that does involve the problem of self-awareness. Fred, a young teenager, had been promised that his father would take him to a college football game that afternoon, and Fred was looking forward to the event. An unexpected business appointment caused Fred's father to call home cancelling his promise, and Fred was intensely disappointed. He went out to play in the backyard, where he met his younger sister. She began to tease him, a behavior that was common for her. He responded very angrily, striking her and screaming at her. The sister began to scream in return and tried to hit him back. The mother soon had to intervene, and sent Fred to his room for the rest of the day. As she comforted her daughter, she wondered why the day turned out so badly. Let us analyze this incident to determine how this social trap developed, and how self-awareness might have led to a different outcome.

The major cause for the incident can be identified as Fred's frustration over his father's failure to take him to the promised football game. To the slight cue of his sister's teasing, the frustrated boy reacted with strong **displaced aggression,** without being aware that anything more was involved than the fact that he had been provoked by her. As in most families, Fred did not show any anger to his father for breaking the promise. Instead, he continued to talk to himself about his lost goal, and this internal conversation intensified his internal distress. While Fred would usually respond to his sister's teasing with counterteasing, this time his unacknowledged anger led to a direct attack. In other words, he displaced his anger from his father to his sister, and this behavior led to a sequence of entirely predictable consequences.

What other alternatives were open? What if Fred's mother had reminded him that feeling angry or disappointed would be a natural reaction to his father's call? She could have encouraged him to label his feelings accurately and to express them verbally to her and to others. She might have warned him that when people are angry they are likely to "take it out on someone." She could have urged Fred to restrain himself under such circumstances. She could have pointed out to him that his sister was at home, and that teasing would be likely to occur. Further, Fred's mother could have pointed out that it would not be fair of him to react to the teasing with undue hostility, since his sister was not the cause of the original frustration. In other words, the mother could have deliberately tried to help Fred suppress his angry behavior, while encouraging him to express the anger verbally. Such a program would have heightened Fred's self-awareness and provided him with alternative behaviors. She also could have suggested that Fred consider how his father might apologize for breaking the promise.

We are suggesting that many social traps develop because we do not adequately understand our own behavior. The important point to be noted is that we can avoid many social traps through greater self-awareness. In the example, the critical issue was Fred's lack of self-awareness of his internal states or feelings. Clearly, one way of enhancing our personal adjustment is to be aware of our feelings and to label them accurately, in order to prevent them from triggering responses that we did not intend.

It is possible for most of us, through a process of self-study (see Dollard and Miller, 1950), to become more aware of our own internal feelings. As was pointed out in

Chapter 4, anxiety can easily become attached to thoughts, resulting in the inhibition of thinking and problem solving. To become more self-aware, we must carefully examine our own behavior chains, looking for those places where our behavior does not "make sense." It is at these crucial places that there are likely to be mislabeled emotional reactions which might account for the seemingly senseless behavior. Only when we are able to accurately label our own behavior and the stimuli (internal or external) that elicit them can we intelligently plan and guide what we do.

It is important to emphasize the crucial difference between identifying or labeling feelings and acting on those feelings. You could be very angry at somebody, so angry that you feel that "you could kill him," and yet be very much aware of that feeling *without* acting it out. The whole point is that the process of accurately labeling one's feelings reduces rather than raises the probability that the feelings will lead to unplanned behavioral consequences. It is when we cannot face our feelings, or when we have deliberately failed to label them, that they elicit problematic behavior, as was true in the example of Fred. Thus, the verbal expression of feelings is legitimate and desirable, but not their direct expression in overt behavior. That is, people should be able to acknowledge that they would like to hurt someone else, but that it is usually not permissible to carry out that action. And the open acknowledgment of the feeling diminishes the probabiity that it will be expressed in direct behavior.

The notion that awareness and accurate labeling of feelings facilitates adjustment flies in the face of much conventional folk wisdom. It is too often believed that the best way to handle feelings is by ignoring or overlooking them. Most of us at one time or another have been told something like: "Oh, it's not as bad as all that. Just pretend it never happened." A more adjustive comment would be: "You're pretty upset with what happened and you have *every* right to feel that way!"

Our major emphasis in this section has been upon the facilitating effects of self-awareness and, in particular, awareness of one's feelings. It was pointed out in Chapters 4, 5, and 6 that the lack of self-awareness and self-understanding is an important underlying factor in much human discomfort. In the present context we wish to emphasize that self-awareness greatly facilitates positive adjustment, permitting us to do a better job of planning our own lives and using our higher mental processes in the management of our own destiny.

Altered States of Consciousness

No discussion of self-directed behavior change would be complete without a survey of the techniques and procedures that bring about what are nowadays called **altered states of consciousness.** There are basically three ways to produce such a state: *chemically*, through taking a psychoactive or "mind-altering" drug; *behaviorally*, through training in hypnosis, meditation, and related procedures; and *electronically*, by enhancing the alpha rhythm of one's EEG (electroencephalographic) pattern through the use of a biofeedback device.

A complete review of this fascinating topic is well beyond the scope of the present book. For further material, the interested reader is referred to the excellent collection of papers and commentaries by psychologist Charles Tart (1975). In addition to the possible use of these procedures for enhancing human potential, three other uses can be identified. The best known is the therapeutic use, when hypnosis is employed to assist a smoker to break the habit, or when psychoactive medication reduces anxiety or relieves depression. Another use, permitted rather reluctantly by society, is the recreational one, such as the use of alcohol or marijuana for personal enjoyment. The third is the employment of these procedures for purposes of escape, and it is this third use that society formally identifies as unacceptable. Included in this category would be addiction or uncontrollable reliance on a chemical substance, and the severe psychic withdrawal states of some schizophrenic patients.

The philosophy that chemical means can be usefully employed to enhance human potential, as opposed to their use for correcting maladaptive conditions, became known in the 1960s as the "psychedelic" movement. After reaching the proportions of a social crisis in the late 1960s, this philosophy is now less widely espoused. The use of EEG alpha-rhythm feedback for the same purpose is newer and has many of the elements of a fad, but as can be seen below, there is some tentative scientific evidence to suggest that this procedure shares certain basic processes in common with at least some of the wide variety of behavioral methods for promoting altered states of consciousness.

Meditation. It has only been in the last twenty years that behavioral scientists have been willing to even consider the possibility that the mental exercises which form an important part of certain eastern religions might have a valid scientific basis. The early credit for this work belongs to investigators such as Anand, Chhina, and Singh (1961), who have demonstrated that during meditation, the EEG alpha rhythms of expe-

There is increasing evidence that the mental exercises which form part of certain eastern religions may have a valid scientific basis, and meditation is now widely practiced as a means of dealing with everyday stress-related problems.

rienced yoga practitioners show marked increases in activity, and that these increases tend to be related to verbal reports of subjective states and to experienced judges' evaluations of the yogis' mental states. Working from the viewpoint of American behavioral psychology, it has also been shown (Kamiya, 1972) that normal individuals can be trained to tell the difference between their own states of enhanced alpha and normal alpha activity. It is also possible to learn to bring about such states voluntarily, an experience that is reportedly so pleasant that potential research subjects beg for the opportunity to take part in these studies.

There is increasing evidence (Benson, 1975; Blanchard and Epstein, 1978) that a combination of meditation and passive relaxation can be very effective in bringing about a physiological state of low arousal that is of considerable benefit in dealing with stress-related problems, such as some forms of hypertension (high blood pressure). It is also possible that the effective ingredient in this procedure and other similar procedures is simply relaxation. Thus, Blanchard and Epstein talk of relaxation as possibly being "the final common pathway to the clinical benefits" (p. 187). As with any new and developing field, these findings must as yet be considered tentative, and we must await future scientific study before we make definitive statements about the usefulness of meditation, relaxation, and related processes for enhancing human potential.

GROUP AND ENCOUNTER EXPERIENCES

In the past ten years or so a variety of different group interaction procedures have developed, all of which aim to enhance the adjustment of the people who participate. These groups, sometimes termed "therapy for normal people," involve a range of techniques and procedures and are variously known as encounter groups, sensitivity training or T-groups, marathon groups, and personal growth groups. Since there is no standardized terminology in this area, it is difficult to describe the various group approaches in any systematic way, but we will attempt to at least sketch them briefly and to discuss their effectiveness. The interested reader will find Jane Howard's book *Please touch: A guided tour of the human potential movement* (1970) a fascinating and highly personal account of one person's experiences during a year spent in participating in over twenty such groups.

There is much enthusiasm for group experiences, and much concern about them. They have been heralded as the antidote for alienation, as an inexpensive alternative to psychotherapy, and as a way of gaining self-understanding. They have been criticized as part of a communist plot to destroy the moral fiber of America, as an alternative form of religion, as undignified, and as a serious danger to the mental health of persons who participate. It must be recognized that we are dealing with a diffuse and disorderly phenomenon, and that the organizers and leaders of encounter groups range from mental health professionals with years of supervised experience to persons whose only qualifications are interest and enthusiasm. Thus, it is entirely possible that all of the above statements may be true in one setting or another.

The group movement had its origins in the 1940s, in the work of the late psychologist Kurt Lewin, who started to train community leaders to work effectively with interracial tensions. These leaders worked together in small discussion groups, analyzing the back-home problems of their members. Each leader's group had a "process observer," who recorded what was said, by whom and to whom, and with what consequences. At the end of each day of training, the process observers fed back their observations to the members. It was soon recognized that these process observations were more important to the group members than the actual content of their deliberations. The observers' feedback enabled the members to learn about the way in which small groups operated and enabled them to recognize the effects of their behavior on others.

This initial experiment, in which members of small groups used process observations to learn simultaneously about small group interactions and about their own behavior, led to the development of the National Training Laboratories (now the NTL Institute for Applied Behavioral Sciences) and a number of other organizations offering basic human relations training, and later, to **T-groups** (for "training") or sensitivity-training groups. In this mode of group experience, group leaders employ such concepts as "feedback," the giving and receiving of interpersonal perceptions, and "participant-observation," the deliberate study of the processes of the group, such as

The recent emphasis in the encounter-group movement has been on learning about oneself through various interpersonal and intrapersonal exercises. Group experiences often include physical touching of others and personal awareness exercises such as meditation and body movements.

leadership patterns, patterns of inclusion or exclusion, and expressions of hostility and affection. Many of the interpersonal exercises that were built into these group encounters, such as those involving decision making, were designed to heighten the participants' awareness of their behavior in group situations.

The encounter group movement has now tended to move away from its early focus upon the acquisition of interpersonal and group process skills, especially in California, where such personal growth centers as the Esalen Institute have developed. Psychologists at these centers have proposed a more diffuse, less easily specified set of goals for their group experiences, using rather vague concepts such as personal growth, developing the full potential of individuals, and the discovery and enjoyment of hidden, untapped individual resources. Emphasis is upon learning about oneself rather than about one's interpersonal or group behavior, and procedures include personal awareness exercises such as meditation, yoga, and body movements.

Thus, one major dimension on which the encounter movement approaches might be classified is that of group versus individual focus, with the original focus being upon group and interpersonal behavior, and the more recent focus upon self-awareness and personal growth. Judging from the various written program descriptions of the many group experiences that are offered to the public, most encounter groups appear to include a combination of these concerns.

Another useful dimension for classification is the degree of structure involved in the encounter. At one end we would place those procedures in which the group is given little or no structure other than to deal with "here-and-now" issues, and in which the leader plays a nondirective, ambiguous role. At the other end would be those encounters in which the group moves from exercise to exercise according to a preset program. In such a program, for example, the participants might first be asked to introduce themselves by identifying their favorite literary figure or movie star, and then having the group discuss this experience. Next, each member of the group might be asked to encounter each other member in some nonverbal manner, again followed by a group discussion. Obviously, the leader in this kind of group follows a more active course in arranging a program of experiences.

Another dimension of encounter groups is the timing of the experience. Encounter groups may last for only several hours, or they may last for several weeks. The shorter experiences are often called "microlabs," and are typically intended to give participants some minimal understanding of what might be experienced in an encounter group. The one- or two-week encounters are usually run at an isolated location where the participants can work together on a sort of "cultural island" without outside distractions. The fact that the participants spend a great deal of time with each other without most of the ordinary concerns and pressures of living serves to heighten the impact of the experience. Another way of heightening the impact of the encounter is through the use of the **marathon,** or time-extended group. A marathon group meets for long and completely uninterrupted periods of time—twelve or twenty-four hours, or even through an entire weekend—and without time out for sleeping. The group experience becomes intensified as familiarity and fatigue combine to strip away superficialities and niceties. Another technique for stripping away superficialities has been to run encounter groups in the nude, typically in a heated indoor swimming pool. On another pattern, encounter groups in colleges and universities are sometimes conducted according to the academic calendar, meeting two or three times a week for the quarter or semester. It should be obvious that there is a wide variety of schedules and arrangements, with different implications for the intensity of the experience and its impact upon the participants. Unfortunately, despite the many claims for the greater usefulness of one arrangement over another by the adherents of each strategy, there is little solid evidence to favor any particular one over another (or over none at all).

Theoretical Viewpoints

Another way of understanding the encounter group movement is in terms of the theoretical viewpoints of the leaders. While many of the leaders who emphasize group and interpersonal aspects tend to be atheoretical, there are a number of more theoretically-based approaches to personal awareness and growth groups. Perhaps the three most important are the transactional analysis groups, the gestalt therapy groups, and the psychoanalytic groups.

Transactional analysis. Eric Berne (1961) first introduced the concept of transactional analysis and developed a distinct style of small-group leadership based upon his concepts. According to **transactional analysis** (TA), each of us has three ego states or "consistent patterns of feeling and experience directly related to a corresponding consistent pattern of behavior" (Berne, 1961, p. 17). These states are the consequence of our prior experience, including our childhood experiences, our perceptions of events, our feelings associated with these events, and the later distortions which we apply to our memories. The three ego states are identified as Parent, Adult, and Child. According to Berne, these states are not abstract concepts but "realities," and each is a separate and distinct source of behavior.

The Parental ego state involves attitudes and behavior that are incorporated from our external environment, principally our parents. In terms of our relations with others, we express our Parental ego state in evaluative, critical, and nurturing behaviors, that is, in behaving like parents toward others. In terms of internal responses, our Parental ego state causes us to evaluate, criticize, and either censure or praise ourselves, in the manner of old parental messages that are recalled from the past.

The Adult ego state is based upon the current reality of the situation and requires the objective gathering of information. The Adult is organized, adaptable, intelligent, and heavily oriented toward reality, computing or estimating probabilities dispassionately. The Adult state tends to be rather free of emotions and is typified by the rational person.

The Child ego state is natural, impulsive, and fun-loving. The behavior stemming from this state is playful or destructive, and relatively unconcerned with consequences.

James and Jongeward (1971) have presented the following case illustration applying transactional analysis:

A client was advised to investigate a private school for his son. When he reported his findings about the school, where the teaching was informal and creativity encouraged, three distinct reactions were easily observable. First he scowled and said, 'I can't see how anyone could learn anything at that school. There's dirt on the floor!' Leaning back in his chair, his forehead smoothed out as he reflected, 'Before I decide, I think I should check with the school's scholastic rating and talk with some of the parents.' The next minute, a broad grin crossed his face, and he said, 'Gee, I'd love to have gone to a school like that!' (p.19)

As James and Jongeward note, the client's first reaction was precisely the way in which his own father would have reacted, and thus represented his Parent ego state. The client's second reaction was made from his Adult ego state and involves the search for more data, the rational man. His final reaction stems from his Child ego state and was based upon the recall of his own unhappy childhood school experiences and his fantasies about the fun that he might have had as a student at the school under consideration.

All of us have Parent, Adult, and Child ego states, and our behavior at any moment may represent one of these states. According to TA theory, it is not necessary to eliminate or change these states, but rather to develop an awareness for which state we are in at a particular time, and of the reaction that the state elicits from others. If, for example, you feel playful and uninterested in studying (Child ego state), while your roommate is busy studying for an important exam, you are likely to elicit a statement such as "Can't you act your age?" (Parent ego state) as your roommate tries to engage in the necessary studying. You will probably feel put down and resentful at this remark, and might even sulk or leave the room, slamming the door behind you as you continue in your Child ego state.

In TA groups, the leader uses Berne's concept of ego states to help the participants understand their own behavior in these terms, and also to understand how these ego states are integrated in continuing "life scripts" that are maladaptive for most of us. TA assumes that the increased self-awareness that is provided through this process of transactional analysis will permit us to rewrite our scripts into more functional ones.

There is a clear similarity between Berne's three ego states and the psychoanalytic concepts of Superego, Ego, and Id, but TA differs from psychoanalysis in being highly practical rather than theoretical. Many persons find TA to be a useful way of observing and thinking about their behavior, and its simplicity and practicality are undoubtedly the major factors in accounting for its present popularity. Critics regard it as overly simplistic, and claim that it tends to encourage its adherents to categorize their thoughts, actions, and impulses into artificial categories that have little value for the serious student or professional.

Gestalt therapy. The second theoretically derived approach to the encounter group movement is that of gestalt therapy, developed by the late Fritz Perls (1969). *Gestalt* is a German word that means roughly an "organized whole," and Perls believed that many individuals lacked this organized wholeness. The aim of **gestalt therapy** is to help people integrate the fragmented parts of their personality, to help them become aware of, admit to, and reclaim the disintegrated and disorganized aspects of their lives. While these goals are to some extent common to all therapy and encounter groups, there are a number of techniques that are specific to gestalt therapy, including, for example, the exaggeration of symptoms or problematic behavior. Others include the use of fantasy and the insistence on the use of the word "I" rather than "it" to help members assume responsibility for their behavior. Thus, one must say "I cannot handle this problem" rather than "It is a very tough problem." Further, gestalt therapy focuses on awareness of one's own bodily senses, on "staying with one's feelings" until they are understood and integrated with one's thoughts and behaviors, and it also uses a special form of role playing (Polster and Polster, 1973).

Role playing has been widely used as a therapeutic technique in both group and individual treatment methods since its development by Jacob Moreno earlier in this century. Indeed, Moreno (1953) has developed a group treatment procedure based upon role playing known as psychodrama, in which various participants in the group

take on different identities or roles, and then act out these roles to clarify their own problems and those of others. Role playing in gestalt therapy, however, differs from ordinary role playing in that other people are rarely used to play different roles. Instead, a single individual plays all the roles, moving from role to role. For instance, in one gestalt therapy group a participant reported that he was having trouble in his relationship with his father with whom he worked in a family business. The group member was therefore encouraged to role play a recent argument he had had with his father. Two chairs were set up, and our young man was told that when he sat in the large easy chair he was to imagine that he was his father, and when he was in the desk chair he was to play himself. He was instructed to move from one chair to the other as the discussion ensued, and as Perls suggested, the group was instructed to note *how* he acted in this role play, and not *why* he behaved in a particular manner. It was extraordinary how this man, a strapping 6′5″ former athlete, seemed to shrink when he assumed his own role opposite his father. Although he gave the impression of being tough and direct in real-life communications, in dealing with his father he became unsure of himself and almost pleading—represented in this case by the empty chair. When he played the role of the father, however, his arrogance and self-assurance reasserted themselves. Interestingly, he had great difficulty in believing the group members when they pointed out to him the changes in his behavior in the two roles. Only when this observation was echoed by every member of the group, and the changes mimicked by one of them, could he begin to appreciate the extent to which his own behavior entered into the problems that he was experiencing in his relations with his father. This same theme, of shrinking in relationships with his father and with other authority figures, recurred a number of times for this patient during the work of his gestalt therapy group.

In another use of role playing in gestalt therapy, persons role play two aspects of their own behavior, aspects which are in direct contradiction and are not integrated. Thus, a young woman who comes across as pleasant, bland, and rather colorless, yet who also complains of hostile, angry feelings which she cannot express, might be asked to have these two aspects of herself intersect directly, using the two chairs. In other words, her pleasant, nonabrasive self would talk to her hostile, angry self with the expectation that this discourse would permit an eventual integration of these disparate elements of her behavior. Although such an exercise might seem fanciful to some readers, most participants in gestalt therapy groups can meet the demands of such a situation, and almost invariably tend to report that their feelings about themselves have been clarified by their experiences. While very few research data are available to support the usefulness of gestalt therapy groups, there is abundant evidence to indicate the willingness of participants to enter into a variety of new experiences, and perhaps this is one of the most obvious benefits to be gained.

Another characteristic of the gestalt therapy groups is that there is very little concern with group process; rather, each participant takes turns in "the hot seat," or as the center of attention, as the leader "works" on that person's problems. The other members of the group take the role of observers, although they are sometimes asked to serve as a Greek chorus, verifying the observations of the leader.

Psychoanalytic groups. The third theoretical approach in encounter groups is that of the psychoanalytic group. While some psychoanalysts would say that a psycho-analytic encounter group is a contradiction in terms, there are a number of orthodox and conservative psychoanalysts who do conduct them. These groups are often run for students in the mental health professions—psychiatrists, psychologists, and social workers. They usually focus on the dynamics, or underlying psychological moti-vations, of the participants, and not on their behavior in the "here-and-now" of the actual group situation. Members are encouraged to bring up concerns or problems, which are then discussed within a psychoanalytic framework. These groups tend to be less emotionally intense than either transactional analysis or gestalt groups, and tend to emphasize an intellectual understanding of group dynamics as well as one's own individual dynamics. However, a psychoanalytically based group approach which does emphasize present ongoing behavior, especially behavior aimed at the leader or therapist, has been developed at the Tavistock Clinic in England (Ezriel, 1950). The Tavistock approach has not been widely adopted in the United States.

Effects of Group Experience

Having now completed a brief overview of the group encounter movement, one might reasonably ask about the consequences of participating in it. Unfortunately, there is no clear-cut answer to this question. On the one hand, almost all the subjective reports from group participants are highly positive. This should not be surprising, since the group experiences encourage and support behaviors that have been largely neglected in our society: the improvement of interpersonal competence, increased self-understanding, improved understanding of the impact of one's behavior on others, an awareness of the way groups function, and the development of one's potential as a complete human being. On the other hand, it is difficult to document changes along these lines in an objective and scientific manner.

As we have noted, there is considerable variety among encounter groups, and many types have never been studied in any way for the purpose of evaluating their outcome. Indeed, the leaders of some of the more *avant garde* groups would not regard an external empirical evaluation as valid or even possible within their particular value system. Most research on the outcomes of encounter groups has involved sensi-tivity training or T-groups, focusing on self- and interpersonal awareness. Gibb (1971) has summarized the results of several research studies that have attempted to evaluate this kind of human relations training. He has organized his report into five kinds of out-comes, each of which is a frequently stated aim or objective of such a group.

1. *Sensitivity.* Encounter groups are often aimed at producing greater sensitivity to oneself, to the feelings and perceptions of other people, and to one's interpersonal

environment in general. Of the seventeen studies surveyed by Gibb, fourteen reported significant increases in sensitivity as a function of encounter group participation, while three reported no changes. Despite some faults, these studies indicated that changes in sensitivity to the general interpersonal environment, especially to group processes, did occur. Increased sensitivity to others or to oneself was less apparent.

2. *Managing feelings.* The awareness and acceptance of one's feelings is usually seen by encounter group workers as leading to a more satisfactory management of these feelings, with lessened discrepancy between feelings and behavior. Gibb cites a number of studies that do tend to demonstrate this change as a result of group experience, but he cautions once again that weaknesses in the design of the research procedures make this conclusion a tentative one.

3. *Managing motivations.* The encounter group literature often lists self-actualization, awareness of one's motives and the ability to communicate them to others, and greater energy level as potential outcomes of group participation. Gibb's review concludes that "there is evidence that participants in human relations training appear to be somewhat more self determining" (p. 846), but emphasizes the clear need for further research data.

4. *Functional attitudes toward self.* Other characteristics that have been suggested as consequences of sensitivity training are self-acceptance, higher self-esteem, and greater congruence between actual-self and ideal-self concepts. Gibb cites a number of studies that support these views and show further that the positive changes in self-acceptance are responsible for bringing about other attitudinal and behavioral changes. Rubin (1967), for example, found that the increased self-acceptance that occurred as the result of a T-group experience led to lowered ethnic prejudice.

5. *Interdependent behavior.* Further qualities that are said to result from group participation are interpersonal competence, being a good team member, increased commitment to democratic ideals, and greater interdependence. A number of studies cited by Gibb give strong support to these views.

Gibb's review concludes by stating that "the evidence is strong that intensive group experiences have therapeutic effects," although most of these human relations training programs are too short to produce really enduring effects. He also notes that training programs aimed at making changes in already existing organizations and institutions seem to be more effective than those that have worked with groups of strangers. We will return to this point later.

Gibb's overall positive conclusions should not be surprising when one considers the nature of a typical sensitivity training experience. The group leader exerts a profound influence on the behavior of the participants, influence that is mediated through two major processes of learning: modeling and reinforcement. As in the case of psychotherapy, the T-group leader is seen as a model of personal adjustment, as someone who has "made it." Even when leaders play low-keyed, passive roles, their ability to remain non-anxious, comfortable, and comforting while others become confused and unhappy serves as a model for optimal behavior under stressful conditions. Group leaders tend to be rather matter-of-fact in their approach to their own behavior and "hang-ups," a quality that facilitates the involvement of other participants in the group.

T-group leaders tend to reinforce certain behaviors among group members; in particular, experimentation with new interpersonal responses. Conversely, they usually discourage group members from reacting negatively to such behavior on the part of others. Thus, they encourage openness and the learning of new behaviors within an environment that is relatively free of threat. They reinforce participants for meeting this norm, and also reinforce them for reinforcing the experimental behaviors of other participants. In this manner, the T-group provides a vehicle for new social learning and interpersonal experimentation that is relatively unique in our society. Many group leaders also attempt to provide positive reinforcement for skills which people use rarely because of restrictive social attitudes. Thus, the leader may both model and reinforce nonverbal communication or increased physical and psychological closeness. The actions of the leader in making these behaviors legitimate are an important example of the way in which the leader affects the behavior of the group members.

Perhaps the most comprehensive study of encounter groups has been that of Lieberman, Yalom, and Miles (1973). These researchers studied seventeen different groups of university undergraduates, each of which had a different leader (including two leaderless groups). They compared the outcomes of these groups, which included almost all the varieties discussed above, both immediately after the conclusion of the group experience and six or eight months later. A series of thirty-three different measures, including ratings by self, leaders, observers, and others, showed that the 206 participants made important and stable changes in self-concept and in their values and attitudes when compared to a matched control group of nonparticipants. The participants showed greater congruence between their ideal-self and actual-self concepts, and perceived themselves as more lenient and more oriented toward change and growth. Changes in greater interpersonal adequacy were somewhat less stable, and all changes were less apparent at reevaluation six months later.

Equally important was the evaluation of the psychological hazards that are often felt to be involved in encounter groups. Lieberman and his colleagues found that sixteen of the 206 participants (7.6 percent) suffered significant psychological injury that could be attributed directly to participation in the encounter group experience. Included were persons who had been made more uncomfortable, or whose behavior was now more maladaptive, and in whom this negative change appeared to be relatively enduring. The casualties included several psychotic episodes, the development of intense feelings of unworthiness, and the disruption of the participant's academic and social life. Of special interest is their finding that these casualties occurred primarily in groups where the leader used highly aggressive stimulation techniques, focused attention upon individuals rather than upon group process, used direct confrontation, and was characterized as highly charismatic. It should be emphasized that all of these leaders were well qualified professionals who were experienced in this role, and that all sessions were monitored by teams of observers. Thus, it is likely that with less qualified leaders or in settings that are less public, the number of casualties might run even higher. While encounter groups apparently do produce positive change in a substantial proportion of the participants, this appears to be accomplished at some risk to other participants. Clearly, caution should be used in deciding to enter into such an experience. Persons with a prior history of psychological disturbance appear to be especially vulnerable in encounter groups, and the risk is intensified when the groups involve charismatic leaders and direct confrontations. These findings of Lieberman and his colleagues have been supported more recently by the work of Hartley, Roback, and Abramowitz (1976).

Organizational Development

Organizational development (OD) refers to the group training of intact organizational units. As we noted above, Gibb (1971) has concluded that human relations training programs aimed at already existing organizations tend to be more effective than programs that are aimed at groups of strangers. Programs usually focus on the development of procedures that enhance group problem solving within the organization, and attempt to promote organizational growth in general (Beckhard and Harris, 1977). In other words, OD attempts to apply many of the group encounter approaches discussed above to intact organizations in order to help these organizations operate more effectively.

All of us have been members of organizations, such as fraternities, sororities, church groups, businesses, and committees, which have been ineffective in getting their work done. The difficulties occurred because the members could not agree on the task of the group or the ground rules for its operation, or because there were unresolved personal issues between group members that interfered with the group's business. OD aims at the resolution of these interpersonal issues that hamper group effectiveness.

Team building, or training the organizational system in the skills of group dynamics and effective interpersonal relationships, is the core of OD as discussed here (Katz and Kahn, 1978). A variety of group dynamics procedures have been developed to help resolve a variety of common organizational problems. Thus, there are techniques to increase the level of trust and support within organizational segments, to increase the openness of the organization in facing its own problems rather than "sweeping them under the rug," to compare the formal and informal structure of the organization, and to increase personal involvement and personal satisfaction.

As an example of OD, consider what happens to most of us in organizational life. We sit through meetings and afterwards we share our reactions with a friend or colleague. "Did you notice that Sally never says anything at our meeting?" or "I'm sick and tired of how Bill tries to push us into doing things his way," or more simply, "What a waste of time!" In an OD program these issues would be identified and discussed in the group when it became apparent that they were interfering with the organizational goals. The OD specialist is usually a consultant, who observes the group in action and then intervenes by commenting on the group process. Called **process consultation** (Schein, 1969), this procedure has been used mainly with industrial and business organizations, but it is equally useful with organizations in the public sector, such as churches, civic groups, hospitals, and police forces (Goodstein, 1978).

OD programs attempt to improve organizational effectiveness on a systemic and systematic basis. The OD consultant raises difficult questions about the purpose of the organization and whether it is well enough organized to meet that purpose. Any lack of clarity about organizational goals and any failure to organize activities for meeting those goals will become obvious in the OD process. It should be apparent that many organizations cannot easily stand such close scrutiny, so that any OD effort requires a total commitment and involvement of the organization's leaders and administrators.

Our description of OD implies that organizational openness leads to organizational effectiveness. Most OD consultants believe that an open, frank discussion of problems in an organization is more likely to lead to organizational health and effectiveness than pretense that problems do not exist. Many times a crisis occurs when issues that have previously been overlooked or ignored are brought to the surface, leading to much anxiety and concern about the utility of the OD effort. The OD specialist, however, believes that these issues should be identified and resolved, and that in the process of doing so, better procedures are developed for solving problems in the future. Thus, openness is thought to lead to the development of a climate that is more supportive for coping with organizational problems.

SUMMARY

1. This chapter discusses some of the procedures that have been developed recently in an effort to enhance human adjustment. The two major approaches are the *self-directed techniques* and *group or encounter experiences.*

2. The concept of self-directed behavior change is a recent one, and it contradicts traditional views that one's important interpersonal learning is completed in the early years of life. Because these beliefs are widespread, however, there are few available opportunities for adults to engage in new learning experiences, either in formal education or in social and interpersonal skills.

3. *Social traps* are those situations in which an individual or a group gets started in some behavior that later proves to be unpleasant and perhaps dangerous. From a behavioral viewpoint, several kinds of social traps can be identified. In one, there is immediate positive reinforcement which serves to maintain the behavior, but also long-term negative consequences that are ignored until it is too late. In a second, there are aversive consequences which the individual is not aware of. A third involves "sliding" reinforcers, which gradually lose their potency. The interpersonal relationships in which social behavior is embedded also become involved in locking the individual into the social trap.

4. Five different methods are suggested for *escaping from social traps,* not all of which are feasible in every situation. First, one might reduce the delay of reinforcement, so that the aversive consequences become more immediate. A second way is to add counterreinforcers to encourage the desired behaviors or discourage undesired behaviors. A third procedure would be to eliminate the aversive quality of the long-term consequences, and a fourth is to provide reinforcement for competing responses that do not have delayed aversive characteristics. Fifth, one might rely on external resources to change the reinforcement patterns.

5. To apply the above analysis to the social trap of *overeating,* we note first that the obvious behavior to control would be amount of food intake. Eating is under the control of external stimuli, so that changing this behavior requires substantial changes in a variety of environmental cues. In addition, its consequences can be modified by some of the methods described above. For example, aversive consequences can be made immediate through the use of aversive visual imagery, a technique that most people can master with practice. Pleasant visual imagery can also be used to reinforce "not-eating" behaviors. Additionally, the help of friends and family can be used to punish undesired behavior and reward desired behavior.

6. It is important to understand the role of self-awareness in developing self-control procedures. Strong feelings often serve as internal cues that trigger maladaptive behavior, and individuals who have not accurately labeled their strong feelings, particularly negative ones, often find themselves engaging in maladaptive behaviors over which they feel no control. Such feelings can be handled adaptively by describing them verbally and expressing the related behaviors in words rather than in actions.

7. Much attention has recently been given to the use of *altered states of consciousness* for the enhancement of human adjustment. These states can be produced either chemically or behaviorally, and have also been used for therapeutic purposes, for recreation, and as an escape. The process of meditation, long practiced as an integral part of eastern religions, has recently become popular in the United States as a method of enhancing personal development. There is increasing evidence that a physiological state of low arousal, brought about by relaxation and meditation, is useful in dealing with stress-related problems.

8. *Group and encounter experiences* began in the 1940s, when it was found that the analysis of discussions among group leaders yielded valuable personal information about the leaders themselves. Such findings formed the basis for the development of encounter groups or T-groups; later, the trend moved toward a focus on individuals, and on procedures designed to enhance personal awareness. Encounter group experiences vary in the extent to which they are structured, and in the length of time the sessions last.

9. While some group experiences tend to be atheoretical in conception, others follow one of three theoretical orientations. *Transactional analysis* groups are based on Eric Berne's formulations, in which each of us has three ego states: Parent, Adult, and Child, corresponding roughly to critical, realistic, and impulsive behavior. In TA groups, the leader assists participants to understand their own behavior in these terms, hopefully leading to increased self-awareness and more adaptive life behaviors.

10. A second encounter group style is that of *gestalt therapy,* in which the participants are helped to focus on their current feelings, and considerable use is made of role-playing procedures. Here, individuals will play two or more roles corresponding to important people in their lives, while the group observes and provides feedback on the process. Alternatively, individuals might role play two different aspects of themselves. The third theoretical approach is that of *psychoanalysis;* here the focus is usually on the underlying "dynamics" and motivations, and the group interaction is less intense emotionally than in other styles.

11. How effective are the various group experience procedures in meeting their goals? Most research has involved sensitivity training groups, and the following results have been reported: individuals tend to improve in their sensitivity to group processes, rather than to other individuals or to themselves; there is some rather tentative evidence for improvement in managing personal feelings and motivations; attitudes toward the self show improvement; and at times there is a greater acceptance of others. It is important to understand the role of the leader and his or her powerful effect as a reinforcer and as a model for mature and nonanxious behavior. A recent comprehensive study of seventeen different encounter groups showed positive changes, but also showed a number of "psychological casualties," particularly from groups where the leader was charismatic and used the technique of direct confrontation.

12. *Organizational development* refers to the group training of intact organizational units, with the goal of helping them to function more effectively. Attempts are made to increase openness in facing problems, to compare the organization's formal and informal structures, and to increase personal involvement and satisfaction. Because questions are often raised about the fundamental nature of the organization, it is important that the leaders and administrators be committed to the OD process.

KEY TERMS

self-help groups

social traps

displaced aggression

altered states of consciousness

T-group

marathon

transactional analysis

gestalt therapy

role playing

organizational development

process consultation

References

Alber, A. E. Job enrichment programs seen improving employee performance, but benefits not without cost. *World of Work Report,* 1978, **3,** 8-11.

Allport, G. W. *Personality: A psychological interpretation.* New York: Holt, 1937.

Allyon, T., and N. Azrin. *The token economy.* New York: Appleton-Century-Crofts, 1968.

Anand, B. K., G. H. Chhina, and B. Singh. Some aspects of electroencephalographic studies in yogis. *Electroencephalography and Clinical Neurophysiology,* 1961, 452-456.

Aronson, E., and J. M. Carlsmith. Performance expectancy as a determinant of actual performance. *Journal of Abnormal and Social Psychology,* 1962, **65,** 178-182.

Bancke, L. Background antecedents of aggressiveness and assertiveness found in academically achieving women. Unpublished doctoral dissertation, University of Cincinnati, 1972.

Bandura, A. (ed.), *Psychological modeling: Conflicting theories.* Chicago: Aldine/Atherton, 1971.

_____. *Social learning theory.* Englewood Cliffs, N.J.: Prentice-Hall, 1977.

Bandura, A., J. E. Grusec, and F. L. Menlove. Vicarious extinction of avoidance behavior. *Journal of Personality and Social Psychology,* 1967, **5,** 16-23.

Barker, R. G., T. Dembo, and K. Lewin. Frustration and regression: An experiment with young children. *University of Iowa Studies in Child Welfare,* 1941, **18,** Whole No. 386.

Beckhard, R., and R. E. Harris. *Organizational transitions: managing complex change.* Reading, Mass.: Addison-Wesley, 1977.

Bem, S. L. The measurement of psychological androgyny. *Journal of Consulting and Clinical Psychology,* 1974, **42,** 155-162.

Benson, H. *The relaxation response.* New York: Morrow, 1975.

Beral, V., and C. R. Kay. Mortality among oral-contraceptive users. *Lancet,* October 8, 1977, 729-731.

Berne, E. *Transactional analysis in psychotherapy.* New York: Grove Press, 1961.

_____. *Games people play.* New York: Grove Press, 1964.

Bieber, I., H. J. Dain, P. R. Dince, M. G. Drellich, H. G. Grand, R. H. Gundlach, M. W. Kremer, A. H. Rifkin, C. B. Wilbur, and T. B. Bieber. *Homosexuality.* New York: Basic Books, 1962.

Blanchard, E. B., and L. H. Epstein. *A biofeedback primer.* Reading, Mass.: Addison-Wesley, 1978.

Bloom, B. L. *Community mental health: A general introduction.* Monterey, Calif.: Brooks/Cole, 1975.

Bloustein, E. J. Man's work goes from sun to sun, but woman's work is never done. *Psychology Today,* 1968, **1** (10), 38–41, 66.

Bowlby, J. *Attachment and loss.* New York: Basic Books, 1969.

Braginsky, B. M., D. D. Braginsky, and K. Ring. *Methods of madness: The mental hospital as a last resort.* New York: Holt, Rinehart and Winston, 1969.

Broverman, I. K., D. M. Broverman, F. E. Clarkson, P. S. Rosenkrantz, and S. R. Vogel. Sex-role stereotypes and clinical judgments of mental health. *Journal of Consulting and Clinical Psychology,* 1970, **34,** 1–7.

Brown, J. S. Gradients of approach and avoidance and their relation to levels of motivation. *Journal of Comparative and Physiological Psychology,* 1948, **41,** 450–465.

———. *The motivation of behavior.* New York: McGraw-Hill, 1961.

Brown, R. *Social psychology.* New York: Free Press, 1965.

———. Schizophrenia, language, and reality. *American Psychologist,* 1973, **28,** 395–403.

Bugental, J. F. T. *Psychotherapy and process: The fundamentals of an existential-humanistic approach.* Reading, Mass.: Addison-Wesley, 1978.

Burchard, J. D., and P. T. Harig. Behavior modification and juvenile delinquency. In H. Leitenberg (ed.), *Handbook of behavior modification and behavior therapy.* Englewood Cliffs, N.J.: Prentice-Hall, 1976, pp. 405–452.

Buss, A. H., and R. Plomin. *A temperament theory of personality development.* New York: Wiley, 1975.

Calhoun, J. F., J. R. Acocella, and L. D. Goodstein. *Abnormal psychology: Current perspectives.* Second Edition. New York: CRM/Random House, 1977.

Campbell, D. B. *Manual for the Strong-Campbell Interest Inventory.* Stanford, Calif.: Stanford University Press, 1974.

Campbell, D., R. E. Sanderson, and S. G. Laverty. Characteristics of a conditioned emotional response in human subjects during extinction trials following a single traumatic conditioning trial. *Journal of Abnormal and Social Psychology,* 1964, **68,** 627–639.

Cartwright, R. D. *A primer on sleep and dreaming.* Reading, Mass.: Addison-Wesley, 1978.

Cattell, R. B. *Description and measurement of personality.* New York: World Book Co., 1946.

———. Personality and mood by questionnaire. San Francisco: Jossey-Bass, 1973.

Chalfant, J. C., and M. A. Scheffelin. *Central processing dysfunctions in children: A review of research.* Bethesda, Md.: U.S. Department of Health, Education, and Welfare, 1969. (NINDS Monograph 9).

Cialdini, R. B., R. J. Borden, A. Thorne, M. R. Walker, S. Freeman, and L. R. Sloan. Basking in reflected glory: Three (football) field studies. *Journal of Personality and Social Psychology,* 1976, **34.** 366–375.

Clausen, J. A. Differential physical and sexual maturation. In S. E. Dragastin and G. H. Elder (eds.), *Adolescence in the life cycle: Psychological change and social context.* New York: Halsted, 1975.

Clopton, W. Personality and career change. *Industrial Gerontology,* 1973, **5,** 9-17.

Coch, L., and J. R. P. French, Jr. Overcoming resistance to change. *Human Relations,* 1948, **1,** 512-533.

Cochran, W. G., F. Mosteller, and J. W. Tukey. Statistical problems of the Kinsey report. *Journal of the American Statistical Association,* 1953, **48,** 673-716.

Colby, K. M. *A primer for psychotherapists.* New York: Ronald, 1951.

Coleman, J. R. *Psychology and effective behavior.* Glenview, Ill.: Scott, Foresman, 1969.

Coleman, J. S. *Youth: Transition to adulthood* (Report of the panel on Youth of the President's Science Advisory Committee.) Chicago: University of Chicago Press, 1974.

Cortés, J. B., and F. M. Gatti. Physique and propensity. *Psychology Today,* 1970, **4,** 42-44, 82-84.

Cowles, J. T. Food-tokens as incentives for learning by chimpanzees. *Psychological Monographs,* 1937, **14,** No. 5 (Whole No. 71).

Crichton, R. *The great imposter.* New York: Random House, 1959.

Davitz, J. R. The effects of previous training on postfrustration behavior. *Journal of Abnormal and Social Psychology,* 1952, **47,** 309-315.

Dennis, W. *The Hopi child.* New York: Appleton-Century-Crofts, 1940.

Diamond, S. *Personality and temperament.* New York: Harper & Row, 1957.

Dollard, J., L. W. Doob, N. E. Miller, O. H. Mowrer, and R. R. Sears. *Frustration and aggression.* New Haven: Yale University Press, 1939.

Dollard, J., and N. E. Miller. *Personality and psychotherapy.* New York: McGraw-Hill, 1950.

Duffy, E. *Activation and behavior.* New York: Wiley, 1962.

D'Zurilla, T. Recall efficiency and mediating cognitive events in "experimental repression." *Journal of Personality and Social Psychology,* 1965, **1,** 253-257.

Elder, G. H., Jr. *Children of the great depression.* Chicago: University of Chicago Press, 1974.

Epstein, C. F. Encountering the male establishment: Sex-status limits on women's careers in the professions. *American Journal of Sociology,* 1970, **75,** 965-982.

Erikson, E. H. *Childhood and society.* Second Edition. New York: Norton, 1963.

Eysenck, H. J. *Dimensions of personality.* London: Routledge and Kegan Paul, 1947.

_____. The effects of psychotherapy: An evaluation. *Journal of Consulting Psychology,* 1952, **16,** 319-324.

_____. *The Structure of personality.* Third Edition. London: Methuen, 1970.

Ezriel, H. A psychoanalytic approach to group treatment. *British Journal of Medical Psychology,* 1950, **23,** 59-74.

Fairweather, G. W. *Social psychology in treating mental illness: An experimental approach.* New York: Wiley, 1964.

Farber, I. E. The things people say to themselves. *American Psychologist,* 1963, **18,** 185-197.

_____. Sane and insane: Constructions and misconstructions. *Journal of Abnormal Psychology,* 1975, **84,** 589-620.

Feldman, H., and M. Rogodd. Medical briefs. *Today's Health,* 1969, **47** (1), 17.

Fenichel, O. *The psychoanalytic theory of neurosis.* New York: Norton, 1945.

Fisher, S. *The female orgasm: Psychology, physiology, fantasy.* New York: Basic Books, 1973.

Ford, C. S., and F. A. Beach, *Patterns of sexual behavior.* New York: Harper, 1951.

Frank, G. H. The role of the family in psychopathology. *Psychological Bulletin,* 1965, **65,** 191-205.

Freud, S. Introductory lectures on psychoanalysis. In *The standard edition of the complete psychological works of Sigmund Freud,* Vols. 15 and 16. London: Hogarth, 1957. (First German edition, 1917).

_____. Inhibitions, symptoms, and anxiety. In *The standard edition of the complete psychological works of Sigmund Freud,* Vol. 20. London: Hogarth, 1959. (First German edition, 1926).

Gibb, J. R. The effects of human relations training. In A. E. Bergin and S. L. Garfield (eds.), *Handbook of psychotherapy and behavior change: An empirical analysis.* New York: Wiley, 1971.

Ginzberg, E., S. W. Ginzberg, S. Axelrod, and J. L. Herma. *Occupational choice: An approach to a general theory.* New York: Columbia University Press, 1951.

Goldiamond, I. A diary of self-modification. *Psychology Today,* 1973, **7** (6), 95-102.

Goldstein, S. B., and R. I. Lanyon. Parent therapists in the language training of an autistic child. *Journal of Speech and Hearing Disorders,* 1971, **36,** 552-560.

Goodstein, L. D. *Consulting with human service systems.* Reading, Mass.: Addison-Wesley, 1978.

Gough, H. G. *California psychological inventory: manual.* Palo Alto: Consulting Psychologists Press, 1957 (Revised 1964).

Gough, H. G., H. McCloskey, and P. E. Meehl. A personality scale for dominance. *Journal of Abnormal and Social Psychology,* 1951, **46,** 360-366.

Gough, H. G., and D. R. Peterson. The identification and measurement of predispositional factors in crime and delinquency. *Journal of Consulting Psychology,* 1952, **16,** 207-212.

Gray, J. *The psychology of fear and stress.* New York: McGraw-Hill, 1971.

Grinker, R. R., and J. P. Spiegel. *Men under stress.* New York: Blakiston, 1945.

Guilford, J. P. *Personality.* New York: McGraw-Hill, 1959.

Hall, C. S., and G. Lindzey. *Theories of personality.* Second Edition. New York: Wiley, 1970.

Hall, G. S. A synthetic genetic study of fear. *American Journal of Psychology,* 1914, **25,** 149-200.

Halpern, J. Projection: A test of the psychoanalytic hypothesis. *Journal of Abnormal Psychology,* 1977, **86,** 536-541.

Hampson, J. J. Determinants of psychosexual orientation. In F. A. Beach (ed.), *Sex and behavior.* New York: Wiley, 1965.

Hare, R. D. *Psychopathy: Theory and research.* New York: Wiley, 1970.

Harlow, H. F., and M. K. Harlow. The effects of rearing conditions on behavior. In J. Money (ed.), *Sex research: New developments.* New York: Holt, Rinehart and Winston, 1965.

_____. Learning to love. *American Scientist,* 1966, **54,** 244-272.

Harlow, H. F., and R. R. Zimmerman. Affectional responses in the infant monkey. *Science,* 1959, **130,** 421-432.

Hartley, D., H. B. Roback, and S. I. Abramowitz. Deterioration effects in encounter groups. *American Psychologist,* 1976, **31,** 247-255.

Hathaway, S. R., and J. C. McKinley. *Minnesota Multiphasic Personality Inventory: Manual.* New York: Psychological Corporation, 1951.

Heidegger, M. *Being and time.* New York: Harper & Row, 1963.

Heider, F. *The psychology of interpersonal relations.* New York: Wiley, 1958.

Henry, W. E. *The analysis of fantasy.* New York: Wiley, 1956.

Herrnstein, R. I.Q. *Atlantic,* 1971, **288** (3), 44-64.

Herzberg, F. Motivation, morale, and money. *Psychology Today,* 1968, **1** (10), 133-141.

Heston, L. L. The genetics of schizophrenia and schizoid diseases. *Science,* 1970, **167,** 249-256.

Hilgard, E. R. *Hypnotic susceptibility.* New York: Harcourt, Brace & World, 1965.

Hilgard, E. R., and R. C. Atkinson. *Introduction to psychology.* Fourth Edition. New York: Harcourt, Brace & World, 1967.

Hite, S. *The Hite report.* New York: Dell, 1976.

Hobbs, N. Sources of gain in psychotherapy. *American Psychologist,* 1962, **17,** 741-747.

Holland, J. L. *Making vocational choices: A theory of careers.* Englewood, N.J.: Prentice-Hall, 1973.

Holzman, P. S. *Psychoanalysis and psychopathology.* New York: McGraw-Hill, 1970.

Hooker, E. An empirical study of some relations between sexual patterns and gender identity in male homosexuals. In J. Money (ed.), *Sex research: New developments.* New York: Holt, Rinehart and Winston, 1965.

Horney, K. *The neurotic personality of our time.* New York: Norton, 1937.

_____. *Neurosis and human growth.* New York: Norton, 1950.

Howard, J. *Please touch: A guided tour through the human potential movement.* New York: McGraw-Hill, 1970.

Hunt, M. *Sexual behavior in the 1970's.* New York: Dell, 1974.

Jacobson, E. *Progressive relaxation.* Chicago: University of Chicago Press, 1938.

James, M., and D. Jongeward. *Born to win: Transactional analysis with Gestalt experiments.* Reading, Mass.: Addison-Wesley, 1971.

Janis, I. When fear is healthy. *Psychology Today,* 1968, **1** (11), 46-49, 60-61.

Jarvik, L. F., V. Klodin, and S. S. Matsuyama. Human aggression and the extra XYY chromosome: Fact or fantasy? *American Psychologist,* 1973, **28,** 674-682.

Jensen, A. R., *et al. Environment, heredity and intelligence.* Cambridge, Mass.: Harvard Educational Review, Reprint Series No. 2, 1969.

Jensen, G. D. Human sexual behavior in primate perspective. In J. Zubin and J. Money (eds.), *Contemporary sexual behavior: Critical issues in the 1970's.* Baltimore: Johns Hopkins University Press, 1973.

Jessor, S. L., and R. Jessor. Transition from virginity to nonvirginity among youth: A social-psychological study over time. *Developmental Psychology,* 1975, **11,** 473-484.

Joint Commission on Mental Illness and Health. *Action for mental health.* New York: Basic Books, 1961.

Jones, E. E., and R. E. Nisbett. The actor and the observer: Divergent perceptions of the causes of behavior. In E. E. Jones, D. E. Kanouse, H. H. Kelley, R. E. Nisbett, S. Valins, and B. Weiner (eds.), *Attribution: Perceiving the causes of behavior.* Morristown, N. J.: General Learning Press, 1972.

Jones, M. C. A laboratory study of fear: The case of Peter. *Pedagogical Seminary,* 1924, **31,** 308-315.

Jones, R. M. *Fantasy and feelings in education: A reply to Bruner.* New York: New York University Press, 1968.

Kagan, J. The acquisition and significance of sex typing and sex-role identity. In M. Hoffman and L. Hoffman (eds.), *Review of child development research.* New York: Russell Sage, 1964.

_____. Discussion on D. A. Hamburg, Sexual differentiation and evolution of aggressive behavior in primates. In N. Kretchmer and D. N. Walcher (eds.), *Environmental influences on genetic expression biological aspects of sexual differentiation.* Washington, D.C.: U.S. Government Printing Office, 1969.

_____. *Personality development.* New York: Harcourt, Brace Jovanovich, 1971.

Kahn, R. L. The work module: A tonic for lunch pail lassitude. *Psychology Today,* 1973, **6** (2), 36-39, 94-95.

Kamiya, J. Operant control of the EEG alpha rhythm and some of its reported effects on consciousness. In C. T. Tart (ed.), *Altered states of consciousness.* Second Edition. New York: Doubleday, 1972, 519-529.

Kanfer, F. H. Self-management methods. In F. H. Kanfer and A. P. Goldstein (eds.), *Helping people change.* New York: Pergamon, 1975.

Kanfer, F. H., and J. S. Phillips. *Learning foundations of behavior therapy.* New York: Wiley, 1970.

Katchadourian, H. A., and D. T. Lunde. *Fundamentals of human sexuality.* Second Edition. New York: Holt, Rinehart and Winston, 1975.

Katz, D., and R. L. Kahn. *The social psychology of organizations.* Second Edition. New York: Wiley, 1978.

Kazdin, A. E. *The token economy.* New York: Plenum, 1977.

Kelley, H. H. Attribution in social interaction. In E. E. Jones, D. E. Kanouse, H. H. Kelley, R. E. Nisbett, S. Valins, and B. Weiner (eds.), *Attribution: Perceiving the causes of behavior.* Morristown, N.J.: General Learning Press, 1972.

Kierkegaard, S. *The concept of dread.* Princeton, N.J.: Princeton University Press, 1944.

Kinsey, A. C., W. B. Pomeroy, and C. E. Martin. *Sexual behavior in the human male.* Philadelphia: Saunders, 1948.

Kinsey, A. C., W. B. Pomeroy, C. E. Martin, and P. H. Gebhart. *Sexual behavior in the human female.* Philadelphia: Saunders, 1953.

Klopfer, B., and H. H. Davidson. *The Rorschach technique: An introductory manual.* New York: Harcourt, Brace & World, 1962.

Krasner, L. Behavior modification: Ethical issues and future trends. In H. Leitenberg (ed)., *Handbook of behavior modification and behavior therapy.* Englewood Cliffs, N.J.: Prentice-Hall, 1976, pp. 627-649.

Kroeber, T. C. The coping functions of the ego mechanisms. In R. W. White (ed.), *The study of lives.* New York: Atherton Press, 1963.

Kuhn, M. H. Self attitudes by age, sex, and professional training. *Sociological Quarterly,* 1960, **9,** 39-55.

Lachar, D. *The MMPI: Clinical assessment and automated interpretation.* Los Angeles: Western Psychological Services, 1974.

Laing, R. D. *The politics of experience.* New York: Pantheon, 1967.

Lang, P. J., B. G. Melamed, and J. A. Hart. Psychophysiological analysis of fear modification using an automated desensitization procedure. *Journal of Abnormal Psychology,* 1970, **76,** 220-234.

Lanyon, R. I. *Psychological Screening Inventory: Manual.* Goshen, N.Y.: Research Psychologists Press, 1973.

Lanyon, R. I., and L. D. Goodstein. *Personality assessment.* New York: Wiley, 1971.

Lazarus, R. S. *Psychological stress and the coping process.* New York: McGraw-Hill, 1966.

Lefkowitz, M. M., L. D. Eron, L. O. Walder, and L. R. Huesmann. *Growing up to be violent.* New York: Pergamon, 1977.

Levin, R. J., and A. Levin. Sexual pleasure and the surprising preferences of 100,000 women. *Redbook,* 1975, **144,** 51-58.

Levinson, D. J. *The seasons of a man's life.* New York: Knopf, 1978.

Levinson, D. J., C. M. Darrow, E. B. Klein, M. H. Levinson, and B. McKee. Periods in the adult development of men: Ages 18 to 45. In A. G. Sargent (ed.), *Beyond sex roles.* St. Paul, Minn.: West, 1977.

Levitt, E. E., H. Persky, J. P. Brady, J. A. Fitzgerald, and A. deBreeijen. Evidence for hypnotically induced amnesia as an analog of repression. *Journal of Nervous and Mental Disease,* 1961, **133,** 218-221.

Levy, L. H. Self-help groups: Types and psychological processes. *Journal of Applied Behavioral Science,* 1976, **12,** 310-322.

Lewin, K. *A dynamic theory of personality.* New York: McGraw-Hill, 1935.

Lieberman, M. A., I. D. Yalom, and M. B. Miles. *Encounter groups: First facts.* New York: Basic Books, 1973.

Linton, R. *The study of culture.* New York: Appleton-Century-Crofts, 1945.

Lorenz, K. *On aggression.* New York: Harcourt, Brace & World, 1966.

Losco, J., and S. Epstein. Relative steepness of approach and avoidance gradients as a function of magnitude and valence of incentive. *Journal of Abnormal Psychology,* 1977, **86,** 360-368.

Lovibond, S. H., and G. Caddy. Discriminated aversive control in the moderation of alcoholics' drinking behavior. *Behavior Therapy,* 1970, **1,** 437-444.

Lykken, D. T. Psychology and the lie detector industry. *American Psychologist,* 1974, **29,** 725-739.

_____. Where science fears to tread. *Contemporary Psychology,* 1978, **23,** 81-82.

Maddi, S. The existential neurosis. *Journal of Abnormal Psychology,* 1967, **72,** 311-325.

Mahoney, M. J., and K. Mahoney. *Permanent weight control: A total solution to the dieter's dilemma.* New York: Norton, 1976.

Malmo, R. B. Activation: A neuropsychological dimension. *Psychological Review,* 1959, **66,** 367-386.

Maslow, A. H. *Motivation and personality.* New York: Harper & Row, 1954.

Masserman, J. H. *Principles of dynamic psychiatry.* Second Edition. Philadelphia: Saunders, 1961.

Masters, W. H., and V. E. Johnson. *Human sexual response.* Boston: Little, Brown, 1966.

_____. *Human sexual inadequacy.* Boston: Little, Brown, 1970.

May, R. *The meaning of anxiety.* New York: Ronald, 1950.

_____. *Existential anxiety.* Second Edition. New York: Random House, 1969.

May, R., E. Angel, and H. F. Ellenberger, (eds.). *Existence.* New York: Basic Books, 1958.

McGregor, D. *The human side of enterprise.* New York: McGraw-Hill, 1960.

McNeill, D. The development of language. In P. H. Mussen (ed.), *Carmichael's manual of child psychology.* Third Edition. New York: Wiley, 1970.

Mead, M. *Male and female.* New York: Morrow, 1949.

Meehl, P. E. Schizotaxia, schizotypy, schizophrenia. *American Psychologist,* 1962, **17,** 827-838.

Meichenbaum, D. *Cognitive-behavior modification.* New York: Plenum, 1977.

Michael, R. P., and J. Herbert. Menstrual cycle influence grooming behavior and sexual activity in rhesus monkeys. *Science,* 1963, **140,** 500-501.

Miller, N. E. Learning of visceral and glandular responses. *Science,* 1969, **163,** 434-445.

Miller, N. E., and A. Banuazzi. Instrumental learning by curarized rats of a specific visceral response, intestinal or cardiac. *Journal of Comparative and Physiological Psychology,* 1968, **65,** 1-7.

Miller, N. E., and B. R. Dworkin. Visceral learning: Recent difficulties with curarized rats and significant problems for human research. In D. A. Obrist et al. (eds.), *Cardiovascular physiology.* Chicago: Aldine, 1974, pp. 312-331.

Mischel, W. Theory and research on the antecedents of self-imposed delay of reward. In B. A. Maher (ed.), *Progress in experimental personality research,* vol. 3. New York: Academic Press, 1966.

_____. *Personality and assessment*. New York: Wiley, 1968.

_____. *Introduction to personality*. Second Edition. New York: Holt, Rinehart and Winston, 1976.

Mitchell, G. D. Paternalistic behavior in primates. *Psychological Bulletin,* 1969, **71,** 399-417.

Money, J., and A. A. Ehrhardt. *Man and woman; boy and girl.* Baltimore: Johns Hopkins University Press, 1972.

Moreno, J. L. *Who shall survive?* New York: Beacon House, 1953.

Morse, N. C., and R. S. Weiss. The function and meaning of work and the job. In S. Nosow and W. H. Form (eds.), *Man, work, and society.* New York: Basic Books, 1962.

Morse, S. J., and R. I. Watson, Jr. (eds.), *Psychotherapies: A comparative casebook.* New York: Holt, Rinehart and Winston, 1977.

Mowrer, O. H. On the psychology of "talking birds"—a contribution to language and personality theory. In O. H. Mowrer (ed.), *Learning theory and personality dynamics.* New York: Ronald Press, 1950.

Munsinger, H. Reply to Kamin. *Psychological Bulletin,* 1978, **85,** 202-206.

Murdock, G. P. Comparative data on the division of labor by sex. *Social Forces,* 1937, **15,** 551-553.

Murphy, G. *Personality: A biosocial approach to origins and structures.* New York: Basic Books, 1966.

Murray, H. A. *Explorations in personality.* New York: Oxford, 1938.

_____. *Thematic Apperception Test: Manual.* Cambridge, Mass.: Harvard University Press, 1943.

Murstein, B. I. *Who will marry whom?* New York: Springer, 1976.

Mussen, P. H. Long-term consequents of masculinity of interests in adolescence. *Journal of Consulting Psychology,* 1962, **26,** 435-440.

Mussen, P. H., J. J. Conger, and J. Kagan. *Child development and personality.* Fourth Edition. New York: Harper & Row, 1974.

Mussen, P., and N. Eisenberg-Berg. *Roots of caring, sharing, and helping.* San Franscisco: Freeman, 1977.

O'Leary, K. D., and G. T. Wilson. *Behavior therapy: Application and outcome.* Englewood Cliffs, N.J.: Prentice-Hall, 1975.

O'Neill, N., and G. O'Neill. *Open marriage: A new life style for couples.* New York: Evans, 1972.

Packard, V. *The sexual wilderness.* New York: McKay, 1968.

Patterson, C. H. *Theories of counseling and psychotherapy.* New York: Harper & Row, 1973.

Perls, F. S. *Gestalt therapy verbatim.* Lafayette, Calif.: Real People Press, 1969.

Pietrofesa, J., A. Hoffman, H. H. Splete, and D. V. Pinto. *Counseling: Theory, research, and practice.* Chicago: Rand McNally, 1978.

Pietropinto, A., and J. Simenauer. *Beyond the male myth.* New York: Quadrangle, 1977.

Platt, J. Social traps. *American Psychologist,* 1973, **28,** 641-651.

Polster, E., and M. Polster. *Gestalt therapy integrated.* New York: Brunner Mazel, 1973.

Rachman, S. Sexual fetishism: An experimental analogue. *Psychological Record,* 1966, **16,** 293-306.

Rees, J. P. Back to moral treatment and community care. *Journal of Mental Science,* 1957, **103,** 303-313.

Ringer, R. J. *Looking out for number one.* New York: Funk & Wagnalls, 1977.

Rogers, C. R. *Counseling and psychotherapy.* Boston: Houghton-Mifflin, 1942.

_____. *Client-centered therapy.* Boston: Houghton-Mifflin, 1951.

_____. The necessary and sufficient conditions of therapeutic personality change. *Journal of Consulting Psychology,* 1957, **21,** 95-103.

_____. *Carl Rogers on personal power.* New York: Delacorte, 1977.

Rorschach, H. *Psychodiagnostics.* Bern, Switzerland: Huber, 1942. (New York: Grune & Stratton, 1951).

Rosenhan, D. L. On being sane in insane places. *Science,* 1973, **179,** 250-258.

Rosenthal, D. *Genetics of psychopathology.* New York: McGraw-Hill, 1971.

Rossi, A. Equality between the sexes: An immodest proposal. *Daedalus,* 1964, **93** (2), 607-652.

Rossman, J. E., and D. P. Campbell. Why college trained mothers work. *Personnel and Guidance Journal,* 1965, **43,** 986-992.

Sarason, S. B. *Work, aging, and social change.* New York: Free Press, 1977.

Scarr, S. Genetic effects on human behavior: Recent family studies. Master Lecture, annual meeting of the American Psychological Association, San Francisco, August 1977.

Schachter, S. The interaction of cognitive and physiological determinants on emotional states. In C. D. Spielberger (ed.), *Anxiety and behavior.* New York: Academic Press, 1966.

_____. Eat, eat. *Psychology Today,* 1971, **5** (4), 45-47, 78-80.

Schein, E. L. *Process consultation: Its role in organizational development.* Reading, Mass.: Addison-Wesley, 1969.

Schofield, W. *Psychotherapy: The purchase of friendship.* Englewood Cliffs, N.J.: Prentice-Hall, 1964.

Seashore, S. E., and D. G. Bowers. Durability of organizational change. *American Psychologist,* 1969, **25,** 227-233.

Seligman, M. E. P. *Helplessness.* San Francisco: Freeman, 1975.

Shaffer, J. W., C. W. Schmidt, H. I. Zlotowitz, and R. S. Fisher. Biorhythms and highway crashes. *Archives of general Psychiatry,* 1978, **35,** 41-46.

Shaver, K. *An introduction to attribution processes.* Cambridge, Mass.: Winthrop, 1975.

Sheehy, G. *Passages: Predictable crises of adult life.* New York: Dutton, 1976.

Sheldon, W. H. *The varieties of temperament: A psychology of constitutional differences.* New York: Harper, 1942.

_____. *Atlas of men: A guide for somatotyping the adult male at all ages.* New York: Harper, 1954.

Skinner, B. F. *Science and human behavior.* New York: Macmillan, 1953.

_____. *About behaviorism.* New York: Knopf, 1974.

Sorensen, R. C. *Adolescent sexuality in contemporary America: Personal values and sexual behavior, ages thirteen to nineteen.* New York: World Press, 1973.

Spence, J. T., and R. L. Helmreich. *Masculinity and femininity: Their psychological dimensions, correlates, and antecedents.* Austin: University of Texas Press, 1978.

Spielberger, C. D. Theory and research on anxiety. In C. D. Spielberger (ed.), *Anxiety and behavior.* New York: Academic Press, 1966.

_____. *Anxiety: Current trends in theory and research.* New York: Academic Press, 1971.

Spitz, R. A. Hospitalism: An inquiry into the genesis of psychiatric conditions in early childhood. In A. Freud et al. (eds.), *The psychoanalytic study of the child,* Vol. I. New York: International Universities Press, 1945.

Stanton, A. H., and M. S. Schwartz. *The mental hospital: A study of institutional participation in psychiatric illness and treatment.* New York: Basic Books, 1954.

Strong, E. K. Permanence of interest scores over 22 years. *Journal of Applied Psychology,* 1951, **35,** 89-91.

Szasz, T. S. *The myth of mental illness.* New York: Harper & Row, 1961.

Tart, C. T. *States of consciousness.* New York: Dutton, 1975.

Taylor, F. W. *The principles of scientific management.* New York: Harper, 1923.

Tharp, R., and R. Wetzel. *Behavior modification in the natural environment.* New York: Academic Press, 1969.

Thommen, G. S. *Is this your day?* New York: Crown, 1973.

Trevor-Roper, H. R. *European witch craze of the sixteenth and seventeenth centuries and other essays.* New York: Harper & Row, 1969.

Truax, C. B., and R. R. Carkhuff. *Toward effective counseling and psychotherapy: Training and practice.* Chicago: Aldine, 1967.

Udry, J. R. *The social context of marriage.* Philadelphia: Lippincott, 1966.

Vaillant, George E. *Adaptation to life.* Boston: Little, Brown, 1977.

Van Lawick-Goodall, J. The behavior of free living chimpanzees in the Gombe Stream Reserve. *Animal Behavior Monographs,* 1968, **1,** 165-301.

Vernon, P. E. *Personality assessment.* London: Methuen, 1964.

Washburn, S. L. Tools and human evolution. *Scientific American,* 1960, **203,** 63-75.

Watson, J. B., and R. Rayner. Conditioned emotional reactions. *Journal of Experimental Psychology,* 1920, **3,** 1-14.

Weatherly, D. Self-perceived rate of physical maturation and personality in late adolescence. *Child Development,* 1964, **35,** 1197-1210.

Weinberg, M. S. The problem of midgets and dwarfs and organizational remedies: A study of the little people of America. *Journal of Health and Social Behavior,* 1968, **9,** 65-71.

White, R. W. Motivation reconsidered: The concept of competence. *Psychological Review,* 1959, **66,** 297-333.

Whiting, J. W. M., and I. L. Child. *Child training and personality*. New Haven: Yale University Press, 1953.

Wiggins, J. S., K. E. Renner, G. L. Clore, and R. J. Rose. *The psychology of personality*. Reading, Mass.: Addison-Wesley, 1971.

Winch, R. F. *Mate selection: A study of complementary needs*. New York: Harper, 1958.

————. *The modern family*. Rev. Ed. New York: Holt, Rinehart and Winston, 1963.

Wolf, S., and H. G. Wolff. *Human gastric functions*. Second Edition. New York: Oxford University Press, 1947.

Wolfe, J. B. Effectiveness of token-rewards for chimpanzees. *Comparative Psychology Monographs*, 1936, **12,** No. 5 (Whole No. 60).

Wolpe, J. *Psychotherapy by reciprocal inhibition*. Stanford: Stanford University Press, 1958.

Zeller, A. An experimental analogue of repression. I. Historical summary. *Psychological Bulletin*, 1950 (a), **47,** 39–51.

————. An experimental analogue of repression. II. The effects of individual failure and success on memory measured by relearning. *Journal of Experimental Psychology*, 1950 (b), **40,** 411–422.

Zigler, E. F., and I. L. Child. *Socialization and personality development*. Reading, Mass.: Addison-Wesley, 1973.

Zubin, J., and B. Spring. Vulnerability—a new view of schizophrenia. *Journal of Abnormal Psychology*, 1977, **86,** 103–126.

Glossary

This glossary defines most of the important terms and concepts used in this book, including both technical terms and common words used in a special or restricted sense in psychology. Wherever possible, the definition is quoted directly from the text, and the meaning given is that which is used in the text. The boldface number in parentheses at the end of each definition indicates the chapter in which the word or concept first appears. For more complete definitions, other meanings, and terms not used in this book, see H. B. English and A. C. English, *A Comprehensive Dictionary of Psychological and Psychoanalytical Terms* (New York: Longmans, Green, 1958).

Abortion Induced termination of pregnancy before the fetus is capable of survival as an individual. **(8)**

Achievement tests Measures of present levels of competence, of what has been learned. **(10)**

Acquired need *See* Secondary drive. **(3)**

Acting-out Unexpected aggressive behavior which is socially forbidden and has direct negative consequences, and is usually interpreted as the "failure" of more adaptive defenses; also called externalization. **(6)**

Adjustment, psychology of The special part of psychology that attempts to understand and explain the complex interpersonal behavior that people exhibit in their daily lives. **(1)**

Adult development Changes in values, attitudes, skills, aspirations, and similar attributes throughout the life cycle, especially after adolescence. **(9)**

Age grading Role behaviors considered appropriate according to age; also the socially defined "right" age for a behavior, such as for weaning, entering school, etc. (*See also* Role.) **(3)**

Agent of socialization A person who, intentionally or unintentionally, transmits to another person the culture to which the agent belongs, principally by reinforcing those behaviors which are regarded as appropriate in that culture or by punishing those which are not. **(3)**

Aggression Vigorous activity or attack in an effort to remove a block to a desired behavior, or in response to the frustration of being blocked; sometimes an unlearned response. **(3)**

Alcoholic A person whose drinking seriously interferes with everyday living. **(7)**

Altered states of consciousness Any state of awareness not typical of normal waking experience; may be induced by lack of sleep, or by drugs, fever, meditation, hypnosis, and other techniques. **(12)**

Amnesia The loss of personal memories. **(7)**

Anal stage In psychoanalytic theory, the second stage of psychosexual development, in which gratification is obtained primarily through the expelling or retention of feces. **(3)**

Androgens Male sex hormones, produced by the testes. **(8)**

Androgynous Above average development of the adaptive characteristics of both traditional male roles and traditional female roles. **(3)**

Anticipatory responses Responses made just before reinforcement is presented. **(2)**

Anxiety An acquired or learned fear (probably learned by association); characterized by feelings of fear or apprehension, physiological changes, and impairment of thought. **(4)**

Anxiety (existential view) A normal and inescapable part of human existence which arises with the growing awareness of freedom and of the gap between what one has achieved and what is possible; the failure to recognize and confront anxiety leads to such neurotic disorders as apathy and resignation. **(4)**

Anxiety (psychoanalytic view) (1) Early view: the internal pressure experienced by an individual as a result of the repression, or barring from conscious awareness, of unacceptable libidinal impulses. (2) Later view: danger signal or symptom that unacceptable libidinal impulses are threatening to break into consciousness, thus alerting the individual to the need for greater use of repression. **(4)**

Anxiety (social-learning view) *See* Anxiety. **(4)**

Anxiety, binding of The "choice" of a convenient object that has some symbolic connection to the underlying problem, which is then used to focus or "bind" free-floating anxiety. **(4)**

Anxiety, displacement of Transfer of fear to an object that is not the real source of the anxiety, as a defensive reaction to a situation that would otherwise be even more anxiety-arousing or dangerous. **(4)**

Anxiety, free-floating A strong, generalized fear reaction; a disabling state marked by a strong sense of impending doom, overwhelming but nameless fears, and a variety of somatic upsets. **(4)**

Anxiety, state Anxiety aroused by a particular situation or stimulus; a temporary level of anxiety. (*See also* Anxiety, trait.) **(4)**

Anxiety, trait Anxiety as an enduring aspect of behavior or personality, the base line or operant level of this characteristic; a habitual level of anxiety. (*See also* Anxiety, state.) **(4)**

Approach-approach conflict A situation in which there are incompatible tendencies to approach two objects with positive valences that lie in opposite directions. **(5)**

Approach-avoidance conflict A situation in which there is simultaneous arousal of approach and avoidance tendencies by a single goal or object that has both positive and negative valences. **(5)**

Aptitude tests Measures of how well a person can perform if given the proper training; a prediction of future competence. **(10)**

Ascientific Predating the development of psychology as a science. **(10)**

Association, learning by Learning that takes place when a conditioned stimulus is paired with an unconditioned stimulus so that the response usually evoked by an unconditioned stimulus is now made to the conditioned stimulus. Also called classical conditioning and stimulus substitution, and conforming to the pattern of Pavlov's experiments. **(2)**

Attachment The predisposition of the infant to initiate reactions to the caretaker. **(3)**

Attribution theory The study of the methods used by people to attain an understanding of the behavior of self and others. **(10)**

Autonomic nervous system A division of the nervous system comprising the smooth muscles and endocrine glands and controlling unlearned internal changes during anxiety or other strong emotional responses. **(4)**

Avoidance-avoidance conflict A situation in which two objects with negative values are so arranged that escape from one would force one closer to the other. **(5)**

Behavior Actions of living organisms. Observable attempts of an organism to reduce or satisfy its needs, both physiological and psychological, as it understands those needs. **(5)**

Behavior genetics The study of the complex relationship between heredity and behavior. **(1)**

Behavioral therapies Techniques for directly changing behavior, based on learning-theory principles, including classical and instrumental (operant) conditioning and modeling. **(11)**

Behavior modification *See* Behavioral therapies. **(11)**

Biofeedback The use of artificial, or mechanical, feedback devices to monitor internal physiological changes of which one usually has little or no awareness. **(6) (7)**

Biorhythms Hypothetical cycles—physical, emotional, and mental—which some persons believe to govern one's day-to-day effectiveness. **(10)**

Birth control pill Pill taken daily by women to prevent pregnancy; very effective chemical method of contraception. **(8)**

California Psychological Inventory (CPI) A standardized questionnaire designed to assess normal personality on a number of socially important dimensions. **(10)**

Canalization The process of learning, through socialization, to satisfy a primary drive with specific satisfiers, rather than through an entire class of satisfiers; e.g., preferences for specific foods and distaste for others. **(3)**

Catharsis The discharge, directly or indirectly, of aggressive energy, thus diminishing the drive and the likelihood of further aggression; regarded as healthy for the person with the aggressive drive. **(5)**

Character disorder A group of behavioral disturbances that principally involve acts which flout societal norms and are not influenced by feelings of guilt or remorse. **(7)**

Chromosomes Tiny rodlike structures present in each cell which contain the genes, or genetic code, for each individual. In humans, each cell contains 23 pairs of chromosomes. **(1)**

Classical conditioning *See* Association, learning by. **(2)**

Client-centered psychotherapy *See* Nondirective psychotherapy. **(11)**

Clitoris A small cylindrical node of tissue in the female which becomes engorged with blood upon sexual stimulation in much the same manner as the penis. **(8)**

Coitus Sexual intercourse between two human beings. **(8)**

Coitus interruptus Withdrawal of the penis immediately before ejaculation; an extremely uncertain and ineffective method of birth control. **(8)**

Compensation The substitution of an alternative goal for an original one which was frustrated, in order to satisfy the original need; also called substitution. **(6)**

Conditioned aversive stimuli Stimuli (including thoughts) present during or immediately preceding punishment in addition to the natural or primary aversive stimulus. **(4)**

Conditioned generalized reinforcer Any conditioned or secondary reinforcer which has been paired with gratification involving more than one primary reinforcer, and has thus become generalized (Skinner, 1953). (*See also* Secondary reinforcer.) **(3)**

Conditioned response (CR) A response produced by a conditioned stimulus after learning. (*See also* Association, learning by.) **(2)**

Conditioned stimulus (CS) A stimulus that is originally ineffective but that, after pairing with an unconditioned stimulus, evokes the conditioned response. (*See also* Association, learning by.) **(2)**

Condom Rubber sheath worn over penis during intercourse; primary mechanical method of contraception; moderately effective. **(9)**

Conflict The simultaneous arousal of two or more imcompatible response tendencies in a situation where one response or the other must be made. **(5)**

Contraception Prevention of pregnancy by rhythm, mechanical, chemical, or surgical methods; birth control. **(8)**

Conversion reaction *See* Hysteria. **(6)**

Correlation The degree of relationship between two sets of scores or factors. **(1)**

Counseling The attempt to solve personal problems by short-term discussions with a professionally trained person; usually involves the uncovering of new information. **(11)**

Counter-transference Feelings that therapists develop toward their patients based upon earlier feelings toward important figures in the therapist's past. **(11)**

Cue value The distinctive elements or properties of a stimulus to which an organism in a state of drive responds. **(2)**

Defense mechanisms Habitual ways of managing adjustment problems involving anxiety, usually including some kind of self-deception; additionally, defending or protecting an individual's sense of self-worth or self-esteem. **(6)**

Defense mechanisms, coping aspects of Those aspects of the defense mechanisms which are positive or adaptive in the individual's behavior (Kroeber, 1963). **(4) (6)**

Delusions Obviously false beliefs. **(7)**

Denial The exclusion from awareness of anxiety- or conflict-arousing material; one of the most common forms of denial is repression. **(6)**

Desensitization *See* systematic desensitization.

Diaphragm Dishlike, soft rubber device inserted by woman into vagina at mouth of uterus; moderately effective mechanical means of contraception. **(8)**

Differential susceptibility to experience Behavior genetic principle which states that the same environmental experience has different effects upon people with different hereditary endowments (Wiggins *et al.*, 1971). **(1)**

Discrimination The ability to make different responses to similar but not identical stimuli. **(2)**

Disease model The view that behavioral abnormalities are simply surface signs, or symptoms, of a basic underlying "mental disease." **(7)**

Disguise mechanisms Learned ways of protecting oneself from anxiety and conflict by changing or disguising both the behavior and the thoughts or motives that underlie the behavior. **(6)**

Displaced aggression Aggression against a more convenient or safer target than the one causing the frustration. **(12)**

Displacement The process of misidentifying the source of anxiety as some object, person, or situation that is less threatening than the correct source. **(6)**

Dissociation The splitting off of feelings from behaviors. (*See also* Emotional isolation.) **(6)**

Douche Rinsing of vagina with water spray to which some spermicidal chemicals may have been added; popular but ineffective method of contraception. **(8)**

Drive The state of psychological tension which exists when an organism is undergoing physiological or psychological deprivation or is suffering some pain or injury. **(2)**

Dynamic psychotherapy The kind of psychotherapy that places strong emphasis on the relationship between patient and therapist and aims at increasing the patient's self-awareness. (*See also* Psychodynamic therapy.) **(11)**

Electroshock therapy (EST) or **electroconvulsive shock treatment (ECT)** Treatment for some psychoses, primarily depression, in which a weak electrical current is applied to the temples, causing convulsions and coma. **(11)**

Ego In psychoanalytic theory, that aspect of the personality which monitors the interactions between the individual and the environment on the basis of the reality principle and controls the impulsive demands of the Id in an effort to delay gratification until socially acceptable means are found. (*See also* Id, Superego.) **(4)**

Embryo The unborn developing human organism through the second month of pregnancy, before it has reached a distinctly recognizable form. **(1)**

Emotional arousal The physiological changes, largely mediated by the autonomic nervous system and involving increases in an individual's level of activation, which accompany anxiety. **(4)**

Emotional isolation A form of withdrawal in which the individual is physically present in the situation but blocks any emotional reaction from occurring. **(6)**

Empathize To become emotionally aware of a situation in the same way as another person experiences it. **(10)**

Empirical validity The demonstrated relationship between test scores and non-test behavior. **(10)**

Encounter groups *See* T-groups. **(12)**

Escapism The combined use of withdrawal and fantasy to avoid conflict or anxiety. **(6)**

Estrogens Female sex hormones, produced by the ovaries. **(8)**

Externalization *See* Acting-out. **(6)**

Extinction Decrease in the tendency to make a particular response when it is no longer reinforced. **(2)**

Extrinsic work reinforcements Satisfactions not directly involved in the work itself, such as salary, fringe benefits, working conditions; a basis of "Theory X" approach to management. **(9)**

Face validity The assumption that a test will predict behavior because the test items "obviously" sample that set of behaviors. **(10)**

Fallopian tubes A pair of slender ducts that connect the uterus to each ovary and through which the ova pass from the ovaries to the uterus. **(9)**

Fantasy The imaginary representation of real-life events. **(6)**

Fear *See* Anxiety. **(4)**

Fear hierarchy A graded list of situations involving progressively greater and greater anxiety. **(11)**

Fetishism Sexual arousal by an object or part of the body not normally considered erotic. **(8)**

Fetus The unborn developing human organism from the beginning of the third month of pregnancy until birth. **(1)**

Formal psychoanalysis Traditional psychotherapy that follows the traditional procedures developed by Sigmund Freud, including daily visits, lying on a couch, the use of free association, etc. **(11)**

Free-floating anxiety Upsetting or disabling episodes of anxiety in which the individual is unable to identify the cause of the anxiety or sense of impending doom. **(7)**

Frigidity Inability of the female to function sexually in a normal or adequate manner; also called orgasmic dysfunction. **(8)**

Frustration (1) the blocking of ongoing behavior; (2) the emotional reaction to this blocking. **(3) (4)**

Frustration-aggression hypothesis The contention that a frustrated organism will vigorously attempt to counter whatever is thwarting or blocking its behavior (Dollard, 1939). **(5)**

Fugue The disorder of finding oneself in a new place with no recollection of how one arrived there. **(7)**

Functional psychosis Psychotic behavioral disturbance in which there is no known associated brain or nervous system pathology. **(7)**

Generalization The phenomenon in which the same response is made to similar, but not identical, stimuli. **(2)**

Genes Individual units contained by the chromosomes, each of which transmits a specific hereditary characteristic. **(1)**

Genital stage In psychoanalytic theory, the final stage of psychosexual development in which gratification is obtained through adult heterosexual behavior. **(3)**

Gestalt therapy An approach to psychological change which emphasizes the need for the person to develop an organized wholeness in his or her life. Focuses on "staying with one's feelings" until they are understood and integrated with one's thoughts and behaviors, and makes considerable use of role-playing (Perls, 1969). **(12)**

Goal gradient The strength of the approach or avoidance tendencies at various distances from the goal object. **(5)**

Gonads The sex glands (ovaries and testes) whose functions are to produce reproductive cells (ova and sperm) and to secrete sex hormones (estrogens and androgens). **(8)**

Guilt Anxiety experienced when one disapproves of one's own behavior. (*See also* Shame.) **(4)**

Hallucinations False perceptions, such as hearing or seeing things for which no real-life stimuli exist. **(7)**

Heredity The manner in which characteristics are transmitted from one generation to the next. **(1)**

Hermaphrodite A person having the sex organs and many of the secondary sex characteristics of both males and females. **(8)**

Hierarchy A systematic list or scale representing increasing degrees of a particular characteristic. **(85)**

Higher-order conditioning Conditioning of a response to a stimulus by pairing that stimulus with another stimulus to which the response has previously been conditioned. **(2)**

Homogamy Tendency for people to choose mates from a similar background, especially from similar economic and social backgrounds. **(9)**

Hypochondriasis The exaggeration of real physical symptoms in order to serve psychological needs. **(7)**

Hysteria The development of physical symptoms which have no physiological basis but serve to interfere with the arousal of anxiety. **(6) (7)**

Id In psychoanalytic theory, that aspect of the personality which is the unlearned source of libidinal energy, the reservoir of primitive biological impulses, and which operates by the pleasure principle, demanding immediate gratification of these impulses without regard for reality or consequences. (*See also* Ego, Superego.) **(4)**

Identification The process by which an individual takes on through modeling the characteristics of a person whom he or she admires. **(2)**

Identity The sense of oneself as a unique functioning individual; an integrated self-concept. **(9)**

Impotence Inability of a male to function sexually in a normal or adequate manner. **(8)**

Instinct An unlearned biological response. **(3)**

Intellectualization Excessive theorizing, often including rationalization, to avoid the emotional reactions that would be expected in a particular situation. **(6)**

Intelligence The capacity for conceptual thinking, for judgment, for anticipating the consequences of one's actions; also a general aptitude, especially the aptitude for learning. **(1)**

Intelligence quotient (IQ) A scale unit used in reporting intelligence test scores, based on the ratio between mental age and chronological age. **(10)**

Interpretation Therapist statements in psychotherapy that attempt to point out aspects of the patient's behavior of which he or she was unaware. **(11)**

Intrauterine device (IUD) Small, irregularly shaped piece of plastic placed by physician in woman's uterus to prevent pregnancy; mechanical method with good effectiveness. **(9)**

Intrinsic work reinforcements Satisfactions yielded by work itself such as pride in accomplishment, self-esteem, utilization of worker's skills and talents; a basis of the "Theory Y" approach to management. **(9)**

Introjection In psychoanalytic theory, the incorporation of parental and societal standards into one's own value system; also called internalization, incorporation, and identification. **(3)**

Kuder Preference Record A standardized questionnaire which inquires into likes and dislikes among a wide variety of activities. **(10)**

Latency period In psychoanalytic theory, the period of development following the phallic stage, in which libidinal gratification is suppressed in the interest of learning about the surrounding world. **(3)**

Learned helplessness A condition resulting from consistent experiences in which one's attempts to influence the environment are ineffective. **(3)**

Learning The process by which behavior is established through the influence of special experience of stimulation, as a result of practice or training. **(2)**

Libido In psychoanalytic theory, the innate sexual needs or impulses which motivate behavior. **(3)**

Lie-detector tests Procedures which record a person's physiological emotional responses while answering a series of carefully prepared questions. **(10)**

Malingering The conscious, deliberate pretense of suffering symptoms in order to cope with an adjustment problem. **(7)**

Manic-depressive psychosis Mental disorder involving mood swings of such intensity that professional care is required. **(1)**

Manifest trait An observable, generalized response tendency, such as conscientiousness (Cattell, 1946). (*See also* Source trait.) **(1)**

Marathon group A T-group or sensitivity training group that meets for a long, uninterrupted period of time—12 to 24 hours or even an entire weekend **(12)**

Maslow's hierarchy A five-level scheme of primary and secondary drives (Maslow, 1954). **(3)**

Masturbation Stimulation of the genital organs, usually to orgasm, by manual or other bodily contact other than sexual intercourse. **(8)**

Maturational behaviors Those behaviors which emerge spontaneously in the developing infant as a function of biological makeup and appear to be independent of experience; for example, crawling and walking. **(2)**

Mediated generalization The use of language, or labeling, to enhance generalization. **(2)**

Meditation A technique of altering conscious states by inner contemplation. **(12)**

Mental age A type of norm. Gives the relative degree of mental development of a child by stating the age level at which the child is performing. **(10)**

Mentor relationship Aspect of adult development in which an older person takes a younger one "under his wing." **(9)**

Middle adulthood A period of life beginning in the middle forties. **(9)**

Minnesota Multiphasic Personality Inventory (MMPI) A standardized questionnaire to assess psychological disorders, based on traditional psychiatric diagnostic categories. **(10)**

Modeling, learning by The process of acquiring new or potential behaviors by observing the behavior of others. **(2)**

Moral development *See* prosocial behavior.

Myotonia An increase in muscle tension in the genital area experienced by both males and females during sexual stimulation. **(8)**

Neurasthenia The condition of feeling tired, listless, and unable to function because of the physiological changes accompanying anxiety. **(7)**

Neurosis Behavior deviations which involve disabling amounts of anxiety or which represent attempts by the individual to avoid disabling anxiety. **(7)**

Nondirective psychotherapy The psychotherapeutic procedure developed by Carl Rogers which emphasizes warmth and empathetic understanding by the therapist, and in which the patient is encouraged to solve his or her own problem with as little direction as possible by the therapist. **(11)**

Normality, biological State of being in which function follows structure; that is, in which an organism fully performs its biologically intended function. **(7)**

Normality, medical The absence of any physiological disorder that might interfere with the organism's fulfilling its intended function; special case of biological normality. **(7)**

Novice phase The first stage of adult life, involving initial exploration of the adult world. **(9)**

Obsessive-compulsive neurosis A behavior disorder marked by rumination, self-doubt, and/or repetitive compulsive acts which impede effective functioning. **(7)**

Oedipal stage In psychoanalytic theory, the stage of development in which gratification from the parent of the opposite sex is desired; concurrent with the phallic stage. (*See also* Phallic stage.) **(3)**

Open marriage An interpersonal contract between the partners which should be frequently renegotiated and which emphasizes change, growth, and flexibility of roles. **(9)**

Operant behavior Behavior which is spontaneous and appears to be voluntary or under the control of the organism; developed and shaped through reinforcement learning. **(2)**

Oral stage In psychoanalytic theory, the first stage of psychosexual development, in which gratification is obtained primarily with the lips and mouth through sucking and biting. **(3)**

Organic psychosis Behavioral disturbance resulting from known injury or disease of the brain or central nervous system. (*See also* Functional psychosis.) **(7)**

Orgasmic dysfunction Inability of the female to function sexually in a normal or adequate manner; also called frigidity. **(8)**

Organizational development (OD) A group of procedures that attempt to enhance the functioning of intact organizational units. **(12)**

Ova Female reproductive cells, produced by ovaries. **(8)**

Ovaries Female sex glands (gonads) which produce reproductive cells (ova) and secrete sex hormones (estrogens). **(8)**

Overcompensation A special form of compensation in which one attempts to cope with what is seen as an area of weakness by excelling in that very behavior. **(6)**

Partial reinforcement Presenting reward or reinforcement for only some correct responses; behavior so learned is extremely resistant to extinction. Also called intermittent reinforcement. **(2)**

Passive-aggressive behavior Behavior which expresses aggression or hostility in indirect, covert ways. **(7)**

Persistent unadaptive reaction A response that meets an individual's immediate needs to some extent, and which is reinforcing in terms of the individual's particular learning history, but which also has longer-term negative consequences. **(5)**

Personality The enduring characteristics of the person that are significant for interpersonal behavior. **(5)**

Phallic stage In psychoanalytic theory, the third stage of psychosexual development, in which gratification is obtained by manipulation of the external sex organs and in which the child forms a romantic or sexual attachment to the parent of the opposite sex. (*See also* Oedipal stage.) **(3)**

Pleasure principle In psychoanalytic theory, the tendency to seek immediate gratification of needs or drives without consideration of longer-term consequences. (*See also* Reality principle.) **(3)**

Phobia Exaggerated fears of specific objects or events in situations where the actual possibility of harm to the individual is rather slight. **(4)**

Prefrontal lobotomy *See* Psychosurgery. **(11)**

Process consultation The attempts by an organizational consultant to point out the processes, such as decision making, which the group uses in its ongoing activities. **(12)**

Projection A disguise mechanism in which one engages in an extreme form of blaming others by "seeing" one's own unacceptable thoughts, behaviors, and needs in other people, often to an exaggerated degree. **(6)**

Projection, complementary Projection in which others are seen as trying to force the individual into engaging in the undesirable behavior. **(6)**

Projection, similar Projection in which others are perceived as having the characteristic that is threatening to the individual. **(6)**

Projective techniques A group of personality tests in which aspects of personal functioning are revealed by responses to rather ambiguous stimuli such as inkblots or incomplete sentences. (*See* Rorschach Test, and Thematic Apperception Test.) **(10)**

Prosocial behavior Behavior involving caring, helping, and sharing; also called moral behavior. **(3)**

Psychoactive drugs Any of a number of drugs that produce different psychological effects such as mood change, anxiety reduction, etc. **(11)**

Psychodynamic therapy *See* Dynamic psychotherapy. **(11)**

Psychogenic needs Secondary drives or motives, as proposed by Murray (1938). **(3)**

Psychological adjustment The process by which one attempts to meet simultaneously all of one's psychological, learned, and social needs. **(5)**

Psychological adjustment (existential view) Each individual is solely and personally responsible for the quality of his or her own adjustment through the exercise of free will in making a continual series of decisions throughout life; the question of evaluation of the quality of adjustment is irrelevant. **(1)**

Psychological adjustment (humanistic view) The quality of one's adjustment should be evaluated in terms of personal progress toward the goal of self-actualization; this progress is innately motivated by positive growth forces. **(1)**

Psychological adjustment (moral view) The quality of one's adjustment should be evaluated according to standards contained in absolute moral guidelines, such as those of religion or other established sets of standards for good and bad behavior. **(1)**

Psychological adjustment (phenomenological view) The quality of one's adjustment can be evaluated only by each individual for him- or herself, using his or her own internal subjective frame of reference. **(1)**

Psychological adjustment (social-learning view) The quality of one's adjustment should be evaluated in terms of problem-solving or coping skills, that is, by the degree to which one is able to meet and master at least three kinds of challenge to existence: (1) from the physical environment; (2) from one's own physical limitations; (3) interpersonal challenges. **(1)**

Psychological crisis A temporary situation in which an individual is under unusual stress and does not have adequate resources to meet the situational demands, often because no previous experiences required development of the necessary coping skills. **(5)**

Psychology The science of human behavior. **(1)**

Psychopath An individual characterized by irresponsible and impulsive behavior and by lack of concern for the appropriateness or consequences of that behavior; also called sociopath. **(7)**

Psychopathy Personality characteristic or disorder associated with a lack of normal consideration for moral and ethical values. **(1)**

Psychosexual stages Stages of socialization, according to psychoanalytic theory, in which different zones of the body provide the major source of libidinal gratification until adult sexuality is achieved. (*See* Oral, Anal, Phallic, Oedipal, Genital stages, Latency period; *See also* Socialization, psychoanalytic theory of.) **(3)**

Psychosis Any severe mental disorder, with or without organic damage, characterized by deterioration of normal intellectual and social functioning and by partial or complete withdrawal from reality. **(7)**

Psychosocial stages A series of stages posited in a lifelong view of socialization developed by Erik Erikson; in progressing through these stages individuals face an ever-widening range of human interactions. **(3)**

Psychosurgery The surgical destruction of portions of the frontal lobes of the brain in order to control psychotic behavior; also called prefrontal lobotomy. **(11)**

Psychotherapist A professionally trained person, usually in the professions of psychology, medicine, social work, education, or the ministry, who attempts to help psychologically distressed persons solve their problems. **(11)**

Psychotherapy The attempt to alleviate psychological distress by discussing one's problems with a professional mental health worker. **(11)**

Puberty The attainment of biological sexual maturity in early adolescence. **(4)**

Punishment The use of an unpleasant stimulus for the purpose of eliminating undesirable behavior. **(2)**

Rationalization A disguise mechanism in which an individual offers a convenient, logical, and often partially accurate explanation for a behavior, leaving a misleading or incomplete impression. **(6)**

Reaction formation A disguise mechanism in which an individual guards against unacceptable thoughts and motivations by developing strong conscious attitudes and behaviors that are their direct opposite. **(6)**

Reality principle In psychoanalytic theory, the ability or willingness to postpone or inhibit need gratification. (*See also* Pleasure principle.) **(3)**

Regression A return to earlier and more childish forms of behavior. **(5)**

Reinforcement, learning by Increases in response following the delivery of reinforcers. **(2)**

Reinforcer Any event whose occurrence, following a particular response, increases the probability that the response will be made again in the future. **(2)**

Reliability The consistency of scores on a test given more than once to the same individuals. **(10)**

Remote compensation A special form of compensation in which one attempts to gain satisfaction through the successes of others, which one counts as one's own. **(6)**

Repression The automatic or unconscious avoidance of anxiety-arousing material; also called cognitive avoidance. (*See also* Suppression.) **(4) (6)**

Repression (psychoanalytic view) Rejection by the conscious mind of memories or impulses which are unacceptable because they threaten to overwhelm the individual or to lead to loss of control, and the banishment of these rejected memories and impulses into the unconscious mind. These companion processes drain the individual's store of psychic energy, leaving fewer resources available for dealing with other matters. **(6)**

Respondent behavior Responses that are commonly regarded as reflexes, such as salivation and simple knee jerks; may be influenced by classical conditioning. **(2)**

Response Changes in the organism as a result of stimulation. **(2)**

Response hierarchy The particular order in which a number of possible responses to a situation are likely to be attempted (trial and error behavior). **(2)**

Role A coherent, organized pattern of behavior defined by a society as appropriate on the basis of an individual's sex, age, occupation, prestige position, group membership, or other similar factors. **(3)**

Role playing A therapeutic technique developed by Moreno (1953) in which persons take on different identities or roles in order to better understand their own behavior and that of others. **(12)**

Rorschach test A projective test of personality, based on a series of 10 standard inkblots. **(10)**

Rhythm method A method of birth control in which the couple refrains from having intercourse during the woman's ovulation, or fertile period; effectiveness depends upon accurate determination of ovulation and is usually low. **(8)**

Satellite relationships Close emotional relationships that a spouse may form outside of marriage. **(9)**

Scapegoating A response to frustration in which aggression is displaced onto an innocent victim; often occurs when the real object cannot easily be identified, or when the real object is a powerful figure who might punish the aggressive response. **(5)**

Schizophrenia Disturbance of behavior and thought processes in which the individual's view of reality appeared to be grossly distorted. **(7)**

Schizophrenia, catatonic Disorder characterized by extremes of stereotyped behavior— either complete, statue-like lack of motion or extreme excitement. **(7)**

Schizophrenia, hebephrenic Disorder characterized by emotional confusion or extreme silliness, inappropriate laughter, childish giggling, repetition of meaningless phrases, bizarre speech. **(7)**

Schizophrenia, paranoid Disorder characterized by absurd, illogical, often changing delusions, usually of grandeur or of persecution. **(7)**

Schizophrenia, process Any schizophrenia which has a gradual onset and is characterized by withdrawal and reduced emotional responsiveness; generally there is a poor prognosis for recovery from the symptoms of the disorder. **(7)**

Schizophrenia, reactive Any schizophrenia which has a sudden, dramatic onset; generally there is a favorable prognosis for recovery from the symptoms of the disorder. **(7)**

Schizophrenia, simple Schizophrenia characterized by gradual withdrawal and seclusiveness and general deterioration of behavior. **(7)**

Secondary drive An aroused condition of the organism based on the deprivation of some learned or secondary reinforcer. (*See also* Secondary reinforcer.) **(3)**

Secondary reinforcement Learning process in which a formerly neutral stimulus acquires reinforcing properties after being closely and repeatedly associated with a primary rewarding event. (*See also* Secondary reinforcer.) **(3)**

Secondary reinforcer A previously neutral stimulus which has acquired reinforcing properties through the process of secondary reinforcement, such as money or words of praise. (*See also* Secondary reinforcement.) **(3)**

Selective exposure Behavior genetic principle that one's hereditary endowment determines to some extent the environmental experiences to which one is exposed (Wiggins *et al.*, 1971). **(1)**

Self-concept The organized set of verbal self-signaling devices by which one interprets one's own behaviors and the circumstances underlying them. **(6)**

Self-esteem One's own personal judgment of one's self-worth. **(6)**

Self-help groups Groups which come together for the purpose of helping the members with a particular psychological problem or an aspect of personal effectiveness. **(12)**

Self-reinforcement Rewarding or providing secondary reinforcement to oneself, thus bypassing or reducing the need for external reinforcement. **(3)**

Self-study The process by which we attempt to become aware of our own internal feelings (Dollard and Miller, 1950). **(11)**

Sensitivity-training groups *See* T-groups. **(12)**

Separation anxiety Initially, the strong emotional reaction of a child to the mother's leaving its presence; later, the reaction engendered by the leaving of any significant other. **(3)**

Settling down Phase of adult development following the novice phase, typically beginning in a person's early thirties. **(9)**

Sex typing Role behaviors considered appropriate according to sex. (*See also* Role.) **(3)**

Sexual response cycle Four phases of sexual response: (1) excitement, (2) plateau, (3) orgasm, (4) resolution (Masters and Johnson, 1966). **(8)**

Shame Anxiety experienced when one recognizes that other people will disapprove of one's behavior (*See also* Guilt). **(4)**

Shaping The practice of initially reinforcing responses which only crudely approximate the final response desired, then gradually raising the standard of response required for reinforcement until the desired response is achieved. **(2)**

Sliding reinforcers Reinforcements that deteriorate or lose their reinforcing properties over time (Platt, 1973). **(12)**

Socialization Process by which the infant is slowly but systematically trained in the expected behavioral traditions of its society. **(2) (3)**

Socialization, Freudian theory of *See* Socialization, psychoanalytic theory of. **(3)**

Socialization, psychoanalytic theory of Changes in the way an individual gratifies biological (primarily sexual) needs as a result of both social consequences and biological maturation; also called Freudian theory. (*See also* Psychosexual stages.) **(3)**

Social traps Situations which provide short-term rewards but which are hurtful or destructive in the long run (Platt, 1973). **(12)**

Sociopath *See* Psychopath. **(7)**

Somatic Of, relating to, or affecting the physical body, especially as distinguished from feeling or emotions. **(4)**

Source trait The mechanisms, including hereditary or constitutional factors, that underlie observed consistencies in behavior (Cattell, 1946). (*See also* Manifest trait.) **(1)**

Sperm Male reproductive cells, produced by the testes. **(8)**

Spermicidal cream, jelly, foam Material inserted into vagina before each act of intercourse, containing spermicidal chemicals; effective method of contraception when used correctly. **(8)**

Spontaneous nocturnal emission Ejaculation of semen by males during sleep without manipulation of the penis; also known as wet dreams. **(8)**

Spontaneous recovery The tendency for a response to reappear after a period of time during which no reinforcement was obtained. **(2)**

Standardization The process of establishing norms for a test. **(10)**

Stanford-Binet Intelligence Scale The oldest major test of individual intelligence, last revised in 1973. **(10)**

Stimulus Any object, event, or internal or external situation that can be reliably specified and that elicits a response from an organism. **(2)**

Stimulus substitution *See* Association, learning by. **(2)**

Stress (1) Certain characteristics in the environment; (2) the reactions of an individual without regard to the situation; (3) characteristics of the situation *and* particular responses of the individual; (4) some characteristic or state of an individual that accounts for behavior. Interchangeable with anxiety. **(4)**

Strong-Campbell Interest Inventory A standardized questionnaire designed to measure the degree of similarity between a person's interests and those of successful persons in a variety of occupations. **(10)**

Sublimation The transformation of socially unacceptable impulses into socially acceptable behavior. **(6)**

Substitution *See* Compensation. **(6)**

Subtle items Questions on a personality inventory whose relevance to a particular behavior is not apparent but can be empirically shown. **(10)**

Superego In psychoanalytic theory, that aspect of the personality which attempts to control gratification of impulses through the mechanism of guilt on the basis of rigid and absolute moral rules which the individual develops through the introjection of cultural values; corresponds closely to what is commonly called conscience. (*See also* Id, Ego.) **(4)**

Suppression The conscious and deliberate avoidance of thoughts, topics, and events that arouse anxiety. (*See also* Repression.) **(6)**

Systematic desensitization The gradual exposure of an anxiety-arousing stimulus so that anxiety is never aroused at a painful level, thus allowing more adaptive responses. **(4)**

Temperament Unlearned or innate differences in the responsivity or activity level of infants **(3)**

Tension (1) Increase in muscle tonus, one of the physiological changes involved in anxiety (not used in this text, because of other vague, common meanings). **(4)**

Testes Male sex glands (gonads) which produce reproductive cells (sperm) and secrete sex hormones (androgens). **(8)**

T-groups Small-group experiences which are intended to heighten one's awareness of one's interpersonal behavior and how groups operate. **(12)**

Thematic Apperception Test (TAT) A projective test of personality, based on a series of 31 cards, each depicting a scene to which the subject responds by making up a story. **(10)**

Theory X Approach to management which views the typical worker as lazy, uninterested, unambitious, motivated only by extrinsic rewards (McGregor, 1960). **(9)**

Theory Y Approach to management which assumes that workers want to be challenged, want satisfaction and achievement from work, respond to intrinsic rewards (McGregor, 1960). **(9)**

Token economy The use of tokens as reinforcers in a controlled environment such as a prison or hospital in order to shape behavior. **(11)**

Transactional analysis A theoretical view of personality developed by Eric Berne (1961) that involves three ego states—Parent, Adult, and Child. **(12)**

Transference The feelings that patients in psychotherapy develop toward their therapists which stem from feelings that they had toward significant persons earlier in life, especially parental or authority figures. **(11)**

Tubal ligation Surgical method of contraception in which the fallopian tubes are cut and tied by a physician so that ova can no longer enter the uterus; very effective, but permanent, method of preventing pregnancy. **(8)**

Unconditioned response (UCR) The response elicited by the unconditioned stimulus. (*See also* Association, learning by.) **(2)**

Unconditioned stimulus (UCS) A stimulus which consistently elicits a response without prior learning. (*See also* Association, learning by.) **(2)**

Unconscious behavior Behavior that is explained by the individual involved in a way that does not agree with the reasons given by other observers. **(6)**

Valence Subjectively determined positive or negative characteristics of all aspects of the environment which elicit approach or avoidance behaviors respectively (Lewin, 1935). **(5)**

Vasectomy Surgical method of contraception in which the vas deferens are cut and tied by a physician so that sperm do not enter the ejaculate fluid; very effective, but permanent, method of preventing pregnancy. **(8)**

Vas deferens The ducts which carry the semen, including sperm, to the ejaculatory duct in the penis. **(9)**

Vasocongestion An increase in the blood supply in the genital area, experienced by both males and females during sexual stimulation. **(8)**

Vicarious problem solving The rehearsing of possible solutions to problems, especially in contrast to trying out these solutions overtly. **(11)**

Vocational interests Those personality characteristics, attitudes, aspirations, motivations, etc., which have implications for vocational success. **(10)**

Wechsler tests A series of individual intelligence tests including the Wechsler Adult Intelligence Scale (WAIS), the Wechsler Intelligence Scale for Children (WISC) for children aged 6-16, and the Wechsler Preschool and Primary Scale of Intelligence (WPPSI) for children aged 4-6. **(10)**

Withdrawal The handling of conflict situations by leaving them altogether, either physically or symbolically. **(6)**

Work enrichment Proposals and procedures for providing more intrinsic satisfactions in the work setting. **(9)**

Worry The anxiety experienced by an individual thinking about a difficult personal situation, either real or imagined, who can see no immediate solution to the problem. **(4)**

Zygote A single fertilized cell, formed by the union of a male sperm cell and female egg cell. **(1)**

Photograph Acknowledgments

Index